Everything You Need to Know About Chemical Dependence

Vernon Johnson's Complete Guide for Families

Everything You Need to Know About Chemical Dependence

Vernon Johnson's Complete Guide for Families

JOHNSON INSTITUTE

Minneapolis 1990

Library of Congress Cataloging in Publication Data

Johnson, Vernon E.
    Everything you need to know about chemical dependence.

1. Drug abuse—United States. 2. Drug abuse—United States—
Prevention. 3. Narcotics addicts—United States—Family relation-
ships. 4. Alcoholism—United States. 5. Alcoholism—United
States—Prevention. I. Title.
HV5825.J625 1990   362.29'13   90-4164

PRINTED IN THE UNITED STATES OF AMERICA

10 9 8 7 6 5 4 3 2 1

Contents

Introduction 1

Part One: Chemical Dependence in Individuals 7
Introduction to Part One 9
1   Chemical Dependence is a Disease 11
2   How Does Chemical Dependence
     Affect Individuals? 19
3   Chemical Dependence in Women 53
4   Chemical Dependence in Adolescents.............79
5   Chemical Dependence in the Elderly..............105
6   Alcohol and Anxiety 117
7   The Effects of Alcohol on
     Sexual Behavior 133
8   Relapse and Slips During Recovery 147

Part Two: Effects of Chemical Dependence At Home
           and At Work 173
Introduction to Part Two 175
9   How Does Chemical Dependence
     Affect Families? 177
10   Enabling at Home..201
11   Enabling in the Workplace.............................213
12   What is Co-Dependence? 227
13   Recovery Through Detachment 255

Part Three: Children of Alcoholics 273
Introduction to Part Three 275
14   What Teenage Children of Alcoholics
     Need to Know..277
15   What Adult Children of Alcoholics
     Need to Know..303

Part Four: Intervention, or How You Can Help Someone Who Doesn't Want Help 323

Introduction to Part Four 325
16 Preparing for the Intervention 327
17 Initiating the Intervention 355
18 When a Teenager Needs Intervention 371

Part Five: How Parents Can Prevent Chemical Dependence in Their Children 401

Introduction to Part Five 403
19 A Job Description for Parents 405
20 Teaching Lifeskills 425
21 Parental Drug Use 465
22 The Recovering Parent 477

Publications Used in This Book 487
National Organizations to Contact 489

Editor's Note

We use the term "alcohol or other drugs" in this book to emphasize that alcohol *is* a drug—just like tranquilizers, cocaine, marijuana, heroin, or any other mind-altering substance. We also sometimes use the term "chemical dependence" because it covers dependence on *all* these mind-altering substances and because it's short and simple.

Too often people talk about "alcohol *or* drugs" or "alcohol *and* drugs" as if alcohol were somehow different from drugs and in a category by itself. True, our culture, our government, even our laws, treat alcohol differently from the way they treat other drugs such as pot, crack, or smack. But the symptoms of dependence are essentially the same for all these mind-altering drugs, and there is an urgent need to find ways to prevent or intervene with their use.

Introduction

At last our country is responding to the drug problem with widespread alarm. Poll after poll lists it as among the three most important problems, if not the most important. Both the administration and the Congress apparently feel pressed to take action. Those of us who have labored long in the field and who have promoted a greater general awareness of the enormity of this problem should feel relieved and gratified. Yet, many of us are feeling sad and frustrated in seeing the actions and responses resulting from this new national alarm. I'm reminded of these lines:

> "When in danger, when in doubt,
> run in circles, yell and shout!"

Two government approaches to the drug problem are particularly discouraging because they seem to complicate the problem rather than to provide solutions. The first approach is interdiction. Lining our borders with armed forces is seen as a significant effort to reduce the drug problem. But such force will never be even a partial solution. Marijuana will remain the largest cash crop in a number of our states, and police will continue to discover warehouses filled with cocaine. Virtually any naturally occurring drug can be duplicated in a laboratory and sold illegally on the street. As long as the demand continues to grow, there will be a steady supply of drugs to fill it.

In trying to solve the problem by meeting drugs at the border, we are ignoring the largest part of the problem. Alcohol remains the most widely used drug, but awareness of that seems to be getting lost in the attacks on the other drugs.

A second approach being adopted at top governmental levels is the appeal being made directly to the addict. The "Just Say No" approach may have some value in deterring those who have not yet begun to experiment. Unfortunately, the public assumes it includes those who are already chemically dependent. They believe that the addict needs only to say "no," and the addiction is put aside.

Contributing to that sadly mistaken understanding of the true nature of chemical dependence is the approach being made through the media which suggests, "If you are having trouble with (name the drug), call this number." This does not take into account that the addict is unable to recognize the need for help, and it immobilizes still further those already immobilized people around the addict. They are told by direct implication that they must wait until the addict takes action, that there is nothing they can do, or are expected to do.

That is tragic, for these people are the keys to effectively reducing this dread disease. We do not need more laws or more people to enforce them. We need to give the public an understanding of the true nature of chemical dependence so that active and constructive intervention by knowledgeable people would be the norm rather than the exception.

Back in the early 1960s, when our work began as a part of a five-year research project in Minnesota, two basic discoveries were made which changed our approach to chemical dependence. At the beginning, we asked the obvious question, "What is the greatest problem in working with alcoholism?" The answer became another question, "Why do alcoholism's victims characteristically resist any legitimate help?" Time and continued experimentation provided the discovery that a characteristic of the disease was a progressive delusion of the alcoholic. We found we could describe how and why that delusion was always present.

That work led to the second discovery, that we could break through that delusion and cause the alcoholic to recognize and accept a need for help using a process which came to be called intervention. Intervention was defined as *meaningful people presenting reality to a person in a receivable way*. We saw that around every alcoholic there was a family of some sort, and we began to work with families to introduce the intervention process. While the primary goal remained intervening with the identified alcoholic, working with these family groups made it clear that most of these people nearly always needed help. We saw that alcoholism organized families into progressively dysfunctional relationships as their behaviors ranged from total immobilization to virtually compulsive attempts to manipulate the environment "to make this go away." We realized that these conditions became self-perpetuating and that all involved suffered emotional costs that varied among individuals and over time. We also learned that these emotional costs were, as with the identified victim, largely hidden from these individuals. They too lacked the insight to be able accurately to evaluate their involvement with the disease. Their attitude was, "If you fix my alcoholic, I'll be O.K. Nothing is wrong with me."

In fact, we found very often that the families of even late-stage alcoholics were failing to recognize or to accept the disease as being a basic cause of the problems they faced. The process of intervention so often had to begin with them. They needed enough accurate information to break through the delusion caused by misinformation. They needed reality presented to them in a way that changed their resistance to action.

The problems families have with chemical dependence are the same now as they have been for years. The numbers of people affected by the disease have grown, but the challenge presented to us is illustrated by an event that happened twenty years ago.

I had come to the closing moments of a three-day workshop for sixty supervisors of a government department in Washington, D.C. The goal had been to train them to recognize the symptoms of chemical dependence in the workplace and to give them skills in on-the-job interventions. My summary and final comments expressed my expectation that they now could be more useful to many who needed their help in that department.

"However," I said, "as we part my concern is in another direction. I believe most of today's families have this disease." I asked them, "Do you have a father or mother, brother or sister, son or daughter, husband or wife, uncle or aunt, grandfather or grandmother, who has displayed the symptoms of dependence?" After a long minute of silence, I asked them to raise a hand if they had such a family member. All but half a dozen hands went up! The head of the department, who was sitting next to me, was thunderstruck. The obvious and final question was, "How will you meet your responsibility to your chemically dependent loved one?"

Today, as then, ignorance is the enemy. Accurate information, widely avaliable to families, is the answer.

After nearly three decades of close observation of our society's involvement with chemical dependence, I have become convinced that there is no easy way available to us. The really productive solutions to the problem have come when we have used specific approaches with families and individuals. Employee Assistance Programs, for example, have been useful.

When we gave information to families, people got well, and family relationships were restored. More people were taking action as they too were confronted by the question of how *they*

4

were meeting *their* responsibility to their chemically dependent loved ones.

These pages are an effort to make essential information about chemical dependence more available to families before trouble begins. Since so much material is now in print, this is an effort to simplify their search for needed information. I am deeply indebted to all the authors who contributed to this collection.

This book has resulted from a diligent effort to collect pertinent material from our published literature for that person asking, "What can I do?"

VERNON E. JOHNSON, D.D.

Chemical Dependence
in Individuals

Introduction to Part One

Part One describes how chemical dependence affects individuals and answers the question, "Why can't they see what they're doing to themselves and quit drinking (or using other drugs)?"

Not only are chemically dependent people caught up in a pattern of self-destructive drug use, but they are kept largely unaware of it because they are being victimized by a pathologically developing psychological defense system of rationalization and projection, and an increasingly distorted memory system that includes euphoric recall, repression and blackouts. In short, they are deluded—out of touch with reality. This material describes how and why these individuals usually claim and truly believe that chemical dependence is **not** the problem. It also describes how dependence can be identified in different people.

Chapters Three through Five deal with how chemical dependence affects adolescents, women, and the elderly. Although they all have the same symptoms, these groups have unique problems which need attention. For example, the conflicts caused by dependence in adults is greatly complicated for adolescents because they have not answered the question, "Who Am I?"

Chapters Six through Eight discuss problems often associated with chemical dependence. Chapter Six describes how drugs affect the brain and perception, details appropriate and inappropriate use of sedatives, and the dangers of medicating

9

anxiety. It confronts some myths which are still widely believed in America.

Chapter Seven gives the reader important insights into common sexual problems that arise from drug use and addresses some persistent old wives' tales.

Finally, Chapter Eight stresses the chronic nature of the disease. It offers information from both the physician's and the layperson's perspective on the dangers of relapse, the warning signs, and what can be done to avoid relapse.

VERNON E. JOHNSON, D.D.

Chapter One

Chemical Dependence
Is a Disease

Over the years we've branded the chemically dependent person (traditionally the alcoholic) as simply weak-willed: "If he really *wanted* to stop, he'd do it." In 1956, though, the American Medical Association recognized chemical dependence as a disease like diabetes or cancer.

The alcoholic, for example, abuses alcohol because he's ill, not because he's bad. Understanding that fact will help clear away some of your confusion, frustration, anger. What do you do with a sick person who can't help himself? You learn how to help, or you get professional help.

Recognizing and accepting chemical dependence as a disease implies several important truths. Like measles or the flu, we can recognize chemical dependence through certain symptoms. One of these is that the sick person has a compulsion, an irresistible urge, to use alcohol or other drugs. The compulsion is evident because this person uses those chemicals in a way that's inappropriate, excessive, and constant. His behavior is also unpredictable: his moods can swing from depression to euphoria in a short time and does so repeatedly. He may deny the compulsion with "I don't *have* to drink; I just *decide to*," but the decision is always ultimately the same: to drink.

Experts used to think of chemical dependence as only a symptom of emotional or psychological disorders. They'd say, "Let's find out what's *really* wrong. Then she won't need to drink." But we now know that chemical dependence isn't the *result* of some deeper hidden problem; it's the *cause* of many mental, emotional, and physical ailments. For instance, alcohol might be involved in from twenty-five to fifty percent of all admissions to hospitals. Such diseases as cirrhosis of the liver, deterioration of blood vessels in the brain, impotence, and mental deterioration grow worse as the patient continues drinking.

A practical conclusion: We must treat the alcoholism *before* we can cure the other ailments. To be blunt, once you have it, you have it for life. No one has measles over a lifetime, but a person who becomes chemically dependent remains so until death. For such a person, there's no moderate use; the only answer is *total* abstinence from *all* mind-altering drugs, including alcohol, cocaine, marijuana, "uppers," "downers," minor tranquilizers, even cough syrups containing codeine or other mind-altering drugs.

The good news is that with outside help one *can* abstain, can arrest the disease, can be healthy and happy. Alcoholics Anonymous members have it right: "The best day drinking is not as good as the hardest day sober."

Like other diseases, chemical dependence runs a predictable course. But unlike many diseases that simply disappear after a while, this one *always* gets worse if not treated. For months or years there may be plateaus, with no seeming increase in the chemical use. There may even be occasional improvement. But without competent treatment the path leads inevitably downward, and deterioration can be physical, mental, emotional, spiritual. It's clear, then, that *early* treatment is the only sensible way—and the earlier the better. The old idea that the dependent person must "hit bottom" before being open to treatment makes as much sense as letting someone jump off a cliff and "hit bottom" before you offer help.

Left unchecked, chemical dependence is 100 percent fatal. If it's not arrested, the victim will surely die from it, and die prematurely. For the alcoholic who continues to drink, death comes at least twelve years earlier than for the nonalcoholic. It's clear, too, that alcoholism is the real culprit in many premature deaths attributed to other causes: heart disease, liver ailments, bleeding ulcers, car crashes, on-the-job accidents, suicides. And, of course, we can say the same for other mood-changing drugs.

How Chemical Dependence Starts

One thing we don't know yet is how the disease of chemical dependence gets started. Various theories have been proposed, although none has yet been proved.

Some suggest it may be hereditary; it does tend to run in families, and there's about a fifty percent chance that the child of one or more alcoholic parents will become alcoholic. But that doesn't explain why the other fifty percent won't or why many alcoholics come from families where chemical dependence hasn't (apparently) been a problem in the past. Other theories claim that chemical dependence is related to a specific personality type. But there are millions of alcoholics who don't fit any particular profile.

It's clear that all sorts of people become chemically dependent, some for no apparent reason. On the other hand, it seems that some people can't become chemically dependent no matter how hard they try!

We *do* know that chemical dependence isn't caused by a lack of willpower, weakness of character, or some flaw in a person's moral structure. And it's not a form of mental illness. Nor is it the result of external influences—an unhappy marriage, trouble on the job, peer pressure. This means that if someone you care about is alcoholic or dependent on other drugs, *it's not your fault*. If you learn only one thing from this section, let it be this: *You're not responsible for the disease of chemical dependence that has taken hold in the person you care about.* You may be feeling guilty anyway; but try to believe—or at least consider—*that nothing you've ever done could have caused that person's illness.*

How To Tell If Someone Is Chemically Dependent

Now that you know this much about the disease, how can you decide whether someone you care about is suffering from it? Needless to say, this isn't something that should be taken lightly. Suspecting that someone is chemically dependent, and saying so to the person's face, are two very different matters!

Some people believe you can't label another person an alcoholic, that this must come from the person himself or herself. But as we'll see, the chemically dependent person is often the last to recognize (or admit) that he has a problem. So it may be up to you to observe the signs and draw the conclusions.

The following test, while not a diagnostic tool, can help you determine if your suspicions are well-founded. Answer each question with a yes or a no.

1. Is the person drinking or using any other drug more now than in the past?
2. Are you afraid to be around the person when he's drinking or using other drugs—because of the possibility of verbal or physical abuse?
3. Has the person ever forgotten or denied things that happened during a drinking or using episode?
4. Do you worry about the person's drinking or other drug use?

5. Does the person refuse to discuss her drinking or other drug use—or even to discuss the *possibility* that she might have a problem with it?
6. Has the person broken promises to control or stop his drinking or other drug use?
7. Has the person ever lied about her drinking or using, or tried to hide it from you?
8. Have you ever been embarrassed by the person's drinking or other drug use?
9. Have you ever lied to anyone else about the person's drinking or other drug use?
10. Have you ever made excuses for the way the person behaved while drinking or using?
11. Are many of the person's friends heavy drinkers, or do they use other drugs?
12. Does the person make excuses for, or try to justify, his drinking or using?
13. Do you feel guilty about the person's drinking or other drug use?
14. Are holidays and social functions often unpleasant for you because of the person's drinking or other drug use?
15. Do you feel anxious or tense around the person because of her drinking or other drug use?
16. Have you ever helped the person to "cover up" for a drinking or using episode—for example, by calling his employer or by telling others he's sick?
17. Does the person deny she has a drinking problem because she drinks only beer or wine? Or deny she has a drug problem because use is "limited" to a few lines of coke, marijuana, diet pills, or some other supposedly harmless substance?
18. Does the person's behavior change noticeably when he's drinking or using? (For example: a normally quiet person might become loud and talkative, or a normally mild-mannered person might become quick to anger.)

19. Does the person avoid social functions where alcohol or other drugs won't be available?
20. Does the person insist on going only to restaurants that serve alcohol?
21. To your knowledge, has the person ever driven a car while drunk or under the influence of other drugs?
22. Has the person ever received a DWI (driving while intoxicated) or DUI (driving under the influence)?
23. Are you afraid to ride with the person after she's been drinking or using?
24. Has anyone else talked to you about the person's drinking or using behavior?
25. Has the person ever expressed remorse for his behavior during a drinking or using episode?
26. If you're married to the person and have children, are the children afraid of the person when drinking or using?
27. Does the person seem to have a low self-image?
28. Have you ever found alcohol or other drugs the person has hidden?
29. Is the person having financial difficulties that seem to be related to his drinking or other drug use?
30. Does the person look forward to times when she can drink or can use other drugs?

If you answered yes to any three of these questions, there's a good chance that the person you care about has a drinking or other drug problem. If you answered yes to any five, the chance is even greater. And if you answered yes to seven or more, you can safely assume the person definitely has a problem with chemical dependence.

Here's the rule of thumb that lets you know whether someone is chemically dependent: If the use of alcohol or other drugs is causing any continuing disruption in a person's physical, emotional, mental, social, or economic life, but the person doesn't stop using, he or she is chemically dependent.

The refusal to stop drinking or using—even when it's clearly having an impact on the individual's life—signals a pathological attachment to the chemical and is one of the surest signs of harmful dependence.

Good News About Chemical Dependence

One thing that we know for certain is that chemical dependence is a treatable disease. There is absolutely no need for any man, woman, or child in this country to remain a victim of chemical dependence.

If one suspects the possibility of chemical dependence, what are some ways to get answers and help? The most easily available resource for help with drinking is Alcoholics Anonymous (A.A.). This group is listed in the telephone directory of every major city and many of the smaller cities and towns. A. A. groups will provide information and support to anyone who has a desire to stop drinking.

Treatment facilities for alcoholism and other drug dependencies are found in all major cities of our country. Many of them now offer help to the family of the chemically dependent person as well. There are also organizations like the Johnson Institute that offer many services related to the problems of chemical dependence. Many treatment facilities are connected with hospitals, some are free-standing institutions. Information on these inpatient and outpatient facilities can be obtained from a family doctor, clergyperson, county welfare office, or from calling Alcoholics Anonymous and asking for information about such treatment facilities. Insurance coverage for the treatment of chemical dependence is quite common today, and information on coverage should be requested from an insurance agent or the company personnel office.

Several larger communities have a council on alcoholism or other drug problems. These agencies frequently perform an information and referral function. Many clergy, doctors, and lawyers are knowledgeable about the problems of chemical dependence and the resources available to people who want help. They are often a reliable source of information or referral. There is a list of national organizations you can contact for more help at the end of this book.

If one senses a problem—or just has a question about chemical use—the first thing to do is to get more information. This first step—asking for answers—is often the most difficult, because for most it is a step into an unfamiliar area. Even though today most people recognize chemical dependence as an illness, thinking about oneself as chemically dependent can be frightening. But dependence is not a moral problem; it is not a sign of a weak character. It is a national health problem with severe effects in this country. It is an unnecessary drain on any person's health, happiness, and success. It is an illness that can bring down the strongest and brightest. Fortunately, no one needs to continue as an unwilling victim of chemical dependence. Recovery is to be had for the asking and the work.

THE JOHNSON INSTITUTE

This section is taken from *Chemical Dependence: Yes, You Can Do Something*, published by the Johnson Institute.

CHAPTER TWO

How Does Chemical Dependence Affect Individuals?

Recognizing chemical dependence as a disease is a giant step toward helping a person with a drug problem. You should now know that he or she will probably be one of the *last* people to accept the problem.

Slow acceptance (or no acceptance) of the problem is another symptom of the illness. The reasons for this denial are found in the ways that chemical dependence affects the individual and the people around him or her, and in the attitudes of our drinking and using culture—which actually serve to *compound* and strengthen the denial.

Alcohol is our most common and widely used social drug, although cocaine and marijuana are being used by more people than ever before—and at ever younger ages. Alcohol, however, is both socially and legally sanctioned; anyone of age can buy it and use it. It is routinely served in public restaurants and private homes, at baseball games and office parties (although this is happening somewhat less frequently these days), at theaters and on airplanes. The popping of champagne corks is required at our celebrations; no dinner is complete without wine; and we even allow our children to take their first sips of beer while sitting on our laps.

At the Johnson Institute, we have seen enough evidence to

arrive at the sad conclusion that many people in our culture will become chemically dependent. But it is not only Americans who are prone to this disease; the dilemma is worldwide. The Soviet Union has a serious alcohol problem that it has only recently acknowledged publicly. There are millions of alcoholics in France, England, Italy, Spain, China, Central and South America—anywhere, in fact, where the consumption of alcohol is not expressly forbidden by a national religion.

The extent of the problem—and the fact that it cuts across all racial, social, economic, and geographic barriers—is further proof that chemical dependence is indeed a disease. Why would so many millions of people choose a behavior that is clearly self-destructive? How could it be possible for people everywhere on the face of the planet to develop the *same* symptoms, the *same* compulsions, the *same* related disorders, if what they really suffer from is a lack of self-control?

Most people, when they come down with a disease, will set about trying to find treatment for it, provided that medical help is available to them. Here is where chemical dependence distinguishes itself as a disease unlike any other. *The people who have it generally do not seek treatment of their own volition because they are not aware that they have it.* This is because chemical dependence is universally accompanied by a unique *emotional syndrome* that keeps people from recognizing their problem.

What We Know About
the Emotional Syndrome

To understand this emotional syndrome, it is necessary to trace the progress of the disease from its very beginnings. We will use a device called the Feeling Chart to illustrate what happens, when—and why. The Feeling Chart is simply a straight-line chart along which we can theoretically place every emotion the human being is capable of experiencing, ranging from pain to euphoria.

THE FEELING CHART

NORMAL

PAIN   EUPHORIA

Now let us imagine a character we'll call Ed. He is an average, normal sort of fellow—so normal, in fact, that he probably doesn't exist![1]

One day Ed drinks his first beverage containing ethyl alcohol. He is feeling okay already, the way he usually feels, but the drink causes him to feel even better—pretty good, in fact.

---

[1] For purposes of simplicity, we have chosen to make our character a male. Of course chemical dependence is no respecter of either sex or sexual preference. We have also chosen to make him an *adult* male to avoid having to explain in this chapter the various additional complications surrounding adolescent chemical dependence. Finally, although this example illustrates alcoholism, the emotional syndrome holds true for *any* form of chemical dependence. Ed could just as well be using cocaine, marijuana, barbiturates, painkillers, or tranquilizers—*any* mind-altering drug.

His mood moves in a welcome direction, from 1 to 2 on our Feeling Chart. He thinks, "This is great! How come I didn't know about this stuff before?" When the effects wear off, he moves back to where he started emotionally.

Ed has just entered Phase I of chemical dependence.

PHASE I: LEARNS MOOD SWING

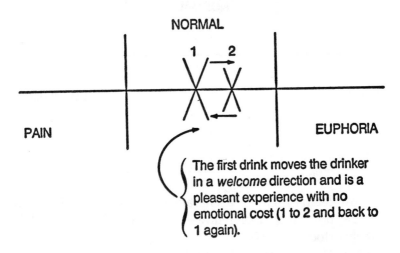

The first drink moves the drinker in a *welcome* direction and is a pleasant experience with no emotional cost (1 to 2 and back to 1 again).

Sooner or later, he makes a profound discovery: If one drink makes him feel good, then two (or three) are even better! He realizes that *he can control the degree of his mood swing* by controlling his alcohol intake. When that dosage wears off, he still returns to where he started from on the Feeling Chart, with no untoward effects.

PHASE I: LEARNS MOOD SWING

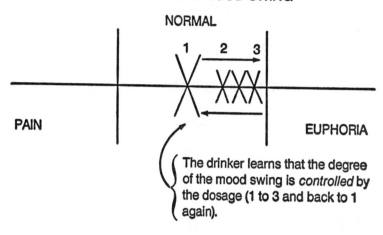

The drinker learns that the degree of the mood swing is *controlled* by the dosage (1 to 3 and back to 1 again).

Ed has had a significant learning experience, and these are the facts he has learned.

- Alcohol *always* moves him in the right direction—toward feeling warm, good-all-over, maybe even giddy;
- He can determine the degree of his mood swing by how much he drinks; AND
- It works every time!

It does not take Ed long to figure out how to select the mood he wants and drink just enough to get there. He accomplishes this *experientially*—by doing—and *emotionally*—by feeling. That, as anyone knows, is the best way to learn something new. Ed is not turning the pages of a textbook on drinking; he is bending his elbow, drink(s) in hand. Whether his drink of choice is beer, wine, or distilled spirits is irrelevant. Each takes him to the same happy place.

With time and experience, Ed comes to know that when he arrives home from work at the end of a long and tiring day, one drink always makes him feel a little better, while two or three

enable him to put his cares aside. And with four, he feels terrific!
He not only enjoys the mood swing, he actively seeks it. Again,
he always returns to the mood he started from; he is not yet
paying any emotional cost for his drinking behavior.

Ed is now in Phase II.

PHASE II: SEEKS MOOD SWING

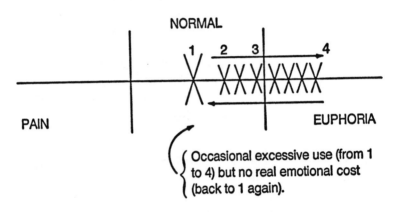

He has gone beyond knowing how to use alcohol to *forming
a relationship with it*. This is a very positive relationship, one of
implicit trust. Ed *believes* in the power of alcohol to relieve his
stress, alleviate his worries, and dissolve his crankiness. He has
graduated to the level of active social drinker—a card-carrying
member of our drinking culture—and drinks fairly regularly
and (usually) appropriately.

Given a little more time and experience, his relationship
with alcohol becomes a deeply embedded one which he will
carry throughout his life. Experience builds on experience to
strengthen and consolidate it.

He may stay in Phase II for weeks, months, or years. There
is no way to predict how rapidly things will progress. Much

later he may exercise hindsight and say, "I don't understand what happened. I used to have a lot of fun drinking. It's only been in the last two years that things have gone to hell in a handbasket." Like most chemically dependent people, he will overestimate the period of happy using and underestimate the period when things went awry.

He may even get deliberately drunk on occasion, provided it's a special one that's worth painting the town for. He'll come home and announce to his wife, "Caroline, honey, I got that raise! Get dressed up; we're going out tonight." He overdoes it, and the next morning he awakens with a first-class hangover. His head is throbbing, his stomach is queasy, and he can't understand why he's so thirsty—he had plenty to drink the night before! But even from his bed of physical pain, Ed can look back emotionally and pay no price. He thinks, "Well, I really tied one on last night. I'm sure not going to do it again tonight! But I had a good reason, I had a good time, and it was worth it."

Many social drinkers never pass beyond Phase II. They continue to drink in appropriate places, at appropriate times, and in appropriate amounts. Drinking still moves them toward euphoria, and when the drinking has stopped they still return to normalcy (albeit with an occasional hangover).

Victims of chemical dependence, however, *always* move past this phase. In Ed's case, there comes a point at which his drinking behavior and excessive use begin to exact an emotional toll. At this point he moves into harmful dependence, and it signals the true onset of the disease. *There is a direct correlation between the degree of emotional cost and the degree of dependence.* The higher the former, the more serious the latter.

How can we differentiate between so-called "normal" social drinking or drug use and harmful dependence? First, we must gather enough data about an individual's behavior to see whether the pattern has changed over time. Then we can begin asking questions.

1. Is there any indication of a growing anticipation of the welcome effects of alcohol or drugs? Does the individual seem preoccupied with those effects?

Ed walks through the door, tosses his briefcase on the table, and announces, "Boy, is it going to feel good to crawl around a dry martini! I need a drink; I've *earned* a drink."

He may adapt his behavior to ensure that he will be able to drink at a certain point (or points) during the day. He knows that he can't drink *all* day long, regardless of how it makes him feel; he realizes that alcohol is powerful stuff, and that he must limit his use. So he formulates a set of "rules" for drinking. One may be the "six o'clock rule": "I'll keep my nose to the grindstone during the day, but the minute I get home—at six o'clock—I'll have a drink."

Ed sticks to these self-imposed rules—for a while. But one day he catches himself looking at his watch. It's only four. Two more hours to go. Two more *long* hours to go. The next Saturday, when four o'clock rolls around, he's at home in front of the television set, or out mowing the lawn. He sees no reason not to have that beer *now*. What's the point in waiting until six?

By the following week he's checking his watch at noon. Lucky it's lunchtime. A glass of wine couldn't hurt.

Slowly, imperceptibly, Ed changes his lifestyle and his rules to satisfy his *growing* anticipation of the welcome effects of alcohol. He sees his co-workers drinking at lunch; he sees his neighbors downing beers while mowing their lawns. Everyone else is doing it, so he can, too.

Ed isn't aware that he has been rewriting his own rules until they are nothing like they used to be. Eventually he may do away with them altogether.

2. Is there a growing rigidity around the times and occasions when the individual has become accustomed to drinking or using drugs?

Does the person feel "put upon" if there is some unexpected interruption or intrusion upon his or her established routine?

Ed is halfway to the liquor cabinet when Caroline announces, "Dinner is on the table; remember, we've got that PTA meeting tonight."

Ed stops in his tracks and says, "What do you mean, dinner is on the table? I'm not ready to eat."

Caroline replies, "If you don't eat now, you won't have the chance. We have to leave in half an hour."

Ed, now irritable, counters with, "But this is when I relax!" (*Translation:* "This is my drinking time—hands off!")

Caroline says, "You can relax later, when we get home. You know I'm counting on you to be there; I'm making my presentation tonight."

Ed sighs. "I had a really hard day. I don't think I'm up to that meeting. I'd love to be there, but can't you go on without me? That will give me a chance to unwind, and when you come back you can tell me all about it. Okay?"

That scene will be replayed, over and over, in countless variations. Ed is not going to let *anything* interfere with his established drinking time.

3. Is the individual drinking or using more to achieve the same effects he or she formerly achieved with less?

Ed used to toss down one martini before dinner; lately he always has seconds. And sometimes thirds. But he *seems* like the same old Ed. Increased use of alcohol has resulted in an increased tolerance for its effects. The alcoholic who claims to be able to "drink everyone else under the table" often can, simply because it takes more to reach the mood shift he or she is seeking.

Another significant change takes place: Now there are times when Ed goes out of his way to get that second (or third, or fourth) drink. And this is why we ask:

4. How much ingenuity is the individual employing to get that greater amount?

You've been inviting Ed to your parties for years, but recently he has begun appointing himself bartender. He's the one who runs around saying, "Let me freshen your drink." Naturally this gives him ample opportunities to pour quick ones for himself. So while everyone else is nursing their second Margarita, Ed is on his third or fourth.

Caroline has noticed a difference, too. Before, she couldn't have paid him to do errands on Saturdays—going to the grocery store, picking up clothes from the cleaners, that sort of thing. Now he volunteers. He also usually includes a visit to the local watering hole somewhere along his route.

Ed is actually *planning* ways to get together with alcohol more frequently. Some of those ways are clever, ingenious, you might say. *The greater the ingenuity, the greater the dependence.*

He may or may not be secreting bottles in various nooks and crannies around the house, just to make sure that he doesn't "run out." Interestingly, this is one way in which most alcoholics are *not* particularly ingenious. They stash their bottles in much the same places alcoholics always have—out in the garage, down in the basement, in the bottom drawer of the built-in buffet.

Users of other drugs have a somewhat easier time hiding their supplies, since they don't take up as much space as alcohol. And the person who finds them may not know the import of what he or she has come across. A marijuana joint can be tucked into a pack of regular cigarettes; mood-changing pills can be stored at the bottom of an aspirin bottle. Cocaine, to the uninitiated, looks like any number of ordinary household substances—baby powder, baking powder, powdered sugar. The discovery of drug-related paraphernalia is often the first sign a spouse or parent has that someone in the house is using drugs.

For Ed, Phase III is on the horizon. There comes a day when he drinks too much, exhibits some kind of bizarre behavior as a direct result, and *for the first time,* when he comes down from that mood swing, he slips back behind normal on the Feeling Chart. The next morning, as he reaches for the aspirin, he thinks about the night before and remembers the rude remark he made to the host, or the lampshade he wore on his head, or the fact that Caroline took the car keys away from him and insisted on driving them home. "What happened last night?" he thinks. "Booze usually doesn't affect me like that." He is uncomfortable, perhaps embarrassed. *He does not feel good.*

PHASE III: HARMFUL DEPENDENCY

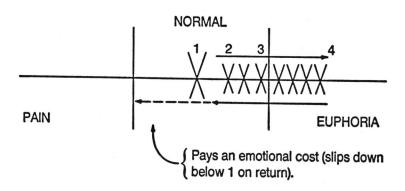

Then—and this is critical—he immediately answers his own question: "Of course! I didn't eat before I started drinking; I drank on an empty stomach! The next time I drink that much, and I won't, I'll eat first."

Notice the ambiguity? He is already planning what he is going to do the next time he *doesn't* drink to excess!

Ed has committed his first rationalization. This is a reasonable, natural, caretaking response to a bruised ego; it is the human being's way of repairing damaged self-esteem.

A few additional words about rationalization are appropriate here.

- First, *all* people rationalize when their behavior has caused them some kind of legitimate discomfort. This is the function of rationalization: to help us feel better about ourselves when we have done something of which we're not especially proud.

- Second, *all* rationalizations must be unconscious in order to work. We cannot be aware that we're rationalizing as we're doing it; in fact, the more aware we are, the less successful our rationalization will be.
- Third, rationalizations are *positive*—as long as our ego strength remains at a normal level and we usually feel relatively good about ourselves. They make life easier.

When a *normal* person rationalizes to atone for feelings of failure, a dose of the facts is usually enough to bring him or her back through the rationalization to reality. ("Don't tell me I never mentioned dinner at my mother's. We talked about it last night, and I reminded you again this morning." "You're right. I guess I just didn't want to go.") But when the chemically dependent person rationalizes, it is a far different story. Rationalization becomes integral to his or her life. *Every* bizarre behavior is rationalized away, and the person is swept further from reality and deeper into delusion. The process grows increasingly rigid and actually helps to victimize the person as the disease progresses. The intellect continues to suppress the emotion and defend against treason until the truth is buried beyond reach.

We do not know *why* an individual slides into harmful dependence from the position of what appeared to be "normal" social drinking or drug use. But we can thoroughly describe the *how*, both behaviorally and emotionally.

It is worth emphasizing, over and over, that *the chemically dependent person remains utterly unaware of the progress of the disease.* As the behaviors become more bizarre, the rationalization simply grows stronger to compensate for the increasing numbers of instances that exact an emotional cost. Rationalizations are no longer trotted out on occasion; they are part of the fabric of everyday life. They are invisible, they are insidious, and they are a necessary—and potentially disastrous—response to the feeling of pain. The more the individual believes in his or her own rationalizations, the further into delusion he or she goes.

To the observer versed in the signs and symptoms of chemical dependence, Phase III is easily recognizable. It can be described, it has distinct symptoms, and it follows a predictable and progressive course.

For Ed, there comes another occasion of excessive use and even more bizarre behavior. The next morning, he not only feels uncomfortable, he experiences a twinge of *remorse*. He no longer wonders, "What happened last night" He thinks, "What happened last night was stupid."

PHASE III: HARMFUL DEPENDENCY

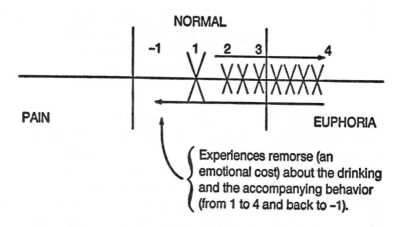

Experiences remorse (an emotional cost) about the drinking and the accompanying behavior (from 1 to 4 and back to –1).

As time goes on and he continues to drink excessively—maybe not every day, but often enough—his behavior goes beyond the bizarre to the outrageous, and his twinge of remorse becomes a stab. Now the morning-after reaction moves from "That was stupid" to "*I* was stupid. How could I have done such a thing?" The emotional pain is harder to bear.

Following the next bender, or the one after that, Ed slides into serious self-castigation. "I was stupid" is not sufficient anymore; now it's "I was a *fool*. I'd better call so-and-so to apologize." He feels awful. His self-worth is at an all-time low.

PHASE III: HARMFUL DEPENDENCY

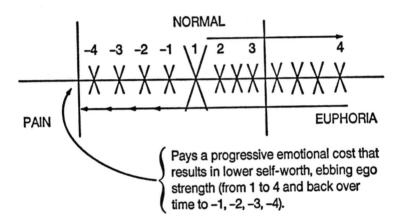

Pays a progressive emotional cost that results in lower self-worth, ebbing ego strength (from 1 to 4 and back over time to –1, –2, –3, –4).

And so goes the downward spiral, ever more painful and difficult to climb out of. Eventually this emotional distress becomes a *chronic* condition; Ed feels awful even when he is *not* drinking. This feeling may be an unconscious one, but it is always present. Initially it may be experienced as a general malaise; invariably, as Ed continues to drink and exhibit bizarre behaviors, it progresses toward sincere self-hatred. The aftermath of each new drinking episode echoes with self-recriminations: "I'm no damn good!" By this stage, Ed is a very sick man.

This is the point at which anyone who is paying attention will notice that something serious is going on. Personality changes and previously unseen mood shifts are evident—bursts of temper, violence, hostility, moroseness. The chemically dependent person may gain or lose weight due to improper eating habits. His or her personal hygiene may not be up to par.

PHASE III: HARMFUL DEPENDENCY

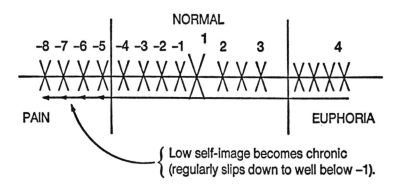

The typical response is to seek what we call the "geographic cure." At no time does Ed admit that his life is a mess because of his drinking; he doesn't admit it because *he still doesn't know it*. Instead, he assumes that the explanation lies in other people or other things. "That Caroline is such a nag; if I could dump her, I'd get better!" Or "I can't stand my job anymore. It's driving me to drink." Or "Maybe it's time to get out of this city—to start over. I need a change!" He may follow up these convictions with erratic actions.

His drinking is totally out of control. He drops into a bar for "a drink or two" after work—and is pushed toward the door at closing time. He brings home a bottle, planing to have a couple of short ones during the evening, and the next morning the bottle is empty.

In the final stages of this phase, self-hatred is replaced by clearly self-destructive feelings and attitudes. "I'm no damn good" is followed by "I'm so rotten that I might as well end it all."

Just flip the wheel at 60 mph and that bridge abutment will take care of everyone's problems, including mine. . . . This office window is high enough; all I'd have to do is lean . . . . Why open the garage door when I start my car? . . . I could take one or two of these pills—or I could take a handful. . . .

PHASE III: HARMFUL DEPENDENCY

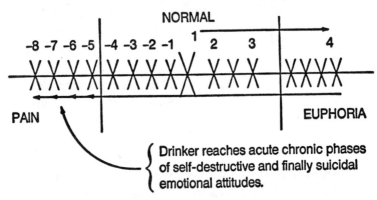

Drinker reaches acute chronic phases of self-destructive and finally suicidal emotional attitudes.

If the disease is allowed to continue, Ed may develop overt suicidal tendencies brought about by the chronic condition known as alcoholic depression—undoubtedly the largest single cause of suicide in our culture today.

Right now, you are probably asking about Ed (or the chemically dependent person in your life), "Why doesn't he see what is happening to him and quit drinking?"

Imagine the ten to twenty million practicing alcoholics who are behaving just like Ed. Now imagine the millions of people who know them and are noticing the same symptoms and behaviors that are evident in the person you care about. *They are all asking the same question*—and it is the wrong question.

To arrive at the right question, leave off the last three words.

Then ask, "Why doesn't he see what is happening to him?" The answer is simple: *He can't.*

That may seem incredible. How can a person who has changed his whole lifestyle not realize what he is doing? How can a person not be able to tell when he is centering his life around a drug? How can he not detect the deterioration in his physical condition, his emotional state, his relationships? Is he blind? In a very real way, he is. The explanation is found in the emotional syndrome we are describing here.

As Ed's emotional need for alcohol has become more and more pressing, and as his drinking behaviors have been followed and reinforced by specific rationalizations, the very process of rationalization (which started out harmlessly enough) has become pathological *mental mismanagement.* His bad feelings about himself have been locked in at the unconscious level by a secure, high, and seamless wall of rational defenses. This is why he can believe what to everyone else seems patently unbelievable.

Because of the wall, he cannot get at those bad feelings about himself. He is not even aware that they exist. But they are nevertheless chronically present in the form of a *free-floating mass of anxiety, guilt, shame, and remorse.*

PHASE III: HARMFUL DEPENDENCY

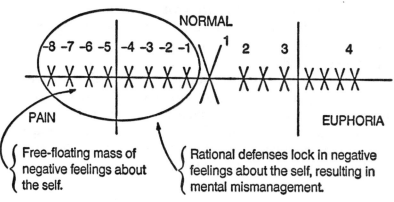

35

As long as he carries this free-floating mass inside himself, Ed can *never* feel good when he is not drinking, *and he does not even feel good when he is.* At this stage he can no longer achieve the happy "high" of the old days. *He drinks to feel normal*—and he enters Phase IV of the disease.

PHASE IV: DRINKS TO FEEL NORMAL

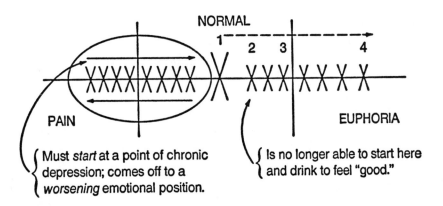

{ Must *start* at a point of chronic depression; comes off to a *worsening* emotional position.

{ Is no longer able to start here and drink to feel "good."

He starts drinking at a point below normal, where he is now living his feeling life. If he drinks enough, he feels the way he used to when he wasn't drinking. The terrifying thing about this phase is that each downswing takes him further and further to the left of the scale. He feels *worse* than he did before he consumed however many drinks it took to feel okay. Eventually he *must* drink because he simply cannot bear being sober. The resulting pain is searing, but it's worth it if he can feel normal even briefly.

As long as the disease continues, this free-floating mass keeps growing. Ed's self-image goes on deteriorating, his ego becomes more battered, and sooner or later rationalization alone is insufficient to do the job of covering up and locking in. At this point, another great defense system leaps to the cause, equally unconsciously. We call this system *projection.*

Projection is the process of unloading one's self-hatred onto others. Like rationalization, it must be unconscious in order to be effective.

Ed sees himself as surrounded by hateful people. If *they* would shape up, *he* would be all right! His boss is a pain, Caroline is a nag, the kids are driving him crazy, the neighbors are bugging him, his mother is pushing him to the limit. He starts dumping his bad feelings onto them.

PHASES III AND IV: HARMFUL DEPENDENCY AND DRINKING TO FEEL NORMAL LEAD TO PROJECTION

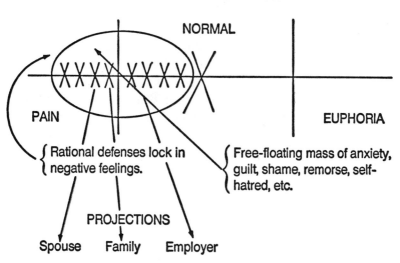

What he *seems* to be saying is, "I hate you all!" What he is *actually* saying is, "I hate myself." But *he* doesn't know this, and *you* don't know this, and besides, you're caught up in some powerful, bad feelings of your own.

What We Know About the Delusional System

We have already discussed how rationalization and projection work together to block the chemically dependent person's awareness of the disease. By keeping the alcoholic or other drug addict out of touch with reality, they eventually make it impossible for him or her to understand that a problem exists.

From the outside, it appears as though the person is lying. (We often hear alcoholics characterized as liars—even *pathological* liars). The people around the chemically dependent person assume that he or she is still responsible to the truth and capable of knowing it and distinguishing it from falsehood. They can't understand why he or she doesn't simply face up to the problem and do something about it.

While rationalization and projection are sufficiently devastating psychological impairments in their own right, three new progressive (and even more bewildering) conditions enter in during the later stages of the disease. *Blackouts*, *repression*, and *euphoric recall* literally *destroy* the person's ability to remember what has happened during any given drinking or using episode. What used to be mental mismanagement evolves into a full-scale *faulty memory system*, or delusional system.

A faulty memory system is typical of the disease of chemical dependence and is almost universally present in sufferers. It is also one of the hardest things for people around them to comprehend.

Blackouts

If any of us experienced a period of time when we walked and spoke and made telephone calls and parked the car, and later couldn't remember any of it (even after talking to witnesses), we'd go at once to a doctor for a thorough checkup and an explanation. But chemically dependent people sense that blackouts are part of their drinking or using—and it's a part they don't want to examine too closely. Instead, they adapt, learning ways to cover up these occurrences, and they continue to drink or use drugs despite them. *The willingness to tolerate repeated blackouts as a normal part of life rarely if ever occurs in the absence of chemical dependence.*

A blackout is a *chemically induced period of amnesia*. This should not be confused with passing out—the total loss of consciousness that sometimes occurs as a result of excessive drinking or drug use. During blackouts, people may continue to behave and function in an otherwise normal fashion, and everyone around them assumes that they are in complete control of their faculties. It is only later that the truth emerges. Victims are unable to recall anything about the blackout period— *and never will.*

Alcoholics and drug addicts experiencing blackouts have driven cars, flown commercial airplanes, performed surgery, and tried and argued court cases. They have traveled to foreign countries, arrived back home without knowing how, made appointments, done household tasks, and carried on at parties. In short, *any* activity a person can do can be performed during a blackout.

The quantity of alcohol or drugs consumed seems to have no direct relationship to the frequency or duration of blackouts. A small amount may cause one while a large amount may not, and vice versa. A blackout may last for seconds, minutes, hours, or days.

As these memory losses occur, victims become increasingly fearful, bewildered, and depressed. With the progression of the disease, the memory losses become more frequent and unpredictable. Anxieties begin to mount. ("What did I do last night after ten o'clock?" "Where did I leave the car?" "Who was I with?" "Where did I hide that bottle?")

Because chemically dependent people cannot remember

what goes on during blackouts, they are denied the specific feeling reactions to the bizarre, antisocial behavior which often occurs during them. In some instances, even blackouts are "blacked out." Large periods of time are totally unaccounted for. Guilt, shame, and remorse are vague and nameless and of no help in self-recognition—as the accurate recall of drinking behavior would be.

One recovering alcoholic used these words to explain the sick feeling that follows a blackout: "I thought I was going crazy. So every time this happened to me, I'd force myself to forget it. I got so good at it that I actually had myself believing that things just 'slipped my mind' from time to time." Another recalled, "I used to think that everyone drew a blank once in a while, when he had drunk too much."

Since the anxiety resulting from a blackout is so great, alcoholics or other drug addicts will tend to minimize, discredit, or disbelieve any firsthand accounts of their behavior during blackouts. "My wife (or husband) is always exaggerating these things," they will say to themselves—and eventually accept as the truth. This conflict between what others say about their behavior, and what they will *allow* themselves to believe, contributes to a growing feeling that others are being "unfair" about their drinking or other drug use. The delusional system cooperates with them to blunt the truth and aid in their ongoing denial of the disease. The eventual result is widespread confusion.

Let's return to our friends Ed and Caroline to illustrate these points. One night Ed and Caroline go to a party at the home of their good friends, Stan and Elizabeth. Midway through the evening, Ed makes a pass at the hostess. Everyone in the room sees and hears it—including Caroline.

The next morning Ed ambles downstairs for breakfast. Caroline is furiously frying eggs and slamming cabinet doors. Ed walks into the kitchen, sits down at the table, and picks up the newspaper—business as usual. A moment later he casually remarks, "Nice party last night. Did you enjoy yourself?"

Caroline is stunned. The very least she had expected was an apology. And there's Ed with his nose in the newspaper, asking her if she had a good time!

"Don't you *remember*?" she asks accusingly.

Ed looks up. "Remember what? I remember driving over, helping Stan fix the drinks, sitting down to dinner, eating, joking with the neighbors, and coming home to bed."

"You made a pass at Elizabeth," Caroline says. "Right in front of everybody. I wanted to die then and there. How *could* you?"

Ed squirms without quite knowing why. "What do you mean, how could I? I couldn't! I didn't! Caroline, I would never do such a thing. You must have been dreaming."

Now Caroline is faced with two awful possibilities. Either Ed is lying outright—or maybe she *was* dreaming. She discards these and moves on to a third: Ed is a cad who doesn't even have the decency to apologize.

Later that day, Ed calls Stan, hoping to borrow his lawn-mower. For the first time in their long acquaintance, Stan is chilly over the telephone. Ed doesn't understand it. Unless. . . . No, that's impossible. He *couldn't* have done that terrible thing.

But he can't remember anything that happened between dinner and coming home.

Repression

While repression results in forgetfulness similar to that caused by a blackout, it is psychologically rather than chemically induced.

Over time, chemically dependent people develop the ability to repress unwanted, shameful memories. They literally shut them out of their minds. They continue to rationalize some of their behaviors (those they can bear to face), and they repress those they cannot rationalize.

Like rationalization, repression is a human survival skill. None of us could endure the memory of *every* shameful or embarrassing moment we've experienced during our lives. When a normal person represses a specific memory, it is usually of no great consequence, since the behavior that led to the memory is unlikely to be repeated. But when a chemically dependent person represses, it is because those actions that produced the pain and shame have occurred more than once and are likely to recur and worsen with the passage of time.

The more bizarre the behavior becomes, the stronger the instinct to repress. Outward manifestations of this can be seen in intensified nervousness, resentment, hostility, and self-pity, and eventually self-destructive and suicidal emotional tendencies.

Also like rationalization, repression becomes counterproductive, even destructive, when it is allowed to go too far. It works to push the chemically dependent person deeper into the disease until the truth becomes virtually unattainable — unless it is brought back forcibly through intervention or a fortuitous grouping of crises.

Let's assume that Stan and Elizabeth are forgiving people, and that they invite Ed and Caroline to their next big bash. Ed's behavior is even worse this time. Not only does he flirt rudely with Elizabeth, he insults Stan, pours a pitcher of martinis over Stan's boss, and manages to break a valuable heirloom while stumbling toward the kitchen.

On awakening the next day, Ed is glad to find himself in his own bed. No telling where he might have ended up! He tries to get out of bed — and sinks back down on the pillows. He has the worst hangover of his life. But it's Saturday, and he's told Caroline that he would run some errands, and he'd better, if only to make up for the fact that he went on a bender the night before . . . he had *promised* her that he wouldn't. So he crawls out of bed, into his clothes, and down the stairs.

Along the way, he is overcome by a feeling of pure horror. He doesn't remember much of anything that happened last night; he just senses that it was *bad*. His unconscious goes to work. It can allow all the memories of the night before to surface . . . or it can close them off, bury them, repress them. In a split second, the decision is made. Note that this is not premeditated, but instinctive; Ed's mind is already heading in a new direction, away from the sheer awfulness of those memories. Ed is thinking about washing the car, doing some shopping, buying Caroline a dozen roses.

Meanwhile, Caroline is beside herself. She isn't even cooking breakfast; if Ed wants to eat, he can find the stove. Instead, she's nursing a cup of coffee and wearing a face like thunder.

Ed strolls into the kitchen and Caroline's resentful glare. What's going on? His beloved wife, the light of his life, looks like hell. Chances are she's about to start in on him again. Maybe he can head her anger off one more time. So he walks over to her, wraps his arms around her, gives her a big smile, and asks, "Is something bothering you?" He feels neither shame nor guilt nor remorse, because he can't imagine any reason why he should. He truly wants to help, to make her feel better.

She pushes him away, bursts into tears, and runs out of the room. Ed is flabbergasted. Upstairs, behind a locked door, Caroline is weeping and pulling her hair. How *could* he be so calm, so collected, so kind? How could he pretend that last night never happened? Unless . . . perhaps . . . it was all in her head.

Euphoric Recall

The third component of the delusional system may be the most devastating; it is certainly the most difficult to comprehend and accept. Most people have some understanding of blackouts. All of us have some familiarity with repression. But euphoric recall seems patently incredible!

It makes it impossible for chemically dependent people to evaluate their current condition accurately while under the influence. They *really don't know* that they can't do everything they're capable of doing under ordinary circumstances. Their subsequent memories of the experience are tied into the inability to evaluate their condition. And those distorted memories are *implicitly trusted.*

Picture the man who is obviously quite intoxicated, yet heads toward his car with his keys at the ready. He perceives himself as perfectly capable of driving home. Everyone else sees that he's *in*capable and highly dangerous, but they can't convince him. When someone finally does manage to take his keys away, he reacts with indignation and sincere bewilderment.

The next morning, while reviewing the events of the previous evening, he *remembers* that he was all right — just as he believed he was the night before. Regardless of what his wife or friends may tell him, he trusts his memory implicitly.

Chemically dependent people who are victimized by euphoric recall remember how they *felt*, but not how they *behaved*. They have no memory whatsoever of slurred words, exaggerated gestures, or the fact that they wove around the room. They *felt* as if they expressed themselves brilliantly and entertained everyone with their wit and humor, and that is what they are positive happened.

One woman listened in disbelief to a tape recording of one of her drinking episodes. Before playing it back, her husband asked her if she could remember *how* she had said *what* she had said on the previous night. "Of course I can," she replied. "I had a few drinks, but I was perfectly coherent." She was convinced that this was the case — until she heard her own voice stuttering, stammering, and slurring through the virtually nonsensical statements she had made the night before. "Then it hit me," she said. How many times have I remembered *feeling* good, when I had actually behaved like a complete idiot?"

One man put it this way: "When I used to tell people that 'I just wasn't myself' last night or last week, I thought I was using a figure of speech. But it was the truth!"

Chemically dependent people who have progressed to the late stages of the disease remember *every one* of their drinking or using episodes euphorically. Although they are incapable of recalling any of the details, they firmly believe that they remember everything. And what they remember most clearly is how good they felt while they were drinking.

Anyone who dares to argue with them is a nag or a party-pooper or just plain wrong. "Whaddaya mean, I already told that joke? You're just jealous because you can never remember a punch line." "You won't dance with me because I step on your feet? Nonsense; I'm a terrific dancer. Maybe I should give you some lessons!" "Don't be ridiculous; hand over the keys. I'll drive."

Imagine how many drunk drivers are on the road every night, convinced that they're in full control of their faculties.

Let's return to Ed and Caroline once more. Ed can't understand why the two of them are never invited to Stan and Elizabeth's parties. He's heard about one just last week, and it sounded like a lot of fun. That Stan is a real spoilsport. Who needs him?

Plus there's this ongoing argument he's having with Caroline. Lately, whenever they go out together — and they don't do that too often anymore — she insists on driving home. He gives her the keys to humor her, but he wishes she'd lay off. He's always been a careful driver, and except for that one DWI he didn't deserve, there's never been a time when he couldn't run circles around every other car on the road.

As if hassling with Caroline weren't enough, his boss is all over him about his production. Apparently you can't please anyone these days. Ed is working as hard as ever, maybe harder, despite the fact that he isn't feeling that well. The doctor says it's his liver, but that's impossible. Drunks have liver trouble, not people like Ed.

And here is where we leave him — with his friends falling away, his marriage in jeopardy, his job on the line, and his health failing. Everything is going to the devil around him. Good thing *he* doesn't have any problems.

VERNON E. JOHNSON, D.D.

This section is taken from *Intervention: How to Help Someone Who Doesn't Want Help*, published by the Johnson Institute.

More On Blackouts

Blackouts often are first noted when a drinker can't remember getting home from a drinking situation. Companions of the drinker may be reassuring and say, "You were all right," that nothing seriously wrong happened. If companions can't remember either, then the drinker—particularly an early-stage alcoholic—may feel relieved and even reassured that this memory lapse is a routine part of the drinking scene. Solitary drinkers may discover the next day that they had telephone conversations they don't recall. Worse, a solitary drinker may discover a broken object in the house, a burned meal, or a bruise on his body.

Two Types of Blackouts

Psychiatrist Donald W. Goodwin, M.D., of the University of Kansas, who had done research on blackouts, has concluded that there are two general types of blackout.

En bloc blackout. This blackout has a definite beginning, and it ends with feelings of lost time and apprehension. The drinker seldom remembers events that occurred during an en bloc blackout, even when they're described by someone else.

Fragmentary blackout. When this kind of blackout occurs, the drinker is unaware of memory lapse unless told of it by someone else. Or the memory of this period may return when the drinker is drunk again. What's more usual is that the drinker is reminded of specific things and then remembers—though hazily—what occurred during a fragmentary blackout.

Who Has Blackouts?

In 1952, Professor E. M. Jellinek of the Yale School of Alcohol Studies questioned 2,000 recovered alcoholics in Alcoholics Anonymous (A.A.) and found that blackouts, just like increased tolerance, were a symptom of early-stage alcoholism. Since then, blackouts have been listed worldwide as a standard early symptom of the disease. For example, the well-known Glatt chart placed blackouts fourth of thirty-six progressive symptoms of alcoholism. However, later researchers have questioned how many alcoholics have blackouts, how soon blackouts begin, and how often nonalcoholics have them.

Dr. Goodwin found that one-third of 100 hospitalized alcoholics never had blackouts. For those who did, blackouts began well along in the course of alcoholism rather than at an early stage.[2] Further, Dr. Goodwin found blackouts beginning at a later average age (35) than had Jellinek (25).

Although nonalcoholics *can* and *do* experience blackouts, most won't drink to the extent of repeating blackouts as readily as do alcoholics. Blackouts are a frightening experience for a nonalcoholic, whereas an alcoholic may experience only mild discomfort from these gaps in memory, especially after more frequent experience with them.[3]

LeClair Bissell, M.D., past-president of the American Medical Society on Alcoholism and Other Drug Dependencies, writes, "Most of us, were we to experience such a frightening event—a real period of time in which we walk and talk and make telephone calls and do business and park the car, yet

---

[2] Donald Goodwin, M.D., with Bruce Crane, M.D., and Samuel B. Guze, M.D., "Blackouts: A Review and Clinical Study of 100 Alcoholics," *American Journal of Psychiatry* 126 (August 1969), pp. 191-198.

[3] *Manual on Alcoholism* (Chicago: American Medical Association, 1977), p. 36.

cannot remember doing so—would go at once to a physician for an explanation. Not so alcoholics, who sense that blackouts are part of their drinking, the part of life that they don't want too closely examined. They will adapt to blackouts, learning ways to cover up their occurrences, and they will continue to drink in spite of them. This willingness to tolerate repeated blackouts as part of one's method of living rarely if ever occurs in the absence of alcoholism. The diagnostic clue, then, becomes the patient's equanimity in the face of repeated blackouts.[4]

Dr. Goodwin found that 83 percent or more of his hospitalized alcoholics who had had blackouts could drink more than a fifth of spirits (or the equivalent) per day, had weekend drunks, morning drinking, benders and tremors, neglected meals, and were diagnosed as "severely alcoholic."

According to one study, alcoholics who frequently experience blackouts share the following characteristics: they have higher tolerance for alcohol; lose control more frequently; more often drink until drunk or asleep; crave alcohol more. However, frequency of blackouts isn't related to beverage preference, delirium tremens, seizures, or family drinking history.[5]

What Causes Blackouts?

Blackouts don't seem to be related either to the amount of alcohol consumed or to one's previous drinking history.[6] Some

---

[4]Stanley Gitlow, M.D., and Herbert S. Peyser, M.D., eds., *Alcoholism: A Practical Treatment Guide* (New York: Grune & Stratton, 1980), pp. 31-32.

[5]Ralph E. Tartar and Dorothea U. Schneider, "Blackouts: Relationship with Memory Capacity and Alcoholism History," *Archives of General Psychiatry* 33 (1976), pp. 1492-1496.

[6]J. Kinney and G. Leaton, *Loosening the Grip* (St. Louis: The C. V. Mosby Company, 1978), pp. 107-109.

alcoholics experience blackouts early in their drinking careers. For others, blackouts occur much later. Some alcoholics may never have a blackout. Some have blackouts frequently, others only occasionally.

Thus blackouts, like alcoholism itself, follow no universal pattern. Even the amount of alcohol needed to cause a blackout can vary not only with the individual but with the occasion. On the one hand, moderate amounts of alcohol, even an amount that would fall far short of having anesthetic or stuporous effect (perhaps even 3 or 4 ounces of hard liquor), may be sufficient to cause blackouts in drinkers whose tolerance to alcohol is elevated.[7] On the other hand, blackouts almost never occur in conjunction with moderate drinking by nonalcoholics.

Do an alcoholic's habits contribute to having blackouts? Dr. Goodwin found blackouts associated with gulping drinks, continuous drinking over long periods, fatigue, not eating, and getting older. Physicians generally don't report blackouts caused by moderate drinking.

Mechanism of Blackouts

No one knows exactly how or why blackouts happen, and there are obvious and serious ethical considerations in conducting legitimate research. To date, research on blackouts depends almost entirely on self-report.

While research hasn't yielded much information on the cause of blackouts, it has told us some things about the memory of a person who experiences blackouts. In a 1975 *Harvard Magazine* article, William I. Bennett said that if an alcoholic can remember something *for* a few minutes or *in* a few minutes, he can remember it the next day. Thus "it would appear that once

---

[7] H. Wallgren and H. Barry III, *Actions on Alcohol*, Vol. 2 (Amsterdam: Elsevier Publishing Company, 1970), pp. 11-12.

an experience has time to get into permanent storage, alcohol has little effect on it"—except, as Bennett pointed out, that some things an alcoholic can't recall when sober may be recalled when he's drunk again.

Dr. Goodwin and other researchers have determined that blackouts actually start during the second, the "short-term" phase of memory function. Alcoholics, even if drunk (with a blood alcohol level as high as .30), can recall things during "immediate" memory, which is the first stage and lasts a couple of minutes. If that memory has disappeared half an hour later, during the "short-term" phase, it will remain missing for the "long-term" phase, which was tested twenty-four hours later, a time when alcoholics were again sober.

Somehow—and only in some people—alcohol inhibits the brain's ability to move short-term memory into the long-term storage system in the brain. Thus for the times of these short-term memories there's total amnesia.

How Blackouts Aid Denial

Because alcoholics can't remember what happens during blackouts, they're spared confronting not only the threatening details but also their feelings about their antisocial behavior during blackouts. Thus their guilt, shame, and self-reproach are vague, nameless, and of little help in self-recognition. Even if someone who was present describes their blackout behavior in detail, alcoholics tend to minimize such reports as exaggerations. They even, in some measure, *believe* the report is exaggerated. This, of course, blunts the truth—and aids overall denial of their alcoholism.

Confrontation and Blackouts

Presenting data on blackouts can be a vital tool in confronting an alcoholic. Experts recommend carefully detailed descriptions of specific incidents. These should be related to the alcoholic by people important to the alcoholic and in the simplest, most direct, and objective manner possible. Dr. Goodwin urges physicians not to ask a patient, "Ever had a blackout?" and let it go at that. He believes that "Have you ever forgotten things you did while drinking?" is far better strategy.

Not everyone who has a blackout is an alcoholic. People who have little experience drinking may black out the first time they drink heavily. However, nonalcoholics tend to avoid drinking to such an extent thereafter. In short, any person who experiences blackouts and continues to drink is manifesting a serious symptom of alcoholism. To continue drinking heavily after such experiences is to court serious problems and to witness the loss of control over one's drinking.

Lucy Barry Robe

This section is taken from *Blackouts and Alcoholism*, published by the Johnson Institute.

CHAPTER THREE

Chemical Dependence in Women

Chemical dependence is one of the greatest problems facing contemporary society. In our eagerness to tackle it, though, there's always the danger of generalizing too hastily, of assuming that all alcohol and other drug users are about the same and that therefore our ways of identifying, diagnosing, and treating their problems should be about the same. This chapter hopes to dispel that myth as it explores our latest knowledge about the special problems women have with drugs.

For now, let's mention just two examples of how women's problems are special.

One problem is that in nearly all human societies, norms for permissible alcohol or other drug use are different for men and women. Although sex-related differences in drinking rules may sometimes protect women, they can also be destructive. In the early days of ancient Rome, to cite an extreme example, the law of Romulus forbade women to use alcohol, and some women were put to death by stoning or by starvation for violating that law. Writers of the time explained that alcohol was forbidden to women because it made them sexually promiscuous. This same double standard of drinking and this same stereotype of the female drinker (or other drug user) as a lewd woman survive in American culture today. And they still provide a basis for the special stigma attached to drug-dependent women. This stigma creates a barrier to identifying and treating these women, for it encourages individual, family, and societal denial and encourages the dependent female to remain in hiding.

A second example of women's problems with drugs relates to their special role as mothers. Recent research has shown that dependent mothers subject their fetus to risks of damage, including fetal alcohol syndrome and prenatal sedative and opiate dependence. In addition, drugs may interfere with normal pregnancy and birth, causing such complications as premature or pathological labor. Moreover, drug dependence often distorts early nurturing and mother-infant bonding. A special problem for many modern women is the responsibility of being a single parent. When she suffers from drug dependence, her children are likely to lack a stable caring adult. And so the damage done by these diseases passes from generation to generation.

Much of our understanding of the drinking patterns and problems of women comes from a comprehensive nationwide survey conducted by Dr. Sharon Wilsnack and her colleagues at the University of North Dakota.[1] This project collected detailed information from over 900 female drinkers (sampled so as to include 500 "heavier" drinkers) and nearly 400 male drinkers. For both men and women the highest rates of alcohol-related problems (such as driving under the influence, belligerence, or interpersonal conflict), as well as the highest rates of alcohol-dependence symptoms (such as memory lapses or morning drinking), occurred in the youngest age group (21-34). In men, the highest rate of heavier drinking was found in the same age group. Among women, on the other hand, the highest proportion of heavier drinkers was found in those aged 34-49.

---

[1] S. C. Wilsnack and L. S. Beckman, eds. *Alcohol Problems in Women* (New York: Plenum Press, 1980).

This curious dissociation of heavy and problem drinking awaits further research.

However, the difference between male and female patterns is relevant to prevention and early intervention. In American men the heaviest drinking occurs in young adulthood, so men who maintain a pattern of heavy drinking or who increase their drinking into their late thirties and forties are atypical and therefore merit special diagnostic attention. Among women, however, the rate of heavier drinking continues to climb (although not to levels as high as it does in males) beyond early adulthood and into middle age. Since women may begin their alcohol dependence at any age, and on the average do so later than men, prevention efforts must continue throughout a woman's life cycle. Programs that teach women how to cope with life problems without relying on alcohol or other drugs are important components of prevention. But such programs shouldn't be limited to teenagers and young women; they should focus on women undergoing important transitions at any point in their lives. Examples would be a prevention component in programs for battered women, displaced homemakers, and women going through divorce.

The Wilsnack study also found that the characteristics of women showing the highest rates of alcohol problems varied according to age. Risk factors for those in the youngest group surveyed (21-34) were being single (never married), childless, and not employed full-time. These were young women who had not assumed expected adult roles. Among the women aged 35-49, the highest problem rates were found among those divorced or separated, unemployed, or having children who did not live with them. These women had assumed but lost at least some of the adult roles. The oldest women in the study, aged 50-64, showed most alcohol problems among those who were married, not employed outside the home, and those having children no longer living with them—traits reminiscent of the so-called "empty nest" syndrome. This important study clarifies the relationship of alcohol problems to changing roles and transitions in women's lives, as well as to age.

Patterns of other drug use and drug problems in women have also varied during recent American history. Women have been the primary abusers of therapeutic drugs (both prescribed and over-the-counter). In the late nineteenth and early twentieth centuries, before accessibility to many drugs was severely limited by law, narcotic dependence was common in American women. Women of all social classes became dependent on a variety of "tonic wines" and medicinals containing opiates and purchased at the local pharmacy. One popular tonic, Vin Mariani, contained cocaine (as did Coca Cola) before the Harrison Narcotics Act of 1914. When such drugs became very difficult to obtain, women didn't shift in great numbers to illegal drugs. Instead, they became dependent on other prescribed drugs, such as the barbiturates and meprobamate of a few decades ago, and the amphetamines and benzodiazepines (minor tranquilizers) of today.

Today, American women remain more frequent users of prescribed drugs and less frequent users of cigarettes, marijuana, cocaine, and other illegal drugs that men are. Although women begin drug use at a later age than men and use them less frequently, differences in use patterns are less marked among young people today than in previous generations. Researchers have referred to the "vanishing difference" between the sexes in the use of drugs by adolescents. Among teens, cigarette smoking has become as common among girls as boys. In addition, data from a 1985 national household survey by the National Institute of Drug Abuse indicate that among women of childbearing age (18-34), 30 percent reported having used an illicit drug at least once during the previous year, and 18 percent had done so during the previous month. So we must be seriously concerned about women's abuse of both illegal and prescribed drugs. Illegal drug use isn't just a male problem.

Physical Factors

Hereditary Patterns

Some of the most important research in recent years has explored genetic factors in one's predisposition to alcohol problems. Family studies over many years have clearly demonstrated that alcoholism is far more common in the relatives of alcoholics than in the general public. However, special techniques are necessary to distinguish inherited from environmental influences. One such technique is the study of twins; another is the study of adoptees. Early studies comparing identical and fraternal twins involved only male subjects. As for adoptees, later research from Denmark showed a probable genetic influence for men but was inconclusive for women. However, the Stockholm adoption study, which involved 1,775 adults adopted by nonrelatives early in life, has yielded much information on heredity patterns of alcohol problems in women as well as in men. By comparing records of alcohol-related problems in the offspring of biological parents with and without records of alcohol abuse, researchers were able to distinguish two patterns of heredity relevant to women.

The more common type of inheritance, called Type 1, was seen in both sexes. This type was characterized by adult onset and less severe alcohol abuse (as measured by health and arrest records). Alcohol abuse by either biological father or mother, or both, increased the risk for alcohol problems by a factor of 3 in these adoptees. Environmental as well as genetic factors were important determinants of alcohol abuse in later life.

In addition, the researchers identified a less common, male-only pattern, Type 2. It involved severe, early-onset alcohol abuse associated with criminality in both biological father and son, and revealed stronger hereditary influence than Type 1.

Neither the biological mothers nor the daughters of these fathers had an increased incidence of alcohol problems, but the daughters had a high incidence of multiple physical illnesses.

At our present state of knowledge it's fair to conclude that a genetic influence is probable in at least some alcoholics. However, the disease shouldn't be looked upon as hereditary—that is, present at birth and not preventable. The demonstration of environmental influences in these studies offers us clear opportunities for prevention, particularly in women.

Less is known about genetic influences on the origins of other drug dependences, but there also may be an increased risk of such problems in those offspring of alcoholic parents who have been adopted and raised by nonrelatives—which indicates an inherited predisposition. A recent study by Cadoret and his colleagues offers evidence for this hypothesis.[2] In that study, as in the studies on alcohol abuse, both hereditary and environmental factors proved to be important.

General Physical Effects

Early studies of the male's physical reactions to alcohol assumed that the findings would apply to both sexes. Recent research has challenged this assumption and showed that women reach higher peak levels of alcohol in the blood than men in response to a standard dose of absolute alcohol per pound of body weight. This is due in part to the higher proportion of water in men's bodies. Since alcohol consumed is dissolved in the total body water, a standard dose will be less diluted in a woman. The study also found that, unlike males, female subjects showed a great deal of day-to-day variability in

---

[2] R. J. Cadoret, et al. "An Adoption Study of Genetic and Environmental Factors in Drug Abuse." *Archives of General Psychiatry* 43 (1986), pp. 1131-1136.

peak blood-alcohol levels, correlated in part with the phases of the menstrual cycle, with the highest peaks occurring in the pre-menstrual phase. In practical terms, then, a woman will react more strongly than a man to an equivalent amount of alcohol and will likely be less able than a man to predict accurately the effect on her of a given amount of alcohol consumed.

Differences between men and women have also been found in their vulnerability to some of the late-stage physical complications of alcoholism. Compared to men, alcoholic women have been found to develop fatty liver and hepatic cirrhosis, as well as hypertension, anemia, malnutrition, and gastrointestinal hemorrhage, at lower levels of alcohol intake (even correcting for differences in body weight) for fewer years.

Although much has been written about changes in emotions and behavior during the menstrual cycle, few investigators have looked at women's drinking patterns in relation to those changes. In one study, nonalcoholic women reported that significantly more negative moods, more drinking to relieve tension or depression, and more solitary drinking had occurred during menstruation. Since these drinking patterns are characteristic of alcohol dependence, the menstrual cycle may influence the early development of pathological drinking patterns in women. Some women suffering from alcoholism have reported that their drinking tended to be heaviest just before their menstrual periods. Others have reported that they were introduced to the use of alcohol to relieve distress when they were given alcoholic beverages during their teens as a folk-medicine remedy for menstrual cramps. This use of alcohol, like other supposedly medicinal uses, should be strongly discouraged.

Very little is known about the effects of alcohol consumption on women's sexual functioning. Heavy drinking has been linked to infertility, lack of sexual interest, inability to reach orgasm, and a wide variety of obstetrical, gynecological, and sexual dysfunctions. An interesting set of experiments looked at changes in the sexual arousal responses of men and women to single doses of alcohol. In men, both self-reported feelings and physiological measurements of arousal increased in response to sexual stimuli when the subject believed he had consumed alcohol (whether or not he had actually received it). In women, however, there was dissonance between subjective feelings of arousal and physiological responses. Women who thought they had received an alcoholic beverage said they felt more arousal, whether or not they had actually consumed alcohol. However, actual alcohol consumption depressed physical arousal, even if the women *thought* they were more stimulated.

In a further study of orgasm in women, it was demonstrated that increasing levels of blood alcohol interfered progressively with the rapidity and intensity of orgasm. In spite of these negative physiological effects, studies of alcoholic women show that they often expect greater desire and enjoyment of sex when drinking (while at the same time they report a high incidence of sexual and reproductive dysfunction). This seeming paradox is probably due to the women's culturally determined expectations that alcohol increases sexual desire ("Candy is dandy; liquor is quicker"). This is an important observation or clinical practice that may well apply to other psychoactive drugs as well. The expectation of a drug's effects and its actual physical effects often differ. A chemically dependent woman, faced with the necessity of abstinence from alcohol and other drugs as a condition for her recovery, is likely to assume that she will have to sacrifice sexual pleasure in the process. Simple education about the deleterious effects of drugs on sexual excitation and orgasm will reassure her that a satisfactory loving relationship is likely to yield far more sexual pleasure during her sobriety than was possible during her time of drug abuse.

Drugs and Pregnancy

The Fetal Alcohol Syndrome (FAS) and other alcohol-related birth defects are a special concern. FAS probably occurs in between one or two cases per 1,000 live births. Along with Down's syndrome and spina bifida, it's one of the three most frequent causes of birth defects associated with mental retardation. Of these three, it's the only one that is completely preventable. However, adequate prevention requires that obstetrical personnel identify women problem drinkers early in their pregnancy or, preferably, *before* pregnancy. Public education about the danger of alcohol to the fetus and the recommendation that pregnant women avoid drinking aren't sufficient prevention for women who are already drug dependent. And when these women do become pregnant, they need treatment in order to become drug-free, both *during* the pregnancy and *afterward*. Resuming drug use after the baby is born will cause relapse, which will both interfere with adequate parenting and reestablish the other symptoms of the disease.

In addition to the fully expressed fetal alcohol syndrome, drinking during pregnancy can result in a wide variety of other problems for the fetus, including miscarriage, low birth weight, and birth defects. The defects, called fetal alcohol effects (FAE) or alcohol-related birth defects (ARBD), are far more common than FAS. While FAS is usually seen in the offspring of alcoholic women who drink heavily during pregnancy, FAE can be observed in women with lower intakes of alcoholic beverages—intakes compatible with social or nonproblem drinking.

Thus it's important to educate all women of childbearing age who may be pregnant or planning pregnancy. Both U.S. and Swedish studies of women who drank heavily early in pregnancy but were helped to stop alcohol use by the end of the second trimester (sixth month) have shown that it's possible to improve greatly the chance for a healthy baby. None of the mothers who managed to stop drinking gave birth to an infant with the full FAS. Infants of those mothers were also less likely to show low birth weight, neonatal distress, or birth defects. Likewise, experiments on animals have shown that the developing fetus can compensate for alcohol-related damage to some degree if alcohol intake is stopped during pregnancy.

The message this research sends to clinicians is clear. Even if a woman is already in early pregnancy and drinking heavily, she shouldn't be made to feel it's too late to help her current pregnancy. She should be strongly encouraged to enter treatment immediately; clinicians can keep her in treatment by taking advantage of her desire to have a healthy baby.

There are no absolutely reliable estimates of the probability that an alcoholic woman who drinks during pregnancy will produce an infant with FAS or FAE. One study found a probability of 40 percent. However, a variety of factors including diet, the use of other drugs, prenatal medical care, physical health, number of previous pregnancies, and length and severity of alcoholism all seem to play a role along with alcohol intake. One retrospective study compared the children of 36 upper-middle-class and upper-class alcoholic women with the children of 48 alcoholic women who were on public assistance. The women differed significantly in race, marital status, parental alcoholism, and beverage of choice, but not in alcohol intake. The women of lower socioeconomic status, who were Black (70 percent) or Hispanic (30 percent) and more likely to drink beer, contrasted with the White upper-class women, who preferred hard liquor or wine. The differences in the incidence of FAS and FAE were striking, with overt effects present at birth in 71 percent of the children of the public-assistance mothers and in only 4.6 percent of the children of upper-class mothers. However, even though these children of upper socioeconomic-class mothers were considered normal at birth, their birth weight was lower, and 21 percent later showed signs of attention-deficit disorder.[3]

While opiates haven't been shown to cause birth defects similar to FAS, women physically dependent on opiates at the time of delivery do put their infants at risk for neonatal withdrawal syndrome. They also increase the risk of stillbirth and complicated labor. Such pregnant women and newborns require intensive and specialized medical care in order to avoid or minimize complications and distress.

Stimulants such as amphetamines and cocaine have been reported to cause miscarriage, premature labor, and other obstetric complications. Infants of mothers who have used these drugs may be jittery and irritable at first, and later depressed. Marijuana use has been suspected as a contributor to birth defects and may act in conjunction with other factors such as alcohol and malnutrition. Cigarette smoking has been associated with decreased birth weight and prematurity.

Sedative drugs, including sleeping pills and tranquilizers, can also present significant problems for pregnant women. Use of Diazepam (Valium) early in pregnancy has been implicated in birth defects in animals, as have barbiturates. All sedatives, if used in large doses up until delivery, can produce infant drowsiness and poor feeding, followed by a neonatal withdrawal syndrome that will cause continuing distress and will interfere with mother-infant bonding.

Alcohol and other drug use during nursing should also be avoided, since alcohol and some other drugs enter the breast milk. The folk-medicine practice of giving alcoholic beverages to nursing mothers to "help the milk" has no basis in scientific fact and should be discouraged.

---

[3] N. Bingol, "The Influence of Socioeconomic Factors on the Occurrence of FAS." *Advances in Alcoholism and Substance Abuse* 6, No. 4 (1987), pp. 105-118.

With the increased frequency of teenage pregnancy in our society, prevention of adolescent drug use (including tobacco) takes on a special urgency. The treatment of a chemically dependent pregnant woman should be considered a medical emergency and given the highest priority. Fortunately, the wish to protect the health of her unborn child is a powerful motivator for treatment in many pregnant women.

Psychological Factors

There's still a great deal of uncertainty about possible psychological factors that may predispose some people to drug dependence. Studies have failed to distinguish factors that might have been present before the onset of illness from those that are caused by the disease itself. These distinctions can only be made in longitudinal studies that follow subjects from childhood or adolescence into adulthood in an attempt to discover which early traits predict later alcohol problems. Few of these studies of drug problems have included female subjects. Mary Cover Jones, in a long-term follow-up study, identified general feelings of low self-esteem and inability to cope as predisposing factors in preteen and teenage girls who later became problem drinkers.[4] This contrasted with the predisposing factors in males, which were aggressiveness and rebelliousness. Unfortunately, the number of problem drinkers in this study was small.

Fillmore, in a 27-year follow-up of drinking among American college students, found that factors predicting problem drinking in later life differed considerably between males and

---

[4] Mary Cover Jones, "Personality Antecedents and Correlates of Drinking Patterns in Women." *Journal of Consultation and Clinical Psychology* 36 (1971), pp. 61-69.

females.[5] The best predictor of later problems for women was a high score on the "feeling adjustment" scale, composed of such items as drinking to relieve shyness, drinking to get high, drinking to be "happy," and drinking to get along better on dates. (Among men, those with mild rather than serious alcohol-related problems in college were most likely to show up in the problem-drinker group at follow-up.) Although these studies don't establish the existence of an "alcoholic" or "addictive" personality, they do tend to confirm the clinical observation that women often begin their drug dependence during periods of emotional distress, using the drug as a medication.

Social Factors

Whatever the genetic and psychological predisposition of any individual woman, to develop chemical dependence she must feel that it is acceptable to use drugs. Social and cultural customs and values that influence access to various drugs and attitudes toward drug use play an important part in the development of chemical dependence. The socialization of women that makes it more acceptable for them to visit physicians, to acknowledge and seek help for physical and mental symptoms, and to use prescription psychoactive drugs helps shape patterns of female drug dependence. Studies of medical practice have also shown that physicians prescribe psychoactive drugs more readily to women than to men for the same complaints. On the other hand, it has been more socially permissible (or even expected) for males to use illegal drugs. And women dependent on such illegal drugs as heroin and cocaine often report that they were introduced to the frequent or heavy use

---

[5] K. M. Fillmore, et al. *The 27 Year Longitudinal Panel Study of Drinking by Students in College.* (National Institute of Alcohol Abuse and Alcoholism, 1975.)

of such drugs by husbands or boyfriends.

Social values and customs are critically important in both causing and preventing alcohol and other drug problems. Educational prevention programs attempt to decrease the acceptability of drinking and other drug use by minors. However, attractive advertising campaigns that glamorize the use of alcoholic beverages remain a major source of influence on the public. In recent years this advertising has increasingly been aimed at women, who, it has been claimed, may be targeted by the beverage industry as a "growth market." After all, the "average" American woman drinks only half as much as her male counterpart. Ads showing glamorous models in fashionable attire, or women in unconventional settings, seek to associate drinking with success, excitement, and being a "liberated woman." Tobacco advertising has done likewise.

As previously mentioned, the drug-use patterns of adolescents have shown progressively fewer male-female differences in recent years. Since females attain higher blood-alcohol levels than males in response to equal doses of alcohol, and since women and girls tend to be lighter in weight, any change in social norms that expects a woman to "drink like a man" (or requires males and females to consume any drug at the same dosage level) will be especially damaging for women. Prevention programs should stress these differences.

Another important social factor affecting use patterns is the stigma attached to women who use alcohol and other drugs. Although it may be argued that this stigma discourages drug abuse, it produces a great many pernicious consequences, particularly for the chemically dependent woman.

As mentioned earlier, Western societies have associated sexual availability or promiscuity with women who drink. This idea persists in twentieth-century America as part of the triple stigma borne by alcoholic women. First, they carry the same general stigma as male alcoholics. Although many Americans accept the disease concept of alcoholism, this acceptance is still very superficial. When asked directly, the same people who agree that alcoholism is a disease also feel that it's a disease that happens to weak or immoral people and that it's "self-inflicted."

Secondly, women in Western society are expected to adhere to a higher moral standard than men, at least in theory, and are therefore more despised when they fail to live up to expectations. This increases the stigma attached to drug dependent women.

Finally, the assumption that women who use drugs are sexually promiscuous is particularly damaging. This assumption hasn't been confirmed by research. Wilsnack and her associates investigated this question as part of the large national survey of American women (mentioned earlier). The women were asked if they had ever had the experience of being less particular about their choice of a sexual partner when they had been drinking. Only 8 percent of them reported such an experience, and although fewer (4 percent) among the lightest drinkers answered yes, the moderate and heavier drinkers (11 percent and 12 percent) didn't differ. Such results do little to support the idea that drinking makes women "loose." On the contrary, the evidence shows that this societal stigma has promoted sexual victimization of women by considering women who drink as acceptable targets for male aggression.

The Wilsnack study also asked if the women subjects had ever had the experience that someone who had been drinking became sexually aggressive toward them. Sixty percent of all women, in approximately equal proportions of light, moderate, and heavy drinkers, responded yes. Similarly, this study by Fillmore on social victims of drinking found that women who drink in bars (that is, who were exposed to others while drinking) were far more likely to be victimized even if they were not themselves heavy or problem drinkers. On the other hand, problem drinkers (those who often drink heavily) were most victimized among both men and women.

Recent direct evidence of this sexual stigma (that women drinkers are sexually promiscuous) has been found by Dr. William George and colleagues, who studied the reactions of college students to a videotape of a young adult date scene.[6] Both male and female students rated the woman in the scene more sexually available and more likely to have intercourse if the scene showed her ordering an alcoholic beverage rather than a soft drink. Furthermore, she was rated even more likely to be available if the male paid for the drinks than if they split the cost.

In light of the above, it's not surprising that many alcoholic women who reach treatment have histories of being the victims of rape and other abuse. And clinical experience with women in treatment for other drug dependence has been similar.

Finally, this social stigma also acts as a major barrier to the identification and treatment of the women who desperately need help. Since the alcoholic woman grows up in the same society as the rest of us, she applies this stigma to herself and keeps her problem hidden because of guilt and shame. She tends to drink alone, often in her kitchen or bedroom, and the nature and extent of her drinking or other drug use is often not appreciated by her family and friends until she has reached an advanced state of her disease. In addition, although she may seek help repeatedly from medical facilities because of her failing health, nervousness, and insomnia, the stereotype of the drug-addicted female as the "fallen woman" makes health professionals less likely to suspect these diagnoses in their well-dressed, socially competent female patients. The chemically

---

[6] William H. George, et al. "Male Perceptions of the Drinking Woman: Is Liquor Quicker?" Presented at Eastern Psychological Association, New York City, April 1986.

dependent woman seldom recognizes the basic nature of her own problem, since to *her* the drugs are not her problem. Rather, they are her attempt at solving the many other problems she perceives as troubling her. It's no surprise, then, that she often leaves the doctor's office with a prescription for additional sedative drugs rather than with a referral for addiction treatment.

Course and Symptoms of the Disease

Most researchers agree that women coming to treatment for alcoholism differ from their male counterparts in a number of ways. Women start drinking and begin their pattern of alcohol abuse at later ages but appear for treatment at about the same age as male alcoholics. This points to a more rapid development of "telescoping" of the course of the disease in women. Alcoholic women are more likely than men to be divorced when they enter treatment or to be married to or living with an alcoholic "significant other." They're more likely than the alcoholic man to relate the onset of pathological drinking to a particularly stressful event. Women are more likely to have histories both of suicide attempts and of previous psychiatric treatment. Their motives for entering treatment and the problems they perceive as relating to alcohol are more likely to be health and family problems, whereas for the male, job problems and trouble with the law, particularly arrests for driving while intoxicated, are more prevalent.

Women alcoholics have a high incidence of obstetric and gynecological difficulties, and they develop cirrhosis more rapidly than males. Various studies have shown that women more often have histories of other drug dependence along with their alcoholism—particularly dependence on tranquilizers, sedatives, and amphetamines. Female alcoholics are also more likely to have such symptoms of psychological distress as anxiety and depression and to have lower self-esteem than their male counterparts. Some of the same characteristics have been reported for opiate-dependent women, particularly the psychological symptoms, low self-esteem, and the "telescoped" course of the illness.

SHEILA B. BLUME, M.D.

This section is taken from *Alcohol/Drug Dependent Women: New Insights into Their Special Problems, Treatment, Recovery,* published by the Johnson Institute.

Special Needs of Women in Treatment

The first and most easily available means of help for anyone—woman or man—is from a Twelve Step Program such as Alcoholics Anonymous, Narcotics Anonymous, Al-Anon or Nar-Anon. Alcoholics Anonymous and Narcotics Anonymous offer the chemically dependent woman the support and insight of other chemically dependent people who are ready to listen to her troubles and help her toward recovery. It is from the group support of those with similar problems that she may take what she needs for recovery, or she might determine a need for more intensive treatment at an outpatient or inpatient facility. Al-Anon and Nar-Anon are support groups for those whose lives are touched by a chemically dependent person and those co-dependents who share in the family disease of addiction. In this group, the members can work on themselves as they strive for recovery from their own emotional problems.

In some areas of the country there are treatment programs designed especially for women. A partial list of these programs is available from the National Clearinghouse for Alcohol/ Drug Information. (The address for this and other national organizations can be found at the end of this book.) There are also many other programs open to all throughout the nation in which women have found help in their efforts to deal with the disease of chemical dependence. In general, several different services are available to an individual: detoxification, health assessment, inpatient treatment, outpatient treatment, halfway houses, and support groups. In recent years, as the needs of women in treatment have been more clearly recognized, changes

71

have been made in many programs that formerly were designed to treat men only.

Women in treatment need the support of female role models or men who are sympathetic to the specific needs of women in the programs. According to Edith Gomberg in *Women in Therapy*[7] and Marian Sandmaier in *The Invisible Alcoholics*,[8] the attitude of the therapist toward chemically dependent women is influential for successful treatment. M. A. Wilmore in *The Alcoholic Woman: Her Crises and Recovery* emphasizes that both male and female counselors need to be aware of their own attitudes and values regarding sex role stereotypes and how their attitudes may affect any individual's treatment progress.[9]

While remembering that chemical dependence is the same illness in men and women, a skillful counselor will remain aware of the many differences between men and women. Although few surveys of the attitudes of chemical dependence counselors toward women have been conducted, research exploring attitudes of professionals in other fields warns of the danger that sexist stereotyping poses for clients. For example, a task force of the American Psychological Association explored sexism affecting women as clients in psychotherapy.[10] The task force learned that psychotherapists, both male and female, often fostered traditional sex roles, devalued women clients, used psychoanalytic concepts in a sexist way, and

---

[7] Edith S. Gomberg, "Women and Alcoholism," *Women in Therapy*, eds., V. Franks, V. Burtle (New York: Brunner/Margel, 1974), p. 183.

[8] Marian Sandmaier, *The Invisible Alcoholics: Women and Alcohol Abuse in America* (New York: McGraw-Hill, 1980), p. 218.

[9] M. A. Wilmore, "The Alcoholic Woman: Her Crises and Recovery," prepared for Women in Crisis Conference, New York, May 1979.

[10] "Task Force on Sex Bias and Sex-Role Stereotyping in Psychotherapeutic Practice, Report of the Task Force," *American Psychologist* 30 (1975), pp. 1169-1175.

responded to women as sex objects, sometimes to the point of physical seduction.

It is not unusual for those working in the field to know of treatment incidents where women have been encouraged to play submissive roles or have been given mixed messages of how to recover from their illness. After a group session on how to become more responsible, one male counselor was heard saying to a woman from the group, "Don't you worry your pretty little head about that." Another woman was told, "You'd have a lot less trouble staying sober if you didn't keep trying to be a leader in a man's world."

The task facing treatment counselors is challenging. Some not only have to unlearn their own views that all women should be passive, submissive, or incapable in a man's world, they must also learn to deal with these attitudes when they are manifested by male clients in treatment. The problem is real. One study of a therapeutic community for drug users found that men in treatment often contributed to the low self-esteem of the women patients and subtly encouraged women's use of sexuality to gain privileges.[11]

There are many different sub-groups of women alcoholics and chemical dependents. Some choose to live with traditional attitudes, others adopt counter-cultural attitudes. Some are married, others single or divorced. Caregivers, both men and women, who have self-awareness and positive attitudes about women are able to pass on their positives attitudes to almost all their clients. Where the needs of women as well as others are met, good treatment facilities are available.

Women in treatment need some supportive services that men do not. First and foremost, women who are also mothers need to know that seeking help for chemical dependence will

---

[11] L. Mandel, J. Schulman, R. A. Montiero, "Feminist Approach for the Treatment of Drug-Abusing Women in a Co-ed Therapeutic Community," *International Journal of Addictions*, 4 (1979), pp. 589-597.

not automatically result in permanent separation from their children against their wishes and that accommodations will be made for their children. A few programs offer childcare as part of their treatment services. Some make special efforts, when appropriate, to refer women with children to outpatient treatment so that they can be home with their children more often. A very few halfway houses provide for women and their children.

Women who are chemically dependent are people first, not role stereotypes, and the treatment process should be designed to arrest the disease and recover the whole person. Women who leave treatment need to know the reality of the world as it is for women. Women need to get in touch with their anger at being told they are helpless, and at society's assumption that they are normally passive. Women need to grieve the theft of their adventurousness, independence, and intellectual curiosity. Accepting their grief for these losses can give them an open-eyed look at the world in which they live and their own emotions in response to that world. They are entitled to reclaim the suppressed sides of themselves.

In treatment women need to do these things, not to give themselves more reasons to drink, not to blame their drinking on conditions around them, but to come to a better knowledge of themselves and their worth as people.

Acceptance of their own feelings will help them cope with their world when they leave treatment and face what they must do and the lives they must live.

As part of treatment, there is a renovation of the personality, a rethinking process. Women may need to learn how to develop their skills of critical judgment and to examine their personal values. Are their values accurately reflective? Or are they conditioned by stereotypes? Do women believe the cliches they have been told about themselves or do they feel and think differently?

Women often need women's groups to deal with sexual

difficulties with sexual activity, personal medical problems, fantasy lives, and the lives they want for themselves apart from men. They need to deal with their nonsexual feelings about men. They need to deal with their own feelings about being a woman so that they can move toward supportive, loving, trusting relationships with both women and men. And, unfortunately, women need to realize that, as society exists today, there are sometimes opportunities which are still limited for them.

Fundamental to recovery, women need to admit that they have a problem with chemical use. This realization, while necessary for progress, may spark stages of either compliance or defiance about how to deal with the chemical dependence problem. The woman choosing to respond to her chemical problem by behaving compliantly wants another—often a male—to tell her what to do. On the other hand, the defiant woman will not let herself get help from others—women or men. In neither of these stances do women come to terms with taking full responsibility for their actions.

Many women have had years of experience in the compliance/defiance posture. Reinforced passivity has historically been part of the shaving down of the aspirations and independence of young women, getting them ready for their adult role. Women often bury many of their feelings about this aspect of their conditioning and comply their way through treatment very skillfully. Counselors who have stereotypic views of women or who have not dealt with their own needs for power and dominance could easily accept this stage of compliance/dominance as a sign of recovery. A woman must work through compliance/dominance if recovery is to be well founded. Skillful counselors can help as a woman moves on to acceptance of the reality that the problem with chemicals is a problem within herself. Surrender is the final stage where a woman realizes her powerlessness over chemicals and her ability to take responsibility for her own life. At that point, like all other people, she may not be able to live exactly as she would choose, but she need not live as a reactor to another person's standards and directives.

Recovery and New Life

Among those women who learn to live without chemicals, some become dependent on other things such as food or people. Since women in our society traditionally have been socialized to express dependency needs and dependent behavior rather than independence, they may need support for their new efforts in dealing with larger dependency issues. Thus, what happens after formal treatment is important.

The stresses in women's lives that may have contributed to their chemical dependence almost surely will be waiting for them after treatment. A complete recovery program includes support and training for women who need to cope with these continuing stresses. Many programs help a client identify problems that contribute to stress in everyday life. Problem-solving strategies are developed before women are discharged; in some cases weekend passes allow women to see how new plans work. Role playing and imagining what steps are involved in successful coping can help prepare women while in treatment. A study published by one program that uses such strategies recommends weekly follow-up visits after treatment. These visits allow time for a woman and her therapist/counselor to continue working on plans to lower stress levels. A Twelve Step (A.A. or N.A.) sponsor might be used in a similar way.

Contact with community support services will enhance women's chances for successful recovery. Some women will need information on how to deal with a physically abusive partner. Others will want to attend assertiveness training groups or make use of community mental health resources for treatment of depression or anxiety. Because the drug use environment of many women is partially maintained by contact with problem drinking or using partners, Al-Anon, Nar-Anon or family therapy may be strongly recommended. One study found that couples who participated in family therapy as a part of the recovery process had a significantly higher success rate than couples who had volunteered for family therapy but were put on a waiting list. By itself, however, family therapy is an inadequate approach to solving the problems of chemical dependence.

Because the self-esteem of chemically dependent women is usually so low, and because women's ability to feel good about themselves is strongly related to their long-term sobriety, a recovery program needs to incorporate building a healthy positive attitude toward the body. A few women's programs suggest daily body conditioning, learning about nutrition, and acquiring health maintenance information. Some women will need to work through feelings about being incest victims. Others need birth control information. Women with children may wish to investigate day care facilities or to enroll their children in community recreation programs.

Employment is a major concern for many women. Recovering women may need extensive employment or career counseling from someone familiar with and sensitive to the problems women face in the job force. Training in resume writing, job skills, and job interviewing can be crucial. Often, women's agencies offer groups which provide emotional support and feedback to women seeking jobs. Because of their low self-esteem, special attention should be given to pinpointing the skills women already possess but may devalue or ignore. Women need support for the formidable process of employment interviews and, for many, the prospect of entering a workplace for the first time in many years. For women already working, career changes may need to be addressed. Such women may wish to enter managerial training programs or further their education in preparation for a job change. Unfortunately, women also need to be prepared for the discrimination they may meet when seeking employment.

Other needs that may be present during recovery are for help in locating adequate housing or in dealing with social service bureaucracies. Many women need legal help for upcoming custody hearings or divorces. Women in crisis can benefit from advice on financial planning, child rearing, and home management. Whatever help is given is best given in a way that affirms each woman's self-worth and efforts toward recovery from chemical dependence.

Changing to a new lifestyle, focusing on her genuine femininity, dealing with the social and cultural expectations that exist around her, these make for a difficult process. Change takes time. A woman can come to terms with her fear and her past. The new woman can now freely, without chemicals, make decisions about her life. She can see herself as a person of worth in her own right, not depending for her meaning on another person, another drink, or another pill. She can have a stronger, more certain feeling about herself, her challenge, and her world. Her relationships can become more open, more honest, and more complete. Taking one day at a time, she can learn that becoming free of chemicals is to become free for herself. But, free for herself, she can say, "I am sober, I am competent, I am responsible."

THE JOHNSON INSTITUTE

This section is taken from *Women, Alcohol and Dependency: I Am Responsible,* published by the Johnson Institute.

CHAPTER FOUR

Chemical Dependence in Adolescents

Every parent of a teenager today worries about drugs. Every teacher knows that some of his or her students are experimenting with them. Every family doctor, pediatrician, and school nurse must be alert to the signs of alcohol or other drug use. Every mental health professional, social services worker, juvenile justice worker, and clergy youth worker must be prepared to deal with chemical use among the young people he or she sees.

If you're a parent, a teacher, or anyone else who spends time around teenagers in your professional or personal life, you have good reason to be deeply concerned about alcohol and other drugs.

Before we discuss chemical dependence among teenagers further, we must first have some understanding of adolescence—the transition between childhood and adulthood.

Generally speaking, teenagers tend to be more out of touch with reality than adults simply because they are teenagers. Adolescence is a time of confusion and uncertainty. The fundamental reality of "Who am I?" has not yet been established. Finding an answer is what adolescence is all about. In fact, adolescence has been called the "stage of identity."[1]

---

[1] Erik H. Erikson, *Identity: Youth and Crisis* (New York: W.W. Norton & Company, Inc., 1968).

In many aspects, adolescence *is* a job—something to be accomplished, not merely endured. Child development professionals have identified four distinct tasks of adolescence— tasks that must be accomplished in order for the teenager to establish an identity. Coupled with these are four basic needs. Understanding these tasks and self-esteem needs can bring us closer to understanding adolescence.

1. To Determine Vocation

Accomplishing this task gives *meaning* to a teenager's life. It includes choosing life work and getting the necessary training—going to trade school or college, joining the military, and so on. Underlying this task is the self-esteem need *to be somebody*. This need is best met by doing things and experiencing some success. The goal of this task is *to achieve independence*. This means that the teenager must be competent in life skills and job skills with the aim of someday being self-supporting.

2. To Establish Values

Accomplishing this task gives *direction* to a teenager's life. As we grow up, we learn values from significant others close to us. Along the way, we question and challenge them. Underlying this task is the self-esteem need *to go beyond*—to experience the spiritual. The goal of this task is *to develop integrity*. This means that the teenager must sort out values and choose which to keep and which to reject, what to believe in and how to believe.

3. To Explore Sexuality

Accomplishing this task gives *a sense of community*. It includes examining roots (heritage) and relationships with both sexes (sexual orientation). Underlying this task is the self-esteem need *to belong*. The goal of this task is *to experience intimacy*. This means that a teenager must develop the capacity to love and win the acceptance of peers.

4. To Establish Authority

Accomplishing this task gives *uniqueness* to life. It involves moving from being externally supported (by parents and other adults) to being internally supported (by oneself). Underlying this task is the self-esteem need *to be oneself*. The goal of this task is *to develop individuality*. This means that a teenager must believe that he or she is special, and have an internal support system.

The growing pains of adolescence make it hard to meet these four self-esteem needs. It's hard to get down to the business of establishing an identity when your body is under siege from within, your emotions are riding a roller-coaster, and you simultaneously feel capable of doing anything and nothing. It's hard to think clearly and act rationally when you're suffering from emotional pain. And it's especially hard when you are out of touch with reality—a common situation for teenagers.

But the average teenager eventually struggles through the pain, accomplishing the tasks and meeting the self-esteem needs and forming ties with reality. After reaching adulthood, the question "Who am I?" is well on its way to being answered.

This is not the case for chemically dependent teenagers. Their emotional development is arrested. They are incapable of working through negative feelings. *All the tasks of adolescence are still before them.* And they *stay out of touch with reality.*

How Chemical Dependence in Teenagers Differs from Chemical Dependence in Adults

We learned most of what we know about chemical dependence from studying and working with adults. Much of that information is relevant to teenage chemical dependence. But there are important differences between adult drug users and adolescent users, and we must understand those differences before we can help teenagers in trouble with alcohol or other drugs.

1. Polydrug use is higher among teenagers than adults.

Adults tend to find and "stay faithful" to one or two mind-altering chemicals. Teenagers are likely to use anything that's available.

Alcohol is the drug of choice and the most widely abused among both populations. In fact, alcohol is the "drug of entry" into the whole drug scene. For teens, marijuana is second, and cocaine is quickly becoming third in many parts of the country. As recent surveys show, the other drugs—uppers, downers, hallucinogens—are still around.

Teenagers tend not to be very picky about what they will and won't use. Since everything but alcohol is illegal, teens can never be too sure of what they're buying, and many kids don't bother to ask.

There is no "truth in packaging" on the streets. It isn't unusual to find pot mixed with PCP (an animal tranquilizer), cocaine or heroin laced with strychnine (a rat poison).

Also, it is believed that the THC (the active ingredient in marijuana) is ten times more powerful today than in the 1970s, so it's easier to get hooked on less.

The characteristics of chemical dependence are the same for both adults and teenagers. And it doesn't make any difference which chemical one becomes dependent on; the addiction process is the same. But young people are apt to use many more different types of chemicals than adults, and this makes it more difficult to tell what and how much they're using.

2. The reasons teenagers use alcohol or other drugs are more "internal" than the reasons adults use.

Generally speaking, adults drink and use for more "external" reasons—the boss, the kids, the spouse, the occasion. Many women blame a stressful life event (such as a death or divorce) for their chemical abuse.

Young people, in contrast, use drugs to have fun, to feel better or stronger, to have more confidence on dates, and other "internal" reasons. Also, young people will admit to the goal of getting high or drunk when they party ("Let's get wasted tonight!"). Most adults won't admit to that, even if it's true. They call it "socializing."

3. The levels of use are harder to determine for teenagers than adults.

When dealing with teenagers, it is very difficult to distinguish between the abuse level and the early stages of addiction. What are considered symptoms of chemical dependence in adults are often nothing more than "adolescent behaviors" in some teens.

For example, one symptom of chronic late-stage chemical

dependence in adults is using alcohol or other drugs in the morning. They usually do this to stave off "withdrawal"—the shakes, nausea, and other unpleasant physical and emotional feelings. They may need drugs to feel normal and be able to function at home or on the job.

In contrast, many teenagers at all levels of use can and often do use drugs in the morning. Going to school high or drunk is the thing to do. Thus what is *always* a sign of chemical dependence in adults is *sometimes*, but not always, a sign of chemical dependence in teenagers.

Here's another example: When adults hide their alcohol or other drugs from family, friends, and co-workers, it's a definite symptom of chemical dependence. In contrast, almost all teenagers who use chemicals hide them at one time or another, usually because of the legal implications or to avoid parental hassles or getting caught by the authorities. Again, what is *always* a sign of chemical dependence in adults *isn't* always a reliable indicator among teenagers.

Other symptoms vary, too. Young people don't have jobs to lose or marriages to break up, and they seldom experience the chronic physical effects felt by adult users. Furthermore, what may *look* like symptoms in adolescents may be special education concerns (such as poor concentration skills, moodiness, hyperactivity, or poor social skills) or behaviors traceable to growing up in an alcoholic home.[2]

---

[2] To learn more about feelings and behaviors of teenagers from alcoholic homes, read *Different Like Me: A Book for Teens Who Worry About Their Parents' Use of Alcohol/Drugs* by Evelyn Leite and Pamela Espeland (Minneapolis: Johnson Institute, 1987), or read Chapter Fourteen of this book.

4. Although the addiction process is similar for adults and teenagers, it happens more quickly with teenagers.

Experience shows that it can take from eight to ten years for a 30-year-old white male to reach the chronic stages of alcoholism from the time he begins using alcohol to meet his needs. (It takes less time for females.) For a young person under age fifteen who is abusing the same amount of alcohol, it can take fewer than fifteen months.

Cocaine gives such an extreme euphoric high that people literally "fall in love" with it and move almost immediately from misuse to abuse. Crack—a form of cocaine which is smoked rather than snorted—works so quickly that a user gets high in seconds. When it comes to creating addicts, crack appears to be the most efficient drug of all.

Young people are especially attracted to crack because of its low cost and widespread availability. In some parts of the country, it is second to alcohol as a drug of choice.

5. The emotional arrestment of chemical dependence takes place earlier in teenagers than adults.

When a person begins to abuse chemicals by getting drunk or high, his or her emotional development is arrested. The person becomes incapable of working through grief or negative feelings or working on relationships.

Many teenagers who stop using are pre-teens *emotionally*. Unlike most adults, they have no emotional development to fall back on. All of the tasks of adolescence are still before them. Adults often remember "how good it was" before they became chemically dependent; teenagers don't have those memories.

Many teenage addicts never had the time to develop life-skills. Rather than talk about adolescents in terms of "rehabilitation," we should use the term "habilitation," since what we end up doing is teaching them how to live.[3]

6. While the delusional system is similar in adults and teenagers, it seems to be more complicated in teenagers.

Chemically dependent adults and teens alike are out of touch with reality due to the denial, rationalization, projection, minimizing, and memory distortions that characterize the delusional system. Young people have another strike against them: their age. It is very difficult for a teen to accept that he or she is chemically dependent when "everyone knows" that alcoholics are guys over 50 who live on Skid Row.

Another factor that strengthens the delusional system for many adolescents is the presence of THC in their bloodstreams. THC is sometimes used to prevent nausea in cancer patients undergoing chemotherapy. Many teens who smoke marijuana or hashish regularly and also drink alcohol rarely experience hangovers. And since "everyone knows" that alcoholics get hangovers, they can't possibly be alcoholics—or so their reasoning goes.

The teenager who is naturally imaginative and creative (or wishes he or she were) has another temptation to contend with. Cocaine, marijuana, and some of the hallucinogens can lead one to believe that he or she is *more* creative under the influence. The high is identified with being a better musician, artist, writer, even a better lover. Some teens use drugs prior to tests, athletic events, performances, and other occasions when they must do their best. They think the drugs will help them.

---

[3] To learn more about teaching children lifeskills, read *Parenting For Prevention: How to Raise a Child to Say No to Alcohol/Drugs* by David Wilmes (Minneapolis: Johnson Institute, 1988), or read Chapter Twenty of this book.

7. Teenagers have more "built-in" enablers than adults.

First and foremost, young people have enablers called PARENTS. For many of us, taking responsibility for our children's behavior is as natural as breathing. When they succeed, we strut around feeling proud. And when they fail, we feel as if it's somehow our fault.

For many youth workers—especially teachers, ministers, and counselors who invest a lot of their time and energy in children—the parent in them gets hooked, even if they don't have kids of their own. They, too, become enablers.

In general, youth tend to have far more enablers than adults. The average chemically dependent adult might have as many as ten to twelve enablers—family, friends, in-laws, the family doctor, the boss, and maybe the court. In contrast, the average chemically dependent teenager might have fifty to sixty enablers—immediate family, grandparents, uncles, aunts, school personnel, church staff, law-enforcement officers, court personnel, medical staff, friends, and parents of friends—all making it easier for the teenager to keep using!

From Use to Addiction: An Overview of Teenage Involvement with Alcohol/Drugs

Chemical dependence is also called the "feeling disease." Dr. Vernon E. Johnson has done much to explain the disease on the emotional level. He describes it in terms of a four-phase progression (see Chapters 1 and 2 of this book). However, the four phases of the feeling disease are not as applicable to youth as they are to adults. For example, what is considered "social use" among adults in Phase II (Seeks Mood Swing) is always "misuse" among teenagers because they are breaking the law.

Furthermore, for adults Phase III (Harmful Dependence)

signals the beginning of chemical dependence. Since it is so hard with adolescents to distinguish between chemical abuse and early stage chemical dependence symptoms, it is better to call this phase "Harmfully Involved" and to put chemical dependence in Phase IV (Drinks/Uses to Feel Normal). And since the average adolescent doesn't know what "normal" feelings are, it is better to call this fourth phase "Harmfully Dependent" when applying it to youth.

Here is how the levels of the addiction process and the four phases of the feeling disease relate for teenagers:

The Addiction Process	The Feeling Disease
Level 1: Use	Phase I: Learns Mood Swing
Level 2: Misuse	Phase II: Seeks Mood Swing
Level 3: Abuse	Phase III: Harmfully Involved
Level 4: Addiction	Phase IV: Harmfully Dependent

You'll find information about intervention with teenagers in Chapter 18 of this book. The kind of intervention needed depends on the teenager's drug use level.

Each level of use is distinguished by certain *characteristics*, *chemicals of choice*, and *consequences of using*. This information can help you to assess a teenager's situation and determine which intervention approach is most likely to succeed.

Level 1: Use <-> Phase I: Learns Mood Swing

The teenager has a first experience with alcohol or other drugs and uses them occasionally. At this level, tolerance to drugs is low; it doesn't take much to feel the effect.

Level 1 Characteristics of Use

Responsible: Uses alcohol or other drugs with parental knowledge:
- In the family setting (at holiday meals and celebrations; in keeping with ethnic customs). Frequency: 4-6 times a year.
- In the liturgical setting (taking communion at church; observing religious rites at church, temple, or home). Frequency: varies.
- For medical reasons (with a doctor's prescription; with parental supervision or at the individual's discretion). Frequency: varies.

Experimental: Uses alcohol or other drugs *without* parental knowledge—sometimes alone, more often with friends. Frequency: varies.

Level 1 Chemicals of Choice

- **Alcohol:** Mostly beer and wine, wine coolers, sometimes hard liquor.
- **Marijuana:** Usually locally grown.
- **Over-the-counter medications, pills, or liquids:** Asthma, hay fever, or cold remedies that contain alcohol or antihistamines. Other drugs that stimulate, cause drowsiness, or dizziness: NoDoz, Nyquil, Actifed, Sudafed, Dramamine, Sominex.

- **Inhalants:** Glue, solvents, aerosols, Liquid Paper, Rush (an over-the-counter stimulant sold in "head shops" that comes in a vial-like bottle and is sniffed).

Level 1 Consequences of Using

- **Social:** Few if any. First episode of intoxication or first drug-related high.
- **Personal:** Few if any, with the exception of toxic inhalants.[4] First hangover.

Level 2: Misuse <-> Phase II: Seeks Mood Swing

The teenager uses alcohol/drugs regularly, but usually only on the weekends (or even less often). Tolerance increases.

Level 2 Characteristics of Use

- Control and choice are still present. Can decide when and whether to use and how much to use.
- Begins to develop pattern of use, but weeknight use is still the exception.
- Starts devising reasons for using without parental permission and at other than acceptable occasions (described above for Level 1). Examples: to impress friends, to "get ready" for a social occasion, to "relax" after a hard day.

[4] *Immediate* effects for some who use toxic inhalants may include heart failure, death by suffocation or depression of the central nervous system, nausea, sneezing, coughing, nosebleeds, loss of appetite, lack of coordination.

- Starts making self-imposed rules to govern using. Examples: "I'll only drink at parties," "I'll only have two drinks," "I'll smoke pot, but I won't smoke hash," "I'll only get drunk on weekends."

Level 2 Chemicals of Choice

- **Alcohol:** Uses hard liquor—whiskey, gin, vodka, rum—more frequently.
- **Marijuana:** Prefers foreign-grown. May also use hashish, hash oil.
- **Uppers/downers:** Amphetamines, tranquilizers, and sedatives: Dexadrine, Benzedrine, Valium, Librium, Quaaludes, Dalmane.
- **Hallucinogens:** Psilocybin (mushrooms) and peyote.
- **Cocaine:** Experiments with drugs by inhaling (snorting); may try smoking crack for the first time.

Level 2 Consequences of Using

Social

- Legal: Increased risk of getting caught. May experience first arrest for MIP (Minor In Possession).
- School: Activities begin to suffer, suspension from extracurricular activities may result, truancy begins. Problems with tardiness, handing in homework late (or not at all). Avoids teachers and leaves the classroom more often.
- Home: Starts sneaking out at night and gives vague explanations or lies about whereabouts and activities. Becomes less responsible about chores.
- Friends: Feels strong peer pressure to use at social events. Associates mainly with other users.

Personal

- Physical: Hangovers continue; "bad trips" (very unpleasant experiences with alcohol or other drugs) may begin. Trouble sleeping on weekends.
- Mental: Spends more time and energy planning the next high; equates social occasions with getting high. Starts minimizing extent of usage. Denies (lies to parents) and makes excuses for using and behavior.
- Emotional: Severe and unexplainable mood swings. Normal emotional tasks (grieving, dealing with relationship issues) are delayed.
- Spiritual: Family values and drug values come into conflict. Questions the need to go to church or temple.

Level 3: Abuse <-> Phase III: Harmfully Dependent

(or Early Stage of Addiction)

The teenager is preoccupied with alcohol or other drugs and uses two to three times a week and on weekends. His or her tolerance continues to increase.

Level 3 Characteristics of Use

- Has less control and choice over whether to use.
- Rituals for using are established. Examples: getting high after school, smoking marijuana while listening to music, weekend keg parties. Begins to acquire and use drug paraphernalia (pipes, bongs, one-hitters, roach clips).

- Starts anticipating and planning times and occasions when he or she can use drugs.
- Becomes more ingenious about hiding use from parents and deceiving authorities. Examples: staying overnight with friends, coming home and going straight to his or her room, avoiding family meals, having parties at home when parents are on vacation, not showing up at family activities.
- Solitary use begins. Examples: Drinks alone in room at home; smokes marijuana in room with window open; uses on the way to or from school or work.
- Self-imposed rules are modified and more exceptions are allowed. ("I'll only drink on Mondays and Wednesdays and at weekend parties," "I won't drink on the job but only after work," "I won't get high at school—but I'll skip school to get high if my friends do.")
- Makes repeated promises to family and authorities about cutting down or quitting.

Level 3 Chemicals of Choice

- **Alcohol:** Prefers hard liquor.
- **Marijuana:** Prefers seedless, if available.
- **Uppers/downers:** "Speed" (White Crosses) and barbiturates (Seconal, Nembutal, Tuinal).
- **Hallucinogens:** PCP ("angel dust"), LSD ("acid"), MDA (methyl dioxyamphetamine), mescaline.
- **Cocaine:** Snorts more regularly; uses crack more than once.
- **"Designer drugs":** Examples include MDMA (a compounded form of methamphetamine called "Ecstasy"), MDEA (a slightly altered form of Ecstasy called "Eve").

Level 3 Consequences of Using

Social
- Legal: Shoplifting, vandalism, dealing drugs, accumulating drug paraphernalia. May run away from home. First arrest for driving while intoxicated (DWI).
- School: Grades drop and truancy becomes more frequent. Starts sleeping in class, has a marked change in attitude and may be suspended from school. Brings drugs to school; forges passes and excuses for absences.
- Home: Experiences money problems; may steal from parents. Spends more time in his or her room with the door closed; stays out overnight. Becomes verbally and sometimes physically abusive. There are more family fights. Promises to change.
- Friends: All are using friends. Drops any remaining straight friends.

Personal
- Physical: Injuries, respiratory problems, weight loss or gain, overdoses. Personal hygiene suffers; doesn't bathe as often and isn't as concerned about the appearance of clothes, hair, and skin.
- Mental: Blackouts begin. (Not to be confused with passing out, a blackout is a period of seconds, minutes, hours, or even days when the user is awake and active but later remembers nothing.) Has a shorter attention span and decreased motivation and drive. Starts blaming others and rationalizing drug use.
- Emotional: Depression, suicidal thoughts. Feels different from friends and cut off from them. Anger, loneliness, hurt, feelings of inferiority, a sense of worthlessness.

- Spiritual: The conflict between family values and drug values grows more severe and causes shame and guilt. May stop going to church or temple.

Level 4: Addiction <-> Phase IV: Harmfully Dependent

(Middle and Late Stages of Addiction)

The teenager uses drugs compulsively, usually daily. Tolerance continues to increase.

Level 4 Characteristics of Use

- Can no longer exercise control or choice over drug use. Can no longer predict amount of drug use or outcome.
- More rituals; rituals become more rigid. Examples: uses in the morning before school or work, during the lunch hour and school breaks.
- Binge use—may remain intoxicated or high throughout the day for two or more days.
- Exhibits grandiose and aggressive behavior. More defiant in school. More risk-taking with police. Physically violent with family members and friends.
- Obsessed with drugs and the need to keep a constant supply on hand. Never uses all of supply with friends. Stocks up on liquor for Sundays; spends a lot of time getting drugs; when dealing, "shorts" customers and keeps part.
- Becomes more careless about hiding drugs and paraphernalia. Isn't aware of self as high, so memory and judgment are impaired. Uses more recklessly; leaves

pipes and drugs in bedroom without hiding them.
- Solitary use increases in amount and frequency.
- Abandons self-imposed rules. Because of the obsession and the compulsion to use, life becomes drug centered. The "love affair" is all-encompassing. Everything else becomes secondary to using.
- Makes repeated efforts to control or reduce excessive use.

Level 4 Chemicals of Choice

- **Alcohol** (Still the drug of choice!)
- **Any other available drug:** Uppers/downers, hallucinogens, cocaine.
- **Narcotics:** Some use Codeine, Percodan, morphine, heroin.
- **Crack:** Smokes regularly. Some drugs may be injected.

Level 4 Consequences of Using

Social
- Legal: Commits crimes such as breaking and entering, robbery, assault and battery, and prostitution. May deal drugs more frequently and in larger quantities, engages in physical violence, and spends more time in jail.
- School: May sell drugs at school. Use during school hours is common. May be suspended or expelled; may vandalize the school. May be fired or change jobs.
- Home: Family fights become more physical. Stays away from home for longer periods of time or may leave altogether. Parents may threaten to kick him or

her out.

- Friends: Friends may show their concern. Responds by avoiding them and may use violence against them. Tries a "geographic escape" by going to places where friends are not likely to be.

Personal

- Physical: More injuries; chronic cough; more severe weight loss; tremors (shaky hands, jerky movements); dry heaves. Withdrawal symptoms. Rapid deterioration of health and appearance.
- Mental: Projects self-hatred onto others. Impaired memory; flashbacks (feelings of being under the influence of drugs even when none have been recently ingested). Regular blackouts.
- Emotional: Deep remorse and despair; suicide plans and attempts; feelings of paranoia (of being watched or "chased" or under suspicion); undefinable fears.
- Spiritual: Complete "spiritual bankruptcy"—the conflict between values and behaviors becomes subconscious and no longer serves to restrain or inhibit using behavior. No peace even when high. Constant, overwhelming feelings of self-hatred, hopelessness, and helplessness.

How to Tell If a Teenager Is Using—And How Bad It Really Is

> ## A Working Definition of Chemical Dependence
> If the use of alcohol or other drugs is interfering with any area of a person's life—whether *social* (legal, school/work, family, or friends) or *personal* (physical, mental, emotional, or spiritual)—and he or she *cannot stop using without help*, then the person is chemically dependent.

Now that you know something about teenage alcohol and other drug use, you can use your knowledge to determine whether a teenager is using drugs and the probable level of usage.

The following questionnaire is not a diagnostic tool. Rather, it is an *assessment* tool that will give you an idea of where things stand.

For the sake of simplicity, the questionnaire has been written to parents. Teachers and other professionals can make whatever modifications are necessary.

Some questions have more than one part. Answer each question with a "yes" or "no." (IMPORTANT: Even if you can answer "yes" to only one part of a question with many parts, answer the whole question with a "yes.")

Section I

YES NO

___ ___ 1. Has your child ever been arrested on a MIP (Minor In Possession) charge or been at a party broken up by the police?

___ ___ 2. Has your child ever been suspended from school activities for using alcohol or other drugs, or for skipping classes? Does he have a poor attitude about school and/or family life? Has she dropped activities that used to be important to her?

___ ___ 3. Is your child becoming less responsible around the house with regard to regular chores or curfews? Have you ever caught your child sneaking out of the house at night?

___ ___ 4. Do your child's friends drink or smoke marijuana?

___ ___ 5. Has your child ever experienced a hangover or a bad trip due to drug use? Have you smelled alcohol or pot on your child's breath or in his room?

___ ___ 6. Has your child lied to you about her activities and friends, or made excuses about drinking/using behaviors (her own or friends')?

___ ___ 7. Has your child exhibited any unexplainable mood changes or emotional ups and downs that seem excessive to you?

___ ___ 8. Does your child question your values about drinking or other drug use? Does he challenge or question the importance of family activities and church or temple attendance?

___ ___ 9. Does your child volunteer to clean up after adult parties where alcohol was served, even if she isn't being responsible about other chores around the house?

___ ___ 10. Have you ever been embarrassed enough by these behaviors that you've made excuses about your child to the court, the school, friends, or even members of your family?

Section II

YES NO

___ ___ 11. Has your child ever been arrested for shoplifting, vandalism, driving while intoxicated (DWI), or possession of alcohol or other drugs? Have you found empty beer, wine, or liquor bottles, drugs, or drug paraphernalia (papers, pipes, or clips—used for holding marijuana cigarettes) in your child's room?

___ ___ 12. Has your child ever been suspended from school for possession of drugs or fighting? Have any of the following occurred frequently: sleeping in school, falling grades, truancy, forging passes, forging excuses from you about missed classes or days?

___ ___ 13. Are you missing any money or objects from the house that could be sold for money? Is your liquor supply down? Has there been more than the usual amount of verbal fighting and arguing? Is your child being more secretive or spending more time in his room with the door closed or locked? Has she been staying out all night?

___ ___ 14. Has your child changed friends from those who don't use drugs to those who do?

___ ___ 15. Has your child experienced a significant weight loss or gain, unexplained injuries, respiratory problems, or overdoses? Has his appearance become sloppy; does she seem less concerned with personal hygiene?

___ ___ 16. Has your child's attention span noticeably decreased? Does he have less motivation or drive than in previous times? Does she blame others more frequently? Has he had memory lapses—times when he couldn't remember going somewhere or doing something?

___ ___ 17. Has your child been depressed or voiced feelings of hopelessness and worthlessness? Has she been saying things like "I wish I were dead" or "Life isn't worth living"?

___ ___ 18. Has your child argued with you about basic family, educational, or religious values? Has he stopped going to church or participating in family activities?

___ ___ 19. Does your child strongly defend her right to drink or use other drugs?

___ ___ 20. Have you ever felt used or taken advantage of by your child—especially at times when you ended up blaming the school, the court, or his friends for problems?

Section III

YES NO

___ ___ 21. Has your child ever been arrested for robbery, drug dealing, assault and battery, vandalism, or prostitution?

___ ___ 22. Has your child been suspended from school more than once or expelled? Has she been fired from a job?

__ __ 23. Has your child ever gotten physically violent with you? Has he stayed away from home for more than a weekend, or even left home "for good"?

__ __ 24. Has your child gotten violent with friends, or started to avoid them to the point where they have begun expressing some concern?

__ __ 25. Have you noticed more weight loss or injuries in your child? What about overdoses, tremors, dry heaves, or chronic coughing?

__ __ 26. Does your child blame you, her friends, and just about anybody else for her problems? Does he show a lot of anger? Are you aware of more times when your child can't seem to remember things that she has said or done?

__ __ 27. Has your child ever made suicide plans, left notes, or actually attempted suicide? Have you noticed him exhibiting feelings of paranoia?

__ __ 28. Would you describe your child as being "spiritually bankrupt"?

__ __ 29. Does your child "turn off" to talks about alcohol/drug abuse or skip classes about them, dismissing them as "a bore" or "a drag"? When confronted with evidence that you know about her alcohol/drug use, does she still deny having problems with using?

__ __ 30. Are you afraid for your child's safety—or even your child's life—because of any of the behaviors and consequences described in this questionnaire?

What Your Responses Mean

- "Yes" answers to questions 1-10 indicate that your child is probably at Level 2 of the addiction process. She is *misusing* alcohol or other drugs and seeking the mood swing.
- "Yes" answers to questions 11-20 indicate that your child is probably at Level 3 of the addiction process. He is *abusing* alcohol/drugs and is harmfully involved with them. She might also be in the early stages of addiction.
- "Yes" answers to questions 21-30 indicate that your child is probably at Level 4 of the addiction process. He is *addicted to* alcohol/drugs and is harmfully dependent on them.

None of this is good news. It hurts to learn that your child is in trouble with drugs. It hurts to see what drug use can do to a teenager. It hurts to feel powerless to stop it, as many parents do.

But you are *not* powerless. You *can* put a stop to the progress of the disease of chemical dependence in your son or daughter. Working together with other caring people, you can arrest the disease and head your child toward recovery. For further information about intervention, see Part 4 of this book. Chapters 16 and 17 provide general information about intervention, and Chapter 18 discusses special concerns when intervening with teenagers.

DICK SCHAEFER

This section is taken from *Choices and Consequences: What To Do When a Teenager Uses Alcohol/Drugs*, published by the Johnson Institute.

CHAPTER FIVE

Chemical Dependence in the Elderly

Today the elderly make up about eleven to twelve percent of our population of twenty-five to twenty-six million people, but as a group they are only one to three percent of all patients that doctors see in outpatient mental health settings. The elderly have a number of drug use and dependence problems which are often not diagnosed or treated. Given the devastation this causes in people's lives, we need to better understand the problem of drug misuse by the elderly and to develop education programs for professionals and family members to deal with these serious issues.

Prescription Drug Misuse

Americans over age sixty-five receive twenty-two percent of all drug prescriptions. Nearly two-thirds of these people use drugs regularly, averaging between five to twelve medications each day and more than thirteen prescriptions each year.

Patients in medical and surgical wards of general hospitals receive at least one psychotropic medication. Some twenty to twenty-five percent of admissions of the elderly to general hospitals are reported to be directly related to drug use or misuse.

Additionally, up to ninety-two percent of the elderly in some institutional settings are being given psychotropic drugs. Over half of these patients report they could not perform daily activities without using a drug. The average nursing home resident receives an average of four to seven prescriptions daily.

Americans spend over twenty-two billion dollars on prescriptions and related items each year. This represents approximately seven percent of all health care costs in the United States.

Alcohol Misuse

Estimates of alcohol use among the elderly range from two to thirty percent. Eighteen percent of hospitalized elderly people show signs of alcohol misuse. As many as twenty-eight percent of elderly individuals in psychiatric institutions have had alcohol problems. One study found that forty to sixty percent of nursing home patients had a history of alcohol problems. In a survey published in the *Archives of General Psychiatry* in 1984, alcohol misuse and dependence was the third most serious mental health problem among the elderly. If five to ten percent of the elderly are heavy alcohol users, this would represent two million older Americans who are showing damage from alcohol use. Alcohol interacting with prescription medications can seriously harm their health and complicate planning their health care. One-third of individuals over age sixty-five become alcoholic late in life, even though they had no problems with alcohol at a younger age.

Aging Effects

As people age, they experience well-known physical changes. Their ability to metabolize alcohol and other drugs changes dramatically and creates problems which were not present at an earlier age. Their gastrointestinal tract absorbs some drugs much more slowly. This can alter drug levels in the blood and change the effects of medications.

As the body ages, it increases in body fat, decreases in muscle mass, and decreases in total body water. The increase in body fat decreases the therapeutic amount of fat soluble drugs available in the body from the same oral dose. On the other hand, the overall decrease in body water to dilute water soluble drugs increases the availability of these drugs in an older person's body. Since alcohol is a water soluble drug, the amount of alcohol in the blood will be higher for an older person than a younger person for the same amount of alcohol drunk. With age, there are also decreases in albumin within the blood, and those drugs which are bound to albumin will also show higher drug levels at the same dose.

There are decreases in the blood flow to the liver and decreases in the metabolism rates of the liver. Many of the enzymes in the liver have altered rates of metabolism and drugs are metabolized more slowly. This means that those drugs eliminated from the body through the liver will decrease at a slower rate, therefore having a higher blood level at the same dose of medications that a younger person might tolerate. Finally, the sensitivity of the brain and other organs to drugs increases, and the side effects become greater and cause more problems.

Overlooked Problems

Both family members and professionals often overlook or don't recognize problems in the elderly caused by drugs which would readily be recognized in a younger person. Alcohol and other drug problems usually appear as:

- problems with family and friends
- employment problems
- legal problems
- financial problems
- problems caused by neglected responsibilities

But with older individuals, these problems often appear to be different from those of younger people, and the problems are sometimes not noticed.

Problems With Family and Friends

The family of an elderly person may have moved and may not be in daily contact with their older relative. The elderly often are widowed and have outlived other relatives, and are living alone. Their problems with drugs may not be recognized because there is no one there to notice. Two-thirds of the elderly talk with their families by phone at least weekly, but in these conversations problems may not be readily apparent. Their behavior may have isolated them socially and they may have become depressed.

Employment Problems

Only about twenty-five percent of people over sixty-five are employed on a regular basis. The majority therefore will not have drug-related problems in work performance or attendance. In fact, they may have taken early medical retirement because of drug-related health problems.

Legal Problems

Young people who use alcohol and other drugs have a high rate of legal problems. This is not usually the case with the elderly. Many older Americans no longer drive a car, so driving while intoxicated (DWI) will not be an issue for them. It's rare that an older person is arrested for drug trafficking or possession, and the elderly are rarely taken to court for sharing their prescription medications with neighbors. The elderly have fewer legal problems than younger people, and legal and law enforcement officials will not be aware of them.

Financial Problems

Forty percent of the elderly live at or below the poverty line. There are a number of older Americans who are suffering from financial problems which are unrelated to drug abuse. If they are suffering a problem, it may be caused by the cost of their prescription medications, and they are therefore more likely to not take their medications rather than suffer the financial hardship resulting from buying them.

Problems From Neglecting Responsibilities

Typically, the elderly have few daily responsibilities and spend less time fulfilling them. Their responsibilities usually are to themselves, and they may be able to function quite well when these responsibilities make few demands.

Early Versus Late Onset

There clearly are two different types of impaired alcoholics in the elderly population: those with lifelong problems and those who acquired problems only later in life. The early-onset alcoholic is more likely to have suffered from legal problems because of drinking, and certainly to have had more work and financially related problems. There typically is a greater percentage with a family history of alcoholism.

An estimated twenty-five to forty percent of the elderly experience problems with alcoholism only after reaching age sixty-five. These late-onset alcoholics are more likely to be psychologically stable, to do better in treatment settings, and to have a lower dropout rate. They are also more likely to be women. This may be because women outnumber men two to one in this age group.

A late onset of alcoholism or other drug abuse is typically caused by many different psychosocial and economic factors. The loss of a spouse brings pain and loneliness, and the elderly may overindulge with alcohol or prescribed medications. The compounding losses of friends, family, jobs, roles, incomes, and housing may eventually overwhelm the older person to the point of seeking relief through drugs. Retirement may be a chief factor for a number of elderly people. Studies show that seventy-one percent of late-onset alcoholism begins at retirement. Loss of friends and social status, as well as income from a job, may create tremendous stress. Companies often don't recognize this when planning retirement programs. Unfortunately, the retired person may not have access to psychological and drug use treatment that was previously available through company insurance.

Family relationships can become strained for older Americans. Family members often visit less. Elderly people may be widowed or may have never been married, and loneliness may trigger drug use. Often the older person will seek relocation after retirement. Moving away from friends or to a new environment without social supports, and having to become familiar with a new city and bus routes may cause isolation. Moving across town can be just as devastating as moving across the country. Often the older person will move to be closer to other family members, but find that they are involved in their own daily activities and not any more available than before the move. Expectations that moving closer will create closer family ties, or that the older person will be entertained or be included in social circles may not be realized.

Under-reported Problems

Problems with alcohol and other drug misuse often are unrecognized and not reported for a number of reasons. Often the elderly are living alone. They seldom leave the house, so friends, neighbors, and family members may not know they are drinking. The older person does not even need to go out to obtain refills of their prescriptions or to buy alcohol because many states have liquor stores and pharmacies which will deliver to the home. Families often conceal the problem when drug abuse is considered a moral problem rather than a health issue. The family may be embarrassed by long-standing drug problems. They may not report alcohol consumption or other drug use to physicians even when an older family member is admitted to a hospital. Alcohol problems may surface only when withdrawal symptoms develop after the patient is admitted for an acute medical illness, which may be drug related.

As older people age, they may drink less because physically they are no longer able to tolerate the same level of drinking. One or two ounces of alcohol may be enough to impair daily functioning, but it may not be recognized because they are only having one or two drinks per day. In a person who is also physically impaired, a small amount of alcohol may worsen already existing medical problems and become life threatening. An older person's failing health may be blamed on their chronic illness, but the worsening of the illness may be caused by drug misuse. A person whose health is precarious can be thrown off balance by a small amount of alcohol or inappropriate prescription drug use.

Symptoms of Drug Problems in the Elderly

Deterioration in abilities and daily care often indicates problems with drugs. Older people who have been quite neat and clean, but now appear with soiled clothes or do not care for their homes may be suffering from drug impairment. Conversely, a neat and meticulous home may also be an indication of drug misuse, as the older person may be trying to conceal their problem. Signs of impairment are cigarette burns on clothing or on the rug or chair where an older person sits, passing out, dropping cigarettes, falls, and other accidents. Bruises from falling may be only noticed during a careful physical examination at a doctor's office. Fractures of arms, legs, and hips may result from falling because of over-sedation or drunkenness. Increased emergency room visits are another indication of drug problems. Inquiring about drug use, even having alcohol levels checked and drug screens conducted in emergency settings, should be included in a comprehensive evaluation.

Alcohol and other drug misuse may mimic other illnesses. Falls may be thought to be caused by small strokes. Gastrointestinal upset may actually be alcohol gastritis. Korsakoff's Dementia from alcohol misuse may be considered Alzheimer's disease if a careful history is not taken. Liver disease and liver impairment may not be linked to alcohol intake if this is not considered by the family or the physicians. Alcohol provides only empty calories, and malnutrition may develop with an increase in alcohol consumption. Medical problems may become more frequent; when there is an increase in infections, pneumonia, or gastrointestinal problems, drug misuse should certainly be included in any differential diagnosis. Physical problems and lack of physical exercise may be caused by sedation from drug use. Finally, social isolation often develops as alcohol intake and medication misuse increase. When an elderly person begins to be absent from social settings such as church, club meetings, and family gatherings, impairment should certainly be investigated.

Treatment

Elderly people have a number of treatment options. The first issue certainly has to be awareness and recognition of any drug problem. Once there are signs of impairment, the family, a physician, and social agency workers should intervene with the older person and recommend treatment. Both outpatient and inpatient treatment is available. Medicare will pay for medication toxicity and rehabilitation in an acute care hospital and will also pay for alcohol and other drug treatment in psychiatric settings. However, not all settings will accept Medicare as payment because of the low level of reimbursement, often only twenty-five to thirty percent compared to other insurance claims.

When older people are enrolled in a treatment program, it may take longer for them to clear alcohol and other drugs from their systems. A twenty-eight day program may not be sufficient, and sixty to ninety day stays may be necessary to allow for adequate treatment. It may be thirty days before the patient is able to think clearly enough to participate in individual and group therapy. Admission into an acute care hospital setting with involvement of a psychiatrist as well as a geriatric internist may be necessary to withdraw the patient from numerous medications, which may include cardiac, respiratory, psychiatric, and gastrointestinal medications. Withdrawal may need to be slower than in younger patients.

Developing a social support system for aftercare will be necessary to prevent relapse, and whenever possible, family members should be included in this planning process. Discharge planning will need to consider housing as well. The isolated older patient often needs to be in an environment where personal care and supervision are provided to prevent drug misuse. Aftercare planning should include monitoring of medications by family members or housing staff. The number of prescriptions obtained by the elderly can be limited by coordinating medical care with one physician. Family members should also go to physician office visits and be included in medical care planning. Prescription drugs should constantly be reviewed and medications should be eliminated when they are no longer necessary. Every patient should be given a trial without medications as often as possible, and the idea that the least medication is best is certainly true for the elderly.

Over-the-counter medications must be included when evaluating medication plans. A full accounting of all the drugs a patient is taking will not be possible without asking for all medications, both prescription and nonprescription. Many times it is necessary to ask the family members or caregivers to bring all medications to the appointment. This should include current medications as well as old prescriptions which are out of date and may be concealed and hoarded by the family member. This may also uncover prescriptions which have been loaned in good faith by friends and neighbors.

Recognizing and Responding to the Problem

Alcohol and other drug misuse is often not recognized in the elderly. No one wants to think of the little old grandmother as a drunk, but as many as ten to twenty percent of the elderly may suffer from drug problems. Yet, the elderly are often under-represented in treatment programs for mental illness. They certainly go unrecognized and their chemical dependence continues to harm them, society and certainly their families.

As relatives of the elderly and as members of society, we need to be aware of and concerned with these issues. Physicians must take them into account when evaluating behavior changes or other medical issues of the elderly. Without a high level of suspicion and awareness, physicians will enable their older patients to continue damaging their health and lives through their misuse of medications and addiction to alcohol. Likewise, social service workers should be concerned with alcohol and other drug misuse by their clients. When making home visits and social evaluations, they must always ask questions about medication use and evaluate the possibility of chemical dependence as a source of or contributing factor in their clients' problems.

There are many services and sources of help available, but these treatment programs will continue to be over-looked and under-utilized unless we are willing to consider the possibilities of drug misuse and alcohol abuse among the elderly. Once the potential problems are identified, family members and caregivers must be educated. Action must be taken to assist the elderly in finding treatment if our older Americans are to be treated with honor and dignity. We all must work to provide the treatment which they deserve.

EDWARD A. LUKE, JR. D.O.

CHAPTER SIX

Alcohol and Anxiety

If you are feeling anxious, alcohol (or any other sedative-hypnotic drug) will probably make you feel better. But if you have too much to drink, the next day you are likely to feel jittery and tense again. While alcohol will make that feel better, too, in the long run if you frequently use alcohol to make yourself feel better when you are anxious, you will invariably feel anxious more often.

Normal Anxiety

We must first understand what anxiety is and what alcohol does before we can understand the complex relationship between them. Most people have strong feelings about anxiety and also about alcohol. Where possible in this chapter, in order to clarify the interactions between alcohol and anxiety, we will stick to definitions of anxiety as a physiological event and of alcohol as a pharmacological substance.

Anxiety is a necessary part of life. We use the words "anticipation" at one extreme and "panic" at the other to describe the emotions accompanying what is commonly called the "fight or flight reaction." The body's ability to respond to danger by increasing the heart rate and diverting blood to body muscles enables animals to survive. With the pounding heart and the dry mouth (two early signs of the reaction) comes an increase in alertness and a heightened attention to external stimuli. All of this prepares the animal to take action. The rabbit poised in the field, ears pricked up, muscles tense and quivering, is in this anticipatory state waiting for the signal to flee. The cat, tail and whiskers turgid, attentive to the mouse hole, is psychologically prepared for the pounce. The elderly woman walking quickly down the dark street alone at night and the young man following her, tensing himself for the quick snatch at the handbag, are experiencing similar physiological states. The names we give to the feelings that accompany these physical states are determined by the situations we experience these states in.

Anxiety is a familiar name we give to the feeling accompanying the physiological response to danger or a threat of danger. In the infinitely complex lives of an urban industrial society, there are more threats to our psychological well-being than to our physical well-being. The possibility of danger perceived, though, from whatever source, rouses us to put out our best performance should the threat materialize. When we are about to face a new situation, anxiety heightens our awareness and sharpens our perceptions so that we are less likely to overlook important features of the new setting. Anxiety before a performance of any kind can provide the initial energy that pushes us to excel, motivating us to focus our thinking on ways to reduce the danger. In short, anxiety is adaptive. From the first day at a new job, to giving a lecture, to climbing a mountain, anxiety helps. It is easy to see that, on the one hand, a mouse without "anxiety" or the associated physiological events would not long escape a determined cat, nor, on the other hand, would a cat without anticipatory "anxiety" be very successful at catching an alert mouse. Likewise, humans without anxiety would not do well at many uniquely human endeavors or, for that matter, at simple survival.

Despite its positive aspects, anxiety registers as being

unpleasant, and we see no particular virtue in having unpleasant experiences unless we can see them as useful in some way. Unfortunately, the usefulness of anxiety is seldom recognized or accepted. This narrow view leads to misguided attempts to eliminate anxiety from our lives.

Abnormal Anxiety

The Diagnostic and Statistical Manual III, published by the American Psychiatric Association, states that two to four percent of the population suffer at some time during their lives from anxiety disorders. It is, of course, always difficult to determine the point at which an unpleasant but adaptive experience becomes unpleasant and also maladaptive, especially given the desire, more urgent in some people than in others, to have a life free from all pain.

Although the specific manifestations vary, the symptoms of anxiety are fairly stereotypical, and, in fact, are an exaggeration and persistence of the old fight or flight reaction. What characterizes an anxiety disorder (in contrast to normal anxiety) is that it occurs without cause or it is excessive in its intensity or duration for its apparent cause.

The signs and symptoms of an anxiety disorder are:

Motor Tension

This takes the form of shakiness, jitteriness, overreactive startle response, and trembling. The person may complain of inability to relax, restlessness, muscle aches, and quick fatigue.

Hyperactivity of the Autonomic Nervous System

There may be excessive sweating, flushing, or pallor. The hands may become cold and clammy. Complaints may include hot and cold spells, heart pounding, dry mouth, dizziness, a tingling upset stomach, diarrhea, and a lump in the throat.

Vigilance and Scanning

The individual may be hyperattentive and feel "on edge" and irritable. Sleep may be disturbed with insomnia. The hypervigilance may make it difficult for the person to concentrate on normal work.

Apprehensive Expectation

The person feels high anxiety and tension.

In an anxiety disorder, these signs and symptoms may be associated with particular objects or situations which are then avoided, resulting in phobias. The symptoms may occur unpredictably and intensely in what is called a panic attack, lasting for minutes or hours. They may persist continuously as a generalized anxiety disorder. Excessive or inappropriate anxiety may also occur in other psychiatric disorders, but in this case it is not the only or necessarily the most dominant symptom.

Biochemical Basis of Anxiety

Alcohol is Alcohol

Whether it is an expensive rare wine, mouthwash, vanilla extract, or boiled sterno gulped to stave off the shakes, alcohol is a drug. For most men and women, the drug effect is only a small part of the enjoyment of a pleasing wine accompanying a good meal. For anyone drinking boiled sterno, the drug effect is all. We are not concerned here with the relative merits of sterno and fine wine, but we will discuss the pharmacology of the drug they both contain.

Pharmacology of Alcohol

Alcohol belongs to a group of drugs called sedative-hypnotics. These drugs act on the brain and generally produce a depression of brain activity. As with all drugs, the effects depend on the dosage and the way the drug enters and leaves the body. The parts of the brain with the most complex circuitry are those affected first and at the lowest dosage. Thinking, judging, and learning centers are first impaired, followed by the brain centers for fine and then gross coordination. Alertness is progressively diminished marked by drowsiness, sleep, stupor, and coma as the dose increases. At very high doses, basic life-sustaining functions such as breathing and regulation of the heart can be lost and, of course, death from overdose can occur.

In low doses, sedating drugs produce calming and relaxing effects; only sometimes do they produce moods of euphoria and mild excitement. Even with low dosage, muscle tension decreases, autonomic excitation declines, and vigilance drops.

The signs and symptoms of anxiety diminish, and the feeling of anxiety changes to one of calm and well-being. Drowsiness and sleep may follow if the setting is appropriate. Drugs which produce this action include the minor tranquilizers or anti-anxiety drugs—predominantly benzodiazepines and mepro-bametes—and drugs marketed as sleeping pills, which belong to a number of chemical classes, including the barbiturates and the benzodiazepines. These drugs are produced, prescribed, and taken specifically for their sedative action on the central nervous system. Nobody uses Seconal because of the enchanting red color, the exquisite circular shape, the sensuous feel as it rolls around the tongue, or its aftertaste of acrid chalk.

With alcohol, the stimulus for use is genuinely more ambiguous. The drug effects, however, are the same. Sedating drugs, including alcohol, counteract anxiety and may be used specifically for that purpose. Most people who drink wine, beer, and spirits are not doing so to medicate anxiety, but some are. The anxiety which is being self-medicated may be simple, situational anxiety, that is, normal adaptive fight or flight. It may be abnormal, inappropriate anxiety, part of an anxiety disorder or other psychiatric illness. It may be, and there will be more about this later, anxiety itself produced by a drug effect. No matter what the cause of the anxiety, the use of alcohol specifically to relieve it is dangerous. As a general principle, self-medication is inadvisable because the ability to be objective about oneself is sadly limited. For treating anxiety due to psychiatric disorders, there are better and less toxic drugs than alcohol, and these should be given under medical monitoring. Sedative drugs—including alcohol—are addictive. So far, the capacity of a drug to produce sedation seems to be inevitably associated with the capacity to produce psychological and physical dependence.

Psychological Dependence

Psychological dependence can occur with any drug which produces a fairly rapid change in mood. This change is most frequently, but not always, in the direction of euphoria. Psychological dependence can result from using a drug which relieves unpleasant feelings such as anxiety or pain without necessarily producing euphoria as well. Obtaining relief from unpleasant feelings is powerfully reinforcing. The swifter the relief, the more powerful the reinforcement. Hence the potent addictive effect of drugs used intravenously where the impact is immediate. When a person who is anxious takes a drink, five to ten minutes are required for the alcohol to reach the brain, and even then the dosage from a single drink may be too low for more than slight relief. Drinking alcohol, then, is not the most powerful drug reinforcement available, but it is powerful enough to set up a cycle of psychological dependence in a susceptible person, and a person seeking relief from anxiety *is* susceptible.

The initial discovery of the anxiety-reducing properties of alcohol may be quite serendipitous. For example, an individual, anxious for whatever reason, going to dinner with a friend may discover that a couple of drinks before dinner eliminate the unpleasant anxiety feelings. It may take several such similar encounters before an individual, as yet unaware of the connection between alcohol and the relief of anxiety, makes such an association. However, when such an association is made in the future, the experience of anxiety may be accompanied by the thought "I feel like a drink." Thought may lead to action, and the cycle has begun. It may be that the anxiety that became associated with the alcohol relief was a very specific anxiety, anxiety over completing a term paper or going for an interview, for example. However, the cause of the feeling of anxiety does not matter. The thought "I need a drink" can easily become generalized as a response to all anxiety-producing situations.

An individual who regularly responds to an anxiety-producing situation by drinking for relief can be said to be psychologically dependent upon the drug alcohol. There are many different routes to psychological dependence, but medication of anxiety is certainly one of them. The anxiety which is relieved by alcohol does not have to be abnormal or pathological anxiety; in fact, the vast majority of people with actual disorders of anxiety do not self-medicate themselves with alcohol. If, though, self-medication does occur in a person with an anxiety disorder, that person may end up with two problems: the anxiety disorder and a psychological dependence on alcohol.

Physical Dependence

Withdrawal or Rebound Effects

Drugs in the sedative-hypnotic class have two particular effects: they depress the nervous system when the drug level is up, and they cause a rebound excitement of the nervous system when the drug level falls. This latter, excitatory state is generally not pleasant. A hangover after a night of heavy drinking is a good example of rebound excitation. The number and inventiveness of methods of prevention and cure of the hangover are testimony to its undesirability and inevitability. Actually, one can prevent a hangover only by not drinking excessively (any amount that is followed by a hangover would seem to be excessive). However, this advice is usually seen by heavy drinkers as counterproductive.

There is a way to cure a hangover, and many drinkers learn

it—with unfortunate consequences. A hangover in more or less intense form consists of a diffuse feeling of jitteriness and irritability; it is usually accompanied by a dislike for loud noises and bright lights, an inability to sleep, a somewhat rapid pulse rate, nausea or a lack of interest in food, dry mouth, and headache. The sufferer may identify the general feeling as anxiety, though usually the context in which these symptoms occur make it easy to say "I am not really anxious, I just have a hangover." The symptoms, though, are indistinguishable from mild anxiety, and in another context they might be called anxiety. The simplest, easiest, and pharmacologically most sensible way to reverse this unpleasant state of central nervous system excitation is to offer sedation. And what more accessible, acceptable, and effective sedation than the "hair of the dog." A few drinks will usually put the situation right, though there will, of course, be another rebound excitation later on.

Pharmacological sense can make for psychological disaster. The swift relief of hangover symptoms, if repeated often enough, can lead to a very powerful conditioned response in the drinker's mind. With the appearance of a hangover, the symptoms can lead to the desire of immediate relief through medication and a very dangerous cycle is set up. A cycle of continuously relieving the pain from excessive drinking with more drinking may indicate chronic alcoholism.

It might be thought that the hangover itself would set up an aversive conditioning tending to decrease drinking, and it probably does for some. For many, however, it clearly does not. Here the problem with alcohol and with other addictive drugs is that the positive reinforcement (pleasure of relief from pain) is immediate, whereas the negative consequences (hangovers, accidents, and other effects of intoxicated behavior) are delayed. Learning takes place much more rapidly with immediate than with delayed reinforcement.

Development of Physical Dependence

With a sedative drug taken regularly, there exists the possibility of producing tolerance in the nervous system. Alcohol is no exception. The more one drinks, the more one can drink, and the more one needs to drink. This means that if, when a person started drinking, it took two drinks to make him merry and four to get him drunk, then after regular drinking, say two nights a week for a few months, it may take five drinks before he gets drunk, but it will also take three drinks before he feels merry.

Tolerance is a universal phenomenon that follows regular exposure to sedating drugs. It occurs in mice, in men, and in monkeys, and it is caused by beer, brandy, and barbiturates. People who can drink other people under the table do so because they have done enough drinking to become highly tolerant to the sedating effects of alcohol. A mouse similarly exposed could do the same to other, nontolerant mice. The problem with tolerance is that although it enables one to drink more than others without looking drunk (an achievement of dubious value), it also makes it necessary to drink more to have either the same pleasure or the same relief from pain.

There is another problem with tolerance that is worse and potentially lethal. As tolerance increases, intake goes up and the rebound excitation or the hangover effect becomes more pronounced. If the drinking is spaced out, that is, for example, drinking on only one day a week, physical dependence will not result. However, for some drinkers, as the amount per drinking session increases, so does the frequency of these sessions. With increased frequency of heavy drinking over time, the rebound excitation can build up to a point where a severe withdrawal sets in when drinking stops. This withdrawal reaction can be so severe in some people who are daily, heavy drinkers that they experience all of the hangover effects multiplied a hundred fold and then some. The additional effects can include convulsions, hallucinations, delirium, and death.

Physical dependence and withdrawal effects range from slight to very severe. A constant feature of all withdrawal pictures is anxiety. The anxiety may be a mild, tolerable jitteriness or a profound, pervasive, overwhelmingly intolerable sense of impending doom. Very often in its early, milder stages, anxiety is not recognized for what it is—part of the aftereffects of heavy drinking. The connection between the anxiety this morning and the drinking last night is not made. Instead, the drinker may mistakenly connect the anxiety with the events of the day or the work situation, or he may conclude that he is just an abnormally anxious person.

Medicating Withdrawal Anxiety

There are a number of possible consequences, none of them good, which may follow the failure to identify withdrawal anxiety to the intake of alcohol. The individual may conclude that the work situation is too anxiety producing and change jobs in a vain attempt to diminish the discomfort. He may seek medical help and be offered pharmacological relief for an anxiety disorder of which he appears to have all the symptoms.

It is very easy for both the patient and the physician to be seduced into medicating anxiety from alcohol withdrawal without recognizing the cause. When a patient complains of anxiety, looks anxious, has a rapid pulse rate, dry mouth, and all the other physiological accompaniments the physician concludes that the patient is anxious. And if there is no obvious cause justifying such anxiety, the physician may reach for the prescription pad. Or, the individual on his (or her) own may decide that he is jittery and tense and needs something to calm down and may reach for a drink, a tranquilizer, or a sleeping pill.

What happens when the sufferer from withdrawal anxiety takes a martini or a Miltown? Prompt relief. Complete relief. Even more than for anxiety stemming from other causes, sedative medication provides the perfect pharmacological answer to sedative withdrawal anxiety. It is, unfortunately, also a perfect set-up to perpetuate the sedative-addiction cycle. Relief of withdrawal symptoms is powerfully reinforcing, and once discovered, it is usually repeated. If the relief has been obtained with a sedative other than alcohol, then there is, of course, a very high risk of a dual dependency resulting.

The Process of Generalization

Some people may develop a psychological dependence on alcohol by self-medicating perfectly normal situational anxiety. A few may be medicating an anxiety disorder. Of these people who are psychologically dependent, some may develop a drinking pattern where drinking occurs on most days in a quantity sufficient to result in physical dependence.

Medicating anxiety is only one of the ways in which people can become psychologically or physically dependent on alcohol. Once, however, a person has experienced withdrawal anxiety and has successfully medicated it with alcohol or another sedative drug, there will be a tendency for that person to generalize the strategy and begin to medicate any anxiety with alcohol.

Alcoholism

In the foregoing discussion of psychological and physical dependence upon alcohol, the word alcoholism has not been used. This was deliberate. The purpose of the discussion was to focus on how people can develop dangerous drinking patterns by using alcohol to medicate anxiety, and how these patterns, once formed, are difficult to eradicate because the conditioning is strong and unconscious. Obviously, not everyone who medicates a hangover with a "hair of the dog" becomes an alcoholic, nor does alcoholism develop in everyone who has a drink to calm the nerves before making a speech. Using alcohol primarily for its medicinal, antianxiety properties is hazardous, though. Repetition of this type of use can result in alcoholism.

Alcoholism can be defined as a pattern of drinking in which repeated harmful consequences result for the drinker who, nevertheless, continues drinking. These harmful consequences may be in any area of life, and very frequently, the problems are in more than one area. The most notable factor is that drinking continues in spite of the adverse consequences. Not everyone who is an alcoholic is physically dependent on alcohol. Some people drink in an intermittent pattern and so do not develop physical dependency. However, the consequences of their drinking can be as serious as with an alcoholic who is physically dependent.

It is not completely clear yet why some people become alcoholics and others do not. There appears to be a definite genetic factor: that is, some biological **predisposition** to develop the disease is inherited. Another important factor is the environment. Some cultures, such as ours, give permission to potentially dangerous drinking habits by approving and laughing at drunkenness, whereas other cultures regard drunkenness as shameful. Some cultures take a stoical attitude to suffering as part of the human lot. Others, such as ours, feel that even minor discomfort should be immediately alleviated, clearly an attitude which would encourage drinking for relief. Obviously there is a complex interaction between individual susceptibility and environmental attitudes.

An Alcoholic Personality?

The idea that there is an underlying personality disorder which predisposes some men and women to alcoholism is attractive. It is attractive both because it explains a puzzling phenomenon simply, and because it agrees with our observation that people who are drinking alcoholically often have a lot of psychological problems. Unfortunately, there is a great deal of evidence against this hypothesis. Drinking alcohol to excess causes anxiety, depression, and a host of maladaptive and unpleasant behaviors. However, there is no evidence that alcoholics as a group have more psychological difficulties than nonalcoholics prior to becoming involved with alcohol.

Such a statement may appear to contradict what has been said about medicating anxiety. It may be helpful, at the risk of being repetitious, to clarify what has been said before. Most people with anxiety disorders do not medicate their anxiety with alcohol. Most people experiencing normal situational anxiety do not turn to alcohol for relief. Some do, however. Doing so places them at risk for developing a pattern of anxiety-relief drinking, which, in conjunction with other predisposing factors, could lead to alcoholism.

Stress?

Another attractive myth is that stress causes people to become alcoholics. Being under stress or feeling tension is very similar physiologically to feeling anxious. The unpleasant feeling can be relieved by alcohol, of course. Some people under stress may deliberately or inadvertently use alcohol to obtain relief. If the pattern of stress-related drinking is repeated, there is a risk of setting up an addictive cycle.

In our society, there is an almost glamorous and certainly sympathetic picture of the high-powered executive, the overworked doctor, the newspaper reporter under constant deadline, soldiering on with the aid of a little alcohol to keep the stress to manageable proportions only at last to be overtaken by alcoholism itself. The problem with this picture of stress causing alcoholism is that it leads one logically to the conclusion that if the stress is removed, the alcoholism caused by it will go away. It does not, anymore than treating an underlying personality disorder with psychotherapy makes alcoholism go away.

The fact is that there is very little evidence that being in a stressful situation by itself is an important determinant of becoming an alcoholic. The incidence of alcoholism in high-stress occupations does not seem to be much higher than in low-stress occupations, when all relevant factors are taken into consideration. There is no question though that stress can exacerbate an already abnormal drinking pattern and that drinking specifically for stress relief, whether the stress is high, low, or middling, can be dangerous.

Use of alcohol is one of the common causes of anxiety. But no matter what explanations you may have for being anxious, self-medicating with alcohol or other sedative drugs may be the source or a contributing factor to your anxiety. Self-medication of anxiety or similar states with alcohol is potentially hazardous.

ANNE GELLER, M.D.

This section is taken from *Alcohol and Anxiety*, published by the Johnson Institute.

CHAPTER SEVEN

The Effects of Alcohol on Sexual Behavior

The relationship between alcohol and sex is a deep and enduring one, lasting from the orgies, seductions, and mating rituals in the bloody, sinister rites of Dionysus in ancient Greece to the singles bars in modern America. This rich cultural history, as well as our local and our personal myths, shape our expectations and affect our reactions. When subjects in experiments say after a few drinks that they are feeling sexier, more powerful, more masculine or more feminine, they are almost certainly not responding to a purely pharmacological effect of the drug alcohol. Indeed, up to a point, such reactions seem to be more determined by what people think they have consumed rather than the actual alcohol content. The power of the alcohol-and-sex mythology in influencing how people feel and behave should never be underestimated. This is not to say that there are no measurable acute and chronic physiological effects of the drug alcohol. There are, and it is these effects we are about to discuss in detail. But these effects are only part of the picture.

Because of its pharmacological action on the brain, alcohol has specific effects on mood, perception, and behavior. These effects, particularly at low dosage, are considerably influenced by the setting in which the drinking takes place and the expectations of the drinker. As the blood alcohol level rises, the pharmacological effects of the drug become increasingly dominant, and the environment and expectations become less important. An individual's prior experience with the drug will alter not only the person's expectations, but will even change the pharmacological response. Though the picture is complex, it is not hopelessly so. There is a reasonably predictable sequence of events that follow increasing intake from "mild intoxication" to coma and death.

Disruption in the Brain

First Stage

Alcohol disrupts communication in the brain, and the more a person drinks, the greater the disruption. The most complex circuits—those involved in logical thinking, problem solving, and judging—are the most sensitive and the first to be affected, even at the lowest doses. As judgments in general become less balanced and well-considered, so, too, do judgments about the person's own behavior. As the delicate cortical control becomes disrupted, behavior becomes more dominated by subcortical mechanisms, which usually monitor and urge such actions as breathing and eating. The initial mild disruption of behavior control is often described—and therefore experienced—as a release from inhibitions. Along with these mood changes, behavior is often more friendly, outgoing, and less restrained. Cognitive restraints on both covert and overt sexual behavior are diminished. Hence, the expression from Ogden Nash, "Candy is dandy, but liquor is quicker."

It should be noted that the "permission" given by the drinking environment for certain kinds of behavior may be of at least equal importance as the pharmacological effects at low dosage. Many actions that would not receive social approval between 9 and 5 become only humorous incidents at the office party. As dosage of alcohol increases, the drinker's control of behavior diminishes, and more areas of the brain become affected.

Second Stage

The second stage of disruption involves the part of the brain called the cerebellum. Disruption of cerebellar connections results in loss of motor coordination, slurred speech, and unsteady gait. By this time, cognitive control of behavior is already considerably impaired. Further increase in blood alcohol results in significant effects on those brain pathways responsible for maintaining alertness. At this stage, fortunately for himself and others, the individual usually passes out. Were there to be a further increase in blood alcohol levels, the centers regulating respiration and heart rate would be seriously affected, and the results could be respiratory paralysis and death. Overdose deaths are rare with alcohol alone because alcohol can usually not be drunk fast enough to avoid passing out before enough is taken to cause death.

Perception

As a person becomes more intoxicated, he or she becomes less sensitive to all external stimuli. This includes the sense of touch, of pain, of position, as well as vision and hearing. Indeed, alcohol is a fair anesthetic. It is quite possible in an emergency to put a few stitches in a bad cut when the patient is intoxicated without using any local anesthesia. Intoxicated people can bang themselves up badly without apparently feeling much pain until sober the next day. This increasing inability to perceive is worsened by the brain's decreasing ability to interpret and judge and its slower reaction time.

Mood

Most people drink alcohol for pleasure. They expect that drinking will produce a pleasant, mildly euphoric mood and make them feel more relaxed. In experimental situations when subjects are told they are going to be given an alcoholic drink, they experience the mood change they expect whether the drink actually contains alcohol or just alcohol-flavored soda. In similar experiments those subjects who are told they will not receive alcohol, but are in fact given a disguised alcohol drink, do not experience the expected alcohol-related mood change. This illustrates the importance of setting and expectation in determining mood as well as behavior with low doses of alcohol.

Regular drinkers and alcoholics can have special problems with mood changes caused by alcohol. Regular drinkers become tolerant to the mood-changing effects so that more drug is required to produce the pleasant mood change. Alcoholics in experimental situations often report increased tension and discomfort after drinking small quantities of alcohol, contrary to their own and the experimenter's expectations. With higher doses, the effect on mood becomes in a sense more predictable. That is, mood becomes increasingly changeable and less controlled by environmental and cognitive input. The actual mood may be angry, depressed, or exhilarated and is subject to wide swings. It may be totally inappropriate to the situation. Behavior, of course, may follow upon mood change. Inappropriately aggressive or weepy behavior is quite common at moderate doses.

It should be noted that the mood associated with a specific

blood alcohol level is reported as more pleasant when the blood alcohol level is rising than when it is falling. Indeed falling blood alcohol levels tend to be associated with unpleasant, tense moods. Alcoholics, and, it has been shown recently, regular social drinkers, have mood changes when the alcohol has been metabolized the day after drinking. These changes are in the direction of increased irritability, tension, and anxiety and are undoubtedly related to rebound excitement reaction of the central nervous system.

Sexual Behavior

From the above, the bumper-sticker assertion that "Beer drinkers make better lovers" seems questionable, at least if they are doing the beer drinking while lovemaking or even doing the lovemaking the day after some heavy drinking. Diminished sensitivity, perceptiveness, and judgment, along with an inconsistency of mood, are not generally considered assets in sexual encounters.

There are some effects of the drug which might improve sexual performance. In low doses, the euphoric and decreased cortical control might increase arousal and overcome psychological impediments to sexual activity. In low to moderate doses, the loss of sensitivity to peripheral stimulation might retard orgasm and thus permit longer, more satisfying intercourse. This might be particularly effective for those men who are premature ejaculators. However, to rely on drinking to achieve satisfying sexual action sets up a potentially dangerous situation of learned behavior. As noted above, regular drinking can set up tolerance so that gradually increased amounts of alcohol are needed to achieve the desired result.

Experimental Observations

In a series of experiments with nonalcoholic volunteers, both male and female, the effects of increasing doses of alcohol on sexual feelings, physiological arousal, and orgasm were studied in a laboratory setting. Shakespeare was right. With increasing doses, the subjects reported increasing sexual feelings and desires. But their actual physical response to erotic visual stimuli, as measured by penile or clitoral tumescence and vaginal lubrication, decreased. It is interesting that this progressive decline in physical arousal was seen in the equivalent of one to five drinks. Impaired arousal at intoxicating doses would be expected, but these subjects were not grossly intoxicated. Decline in physical arousal at low doses is not expected because it runs counter to the psychological effects of increased sexual feelings.

In another series of experiments, the time taken to masturbate to orgasm increased with increasing blood alcohol levels. The mechanical efficiency of the sexual response, namely, lubrication, erection, and orgasm, thus decreases as the blood alcohol level rises.

For some who consume only a little alcohol, the decline in efficiency may be more than offset by the psychologically facilitating effects of the drug. However, at higher levels of alcohol intake, the physical, behavioral, and psychological effects increasingly hinder mutually satisfying sexual encounters.

Effects of Prolonged Heavy or Alcoholic Drinking on Sexual Function

Males: Heavy alcohol use can produce impotence in males. About five percent of alcoholic men have complete impotence and an additional forty to fifty percent have varying problems in achieving or maintaining an erection or achieving orgasm, beyond what is expected for their age group. Prolonged heavy alcohol use can cause this dysfunction in at least four ways: by a direct toxic action on the testes; indirectly by liver damage; by damage to the hypothalamus of the brain; and by damage to the peripheral nerves.

Alcohol directly damages the sensitive testicular cells. For example, doses of alcohol sufficient to cause drunkenness in young male volunteers lowered their serum testosterone within one to two hours. When the dose was repeated on a daily basis, the lowering of the serum testosterone became more profound and more prolonged. Similar observations have been made with experimental animals, and severe testicular damage with very low serum testosterone occurred when the drug is given over a long period of time. In humans, prolonged alcohol use results in lowered serum testosterone and a lowered sperm count. There may, in severe cases, be loss of testicular tissue, and noticeably shrunken testicles. However, the relationship between lowered serum testosterone and overall sexual performance is not clear.

When the liver has been damaged to the point of cirrhosis, an increase in estrogens may be seen. Feminization, with loss of body hair and gynaecomastia (enlarged breasts), may be a consequence. Loss of libido and impotence commonly go along with this picture.

As a normal response to lowered testosterone, the hypothalamus in the brain induces the pituitary gland to pour out another hormone, luteinizing hormone, which in turn stimulates the testes. However, this does not happen when alcohol is the cause of the lowered testosterone because the alcohol also interferes with normal hypothalamic function.

The final contributor to potency problems in male drinkers may be damage to the peripheral nerves. Abnormalities in peripheral nerves are not uncommon in alcoholics (sixty percent in one study). These abnormalities can cause funny skin sensations, tingling, itching, burning, "pins and needles," and loss of skin sensitivity to touch. They can also contribute to potency problems. Delicate sheaths of nerves going to skin and muscle around the penis provide a sexual feedback loop for the continuation of intercourse. When this feedback is disrupted, as in drunkenness, or damaged by prolonged alcohol use, orgasm may not occur or the erection may be lost.

Females: Very little is known about the effects of chronic or acute alcohol use in females, though menstrual irregularities, infertility, and loss of libido are reported. Damage to liver and peripheral nerves certainly occurs in women as well as men. Alcohol also causes direct damage to the ovary, decreasing fertility by causing cycles without live ova, and can ultimately lead to ovarian atrophy. Little is known of chronic alcohol effects on sex hormones in women, though in the few studies done on human females, doses of alcohol sufficient to cause drunkenness had no effect on sex hormones.

Alcohol and Sexually Deviant Behavior

Because alcohol decreases clarity of thought, fineness of judgment, and control of impulses, and generally increases the probability of aggressive or belligerent mood, maladaptive social behaviors are bound to increase as the intake of alcohol increases. Of course, at higher doses these effects are reduced by increasing physical incapacity. Still, incest and rape have been associated with the use of alcohol and other drugs, as have physical battering of family members, robberies, and homicides.

Although the effects of alcohol pharmacologically are the same for all individuals, obviously the end results are different. Social setting, sociocultural training, individual and social expectations, as well as individual psychopathology all determine the outcome.

The action of the drug itself increases the likelihood of sexually inappropriate behavior, and social attitudes toward intoxication may encourage inappropriate behavior. In societies where drunkenness is regarded somewhat benevolently, there are fewer demands upon the individual to control intoxicated behavior. Considerable permission may be given to behave in quite unacceptable ways, as long as intoxication is the excuse. Individuals may thus be implicitly encouraged to act on impulses even though they may still be capable of controlling their behavior.

Individuals also vary enormously in their ability to maintain cognitive control over their impulses when sober. The more difficult this control is for an individual, the more easily will it be disrupted by alcohol.

Promiscuity

This word is used here in spite of its pejorative connotations because it frequently comes up in discussion of alcohol and sexual behavior, particularly as applied to women. The likelihood of multiple, sequential sexual partners is probably increased by regular intoxication, though there is little hard data on this point. Alcohol increases erotic feelings and decreases discrimination and reserve. People behave in more sexually provocative ways in certain settings while drinking. The chances of sexual intercourse will increase. This is not necessarily a problem, but lack of foresight, planning and discrimination may lead to sexual exploitation, unwise choice of partners, and unwanted pregnancies.

Some alcoholics frequently report with horror or amusement sexual incidents which are incomprehensible to them in their sober state. Or a part or all of the inappropriate event may take place in a blackout, when the ongoing memory mechanisms in the brain have been so disrupted by alcohol that nothing has been recorded. Awakening the next morning, the alcoholic discovers a total stranger in bed and desperately begins a search for the missing memory. The average member (lay or professional) of the post-Freudian generation, is likely to react with a knowing smile when told of complete amnesia for a sexual encounter. The more bizarre the encounter, the more knowing the smile. But the blackout is not a handy psychological mechanism for repressing unpleasant happenings; it is an often inconvenient physiological consequence of the toxic effect of alcohol on the delicate operations necessary to store memories in a retrievable form. In normal adults, complete amnesia for a recent event on a psychological basis is rare. In alcoholic adults, complete amnesia for a recent event on a physiological basis is common.

A substantial group of people have a decrease in sexual interest and activity as a consequence of drinking. Some people drink in a solitary fashion. For them drinking decreases the chances of sexual encounter. As drinking increases, the solitary drinker spends more and more time alone and becomes more and more preoccupied with the bottle. Quite independent of organic damage, interest in sex declines as do many other interests.

Reported Sexual Problems

A high proportion of alcoholics, women and men, upon coming into treatment will complain of sexual difficulties when asked. Whether this proportion is fifty or ninety percent will depend on the population and the sensitivity of the questions. It is substantial in any case. Difficulty with arousal, erection, lubrication, and orgasm are common and predictable, based on the known effects of the drug. Alcoholics have more multiple sexual contacts as well as more frequent loss of libido and sexual withdrawal than the norm.

In rather informal studies, a greater proportion of alcoholics than nonalcoholics are said to report sexual abuse during childhood and adolescence. This is particularly true of women. It is not surprising since alcoholism is in part a genetically determined disease; it runs in families. Alcoholic parents, grandparents, uncles, and aunts are more likely than nonalcoholics to violate incest taboos and less likely to adequately protect children.

Sexual harmony is rarely a feature of the alcoholic marriage. It is rare that alcoholics are described as exciting or considerate lovers. Spouses, if questioned carefully, are likely to be even less enthusiastic about sex than the alcoholic. Sometimes they have tried withholding sex as a means of controlling drinking. Sometimes they abstain because sexual encounters with a drunken partner are distasteful and unsatisfying. Few people are able to regard with equanimity the spectacle of a drunken partner passed out in the middle of lovemaking. Some take it personally. Recurrent cycles of disappointment, bitterness, and humiliation may result in a buildup of tension prior to the sexual act, something that almost ensures failure. These problems are not exclusive to an alcoholic marriage and many of them may also occur when one partner is a heavy drinker.

Many alcoholics and some heavy drinkers not identified as alcoholics have rarely had intercourse without some alcohol in their bloodstreams. Much of their learning and experience has occurred in the drugged state. Information acquired in the drugged state does not transfer completely to the nondrugged state, a phenomenon known as state-dependent learning. It is not surprising then, that for them, sex in the sober state is experienced as awkward and unfamiliar and somehow not quite right This discomfort with sex when sober tends to reinforce drug taking and to perpetuate the vicious cycle of compulsive drug use.

Sex and the Recovering Alcoholic

In spite of the harmful effects of alcohol on sexual performance, effects of which most problem drinkers are aware, sexual encounters are frequently implicated in relapse in a newly abstinent person. Sexual activity is thought to contribute such a hazard that, in many groups of Alcoholics Anonymous, newcomers are warned not to begin any new sexual relationships until they have been sober for a year. As with much folk wisdom in this field, data to support this position are just not available. Puritanical as it sounds, it does, though, appear reasonable. Two factors which have been identified as significant causes of relapse are anxiety and blows to one's self-esteem, which are possible, even probable, in a new sexual encounter for anyone. The newly abstinent person may be having his or her first sober sexual experience, may have had performance problems in the recent past, may have suffered rejection and humiliation as a consequence of drunken sexual behavior, and, moreover, is quite likely not experiencing great self-esteem to begin with.

Sexual Recovery in the Alcoholic

As with any complication of alcoholic drinking, recovery of sexual function will only follow successful resolution of the drinking problem. Treatment of potency problems in the face of continued drinking is doomed to failure. With abstinence, alcohol-induced sexual problems will, for the most part, resolve spontaneously in a few months. A small proportion of male alcoholics will remain permanently impotent, though abstinent. Alcoholics who continue to have sexual difficulties in spite of successful abstinence for several months should seek medical treatment.

ANNE GELLER, M.D.

This section is taken from *Alcohol and Sexual Performance*, published by the Johnson Institute.

CHAPTER EIGHT

Relapse and Slips During Recovery

For the men and women who have embarked upon a life-style of sobriety—one day at a time—the rewards of recovery are substantial, sometimes even miraculous. As the months of sobriety turn into years, most men and women who are chemically dependent become increasingly aware of the value of what they have discovered and more and more appreciative of their new-found way of life.

The possibility of going back to drinking or chemical abuse, however, always remains. True, as years of sobriety and abstinence increase, the likelihood of relapse diminishes, but it never disappears completely.

The material in this chapter offers an interplay of two authors' ideas on how relapse begins, what signs bear watching and what can be done to avoid it. These authors discuss recovery as it relates to alcoholism, but the principles can easily be applied to chemical dependence on other drugs as well.

Definitions of Relapse

In spite of the voluminous literature on alcoholism, relatively little has been written on the subject of relapse. There is also no universally agreed-upon definition of the term as it applies to chemical dependence. *Blakiston's Gould Medical Dictionary* (4th edition, McGraw-Hill) defines relapse generally as "the return of the symptoms and signs of a disease after apparent recovery." The American Medical Society on Alcoholism states, "Because relapse is possible even after many years of remission, we cannot use the term 'cure'.... One index for recovery is sobriety; comfortable abstinence from alcohol and/or other dependency-producing drugs."[1]

Since the concept of "apparent recovery" in the above definition necessarily involves abstinence, a single drink (or comparable drug use) would represent a "return of the signs of the disease." The accumulated wisdom of Alcoholics Anonymous (A.A.), distilled from thousands of case histories, states it simply: "For an alcoholic one drink is too many and a thousand are not enough."

A.A. literature refers to relapses as "slips," as "falling back into the old drinking patterns." Unfortunately, these A.A. statements may be misunderstood and misinterpreted. Alcoholics themselves may even attempt to refute them in the interest of self-confusion and denial of their illness. For example, after a period of abstinence many alcoholics will "suddenly" decide to test the above dictum and take a drink. Can this experience of a single drink (or more) be called a "relapse" when, as often happens, alcoholics may not immediately become intoxicated, suffer any observed harmful consequences, or show any other obvious "signs and symptoms of the disease"?

In some individuals this "controlled" drinking period may last for a considerable period of time, weeks or months, even extending to a year or more. Some investigators have therefore concluded that a return to drinking *may* be an acceptable and

---

[1] *Definition of Recovery, Policy Statement* (New York: American Medical Society on Alcoholism, 1982).

safe alternative to abstinence for some alcoholics.[2] However, a ten-year follow-up study refuted the experiment which seemed to support this conclusion. "Of the original twenty experimental subjects . . . only one, who apparently had not experienced physical withdrawal symptoms maintained a pattern of controlled drinking." Six decided to become abstinent and the other thirteen relapsed; they experienced a "return of symptoms and signs of the disease." (Nine went on to excessive drinking in spite of repeated damaging consequences and four died from alcohol-related causes.)[3]

It is, then, important to recognize the validity of A.A. experience, that when an alcoholic takes one drink, the process of relapse has already begun. Where a pattern of controlled drinking may be maintained as in the single subject above, the diagnosis of alcoholism may be questionable. Alternatively, since rare spontaneous recoveries without treatment have been known to occur in other diseases, including cancer, one may theorize that a similar phenomenon may occur with alcoholics. However, in the light of the impossibility of making a prediction and anticipating such a result with any degree of accuracy, for any physician or other professional therapist to ignore the need for treatment, once the diagnosis of alcoholism is made, would be tantamount to malpractice.

The term *relapse* may, strictly speaking, not be applicable to many alcoholics in the early stage of their A.A. attendance. They cease drinking and thus seem to be "convalescing" or in "apparent recovery." They attend several meetings over several days; but then they return to drinking. What happened?

---

[2] David J. Armor, J. Michael Polich, and Harriet B. Stambul, *Alcoholism and Treatment* (New York: John Wiley and Sons, 1978).

[3] Mary L. Pendery, Irving M. Maltzman, and L. Jolyon West, "Controlled Drinking by Alcoholics? New Findings and a Reevaluation of a Major Affirmative Study," *Science* 217 (1982), pp. 169-175.

The most obvious explanation seems to be that they were attending A.A. meetings while *still* drinking. They came to A.A. hoping to find a way to continue drinking in a "controlled" fashion without suffering harmful or painful consequences. Not finding it, they experimented with a brief "respite" from drinking for a few days or even weeks to address perhaps the need to feel better physically, to "get things back together," to pay a few bills, and even to convince themselves and others they were not really alcoholics. Since their need to stop drinking—and especially how to do it—had not been addressed, the experiment soon ended. Such a return to drinking is not technically a relapse, since a commitment to abstinence had never really been made and no change toward recovery had begun. Such individuals are actually continual drinkers with interruptions (or what have been called "sabbaticals") in their drinking.

Causes of Relapse

It is clear that the resumption of drinking begins sometime *before* the actual "first drink." So it is logical to ask, "Can we detect a pattern in attitudes and expressed behavior which precedes that relapsing drink?"

Although some alcoholics report that the desire for a drink has left them, many, perhaps most, report that they experience periods of wanting to drink. In some, the urge may be so intense at times that lurid dreams of drinking may occur. Sometimes the sober alcoholic will awaken in a panic fearing that the dream had been reality.

Sobriety for the the alcoholic is, then, an equilibrium, a balance between the forces driving him or her to drink uncontrollably and the new-found strength to keep those forces in check. The struggle is, at first, conscious but then submerges into the unconscious with the potential of reemerging into frightening reality.

The essential state preceding relapse seems to be one of isolation. The bonds tying the individual to fellow humans, to his or her "Higher Power," to the mysterious joy of living, seem lost or dissolved. The individual is adrift and rudderless and cannot mobilize the positive forces which had so recently been embraced in achieving abstinence. As a result, the negative forces become powerful enough to cause a relapse.

Denial: Cunning, Baffling, Powerful

Denial is a fascinating phenomenon. An interesting analogy may be made between denial of alcoholism and the denial of physical illness, a condition called *anosognosia*. Anosognosia is chiefly found in cases where there is a lesion on the right thalamus of the brain and paralysis on the left side of the body. The limbs themselves seem to pass out of the patient's consciousness as though they did not exist and the paralysis is consequently denied. Often the bizarre attitudes and behavior which result are incomprehensible to the observer.

In alcoholism, of course, there is no such specific organic lesion. Whatever the cause, the people who are close to the alcoholic come to realize that the drinking alcoholic is a sick individual. But it is still astonishing and utterly incomprehensible to all these people that alcoholics can *deny* having a problem of control in spite of repeated evidence to the contrary.

When someone denies an allegation which is clearly a fact and of which he or she is aware, that person is defined as lying. In the case of alcoholism the process is not that simple. The statement is often made that "the alcoholic is the last to know he or she has lost control." But, careful, empathic history-taking will often reveal that the alcoholic, on *some* level of consciousness, is aware that the difficulty, the harm, and the crisis stem directly from the excessive use of alcohol. In one sense, the alcoholic may be the first to know and yet also does not know. There are opposing forces so that the denial stems not from any conscious lying but from the strength of an unconscious defense mechanism which prevents this awareness from surfacing. It remains deeply hidden in the unconscious to prevent the intolerable anxiety which would otherwise ensue.

For recovery to take place, this denial must be pierced and the alcoholic must "surrender" to accepting his or her condition. The process of surrender, however, is just as unconscious as the mechanism of denial.[4] It culminates in what is sometimes called the "moment of truth," when the unconscious forces are confronted by a crisis that the conscious mind cannot overcome. This conflict of opposing forces is resolved by surrender and a new phenomenon emerges—an awareness of powerlessness over alcohol.

It is often difficult to understand how denial can continue to operate, causing relapse among alcoholics who were abstinent for many years and were, apparently, convinced from their own experience and personal growth of the benefits of sobriety. Careful history-taking confirmed by the testimony of many A.A. members reveals that they had reservations, either from the very beginning or gradually developing over time. These reservations can be about the validity of the idea that chemical dependence is a disease, or whether the idea applies to them, or any number of other factors.

It is apparent that denial has the capacity to recur or persist over long periods without being recognized. Denial can be exquisitely subtle. It must be countered with an equally persis-

---

[4] H.M. Tiebout, "The Ego Factors in Surrender in Alcoholism," *Journal of Studies on Alcohol*, 15 (1954), pp. 610-621.

tent and long-term focus on the necessity of abstinence. Regular and frequent attendance at A.A. meetings, especially at the very beginning of a program of recovery ("90 meetings in 90 days" is a familiar saying) and the simple A.A. slogan "One day at a time" help the alcoholic recognize the necessity of avoiding that first drink.

The Dry Drunk

Despite suggestions that there may be a similarity between the altered state of consciousness that leads to relapse and the withdrawal-induced changes in blood chemistry found in hypoglycemia, no objective physiological changes have been identified which are invariably found in such an altered state of consciousness. Nevertheless, heightened feelings of anxiety and uncomfortable physical accompaniments such as mild tremors and slight sweating are common before a relapse. Vague symptoms of depression surface, and sleeping and eating habits are disturbed.

Sleep may be fitful and restless with long periods of insomnia alternating with feelings of exhaustion and excessively deep sleep for hours. Appetite diminishes, meals are missed, or "junk food" is craved. The person feels irritable, is easily moved to anger, and is generally more unpredictable emotionally. A feeling of withdrawal, of boredom and listlessness, of inability to go to A.A. meetings, may alternate with intense feelings of resentment against family and friends, and explosive outbursts of violence. With the passage of time the depression becomes deeper, nothing seems worthwhile, and feelings of helplessness and hopelessness take over.

Members of A.A. have long been aware of the above progression and have termed it a "dry drunk." Their experience suggests that the origin of the "dry drunk" can be found in both physical and psychological factors. The acronym H.A.L.T. (avoid being Hungry, Angry, Lonely, and Tired) calls attention to the need for good nutrition, emotional equilibrium, relaxation, recreation, and socialization to prevent a relapse.

Most of these symptoms are reminiscent, of course, of the period when drinking, and a return to alcohol consumption may even be considered. The alcoholic who may be attending A.A. regularly, even several A.A. meetings a week, is completely unprepared for these symptoms and wonders, "How can these things be happening to me sober?" These feelings are so alien to expectations when "things have been going so well," and so gradual in onset that the alcoholic may again deny their existence, although their development is obvious to his or her family and associates. However, a careful exploration of these facts and a reassurance that this is a common experience that can be successfully overcome will begin to reverse the process and speed recovery. Unfortunately, if the process remains untreated, it is likely to proceed to a relapse into active alcoholism.

Although alcoholism, like coronary artery disease and other chronic conditions, *does* tend to relapse, a "dry drunk" is not inevitable and relapse *can* be prevented. The history of many alcoholics in A.A. attests to the fact that once they have discovered the fellowship and pursue the program honestly and devotedly, even those who were considered "hopeless," relapsing time and again, now almost miraculously begin to lead lives of increasingly improving quality.

Preventing Relapse

While accurate figures about percentages of relapse are difficult to calculate, the best studies indicate that the longer an alcoholic remains sober, the less the risk of relapse. The classic

154

survey of nearly 25,000 members in A.A. revealed that relapse occurred in almost sixty percent of those who had been sober for only one year but fell to less than ten percent among those who had maintained sobriety for five years or more.[5]

Obviously, a sensitivity to what is happening to oneself is extremely important, but it does not necessarily develop by itself without help. Regular communication with and feedback from a close friend or a knowledgeable family physician or counselor can be enormously helpful. The first signs of "back-sliding" and of the destructive behavior mentioned above can be monitored, discussed, and addressed. A good, firm A.A. sponsor is invaluable for this feedback.

An increase in the frequency of attendance at A.A. meetings will counter the tendency to isolate oneself, and more open sharing at such meetings will usually subdue any tendency to resort to tranquilizers or sedatives as substitutes for alcohol. A.A. membership is a substitute for the dependence on alcohol. The Twelve Steps provide the alcoholic with what he or she had sought in the drug and never really secured: fellowship, self-esteem, freedom from guilt, meaning and purpose, and a source of help for the future.

For a successful program of recovery to reduce the risk of relapse it must constantly emphasize the pain of drinking while revealing the joy and pleasure of abstinence. Sharing and hearing "drunkalogs" at A.A. meetings serve this function, as does the oft-heard expression, "Nothing is so bad that a drink won't make it worse." A.A. meetings also provide vicarious positive experience through other members' success stories. Fortunately, personal sobriety is its own "reinforcer" since almost everything that went wrong because of drinking tends to get better with continued abstinence and treatment.

---

[5] *Survey of Membership of A.A.* (New York: Alcoholics Anonymous, 1980).

Finally, to reduce risk of relapse, a recovery program must recognize the influence of the alcoholic's surroundings. The immediate family is now recognized as the most important support system in preventing relapse. Involving the spouse and the children as well as the alcoholic in treatment has become an integral part of many recovery programs. The implication is *not* that interaction with the spouse or the children is the cause of alcoholism, in spite of the feeling of guilt with which many family members may be burdened. On the contrary, it is the alcoholism in the family which is the cause of much of the pathology which *every* family member manifests, spouse and children, just as the direct victim of the disease does.

Although a direct, causal connection cannot be made, it is clear that the family acts as a "system" with an interlacing network of relationships and behaviors which often reinforce the illness. When a family member of an alcoholic, however, becomes involved in treatment for his or her own sake, either separately or in conjoint family therapy, there is significant improvement in the drinking history of the alcoholic. Small wonder, then, that Al-Anon and Alateen play such important roles.

And here the family, in the broadest sense of the term, is crucial. Such a support system must extend throughout the warp and woof of the entire social fabric, penetrating industry, the school system, including professional structures, the criminal justice system, the social welfare system, the health industry complex, the leisure and entertainment world, and in fact all else. In a sense, every individual coming in close contact with an alcoholic is touched by the illness and consciously or unconsciously may be changed by the disease process. Thus, the treatment program itself may more markedly reduce the risk of relapse by encouraging change in the alcoholic's surroundings. It must, for example, work with the spouse to refuse to be an "enabler" of continued drinking, and with the employer to retain a recovered alcoholic with clearly defined limits of behavior. Both cases will support the growth of responsibility in the alcoholic.

MAXWELL N. WEISMAN, M.D.

This section is taken from *Relapses/Slips: Abstinent Alcoholics Who Return to Drinking* by Maxwell N. Weisman, M.D. and Lucy Barry Robe, published by the Johnson Institute.

Slips

To A.A. members, a relapse, or "slip," means simply taking a drink. Because avoiding the first drink is essential to sobriety, the program's wisdom includes many messages about the first drink: "Stay away from one drink, one day at a time"; "It's the first drink that gets you drunk"; "One drink is too many and a thousand are not enough."

When long-time A.A. members talk about relapses or slips, they invariably talk about denial. All alcoholics suffer from denial and come to A.A. verbalizing it; in one way or another, they challenge the idea that they have the disease. Paradoxically, through working the A.A. program, a recovering alcoholic learns much about the denial system, and in time, denial may seem to disappear. However, it remains in the subconscious mind, and it can leap to life at the most surprising and inconvenient times.

Even after a long period of sobriety, an alcoholic's denial system can be powerful, earnestly defended, and cleverly camouflaged. Once it begins to operate, it will intensify if not detected, confronted, and discarded.

According to observations by A.A. members over nearly five decades, if a recovering alcoholic wants to stay comfortably sober (in contrast to being dry) he or she must change the attitudes and actions integral to the denial system.

The Dry Drunk

A.A. members use the term "stinking thinking" when some—or even more ominously, all—of a recovering alcoholic's old attitudes from the drinking days reappear. If the person talks and behaves somewhat as if he or she were still drinking, members call it a "dry drunk." A recovering alcoholic on a dry drunk is, in effect, building up to a drink (B.U.D.) He or she *will* drink if a dry drunk runs full course.

How do A.A. members cope with dry drunks to avoid slipping? The acronym "H.A.L.T." is a standard emergency tactic. H.A.L.T. means: Am I (or are you) Hungry? Angry? Lonely? Tired?

Hungry. Hungry active alcoholics find quick relief from a drink. Recovering alcoholics may not realize at first—or they may forget—that the urge to drink may simply indicate hunger. As soon as it is comfortable for the recovering alcoholic, eating habits should be investigated. Are meals regular? Well balanced? Nutritious? Has the alcoholic on a dry drunk eaten enough that day?

Angry. A.A. members believe that they cannot afford unbridled anger or resentment. Attending an A.A. meeting, discussion with another member or running the problem through the Steps usually relieves the anger enough to ward off drinking. The Serenity Prayer is often the most effective tactic in emergencies.

Lonely. Alcoholics—even bar hoppers—are inherently lonely people. The A.A. Fellowship is designed to alleviate loneliness through meetings, meetings, and more meetings. Using the telephone to call another A.A. member is the best known emergency measure when a recovering alcoholic is about to pick up a drink.

Tired. When they are tired, active alcoholics use booze as a quick "pick-me-up"—traditionally in the evening, frequently at lunch, sometimes in the morning. A recovering alcoholic who craves a drink may simply be tired, and a short nap can alleviate this. However, there is no substitute for adequate sleep patterns.

Attitudes Are Part of the Denial System

Looking at the "build-up to a drink" process, there are certain attitudes that signal that a recovering alcoholic's denial system is operating again, and relapse could be the result.

Mental reservations about being an alcoholic

Once an alcoholic has crossed the invisible line into the chronic phase of drinking, A.A. members' experience is that there is no going back to "normal" drinking. However, a recovering alcoholic with mental reservations may still harbor some "evidence" that maybe he or she does not *really* have the disease, so it may be safe to drink again.

Illusions that alcoholism can be cured

Virtually all A.A. members with long-term, comfortable sobriety believe that alcoholism is never "cured"—but is arrested by means of abstinence and important changes in attitudes and behavior.

Belief that alcoholism was caused by problems no longer present

This belief implies that the disease may have abated along with the problems, and that it might be safe to try drinking again.

Disappointment in sobriety

A recovering alcoholic can be in danger of relapse if he or she tumbles abruptly—or with inadvertence to warnings—from the legendary euphoria of newcomers to A.A. The same can happen if problems seem to be worse in sobriety than they were during drinking days. Alcoholics are accustomed to drinking in order to cope, and it is tempting to turn back to alcohol for certain, albeit temporary, relief from pain.

Insistence on permanent sobriety

A.A. members stay away from one drink, one day at a time. Asserting that one will absolutely never drink again can lead a recovering alcoholic to believe that he or she has the willpower to conquer alcoholism. Trusting his or her own willpower can "excuse" an alcoholic from attendance at A.A. In time, the denial system may grow to the point that the alcoholic decides to exercise his or her willpower in "controlled drinking."

Drinking reveries

A recovering alcoholic can be headed toward relapse if he or she regularly entertains reveries (thoughts or memories) about drinking. If, with increasing frequency, good times are recalled without the bad, a recovering alcoholic may underestimate the disease's damage. All too soon, the denial system can resurface, and the rosy memories may lead to a drink. A 1940 *Grapevine* (A.A. monthly magazine) article on relapse stressed this point, with the writer suggesting that the recovering alcoholic force the recollections of drinking through to the bitter end, whether it be the following morning and its hangover or several years later with all the mess of alcoholic problems. A.A. members now call this "thinking through a drink."

Wishing to be able to drink again

In 1965, when researchers Bailey and Leach asked A.A. members with five years' sobriety whether or not they would drink again if they could, nearly three times as many who had relapsed said "yes" as did those with continuous sobriety. If the sober life seems better than the drinking one, a recovering alcoholic with comfortable sobriety would not trade—even if alcohol intake were somehow to become pharmacologically safe for alcoholics.

Complacency about sobriety

If a recovering alcoholic says "It can't happen to me," particularly with conviction, he or she may be headed for trouble. Most A.A. members have heard "slip stories" involving this attitude. Many of the relapsers later say that drinking was the furthest thing from their minds when they took the first drink.

Imposing sobriety on others

These compulsive attempts take the spotlight off the recovering alcoholic's *own* program—*own* need to change—and shroud problems that could lead to a drink with an inappropriate concern for others.

Ashamed to be known as a nondrinker

Some alcoholics inordinately protect themselves after some length of sobriety from being known as alcoholics in social or work situations that feature regular drinkers. In certain situations, some recovering alcoholics feel comfort in holding a glass of ginger ale. This is traditional camouflage at cocktail parties, for it resembles an alcoholic drink, and thus deflects potential pressure from strangers—or acquaintances—to have a drink containing alcohol. This subtle form of denial may pressure the recovering alcoholic in a social setting to pick up a drink as a safeguard against criticism from companions. Regularly concealing the truth from friends not only fuels the denial system, it can also leave the door open for drinking again without criticism from a group of unaware friends.

Listening to contradictions

It is dangerous for the recovering alcoholic to seriously listen to the opinions of family, friends, or co-workers that he or she is not like alcoholics they have known. A premise of A.A. membership is that alcoholism is a self-diagnosed disease. Believing the contradictions of others can weaken a recovering alcoholic's decision to avoid the first drink. And, unfortunately, such critics frequently turn out to be active alcoholics expressing denial of their own alcoholism.

An antagonistic mate

A heavy-drinking or alcoholic spouse who refuses to attend A.A. or Al-Anon meetings, or any person who resents the recovering alcoholic's time spent at A.A., may become a problem. Having lost his or her best drinking buddy to A.A., the mate can put tremendous pressure on the recovering alcoholic's denial system. The drinking alcoholic mate may want his or her drinking buddy back, and this person may want, consciously or unconsciously, the recovering alcoholic to drink again.

Preserving old patterns

Continuing to socialize with heavy drinkers, particularly without an adequate counterbalance of new, sober friends is not helpful. Consistently giving priority to attending functions that provide an opportunity to drink rather than regular A.A. meetings can result in trouble.

Considerable contact with heavy drinking

Recovering alcoholics who work as bartenders and cocktail waitresses are obvious examples in this category. However, no matter *what* the recovering alcoholic's job, being present while others drink or being pressured to drink by co-workers and friends can be a continual threat to sobriety.

Still the host

Some recovering alcoholics consistently encourage others to drink. They insist on keeping booze at home, allegedly for family members or for entertaining. Besides having a supply of liquor ("protecting the supply"), the alcohol is prominently

163

displayed, such as on a bar, or heavily stocked, often by the case. And all this is done for moderate-drinking family members and friends. Beyond stocking liquor, these hosts may urge others to drink by ordering, pouring, and serving drinks for them.

Speculating about amounts

Rationalizing that a drink with a lower alcohol content would be safe: e.g., beer vs. whiskey, wine vs. vodka, is but a step or two away from drinking. This ploy is frequently used by active alcoholics in their desperate attempts to control their drinking, and may be a sign that the denial system is resurfacing.

Redeciding about drinking

If a recovering alcoholic thinks seriously about attempting social drinking, he or she may be headed for a relapse. This is a very serious sign that the person is about to relapse.

The Importance of A.A.

After the late Charles W. Crewe had counseled almost 500 patients in a program for relapsers at Hazelden, he concluded that between eighty and ninety percent of these repeaters to the Minnesota treatment center shared at least one significant characteristic: deficient A.A. attendance. According to Crewe, this meant either no attendance, brief attendance, or ending participation in the program prior to relapse. These findings will not surprise A.A. members, whose standard message to thirsty friends is "Don't drink and go to meetings."

Irregular attendance at A.A. is considered risky by members with successful sobriety. Irregular attendance means that A.A. does not have top priority. It also means that other members cannot really get to know the recovering alcoholic well, and that the erratic attendee may not be in touch with A.A. at the crucial time when the urge to drink hits.

Limited participation in A.A. is another danger zone of potential relapse. This kind of member may show up at meetings with some regularity, but his or her participation in the home group is obviously restrained. Habitual signs of limited participation include:

- arriving late, leaving early
- sitting alone in the back of the room
- coming to the meeting hall, but skipping the meeting itself in favor of reading A.A. literature or chatting inconsequentially with an A.A. friend who also wants to avoid the actual meeting
- avoiding making any close A. A. friends
- having no real commitment to a home group, but instead dropping in to meetings at several different groups so nobody really gets to know him or her
- making excuses for a consistent refusal to make coffee, clean up, speak, chair meetings, hold office, celebrate anniversaries, or do Twelfth Step work

Compromises Cause Relapse

Members call A.A. "a simple program for complicated people." In theory, its contents are but suggestions. However, most members with comfortable sobriety find that in order to avoid relapse, the following suggestions should be followed as directions. Members who have slipped realize later that trouble stemmed from one or more of the following areas.

Disbelief that one's life is unmanageable

Working the Twelve Steps of A.A. is vital to recovery from alcoholism, beginning with the First Step: "We admitted we were powerless over alcohol—that our lives had become unmanageable." If a recovering alcoholic does not believe that his or her life became unmanageable through alcohol, there is no incentive to change—or to take the next eleven Steps. Without change, a detoxified alcoholic may begin to feel better, then may rationalize that he or she is not, after all, powerless over alcohol. This faulty belief leads right back to a drink.

Compromise in working the A.A. program

Compromise means that some suggestions are not followed. For example, an A.A. member may refuse to work certain Steps. Instead, he or she takes the Steps "cafeteria style." This compromise is dangerous because the Twelve Steps are ingeniously designed to follow one another. Sober members constantly use all the Steps to keep themselves sober, and specific Steps can be useful tools to help thirsty members avoid the first drink. Many old-timers ask "slippees" which Step they were working on when they picked up a drink. The answer is usually "none." It is particularly dangerous to avoid Steps Four and Five—the housecleaning Steps.

Not practicing the A.A. program

A member may refuse to retake certain Steps, even when other members believe that his or her sobriety is at stake. Members who believe that taking the Steps is a one-shot deal are also compromising—they do not grasp the importance of continual change as vital to continual sobriety. Some may refuse to "be an active member" of the Program, limiting their participation in the ways listed earlier. Compromise here is dangerous because, if trouble hits, the alcoholic may be too isolated from the group to ask for help in avoiding that first drink.

Dissatisfaction Leads to Relapse

An A.A. member who is overly critical of the program may be headed back to a drink. If criticisms remain unresolved, this member may become convinced that the program is inappropriate for him or her. Some commonly heard criticisms of A.A. by relapsers include:

A general disparagement of the program

Sometimes a recovering alcoholic is broadly critical of A.A. members and of their groups. Complaints that other members are all richer (or poorer), older (or younger), more outgoing (or more withdrawn), Black (or White), and so on indicate that the person is looking for differences instead of identifying with other alcoholics. Such sweeping complaints also indicate lack of tolerance in other areas of life.

Boredom with A.A. meetings

A member may con himself into believing that he does not need meetings, complaining "I'm sick of hearing nothing but drunkalogs." Old-timers tell these complainers that the "how we were" part of a speaker's story keeps the memory green about the drastic effects of alcoholic drinking, that this memory is important to continued sobriety.

Criticism of meetings

Some A.A. members may complain that a group's meetings are not "as good" as those attended elsewhere, such as in a rehab center or a former home town, because they are too big, or too small, meet at inconvenient times or places, have too much smoke, or no smoking allowed, offer only decaf coffee, or don't offer decaf, use a different format, have open discussion or closed discussion, and so on. By focusing on negative comparisons, a critical member can become so annoyed with the differences that he or she decides it is a waste of time to attend *any* A.A. meetings.

Trivial as some of these criticisms may seem, all have been seized as reasons for alcoholics to miss A.A. meetings. All are, therefore, at least indirect and partial reasons for slips.

Newcomers are always urged to try as many A.A. groups as possible. Eventually they will begin to identify, and once a compatible group is found, the generalized complaints will diminish, along with the intensity of the denial system.

Faulty Twelfth Step Work

Helping alcoholics get sober and stay sober in A.A. is vital to the program's very existence. However, certain ways of working the Twelfth Step can be dangerous to the Twelfth Stepper's own sobriety.

"Two Stepping" is a term for members who jump from the First Step right to the Twelfth, ignoring the Steps in between. The Twelfth Stepper's sobriety may be just as shaky as the newcomer's, and *both* may slip. Newcomers who are eager to do Twelfth Step work are usually encouraged to accompany an old-timer.

On the other hand, some members refuse to even try Twelfth Step work. Such a refusal goes against one of the basic A.A. messages: "I am responsible.... When anyone, anywhere, reaches out for help, I want the hand of A.A. always to be there. And for that: I am responsible." A.A. members believe that they have to give sobriety away in order to keep it. They call this principle "Use it or lose it." If *everyone* refused to do Twelfth Step work, the A.A. Program would die out.

Other Common Pitfalls

Comparing instead of identifying

Some recovering alcoholics persist in favorably comparing their own drinking, and its effects, with the experience of other people at A.A. meetings. Comparisons include quantity drunk regularly and on sprees ("She drank a quart a day—*I* only drank a pint"); breaking the law ("He went to jail four times—*I've* never even been arrested for speeding"); employment problems ("She was fired five times—*I* only lost one job and that wasn't really for drinking"); marital discord ("His wife left him—*mine* is still at home"); academic difficulties ("She couldn't even get through high school—*I'm* a sophomore in college"); family feuds ("His relatives won't speak to him—*mine* hung in with me"); hospitalizations ("She went through three drying out places—*I've* never been put away for drinking"). Through such comparisons, an alcoholic can become convinced that his or her drinking is not as serious as that of others—and thus that it would be okay to drink again.

Romance or sexual relations with newcomers

Such emotional involvements are particularly dangerous for newcomers, who are simply too sick and vulnerable to make good judgments. *Any* romance can create problems, and problems can lead an alcoholic back to a drink. Casual sexual relations entered under the pretext of "helping someone's recovery" are usually harmful to the emotions of those who are but newly sober. The dishonesty is always harmful to the phony helper.

Mental reservations about A.A. spirituality

In order to stay sober, A.A. members believe that they need to surrender the will that kept them drinking to some sort of Higher Power. This is the basis of the spiritual part of the program.

Lessening of mental discipline

Steps Ten and Eleven suggest daily inventory-taking, meditation, and prayer. They include asking a Higher Power every day for help to stay sober, and then turning problems over to the care of this Higher Power. Some A.A. members find that slacking off on these disciplines leads back to a drink.

Lack of honesty (sometimes unconscious)

Active alcoholics are characteristically dishonest during their desperate attempts to continue drinking; this habit must change if they are to stay sober.

Bottom Lines

Nobody is barred from an A.A. meeting after a slip. A lesson *can* be drawn from a slip, both for the alcoholic who drank, and for those who learn enough to stave off slips of their own. Since A.A. members function by sharing their "experience, strength and hope" with one another, "You drank for me" is commonly heard at meetings when a member slips.

While helping the relapser to review why he or she picked up the first drink, members concurrently assess their own attitudes toward whatever triggered the person to drink, and then they describe how they handle such situations without drinking.

A slip strongly indicates that the recovering alcoholic must make one or more important changes. If not, he or she will probably drink yet again. Next time, the member might not make it back to the program.

LUCY BARRY ROBE

This section is taken from *Relapses/Slips: Abstinent Alcoholics Who Return to Drinking* by Maxwell N. Weisman, M.D. and Lucy Barry Robe, published by the Johnson Institute.

PART TWO

Effects of Chemical Dependence
At Home and At Work

Introduction to Part Two

In Part One of this guide, I selected material that addresses the disease of chemical dependence and the ways it affects the individual who has developed the disease. Part Two describes the effects of chemical dependence at home and at work.

Chapter Nine explains why chemical dependence is often called the "family disease." It describes the family as a system, how members of the system are affected by the chemical dependence of one member, and how each member contributes to the dysfunction of the system.

Chapter Ten provides a general description of enabling—behaviors engaged in by an uninformed family member that unintentionally encourage the dependent person's drug use. It outlines how to recognize, avoid, and stop such behaviors.

Chapter Eleven discusses how enabling gets started in the workplace and how a supervisor or co-worker of a chemical dependent can learn to stop enabling. In selecting material for this chapter, I was gratified to discover how much has been written on chemical dependence and its effects in the workplace. Only two decades ago, the Employee Assistance Programs we helped establish at the Cargill Company in Minneapolis and at the Minneapolis Star and Tribune made those companies "pioneers."

I am particularly grateful to Dr. Timmen Cermak for contributing so much of his work on co-dependence to make Chapter Twelve a comprehensive discussion of this important subject. Dr. Cermak clarifies why chemically dependent families can be breeding grounds for the development of serious psychological problems.

Finally, I am confident that readers who recognize chemical dependence in their families, and enabling or other co-dependent behaviors in themselves will find the information on detachment in Chapter Thirteen particularly useful. This chapter raises the important distinction between feeling responsible **for** the chemical dependent and the productive acceptance of responsibility **to** the chemical dependent. Readers will learn how to detach—how to stop reacting to the chemical dependent and start choosing family recovery.

VERNON E. JOHNSON, D.D.

CHAPTER NINE

How Does Chemical Dependence Affect Families?

We all grow up thinking we know what a family is and how it functions. So when someone in our family becomes dependent on alcohol or some other drug, we think we *ought* to know what to do. Actually, most people don't. But they can learn. This information is meant to help you understand what's really happening to the chemically dependent person, what's happening to you (someone close to that person), and what's happening to the whole family.

We've all heard about alcoholism and drug addiction, but some of us might not know the term *chemical dependence*. Before discussing it, we need to make it clear that alcohol is a drug just as much as cocaine, marijuana, heroin, "uppers," and "downers" are. Over the years, experts in treating chemically dependent people have learned that no matter which drug one is dependent on, the disease—and it truly is a disease—is basically the same. We can recognize it by the same symptoms, and the ways of recovering from it are the same.

All mind-altering chemicals have one effect: to change the mood, the feelings, of the person who uses the chemical. Chemical dependence, then, refers to a harmful dependence on *any* mind-altering drug, alcohol and others alike. What we now want to emphasize is that chemical dependence of any member of the family is a *family* disease, not just a disease in that individual, for the family is inevitably affected and involved in many important and harmful ways. However, as we'll point out, this disease can be arrested, and all members of the family can be restored to live healthy, happy lives.

By inquiring what you can do about chemical dependence in your family, you've already made a good start. Keep up the good work. And remember—help *is* available for you, for the chemically dependent person you love, and for your whole family.

The Family System and Chemical Dependence: An Overview

No two families are alike. Yet all families have some traits in common; there's a *family system* at work. For instance, we've learned that all families tend to react in patterned, predictable ways when a family member becomes chemically dependent, whether on alcohol or on any other drug. Understanding this family system will help you understand what happens when chemical dependence strikes a family.

First, what is a family? It's those people—traditionally a mother, a father, and some children—who depend on one another for meeting their social, emotional, spiritual, and physical needs. "Family" could be extended to include others who become family members through birth, marriage, legal adoptions, or in less formal ways such as participating in family functions, lending support during troubled times, or sharing in other family activities.

Each family member is somehow a part of every family activity and situation. Each one somehow experiences the pains, joys, and successes of the whole family and of each person in it. And the family as a whole is touched by events in a way that nonfamily members can never experience.

What goes on in a family might be charted this way:

Dysfunctional ———————————— Nurturing

At one end of the line is a *nurturing* atmosphere: not necessarily problem-free, but a situation in which family members love and like one another, respect one another's qualities and capabilities, and accept one another's shortcomings. The members trust and support one another, and the family is relatively happy and emotionally secure.

At the other end of the line is a *dysfunctional* atmosphere—one in which the family system functions abnormally. In that situation, there are big problems that cause family members much pain and insecurity. Family members often show this pain and insecurity by such negative behavior as inappropriate anger, aloofness, resentment—and sometimes very clearly through chemical dependence.

Every family system can be graphed on the line that moves between a nurturing atmosphere and a dysfunctional one. Every family is somewhere on this continuum at any given time, and the family can move in either direction as a result of events that occur in the system. Moreover, *the family tends to move as a group*, not as unrelated individuals.

When a family system is healthy, all the members are able to feel a full range of emotions, and they feel free to express their emotions to one another. They don't avoid conflict or problems at any cost: differences can be talked over. Individuality is accepted, and family members listen to one another. Every person's mistakes are at least tolerated, but each person is held responsible for his or her own behavior. The members of this family system are able to face stress and pain as they work through their problems and their differences. In this open and supportive system, all the members have high self-esteem, respect for one another, energy, and love.

When a family member becomes chemically dependent, however, the family begins to move toward the dysfunctional end of the continuum. A family with a chemically dependent member is a "chemically dependent family," and we'll look closely at the dysfunction that such a family is apt to undergo and what family members can do to restore the family to health and happiness.

Chemical dependence—alcoholism or other drug dependence—is a disease that may start with one person, but eventually it involves *every* member of the family. (How this happens will be explained later.) This involvement in turn makes it possible, in a sense, for the chemical dependence to continue—indeed, to grow worse. Sometimes the chemical dependence will develop in other family members. Even apart from actual chemical dependence, though, the emotional life in a chemically dependent family is almost certain to become less healthy. Every member of a chemically dependent family inadvertently plays a part in this malfunction, and each family member requires help in breaking this destructive pattern. Unless there's a constructive interruption—technically called an *intervention*—each person's negative patterns will continue, and the children in the family will carry their negative patterns into new family systems as they mature, marry, and have children of their own.

Living in a constantly shifting, distressing family and not daring to talk about that situation is a difficult, emotionally painful experience for all family members. The family experiences fear, anger, loneliness, hurt, guilt, and shame as the disease progresses, and typically the family members themselves unwittingly and literally become part of the problem. In short, chemical dependence becomes a family illness. Many professionals refer to this family illness as co-dependence (more on that later).

To protect themselves against the painful feelings resulting from chemical dependence, family members develop defenses that help them meet their emotional needs. Their occasional defensive behavior at the beginning of the dependence grows into a steady defensive posture as the family disease of chemical dependence progresses. There are several stages in each member's progression into dysfunction. Not all family members will be in the same stage at the same time. But as the disease of the chemically dependent person progresses, the family members progress in their own illness in a series of stages very similar to those that the dependent person goes through. Before we discuss those phases, however, it will be useful to discuss the particular feelings manifested in each of the phases and the ways those feelings come out in the members of the family. We'll then briefly investigate three general behavioral patterns that family members use in coping with their own problems and with the chemically dependent person.

Family Feelings and Ways of Showing Them

Chemical dependence, especially in its later stages, is stressful for all members of the family. As dependence progresses in any one member of the family, all members experience certain emotions. Though they may not talk openly about anger, guilt, shame, hurt, fear, and loneliness, they do experience all these feelings. Family members need to learn that they're neither bad nor abnormal if they have these feelings. They also need to learn how to express these feelings appropriately and how to fulfill their own emotional needs.

Anger

Among family members, anger can often be explained as a love/hate relationship. Family members love the dependent person, but they hate the painful experiences that everyone goes through because of his or her chemical dependence. The painful experiences bring about anger and resentment toward him, and it's not easy to separate the dependence from the person.

Shame

During some of the painful experiences resulting from the dependent person's use of alcohol or other drugs, the family has felt ashamed of him. As the situation in the family becomes worse, shame grows to include being ashamed of the whole family—the dependent, the other members of the family, and even oneself. Shame produces feelings of low self-worth in each member of the family.

Guilt

The family members begin to blame themselves and one another for their painful experiences. Each family member may secretly feel that somehow he or she is responsible for the drinking and that "if only I could change," everything would be all right. Such self-blame produces more feelings of guilt and shame.

Hurt

Emotional pain can be broad and deep. It's painful to see a loved one deteriorate as chemical dependence progresses. It hurts to become involved in arguments or to witness angry exchanges between members of the family. Many times the dependent blames others for his or her alcohol or other drug use. Messages such as "If you wouldn't nag, I wouldn't drink" or "You want to know why I drink? Look in the mirror" cause deep emotional hurt and deepen feelings of guilt and shame.

Fear

Living in a constantly shifting, distressed family produces fear: fear of arguments, fear of financial problems, fear about the dependent's usage, fear that the dependent will get drunk, or even fear that everything will remain the same. And there's fear of the future: what will happen to the family if things keep getting worse? The fears compound proportionately with the internalized emotional stress each family member already feels.

Loneliness

The stressful family situation results in a breakdown of normal, rewarding family communication. Family love and concern are lost in the stress and crisis of day-to-day living. The isolation created by the lack of nurturing communication in the dependent family results in more loneliness for everyone.

Defensive Behavior of Family Members

To protect themselves from further emotional pain and to hide the emotions they're experiencing but don't want to admit, family members begin to take on protective defensive behavior. At the Johnson Institute, we speak about three generalized categories of defensive behavior an individual can adopt in a stressful dependent family situation: being too good to be true, being rebellious, and being apathetic.

Being Too Good To Be True

This defensive behavior disguises the pain of the individual and of the family. Being "too good" gives the illusion that the family has no problem. When an individual is being "too good," he's looking for rewards that being good may bring. He's also looking for rewards that are just not available in a dysfunctional family—rewards such as recognition, praise, special family treatment, and more responsibility. Beyond the matter of rewards is the hope that the "being-too-good" behavior will somehow bring about a positive change in the chemically dependent person's behavior. Children often think, "If I'm good enough, maybe Mom and Dad won't have to drink so much."

Being "too good" includes exaggerated behavior such as:
- achieving for the family: in school, at work, in sports, in the community
- doing more than one's share around the house
- counseling the family, patching up family fights and relationships
- being cute and funny at inappropriate times; entertaining to relieve stressful situations
- struggling for perfection, not allowing for any mistakes, denying mistakes
- intellectualizing: acknowledging family stress and pain only on a thinking level; denying feelings about stress
- parenting: children acting as parents, disciplining other children, worrying about family finances; adults acting as parents to other adults
- meeting everyone's expectations, trying to keep everyone happy
- being rigidly obedient, *always* following *all* the rules

What's unhelpful about "being too good"? While admirable in some ways, this behavior insulates the chemically dependent person from having to experience the harmful consequences of dependence. To insulate or protect the chemically dependent person is to enable, because doing what the dependent person ought to be doing or covering up for him or her enables the dependence to continue.

Being Rebellious

Some family members react to chemical dependence with their own kind of misbehavior. The effect is to remove the spotlight from the behavior of the chemically dependent person. By being rebellious and acting out, a family member draws attention away from the primary family problem of the dependence. Most often, a rebellious family member receives negative recognition—i.e., blame for the family stress. There's a payoff for the rebellious person, however. Being rebellious is effective in disguising pain, and such behavior rewards the rebellious individual with family attention, even though it's negative.

Rebellious behavior may involve:
- being dishonest
- being late for work
- acting out in school and at home
- breaking house rules
- defying authority at home or on the job
- starting arguments with neighbors
- bullying, playing hurtful pranks
- bossing the neighbor's children
- rejecting the family: developing a "family" of friends of whom the parents wouldn't approve
- neglecting one's children or becoming abusive

Being Apathetic

This defensive behavior disguises a person's pain and provides relief for the apathetic person and the family. It's difficult to describe this passive, defensive behavior because the apathetic or passive person does very little, shows little emotion, takes no action that's not absolutely necessary. Passive behavior is manifested in the many ways in which the person quietly withdraws from frightening, stressful, or painful situations in a dependent family. Rewards for being apathetic are contained in feelings of safety and self-pity. What's seen as calmness and a philosophical attitude toward trouble is really rigid, deliberately unfeeling behavior. Being apathetic isn't the same as a healthy "I don't-care" attitude. On the surface, apathy often looks like serenity and acceptance. But the apathetic person simply refuses to see the problem and its effects on the whole family. While apathetic people may appear calm, their behavior doesn't quiet the turmoil and anxiety they feel inside.

Being apathetic is often indicated in the following ways:

- withdrawal
- habitual quietness
- separateness from others
- passive rejection of the family
- fantasy, daydreaming
- passive rejection of relationships, inside or outside the family

The apathetic family members actually enable the disease to progress. By refusing to confront the disease, by not recognizing the problem for what it is, they help maintain the illusion that nothing is out of order in the family.

The Four Stages of Family Co-Dependence

Now let's turn to the four phases of the illness of family members who aren't chemically dependent. Helping professionals commonly refer to the illness of family members of chemical dependents as "co-dependence." Co-dependence is the consistent pattern of traits and behaviors recognizable in individual family members that can result in physical, emotional, mental, or social dysfunction often as severe as that of the chemically dependent family member. First of all, it may seem strange to hear that the family members who aren't alcoholic or otherwise drug dependent have an illness. But once we look at the behavior that family members use in coping with the chemically dependent person, it won't seem strange at all to call their behavior and accompanying emotional states ill or at the very least "dis-eased." Family members can become just as abnormal in their behavior, just as emotionally mixed up, just as self-destructive as the dependent person. For simplicity's sake, we'll use the term "co-dependent" to refer to nonchemically dependent family members.

Remember that these phases can begin at different times for different members of the family. While it's likely that family members will progress through the phases at approximately the same time, they don't necessarily do so. Few family members, in fact, begin their own illness process until the chemically dependent person is far down the line into his dependence. Usually family members won't show signs of their co-dependence until the dependent person has begun the harmful Dependence Phase. When he or she enters this phase, the family has a need to develop its own protective defensive behaviors. Let's look at these family phases.

The Learning Phase

The first phase, as with the chemically dependent individual, is the Learning Phase. The process of harmful dependence takes some time before it becomes an observable problem for a family. As the disease process develops, everyone in the family knows that stress is present and that family life is changing. The stress may show itself in increasing arguments, tension, less communication, or strained spousal and parent/child relationships. In an attempt to protect themselves and bring back family stability, family members experiment with the three forms of defensive behavior (being too good, being rebellious, or being apathetic). As they try these different ways of coping with the developing "chemically dependent family" experience, they're learning what defensive behavior works best for them in times of crisis and stress. Although this learning may not be conscious, it's a strong and habit-forming experience.

The Seeking Phase

In this phase the family tries to discover what the problem is and how to solve it. In the Learning Phase there's no awareness that drinking or other drug use is the problem. In the Seeking Phase there are hints—flashes of awareness—that maybe drug use is the problem. Family members may even mention this idea to one another. However, the thought is quickly rationalized away and replaced by the false hope that it's really not the problem. This process is called family denial.

In time, the evidence is too clear to ignore. As family members recognize, however sketchily, that alcoholism or other drug dependence is a problem in their family, individual family members use defensive behavior in a manipulative way. They consciously choose what helps them live their lives most smoothly: being too good, being rebellious, or being apathetic.

A rather serious problem for the family members at this point is that they sincerely believe they can control the dependent person's chemical use by manipulating the family environment. Being more loving, achieving, acting out, blaming, being angry, or withdrawing from the dependent person can all be ways of trying to manipulate or control his or her chemical use. This sincere belief that the family can control the chemical use is called family delusion. The hard fact is, though, that neither manipulation nor defensive behavior by the family can control either the alcohol or other drug use or the chemically dependent individual.

Denial and delusion on the part of the family enable the chemically dependent family member to move farther and deeper into the self-destructive dependence. The family members may not be reacting much differently to the chemically dependent person than they did when they first noticed problems, but a major change has been made in the whole situation. The chemical dependence is now recognized, at least by the co-dependent family members.

Early on, their reactions to the chemically dependent person were random and experimental. They really didn't know what the problem was. Now they do, even if only vaguely. By continuing to practice their acquired styles of coping with the chemically dependent person, they may be helping themselves feel better temporarily, but in the long run their own unhealthy co-dependent behavior will catch up with them and turn them into angry, resentful, emotionally impaired people.

The Harmful Phase

In this phase the family's defensive behavior becomes compulsive. Their reactive behavior becomes just as predictable and automatic as that of the dependent person. It's at this point that the co-dependent traits and behavior of individual family members often become fixed and rigid as members try to control the chemically dependent family member. The family becomes locked into its defensive behaviors (being too good, being rebellious, or being apathetic) and the behaviors become roles: being too good becomes "the Good Kid"; being rebellious becomes "the Family Rebel"; and being apathetic becomes "the Passive Adult" or "the Withdrawn Child." Because of the stress and repeated use of these defensive behaviors, the defenses become habitual roles for the family members.

In this Harmful Phase no one confronts the dependent person about his or her compulsive use of chemicals. Rather, the family blames that person just as if he or she had freely chosen to be dependent and had knowingly caused all the problems. The family illness of co-dependence grows more and more rigid. Family members rightly feel helpless to control the chemical use, but they become so deluded that they often begin to believe that they and their behavior caused the dependence in the first place.

The resulting feelings of guilt, shame, and self-blame add to the family member's feelings of isolation and loneliness. In order to cope with growing pain, family members unwittingly build a denial system around it. As strange as it may seem, if asked about their emotional pain, most family members would think they were being truthful when they responded that everything was all right. Effectively denying the pain, each individual accepts the defensive, painful, dependent family lifestyle as normal. Only when this lifestyle become undeniably painful will individuals begin to look for a way out.

The Escape Phase

This is the final phase of the family disease process. It's marked by repeated major crises: financial problems, work problems, physical, emotional, and social problems become routine occurrences. Family members who have suffered over-powering feelings of guilt, rage, and disloyalty regarding the chemically dependent member begin to act on their bad feelings and seriously begin to search and find ways to escape. Separation and even desertion can occur during this phase, and, worst of all, suicide is sometimes chosen as a way of ending the problems.

Family members do arrive at the point where they feel emotionally exhausted, unable to cope any longer, and numbed by a false sense of guilt. Walking away from the situation seems to be the last, the best, and sometimes the only way to survive or to find peace.

If the co-dependent family member has reached this point, however, separation from the situation doesn't eliminate the painful emotions, the protective, defensive lifestyle, or the resentments that have grown up in the family. By now, each individual in the family needs some kind of personal help if he or she is ever to return to a happy, healthy lifestyle.

Treatment and Recovery

Because the need for treatment for the chemically dependent person is so desperately evident and is generally beneficial for the whole family, the fact that the family also needs treatment for its own problems is easily overlooked. At the outset, when talking about treatment for the family, it's important to dispel certain misconceptions. First, the family doesn't undergo treatment for the sake of the chemically dependent person. Second, the sobriety of the chemically dependent person doesn't depend on the rehabilitation of the chemically dependent family. Third, family recovery doesn't depend on the future sobriety of the chemically dependent family member.

When we talk about family recovery, the point is this: because chemical dependence develops into a family illness, virtually all members of the family need some kind of help toward recovery. Furthermore, if the chemical dependence has existed in the family over a long time, it's very likely that most members of the family will have developed harmful co-dependent traits or behaviors and will need some kind of outside help in restoring themselves to a state of health and happiness. For the chemically dependent family member, this begins in treatment and continues through aftercare and then through regular participation in Alcoholics Anonymous, Cocaine Anonymous, Narcotics Anonymous, or other comparable groups. For the other family members, this usually means a program of family care, individual counseling, and regular, active involvement in Al-Anon, Alateen, Adult Children of Alcoholics, or comparable self-help groups.

Why must a family have a program for recovery? Families who've lived with chemical dependence for a long time are usually so close to it that they can't begin to realize the scope of the problem. In their efforts to protect themselves from the pain and ravages of the disease of chemical dependence, they've developed their own limiting and emotionally insufficient ways of coping with the problem and have gradually slipped into an emotionally crippled life. Although their problems originated around someone else's chemical use, those problems won't necessarily go away even if that person begins to recover.

The best-known method of family care, and certainly the most easily accessible for people all over the United States, is active participation in the organization known as Al-Anon and in its junior counterpart, Alateen. These two organizations were founded to provide group support and a program for living that would help people recover from the problems they suffer from living with a chemically dependent person. Al-Anon and Alateen members follow a program almost identical to that of Alcoholics Anonymous, and they operate on confidentiality and self-help group principles. For more information about Al-Anon or Alateen, consult your local telephone directory.

A more recent development in self-help is the Adult Children of Alcoholics groups that have sprung up across the United States. These groups specialize in offering group support for adult children of alcoholics—children who usually no longer live with a chemically dependent parent or family member but who still suffer the crippling effects of having been raised in a chemically dependent family. The address and phone number for The National Association for Children of Alcoholics, Al-Anon, and other national organizations can be found at the end of this book.

Families of chemically dependent people tend to have problems that are very similar to the ones the chemically dependent person has. Families need to break through their own denial systems. They too must learn that chemicals are the focus of the problem; and they need to realize that each person in a chemically dependent family is responsible for his or her own behavior.

Families sometimes have a very difficult task in breaking through the denial and delusion that have grown up around the chemically dependent family. They must somehow learn that while they're not responsible for all the problems in the family, they're indeed responsible for their own feelings and their own recovery. For family members, breaking through denial and delusion means that they discover that they have choices in how to behave, that their enabling behavior didn't and won't help the dependent person give up the chemical use, and that enabling behavior won't help them fill their own emotional needs.

Like the chemically dependent member of the family, other members of the family must learn that they have choices regarding their behavior; they can try out new behaviors and search for ways to fulfill their legitimate emotional needs.

Most people raised in a chemically dependent family have never developed the ability to experience a full range of feelings. Recovering the rich and rewarding feeling of life that's part and parcel of the healthy family system may take a long time.

Whatever time it takes, recovery is worth the effort. And the chief point of this chapter is worth repeating: chemical dependence and recovery are a family affair.

THE JOHNSON INSTITUTE

This section is taken from *Chemical Dependence and Recovery: A Family Affair*, published by the Johnson Institute.

Recovery

What happens within a dysfunctional family system when a chemically dependent person, after going through treatment, returns home? What problems arise, and what can families do to counter the deterioration of their family unit?

The expectations of the recovering patient and of other family members play a major role in the problems encountered by the recovering family. In fact, these expectations probably direct the behavior and attitudes of all family members during the post-treatment period. Some typical questions are:

"Will she stay sober?"

"How angry is he with me?"

"Will it be like it was in the old days?"

"What's Dad like when he's sober, anyway?"

"Whew, our problems are over! Mom's finally sober."

Generally, however, these expectations fall into two areas: those concerning the *roles* that family members expect to assume or continue; and those concerning the *new family environment* and what it'll be like. Let's look at these two areas.

Roles

When the patient is actively involved with chemicals, he eventually abdicates his family role. This drastically affects the family structure; and usually by the time the patient has gone through treatment, the family has reorganized around the new framework that no longer includes the patient in a functioning role.

This is obvious where the patient has left the family or lost her job. But even where the patient holds a job and is still present in the home, other family members actually run the show: taking care of the bills, taxes, and other business matters, or attempting in other ways to keep the family together. So when the patient comes home after treatment or after achieving sobriety, there's often conscious, as well as unconscious, resistance to accepting him as a responsible family member and turning his role back to him, whether it be as decision maker, financial manager, or as someone from whom other family members seek counsel or emotional support. A daughter who's had to assume the full responsibilities of the mother, or a son who's had to assume the father's role, is often reluctant to give up these responsibilities just because Mom or Dad is back home.

The patient, too, has her own set of expectations about her role:

"Will they accept me?"

"Will I be able to fulfill my role in the family as I feel I should?"

"I wouldn't blame them if they didn't want me back."

"Do the kids hate me?"

"Will I be able to deal with all our problems and stay sober?"

Or the patient may fully expect that the family is waiting appreciatively with open arms to welcome him back to his former role as "loving" father and husband, and that his children will "shape up," be responsible, and be open to communication with him—ready and willing to help things run as smoothly as possible. What the patient doesn't realize is that the family has *not* been through treatment (at least treatment as intensive as his, and certainly not with corresponding impact) and that they're probably a long way from accepting him back into their midst with open arms. Even if they wanted to do this, they couldn't, because there are just too many unhappy experiences in the way. These are the feelings that the family must work together to identify, share, and work out if they're going to develop a successful relationship together. A great many hostile feelings relating to the chemical experience remain, sometimes on the surface, sometimes hidden very deep. Many of these hostile feelings relate directly to the role changes and expectations of both patient and family members. These role expectations will have a direct effect on the relationship that will be developed within the recovering family environment.

New Family Environment

The second area involves the family members' expectations about the new family environment. They expect the patient to be "fixed" after treatment—that she'll be as they remember her before she started actively using chemicals. They also expect that the family itself will be different—maybe happier and more relaxed, functioning efficiently and smoothly. So when these expectations aren't met, disillusionment, hostility, anger, and sadness result.

The fact is that in many post-treatment families, some problems become more evident. The problems of trying to reestablish roles are formidable, and the patient may be very nervous and irritable, often loaded down with feelings of guilt and remorse. The patient may be trying to deal with new financial problems. Children may be acting disturbed in school or in the home. So some problems are still there. The only significant difference is that the patient isn't actively using chemicals on a day-to-day basis—at least the family hopes not. There's still fear among family members that the patient will slip back into using chemicals. This fear is one reason why family members tend to "take care of" the patient after treatment. This usually results in a honeymoon period during the immediate post-treatment weeks. Here the family is trying extra hard to keep the peace and avoid conflict. They're afraid the patient will go back to the old ways and that once again the family will plunge into chaos. This "honeymoon" period may last for two weeks or as long as a year, and by this time the suppressed hostilities of all family members may begin erupting—the kids acting hostile, arguing and fighting with both parents, spouses fighting openly and covertly with each other and with the children.

Another factor that probably motivates this honeymoon behavior is the family's relief at having the conflicts and hassles of active chemical dependence over. The family is floating on its good feelings and expectations about how things will be from now on. Initially, this may be a necessary part of the reentry and readjustment period, but the honeymoon should end quickly or it'll just intensify the pressure and building up of all the latent hostility and negative feelings that family members have had throughout the active dependence period.

We can see that communication within the recovering family is crucial, and herein lies another problem concerning family expectations. As a part of the new environment, family members tend to feel that their contact and communication with one another will improve. But this is extremely difficult, since they have no model. They don't know how to communicate openly and honestly with one another. They don't even know what a good communication system in a family looks like. In the past, the pattern has been just the opposite of this. People have repressed feelings and haven't communicated their fears and frustrations about the chemically dependent person and the effects this has had on the family. They're really caught in a trap. They must communicate to get well and begin positive growth and recovery both as a family and individually, but they don't know how to begin. In addition, many of the post-recovery problems will force them to continue in their noncommunicating roles (problems such as taking care of the patient, not expressing their anger, resentment, fear, hostility, or sadness).

But the pattern must change if the family is to continue recovery in all areas—not just to keep the patient from using chemicals, but to learn to communicate and get back in touch with their own feelings, so they can deal with their sadness, anger, and frustration. There must be recovery for *all* members. At some point the whole family must get together and begin working on their problems.

We see a real need for all chemically dependent families to have follow-up work together in order to break the rigid, sick family system described earlier. It's usually not enough for Dad to go to A.A. meetings, Mom to Al-Anon, and the children to attend Alateen groups. There must be time when the whole family is working *together* for recovery. This can be accomplished best by seeking help from outside sources such as family counseling groups, courses in family communications, and post-treatment family counseling (Aftercare).

Let's summarize the situation of the recovering family. Many of the problems of such families are caused by the expectations of all family members. Generally, people assume that after reaching sobriety, the family will begin to function smoothly and efficiently and that things will easily and quickly return to the happier days of the past. But each family member harbors a lot of resentment, anger, and sadness that has built up during the period of active chemical use, and now the whole family must deal with this. The real problem is that the family really doesn't know what good communication is or how to learn it and put into practice.

Thankfully, today most chemical dependence treatment centers recognize chemical dependence as a family illness and offer educational and therapy sessions to the family members during the patient's treatment. In addition, many of these centers offer Aftercare (post-treatment counseling) to both patient and family members. If this isn't the case at the center where your patient receives treatment, we suggest that as soon after treatment as possible, your whole family get together in some counseling setting to begin learning how to get back in touch with yourselves and with one another. Remember this: a major characteristic of the chemically dependent family is that members don't share their real feelings openly. The walls of communication have been built high and thick, and family recovery is the long, difficult, but worthwhile process of learning to break down those walls. Don't be afraid of the challenge.

THE JOHNSON INSTITUTE

This section is taken from *Recovery of Chemically Dependent Families,* published by the Johnson Institute.

CHAPTER TEN

Enabling At Home

Chemical dependence has far-reaching effects for American society. However, few people feel the pain of chemical dependence as it affects society. Most men and women feel the pain, and they feel it grievously and sharply, only when it hits their own families and friends.

For families in which one member—father, mother, or child—is an alcoholic, there are three major problems at the outset. The first is correctly identifying the problem as alcoholism.[1] Identification is a problem because alcoholism is a great master of disguise. So effective that many people don't recognize it though they live with it every day in the family. Still, once alcoholism is recognized, there's a second problem: what can family members do that will really help? The third problem concerns how family members have been affected and what help they themselves may need.

The purpose of this chapter is to help those close to an alcoholic address these problems by letting them in on some very important insights into the alcoholism process in families.

This is the first insight: there's a subtle and specific way in which alcoholism can involve the nonalcoholic. For an

---

[1] This chapter speaks mostly of alcoholism. But what we say here applies to any chemical dependence, regardless of the drug used: alcohol, cocaine, marijuana, heroin, "uppers," "downers."

alcoholic to continue drinking, nonalcoholics must be unwittingly involved in enabling (that is, encouraging) the alcoholic's drinking. Applied to families, this is sadly ironic. The second insight is this: those close to an alcoholic are inclined to develop behavior and/or emotional problems of their own as they attempt to make adjustments to the alcoholic's progressive disease of alcoholism. They can become so caught up in the alcoholism system that they find it almost impossible to let go of the merry-go-round without some outside help.

Those who are closest to an alcoholic, most concerned about that person, and most hopeful that the alcoholic will stop drinking, often unwittingly play into the alcoholic's progressive drinking pattern. By their actions, the alcoholic can be enabled to drink more comfortably, and family members and friends become drawn into and affected by the very problem they'd like to prevent.

Thus a circular process is set up that can gather a momentum of its own that's difficult to halt.

Enabling Alcoholic Behavior

No one knowingly encourages the continuance of alcoholism or of other drug dependence in another family member. Enabling usually happens because people think they're doing the appropriate thing to help the alcoholic or remedy the situation. Enabling may sometimes occur against one's better judgment; it always occurs without the enabler's full realization of what's going on. In understanding enabling and what do do about it, family members must realize that alcoholism is a disease; it isn't something that anyone who drinks chooses fully and freely.

An alcoholic—and those around the alcoholic—cannot predict with certainty if or when the alcoholic will stop drinking once he or she starts. Because the time and amount of drinking are uncontrollable and unpredictable, the alcoholic, unexpectedly and repeatedly, is likely to engage in such disruptive and destructive behaviors as

- breaking family commitments, both major and minor
- spending more money than planned
- driving while intoxicated, and getting arrested
- making inappropriate statements to friends, family, and co-workers
- arguing, fighting, and other antisocial actions

The alcoholic would probably neither do such things nor approve of them in others unless he or she was drinking. In fact, such behaviors violate the alcoholic's conscience and cause feelings of guilt, remorse, and self-hatred. The alcoholic takes care of these intense negative feelings by spontaneous rationalizations and projections. The effect of such psychological defenses is to remove the person from reality. The alcoholic's view of life can, in fact, become so distorted that he or she will be the last person to recognize that drinking represents any type of personal problem.

Who Is an Enabler?

Now, how does enabling fit into all of this? Usually enabling means helping or supporting something or someone. However, in the alcoholic family, what's being enabled (supported) is the alcoholism—the drinking itself—instead of the drinker as a person. Who is an enabler? An enabler is a person who reacts to an alcoholic in such a way as to shield the alcoholic from experiencing the full impact of the harmful consequences of alcoholism. Enablers help alcoholics delude themselves that drinking isn't the problem. When enablers cover up for an alcoholic, the alcoholic doesn't realize the effects of drinking and thus has little reason to change. Further, the alcoholic misses an opportunity to gain what he or she needs most: significant insight that alcoholism is the problem. Without insight, the alcoholics will remain victims of their drinking. It's in the very nature of the disease that alcoholics really can't recognize that they need to stop drinking and to seek appropriate help.

So family members who go along with the alcoholic's drinking "to calm his nerves," "to help her endure her loneliness," "because he works so hard," or for any other reason, are all engaging in enabling behavior.

Family members who take on the responsibilities of the drinking person are enabling. Teenage (or younger) children who take on responsibilities in the home beyond their years or maturity while a parent is drunk or hung over are enablers. A husband who hides his wife's alcoholism "because I love her too much to embarrass her" is an enabler. A wife who cuts back on her own social life or family activities because a husband is drinking is an enabler in the sense that she's letting the drinking behavior run her life.

In short, family members who do for alcoholics what alcoholics normally would be doing for themselves are enabling.

Refusing to be an enabler can certainly lead to some difficult situations for the alcoholic: loss of job, loss of driver's license, a jail sentence, moving out of the family home, loss of contact with the family. But matters needn't go that far. And if enablers stop their enabling behavior, it's virtually certain that although some difficult situations will arise with the alcoholic in the short run, in the long run he or she will be forced to face problems more honestly.

Tragically, as a person in an enabling role continues trying to "help," the disease progresses, and everyone—both the alcoholic and the family—suffers. If the enabler's role is so harmful, why would anyone assume it? Usually enablers see all that's being done as a sincere effort to help both the family and the drinker, or as the best that can be done in the situation. They're often afraid of how the problems the alcoholic gets into will affect the family, and so they try to shield the family from the consequences. Like the alcoholic, enablers can become demoralized and see no alternative. Lacking the knowledge of how alcoholism works, enablers act out of misguided kindness and sympathy. Sometimes the problem just escalates as the enablers become more emotionally constricted because their blinders narrow their vision.

Rationalizing

Alcoholism is a progressive disease that initially may present only a few episodes of loss of control. Unfortunately, most people close to an alcoholic perceive such episodes as isolated instances of intoxication and not as a pattern of harmful dependence. Early on, few people would see themselves as entwined in a harmful pattern. Rather, they see themselves as concerned people who want to help someone they care very much about. They may receive credit and kudos for their "self-sacrifice," and even as the situation worsens they may begin to feel pleased with their effort, hoping it will bolster their own self-esteem. Consequently, they try to understand why the dependent person became intoxicated and acted so inappropriately. The enabler seldom views the drinker as someone who can't control drinking, but rather as someone who simply chooses to drink in order to cope with some pressure and "lets things get a little out of hand." But the drinking continues, and life for the family most likely gets worse.

The enabler, not recognizing the presence of alcoholism, usually responds to episodes of intoxication in either of two ways.

1. Excusing the behavior as unusual, perhaps, but still normal. The enabler might reason:

- "Who doesn't need to blow off steam once in a while?"
- "It's vacation time. Why shouldn't a person be allowed to let loose?"
- "Lots of people get loaded at that kind of party" (for instance, New Year's, "kegger," promotion, wedding).
- "It was no big deal last night. Why dwell on the broken lamp, cigarette burn, accident, or argument? It'd just be upsetting."

2. Excusing the behavior because it's seen as the result of another problem. The enabler might think such things as:

- "With those job pressures, anyone would drink."
- "She's just going through that phase of life."
- "The peer group's to blame."
- "The problem is loneliness and not knowing how to mix very well."
- "Maybe it's my fault. I shouldn't have been so critical."

Often the enabler either believes that a problem with alcohol doesn't exist or that, if it does, it'll disappear when the "real" problem is resolved.

In this way, the enabler too becomes highly vulnerable to the same developing defenses and denial that victimize the alcoholic. The rationalizations of both people now are supporting their misunderstanding of the nature of the problem. "He drinks because of job pressure," says the enabler. "I'm not having problems at work because of drinking; I'm nervous because they demand so much of me. And my home life just makes things worse," says the alcoholic.

Projecting

The disease continues to have an increasingly adverse effect on both the alcoholic and the enabler. The alcoholic's growing negative feelings about himself, resulting partially from inappropriate behavior while intoxicated and partially from the general devastating (and depressant) effects of alcoholism on the human system, are unconsciously and more frequently projected as the problems of the enablers. The enablers become the target of such statements as:

- "With the work load you're dumping on me, it's no wonder I need long lunch hours."
- "I come home from work and all I hear is you kids fighting over which program to watch on T.V. You're enough to drive anyone to drink."
- If you cared about me half as much as you care about your friends, maybe I wouldn't want to drink so much."
- "If you'd shape up, I'd be all right."
- "School's a bore, the teachers are stupid, and you just don't understand my friends. So I got caught smoking grass—big deal!"

Projection consists of accusing others of failings we dimly see and dislike in ourselves but don't want to admit. Projecting them onto others allows us to attack them safely. When an alcoholic can blame other people or circumstances for his or her bad feelings, he or she experiences an unconscious venting of those emotions. He or she temporarily relieves some of the internal stress that's part of alcoholism. Obviously, this is a false solution to the problem, which will only become worse as time goes on. Projection as a solution or survival mechanism, of course, helps the alcoholic avoid the truth of the situation. Avoiding the truth is counterproductive, though, because the alcoholic will experience more pain, which will produce further unconscious projections.

When the alcoholic verbalizes a projection such as "If you'd shape up, I'd be all right," there's little realization on either the dependent's or the enabler's part that the alcoholic speaks out of fear and self-hatred. For example, both people are apt to believe that the dependent does hate the enabler—and has good reason to do so. One common effect of projection is that both people focus on the enabler's behavior, not on the alcoholic's, and this distraction allows the disease of alcoholism to continue undetected.

Understanding projection makes it possible to see how this defense can and does have a devastating emotional impact on the enabler.

Trying To Control

Enablers need to learn what's happening to them at an emotional level. Because of feelings of decreasing self-worth, the enabler becomes more and more compulsive in reactions to the alcoholic. The alcoholic's drinking becomes a virtual display of the enabler's internal guilt and sense of inadequacy. In other words, the enabler's self-worth becomes tied directly to the alcoholic's drinking. The more the alcoholic drinks, the more the enabler feels responsible, guilty, and inadequate. The only way for the enabler to feel any positive self-worth, so the enabler believes, is to make sure the alcoholic's drinking doesn't get out of control. It's as if the enabler thought, "If there were some things I did to cause this, there must be things I can do to make it go away."

At this point in the disease process, the enabler may have lost the ability to initiate action or to behave autonomously without reference to drinking. It may be almost impossible to retain the emotional stability and insight needed to deal with the disease effectively. Without help, the enabler is likely to become increasingly depressed, discouraged, and dysfunctional.

Having "agreed" that he or she is to blame and must by his or her own effort control the drinking, the enabler ends up trying to control the family life by adopting reactive behavior in such typical ways as:

- canceling social events where there's drinking
- disposing of extra quantities of liquor or other drugs
- calling home at midday to determine whether the alcoholic is sober
- relieving the alcoholic of a portion of office work and personally doing the job
- explaining to the school counselor or teacher why there are problems in school (but never mentioning alcohol) and agreeing to see that the problems get resolved
- assuming household responsibilities that the alcoholic used to hold

These typical reactions of enablers are self-protective efforts to keep control and retain some shred of self-respect. But they can look like attempts to manipulate the drinker and hide the drinking. They're doomed to fail because the enabler is engaged in trying to control the uncontrollable. Neither the alcoholic nor the enabler can control the alcoholic's drinking. Every time the alcoholic drinks, the enabler's self-worth diminishes. Most enablers respond by making even more desperate attempts to control. On and on the vicious cycle goes as both the alcoholic and the enabler become increasingly alienated and dysfunctional.

Help For Enablers

At this point the enabler needs help as much as the alcoholic does. Breaking the cycle requires the enabler to gain knowledge and awareness in the following areas:
- how the disease of alcoholism works
- how enabling fosters continued drinking
- how concerned, loving people with the best of intentions can be enablers
- that enabling behavior can be stopped—there's hope

With knowledge and insight into oneself, the enabler can begin to see what's happened in the gradual building of the dysfunctional patterns and can respond to the alcoholic in more effective ways. The cycle of drinking and enabling can be broken. New and different interaction with the alcoholic will help the enabler to "let go" of responsibility for the alcoholic's drinking and subsequent behavior and to realize that, as close as anyone is to another, no one is responsible for another person's drinking. With a new sense of freedom, the enabler can stop shielding the alcoholic from the harmful consequences of the drinking and can realize that to do so is neither cruel nor uncaring. The enabler may be of help to the alcoholic by presenting the specific ways in which the disease causes and worsens problems for both of them. Talking directly about drinking and behavior, the enabler stops hiding the problem. At last the enabler changes roles and becomes a helper, providing the alcoholic with the data necessary to see the serious nature of the situation. With insight into alcoholism and into their own role in it, the former enablers can seek the appropriate help they need to lead happier and healthier lives.

One of the first and best steps that family members can take is to start on their own self-help program. Al-Anon and Alateen are excellent groups that have provided assistance and advice to thousands of men and women who live with the problems of alcoholism in the family. Both groups can be located by looking in the telephone directory or in the list of national organizations at the end of this book.

Family members who live with alcoholism don't have to live as unhappy, troubled, angry people with low self-esteem. When the enablers change, their new ways of dealing with alcoholism will provide hope and even motivation for the drinking people to seek help for themselves.

THE JOHNSON INSTITUTE

This section is taken from *The Family Enablers*, published by the Johnson Institute.

CHAPTER ELEVEN

Enabling in the Workplace

Much has been written about the ways in which chemical dependence affects the "other victims" of the illness. Immediate family and close friends easily understand the oft-cited statistic that an alcoholic's drinking causes problems for at least ten other people.[1] Among those others are people who work with the alcoholic: supervisors, managers, union representatives, and co-workers. When an alcoholic comes to work, the problems associated with alcoholism come along. Dealing with an alcoholic in the workplace can be a frustrating experience, especially for supervisors and managers. Most people would like to do something about the problem, but it's difficult to know where to begin.

Even in organizations that have formal Employee Assistance Programs—designed to help identify people who have personal problems and refer them to professional help—the alcoholic sometimes continues to drink. Although anyone who works with an alcoholic can refer him or her to the Employee Assistance Program, supervisors play especially important roles, since they're held responsible for overseeing job performance. The task for the supervisor isn't easy, and many find

---

[1] This chapter speaks mostly of alcoholism. But what we say here applies to any chemical dependence, regardless of the drug used: alcohol, cocaine, marijuana, heroin, "uppers," "downers."

it difficult to take the first step—identifying the pattern of inappropriate behavior.

The problems facing the supervisor concerned about the alcoholic in the workplace are similar to those facing the alcoholic's family and close friends. First, it's difficult to recognize a whole pattern of inappropriate behavior that may indicate alcoholism. For many, it's still hard to admit that alcoholism is truly a disease and that a certain person has it, whether it's oneself or others. Second, it's difficult to know for certain what to do once we've recognized the problem. Not only do supervisors feel helpless; they often believe the workplace isn't the best place to deal with personal issues. Third, because of the subtle ways in which alcoholism develops, concerned others belatedly find they've inadvertently cooperated in the disease process. They too have become caught up in the emotional swings, the denial, and the confusion that characterize alcoholism. As we'll go on to explain, at the workplace these three problems contribute to certain supervisory actions—carried out with the best intentions—that actually make it more difficult for the alcoholic to get help.

In general, supervisors are sincerely concerned for the alcoholic. Yet as it becomes clear that the alcoholic isn't meeting his or her job requirements, the supervisor also worries about output and performance. Balancing concerns for the worker and for the job can be emotionally straining to the supervisor and can lead to anxiety, anger, frustration, and even despair. In short, supervisors are among the "other victims" of alcoholism.

Alcoholism establishes itself through denial, covering-up, and a series of other behaviors on the part of both the alcoholic and concerned others that permit the drinking to continue unabated. The actions of concerned others—including supervisors—that indirectly contribute to the problem are known as "enabling" behaviors (more about them later). Thus a seemingly endless pattern of pain develops, built on the negative actions of the alcoholic and the enabling actions of concerned others. This chapter offers insights and suggestions to help break this pattern—for both the alcoholic and the supervisor.

An Alcoholic's Behavior

A supervisor must learn from the outset that an alcoholic's behavior, though uncontrollable and unpredictable in regard to specific actions, is nevertheless typical for an alcoholic. Supervisors often report outrageous behavior on the part of problem employees—such as temper tantrums, blaming others for personal mistakes, inappropriate outbursts of anger or frustration at minor inconveniences, curtness or sarcastic remarks to customers or other employees—and are incredulous that anyone could do the things they see. Or they complain of constant and repeated irritation from a variety of small infractions that occur at unpredictable intervals. They seem to feel that their problem employee is unique.

Although not all unusual or troublesome behavior stems from alcoholism, certain *patterns* of behavior may indicate excessive drinking.

Some of the most common job behaviors associated with alcoholism are:

1. Patterns of absenteeism and tardiness, such as:
   - late arrival and early departure
   - long lunch breaks
   - Monday and Friday absences
   - absences before and after paydays or holidays
   - absences due to accidents, both on and off the worksite
2. Patterns of unusual behavior at work, such as:
   - frequent absences from the work area
   - inability to concentrate

- work quality and quantity that fluctuate between excellent and hopelessly inadequate but are increasingly unsatisfactory
- irresponsibility in completing tasks
- wasted materials or damaged equipment

3. Patterns of abnormal interpersonal interactions, such as:
- mood swings, especially between morning and afternoon
- inappropriate statements
- overreaction to criticism
- outbursts of inappropriate anger, tears, or laughter
- complaints from co-workers, associates, or the public

It's important to note the alcoholic's feelings about inappropriate actions at work. Upon realizing what has occurred, the alcoholic is usually overcome with guilt, remorse, and even fear. Then he or she is obliged to come up with excuses for the behavior. The truth—"My drinking seems to cause so many problems, maybe I *am* an alcoholic"—is simply too painful to accept. But the only alternative explanation in the alcoholic's view—"I must be a really terrible person to have done these things"—is also painful. So he or she invents excuses.

The supervisor now has an employee who has gradually become unreliable and difficult to work with. To complicate matters, the supervisor is faced with a multitude of elaborate explanations. Instead of taking responsibility for his or her actions, the alcoholic blames everything and everyone else, including supervisors and co-workers. Supervisors and co-workers who wish to break out of this cycle of blame and frustration must first recognize it as a *cycle* and try to understand it better.

Who Is an Enabler?

Much has been written about the ways in which family members enable drinking to continue. Sometimes the actions of family members enter the workplace. For example, a family member phones in that the alcoholic is sick, when the problem is specifically a hangover. This is enabling. But the supervisor who overlooks the pattern that such calls occur regularly on Mondays or after long weekends is also enabling. Another common way in which supervisors and co-workers enable drinking to continue is by doing work for the alcoholic. As long as others are willing to pick up the slack, they encourage the alcoholic to avoid acknowledging a problem.

Family members cover up at home; supervisors and co-workers cover up at the workplace. Family members live with and accept a variety of excuses from the alcoholic. One of the most common is "There's so much stress on the job, I have to drink to deal with it." Conversely, the supervisor hears, "I have a lot of problems at home that have been distracting me at work." When family and supervisors accept these excuses without holding the person accountable for family and job responsibilities, they're enabling.

Upon hearing these explanations, a supervisor may become overinvolved with the employee and personally try to provide counseling. The supervisor may develop his or her own "diagnosis" of what the problem is and what the "cure" should be. Such "cures" may include giving the person less work, more time, fewer requirements, more personal attention, more private talks. When a supervisor accepts yet another broken promise or once again makes special arrangements for an alcoholic, he or she is enabling.

In short, anyone who does for the alcoholic what the alcoholic normally would be doing for himself or herself is enabling.

Unfortunately for most supervisors, it's easy to permit the enabling to continue. Dealing with difficult employees almost always creates tension in the supervisor. Just the thought of complicated disciplinary procedures may be enough to deter even a dedicated supervisor from taking action. In addition, when the problem employee is an alcoholic—and it must be remembered that the supervisor usually doesn't know the employee is an alcoholic—an intricate set of emotional barriers comes into play. These barriers aren't the result of the employee's hostility or of the supervisor's inability to cope. Rather, they're simply typical of the patterns of manipulation that characterize the disease of alcoholism.

The Effects of an Alcoholic's Manipulation on Supervisors

Alcoholism is a progressive disease. It seldom descends dramatically upon a person; rather, it creeps up slowly, frequently unobserved. Recognizing it is difficult because alcoholism involves the most commonly accepted drug used in business and social situations. Initially, only a few episodes of uncontrolled drinking may occur; only an occasional inappropriate act or comment may result. Such behavior is easily rationalized; many people have been drunk at least once in their lives. At the workplace, where the supervisor may be completely unaware of the employee's drinking problem, the alcoholic may miss only one deadline or cause one machine to break down. It's also easy to rationalize this; many people have had bad days at work.

Particularly if the supervisor has previously had a high opinion of the employee's work, it's easy to overlook these "isolated problems" and miss the developing *pattern* of decline.

The supervisor retains a mental image of how the alcoholic was *before* drinking became a problem.

The supervisor may have a few informal conversations with the employee to try to understand what's been happening lately. Wanting to believe there are no major problems, the supervisor is all too eager to accept the explanations offered. If asked by higher management to explain the situation, the supervisor simply repeats the employee's excuses. In so doing, he or she becomes committed to that same view of reality. This agreement to see things as the alcoholic sees them is the first step in the supervisor's denial, the first step in enabling.

As the pattern continues and the disease of alcoholism progresses, the alcoholic and the enabler together become more involved in denial and covering-up. The supervisor insists that the alcoholic's work improve. And for a while, things do get better. The supervisor feels confident, perhaps even proud, of his or her skill. But eventually another incident points out that the gain is false. So the supervisor may cover up, do the alcoholic's work, assign someone else to do it, make more elaborate excuses to upper management, and thereby enable the alcoholism to continue.

Because most managers and supervisors would consider such a situation extremely unpleasant, why do so many permit it to continue? Why are so many of them reluctant to confront the employee and make a referral to professional help? We've already seen that part of the reason is their lack of awareness that alcoholism—or another personal problem that causes similar job performance declines—is the problem. Another part of the answer lies in a series of beliefs and emotions that impede the supervisor's actions.

Beliefs That Permit Supervisory Enabling

Even supervisors who've had formal training in identifying troubled employees through deteriorating job performance may still be reluctant to act on that information. In fact, because of the denial described above, they may actually be unable to see the patterns they've been trained to observe. Sometimes their personal beliefs may contribute to the denial process and prevent them from applying their usual supervisory skills and knowledge. Here are a few examples:

Belief: " Someone as intelligent as Joe couldn't have these problems." This belief comes in numerous variations: "Someone as nice as Al," "Someone as pretty as Sally," "Someone with such a nice family as Marilyn," "Someone as young as Tony."

Effect: If the supervisor has defined the employee as intelligent, nice, pretty, young, or as having whatever characteristic *isn't* associated with alcoholism, it's difficult to see that employee as having job problems that may indicate alcoholism.

Belief: " Taking action would be so painful, it's better just to leave the situation alone."

Effect: Believing that a confrontation would be worse than just putting up with the problem limits the supervisor greatly. The belief is mistaken, too. The situation won't simply continue as is; it will get worse.

Belief: "Referring the employee to the Employee Assistance Program for counseling and treatment will damage his (or her) career."

Effect: Any supervisor who believes that making a referral will harm an employee's career will naturally be reluctant to do so. Fortunately, this belief is erroneous. Actually, Employee Assistance Programs are strictly confidential, and records of participation don't go into formal personnel files. Moreover, saving a job is hardly worth losing a life.

Belief: "The management system here doesn't encourage supervisors to get involved in personal problems." Some of the barriers that supervisors may perceive in the system include:

- complex disciplinary procedures
- unsupportive upper management
- unsupportive union
- unclear performance standards

Effect: This behavior promotes inertia in the supervisor. Even if there are real barriers preventing supervisors from becoming healthily involved in employees' personal problems, supervisors must take action. Failure to do so will inevitably mean a decline in the alcoholic's performance and an increasing number of problems in the work group. As others become affected and the total quality of the work output decreases, the supervisor's own performance becomes impaired. Then the supervisor really has a problem.

These few examples illustrate how a number of common erroneous beliefs—about alcoholism, about the ways to help someone, and about the worksite itself—can keep a supervisor from taking appropriate action to deal with an alcoholic employee. But every day on which a supervisor delays making a referral is a day on which both the workplace problem and the employee's illness get worse.

Emotions That Permit Supervisory Enabling

As the illness of alcoholism progresses in a person, the situation at home and in the workplace deteriorates accordingly. The alcoholic becomes more confused and frightened about the negative effects of his or her drinking but is even more unwilling to identify drinking as the problem. Thus the unpleasant emotions of anger, guilt, fear, hurt, isolation, and low self-esteem become stronger. Often those close to the alcoholic suffer from exactly this same set of unpleasant emotions as they attempt to cope with the unpredictable alcoholic. While this is especially true for the alcoholic's family, it's also true for the alcoholic's supervisor and co-workers.

The supervisor (or co-worker) usually becomes angry when the employee breaks repeated promises to improve or misses deadlines and when the supervisor is then forced to cover up or lie for him. Often the supervisor's anger grows quietly; he or she experiences it only as an underlying tension and frustration. If a particularly unpleasant incident occurs, the supervisor may burst out in anger that's inappropriate to the specific infraction.

When this happens, the supervisor is really reacting to a series of problems and annoyances. He or she feels angry and hurt. The employee was once a trusted worker, maybe even a friend. The supervisor wonders, "Why me? What have I done to deserve this?" Hurt mixed with frustration leads to a smoldering supervisor who finally explodes.

After the explosion, the supervisor may feel guilty about having become so angry over what in retrospect appears to have been a small issue. Sometimes a supervisor's regret comes from knowing or suspecting that the employee has personal problems. In such a case, guilt feelings multiply: "I shouldn't be putting any more pressure on; I overreacted." To compensate, the supervisor is likely to accept more excuses, ease off on expectations, and hope the situation will improve.

The supervisor is now caught in a complex web of emotions that lead to feelings of incompetence and low self-esteem. He or she may begin to feel responsible for causing the situation. "Why can't I handle this one? Maybe I'm not as good a supervisor as I thought I was." If the supervisor feels this way, chances are the employee is also blaming the supervisor. So not only does the supervisor face self-doubts, but the employee reinforces them with a constant barrage of criticism.

These negative behaviors aren't due to malicious intent on the part of the alcoholic. They're part of the denial process, part of the employee's ongoing attempt to avoid seeing that drinking is the problem. It's easy for the supervisor to participate in this denial, because the employee keeps the situation off balance with emotional outbursts, excuses, and accusations.

The supervisor is feeling angry, hurt, guilty, and discouraged, and by now is usually isolated. Embarrassed at having such a problem in the work group, the supervisor may avoid telling co-workers or upper management what's really going on.

Thus the supervisor may have the *knowledge* and the *skills* to make an appropriate referral but be unable to do so because of the *emotions* connected with the disease of alcoholism.

Help for Enablers in the Workplace

Although most of the above description has focused on how supervisors become enablers in the workplace, co-workers and union representatives can also be drawn into a similar process. When enabling has gone on for some time, the enabler in the workplace may need help almost as much as the alcoholic does. Perhaps the most important first step is *knowing when to ask for help*.

The enabler needs to be able to:
- recognize that an unhealthy pattern of interaction is occurring
- know that this pattern may indicate alcoholism
- understand that if the problem is alcoholism, enabling merely allows the drinking to continue and the problem to get worse
- realize that even concerned, loving people with the best of intentions can become enablers
- ask for help

Many organizations have Employee Assistance Programs sponsored by management, by labor, or by both. These programs provide confidential assistance to people with personal problems that interfere with their ability to function at work. They also provide important advice and assistance to supervisors, managers, union representatives, and co-workers who feel they may be involved in enabling behavior.

Breaking the cycle of enabling means helping the alcoholic to face the unpleasant effects of his or her drinking. This means that the enabler must be honest and willing to confront the employee about inappropriate behavior and poor job performance. This means also being willing to stop taking responsibility for the alcoholic's actions. It's not always easy to change, but the enabler will find that what appears to be harsh and uncaring behavior is really helpful to the alcoholic. The enabler will also find a sense of relief in being freed from the obligations of denial and covering up.

Employee Assistance Counselors can help enablers to become true helpers, and alcoholics to become sober. Just ask them.

A Special Note About Women

It's likely that as you were reading this chapter you were examining your own mental images of what an alcoholic looks like. You've probably come to accept the idea that you have an alcoholic in your workplace. But you've probably not pictured that employee as a woman. All our stereotypes about alcoholics—especially the negative ones that create the terrible stigma associated with the illness—are even more undesirable when applied to women. Thus most people somehow seem, because of our cultural conditioning, extremely reluctant to think a woman may have a drinking problem. The alcoholic woman herself believes these stereotypes. As a result, she has very low self-esteem and makes extraordinary efforts to cover up and deny her problem.

Consequently, supervisors—both men and women—should be careful not to let their own views about women—possibly slanted views—prevent them from taking appropriate action. All of us can benefit from examining our own attitudes. Supervisors need to apply their knowledge about performance patterns fairly to all their workers, including women, and make referrals for help when prudent judgment seems to demand them.

A Word of Caution

Although this chapter has dealt primarily with the issue of alcoholism, it should be noted that a variety of personal problems other than alcoholism can cause similar patterns of declining performance in the workplace. Many drugs, when used inappropriately or in combination with alcohol or other drugs, can cause both personal and job-related difficulties. Undiagnosed physical ailments, such as diabetes or hypoglycemia, can upset emotions and thinking. Mental illness, both chronic and acute, and family crises, such as a divorce or death, can also influence behavior on the job.

Any and all of these problems damage a person's health and well-being. Like alcoholism, many of them are surrounded by negative feelings such as confusion, denial, and cover-up. The supervisor doesn't need to know for certain what the problem is. The supervisor *does* need to keep the focus on job performance. The important point is to avoid enabling the problem to continue. Like alcoholism, other illnesses may be life-threatening if they run their destructive course. In any case, enabling must be avoided.

A Word of Hope

Supervisors should know the great benefits of breaking out of the enabling cycle and referring someone to professional help. With the aid of Employee Assistance Programs and community treatment facilities, hundreds of thousands of employees have dealt successfully with a wide range of problems. Recovery rates from the disease of alcoholism are particularly high when the treatment process is initiated at the workplace. The result is often a job maintained, a family preserved, and a life saved.

In addition to these tangible benefits to both employer and employee, there are intangible rewards for the individual supervisor or manager. Imagine the good feeling a supervisor or manager would experience watching a valued but impaired employee regain his or her health and performance level. Supervisors and managers who witness this in an employee usually experience the change themselves. The thousands of supervisors and managers who've made the transition from enabling an employee's illness to aiding in his or her recovery highly recommend the move. The results are worth it: to the employee, to the employer, and to the supervisor.

BRENDA R. BLAIR, M.B.A.

This section is taken from *Supervisors and Managers As Enablers*, published by the Johnson Institute.

CHAPTER TWELVE

What is Co-Dependence?

Co-dependence is a term that is often used, but without a clear agreement about what it means. This is due, in part, to the fact that different people use it for different reasons.

In dealing directly with family members of chemical dependents, therapists use co-dependence as an important teaching tool. The word itself legitimizes many of the family members' feelings and gives them permission to begin focusing on their own dysfunctional behaviors.

Co-dependence implies that family members have their own "something" to recover from. Its value in education is sufficient reason for mental health professionals to take co-dependence seriously.

Many definitions for co-dependence have developed precisely because of their practical value in dealing with people in denial. In reality, such definitions rarely go beyond examples designed for maximum emotional impact. For example, Charles Alexander characterizes co-dependence as being like a lifeguard on a crowded beach, knowing you can't swim, and hesitating to tell anyone for fear of starting a panic.[1] When confronted with such a description, many co-dependent people

---

[1] Charles Alexander, "The Definition of Co-Dependence," San Francisco Conference on Children of Alcoholics, The National Association for Children of Alcoholics, July 11, 1985.

are amazed to discover that anyone else might have an idea of their internal sense of dilemma and desperation.

On the other hand, therapists and clinical theoreticians use the term co-dependence in the same way they use other psychological concepts such as defense mechanisms, the ego, homeostasis, and enmeshment. These concepts enable them to organize the raw data of human behavior into coherent frameworks, enhance communication about psychological phenomena, and suggest potentially valuable research and treatment approaches.

Whether or not co-dependence is eventually found to be a specific personality disorder, it will likely remain an important concept precisely because it serves these same purposes for chemical dependence (CD) professionals. Viewed in this light, co-dependence becomes a highly sophisticated psychological concept deserving further consideration.

Finally, for the purposes of clinical assessment of individuals, co-dependence can best be seen as a disease. CD therapists speak of family members as being affected by co-dependence, or as being actively co-dependent. Such assessments imply that a consistent pattern of traits and behaviors is recognizable among individuals, and that these traits and behaviors can create significant dysfunction. In other words, co-dependence is used to describe a "disease entity," just as phobia, narcissistic personality disorder, and Post-Traumatic Stress Disorder are disorders that can be diagnosed.

The origins of the term "co-dependence" to describe a disease entity are obscure; it probably evolved from "co-alcoholic" when alcoholism and other drug dependencies began being lumped together under the generic "chemical dependence." In any event, the more generic term became common parlance in the CD field fairly quickly. Before long, lots of people were speaking of co-dependence as a disease, but everyone had his or her own definition of it. While these definitions appear to point to the same thing, they do not form a clear picture.

Most of these definitions do, however, assume that co-dependence exists independently within members of chemically dependent families, and that many of its symptoms become more overt in a committed relationship—especially with another co-dependent or chemical dependent. These are important insights.

Co-Dependent Trait or Disorder?

A major roadblock to diagnosing co-dependence has been its apparent scope. Described by some as "a condition of the Twentieth Century," co-dependence is often dismissed as social commentary. If nearly everyone appears to be co-dependent, the argument goes, then how can it be considered a disease?

The answer lies in the distinction between personality **traits** and personality **disorders**. Personality traits shape how we see the world and the ways we relate to it over a long period of time. Personality traits only become disorders when they become inflexible and interfere significantly with our social or work lives, or otherwise cause significant distress.

The critical point for our purposes is that while co-dependent **traits** *may be widespread, a person can only be diagnosed as being co-dependent when these traits have become rigid or intense, and caused the person to become dysfunctional.*

Diagnostic Criteria for Co-Dependence

It remains to be proven through clinical research whether relatives of chemical dependents develop a recognizable and diagnosable pattern of personality characteristics, and whether these characteristics can become sufficiently inflexible and maladaptive to produce clear dysfunction or significant distress. Such research cannot be conducted until diagnostic criteria for co-dependence have been defined. I proposed the following criteria to other professionals to further such research. These criteria may also help the lay reader define co-dependence in terms of a recognizable and predictable pattern of traits.

Criterion A:

A Person's Self-Esteem Comes From the Ability to Control Oneself and Others Despite Serious Negative Consequences

This criterion includes four distinct elements: a distorted relationship to willpower, a confusion of identities, denial, and low self-esteem.

Distorted Willpower: Like chemical dependents, co-dependents believe they can control their lives by sheer force of will. Chemical dependents show this by repeated efforts to control their drinking or other drug use. ("I *know* I can stop after one drink." Or, "I swear, I'll never take another drink again.") Co-dependents show it by repeated efforts to control the feelings and behavior of the chemical dependent, as well as their own feelings and behavior. ("If only we all try hard enough and pull *together*, we can get your father to stop drinking.")

In both cases, the end result is isolation—from others, from their own authentic selves, and from their spiritual and unconscious resources. It becomes an either/or situation: *either* they continue to rely totally on willpower, *or* they succumb to utter hopelessness. There is nothing in between.

It is important to understand the distinction between will*ful*ness and will*ing*ness. The willful person believes that everything can be controlled if one's willpower is strong enough and focused enough. Failure leads to a sense of inadequacy. The willing person, on the other hand, recognizes the value of determination where it is possible to exercise influence or control, while accepting the fact that some things simply can't be controlled.

Confusion of Identities: There are important differences between co-dependence and excessive dependence. One difference lies in the previously mentioned sense of willpower found at the core of co-dependence. Another lies in the confusion of identities which co-dependents invariably feel.

Becoming dependent upon another person means giving that person power over one or more aspects of one's life. What usually results is a sort of *inter-dependence*. Partners strike implied "bargains": "I'll take care of the kids, and you'll put food on the table and pay the rent." If either partner fails to uphold the bargain, the other person suffers. But his or her sense of self remains relatively unaffected.

When the line is crossed into co-dependence, that sense of self is confused and even lost. The co-dependent's self-worth rises or falls with the partner's success or failure.

Now picture what happens when this confusion of identities is combined with the belief that one can control almost anything with willpower. In order for the co-dependent to feel good, the partner must be happy and behave in appropriate ways. If the partner is not happy, the co-dependent feels responsible for *making* him or her happy. If the partner is drinking or using other drugs, the co-dependent feels responsible for *making* him or her stop. All of this becomes a matter of intense personal importance. And it is seen as possible, if only the co-dependent puts enough effort into it.

Denial: To continue using alcohol or other drugs despite negative physical, social, and emotional consequences, the chemical dependent must construct a denial system. The co-dependent also builds a denial system. They both go about it through suppression, repression, rationalization, and projection.

Uncomfortable facts and feelings ("This marriage is not working"; "Her drinking is clearly not normal") are consciously pushed out of one's awareness (suppression). Or they are filtered out of awareness before they even have a chance to rise into the light of consciousness (repression). Or reasonable causes for their existence are substituted for actual causes (rationalization). Or the cause of one's problems can be seen as lying outside oneself, rather than in one's own behavior (projection).

At the core of the chemical dependent's world is the prideful insistence that he or she can use drugs without incurring lasting harm. As long as this belief is not challenged, then every misfortune and discomfort must be assigned the next most logical explanation. The consistencies among these explanations become part of the denial system.

The co-dependent also maintains the unchallenged core belief that he or she ought to be able to change his or her partner's behavior. When the partner behaves appropriately, this is seen as proof of success. When the partner behaves inappropriately, this is seen as proof of failure due to inadequacy. In either case, the co-dependent perceives himself or herself as playing a central role that is quite powerful.

Seeing oneself in this role, like seeing oneself as being able to use alcohol or other drugs with impunity, requires denial. The co-dependent either chooses not to see the chemical dependent's inappropriate behavior or rationalizes his or her own failure to keep the person from using drugs. In the latter case, the failure is attributed to not having tried long enough or hard enough, or to having tried the wrong way. Personalizing the failure offers hope that increasing one's efforts can keep things from getting further out of control.

Thus the denial of the chemical dependent and the denial of

the co-dependent are the same. Both work to preserve the status quo, since denial is inconsistent with recovery. And each legitimizes and reinforces the other. Until the pain of continued denial outweighs anxieties about recovery, the chemical dependent will continue to use and the co-dependent will continue to feel responsible.

Low Self-Esteem: Most healthy people avoid relationships with active co-dependents. As a result, co-dependents are often left with some very poor choices for partners.

If self-worth is tied to another person's behavior, it would be best to find a high-functioning, successful partner. But high-functioning, successful people are not likely to want to carry the burden a co-dependent expects them to carry. This burden may be disguised as sincere caring, loyalty, or martyrdom, but the healthy person will not be fooled for long. What the co-dependent is really saying is: "Tell me how to feel and act. When you're sad, I'll be sad. When you're happy, I'll be happy. My self-esteem is in your hands." What healthy person would accept such power?

With their options severely limited, co-dependents usually end up with people with strong narcissistic needs to feel special, such as non-recovering chemical dependents. Unfortunately, chemical dependents are bad bets when it comes to taking care of someone else's self-esteem. There is no one more apt to disappoint the co-dependent as the unrecovering chemical dependent. As the disease progresses, the co-dependent's self-esteem is virtually guaranteed to end up as a bust.

Criterion B:

The Person feels Responsible for Meeting Others' Needs and Does Not Acknowledge Own Needs

> *Partner:* "What would you like to do tonight?"
> *Co-dependent:* "I don't know. What would *you* like to do?"
> *Partner:* "How about a movie?"
> *Co-dependent:* "That sounds nice."
> *Partner:* "Do you have any preference?"
> *Co-dependent:* "Whatever you choose is fine with me."

This conversation appears benign, but the realities for the co-dependent are deeply self-destructive. *Everyone has preferences, however subtle, about nearly everything.* Professing not to care when asked to state a preference is fundamentally dishonest. It is not being "flexible," it is not being "polite," it is not the simple act of generosity it might seem on the surface. If the co-dependent were going to a movie alone, there would be little hesitation about making a choice.

But making a choice in a relationship means taking a concrete stand, and that implies risk. The co-dependent prefers to attend an uninteresting movie rather than risking the partner not enjoying it.

Assuming responsibility for meeting others' needs and not acknowledging one's own is a classic symptom of co-dependence. At its root is the fear of being alone or abandoned. Eventually the co-dependent cannot distinguish his or her own needs from those of the other person and takes on the wants and desires of the other in a series of desperate compromises. Denial of the self for the sake of feeling connected to others is a hallmark of co-dependence. It creates a profound void within the self.

The other side of the coin is the co-dependent who avoids relationships with others. This person is suffering essentially the same disorders as the co-dependent who ignores personal needs in favor of a partner's. Rather than take the chance of being abandoned, he or she goes one step further and refuses to get involved at all. In a similar vein, there are teetotalers who remain as tightly focused on alcohol as active alcoholics.

According to the rules of co-dependence, you can't have a relationship with another person and take care of your own needs and feelings. As a result, co-dependents tend to choose one extreme or another: denial of themselves to keep someone else happy, or compulsive avoidance of others to keep themselves safe.

Criterion C:

The Person Feels Anxious and Has Unclear Personal Boundaries in Regard to Intimacy and Separation From Others

The co-dependent equates closeness with compliance and intimacy with fusion. As he or she becomes more involved with another person, the tendency is to take on many of that person's values, wishes, dreams, characteristics, and denial system. The co-dependent becomes a mirror.

Experiencing others' feelings is rationalized as being "sensitive." The co-dependent involved with a chemical dependent actually feels that person's pain, rather than feeling empathy for the pain. This helps to fill the void caused by not honoring one's own needs and feelings.

Anxiety and unclear personal boundaries are most intense when there is no structure defining the relationship. (An example of such a structure is the work environment, in which relationships and roles are clearly defined.) Without a structure, people in a relationship must continually negotiate the interpersonal distance between themselves. When the interpersonal distance decreases, the co-dependent's grasp on his or her true self becomes even more tenuous. When it increases, the co-dependent fears total abandonment, and consequently the loss of the false self he or she has created for the relationship. *Any shift in the status quo will be seen as a threat to the co-dependent's identity.*

When the interpersonal distance changes, the co-dependent may experience rapid swings between seeing one's partner as all good or all bad as the co-dependent lurches back and forth between feeling totally inadequate and feeling in control. As black-and-white thinking increases, the world is split into friends and enemies. Friends are often those who support co-dependents' denial and commiserate with their pain; such friends often are idealized. Enemies are often those who insist on speaking the truth, and they may become the target of intense rage. The co-dependent frequently makes impulsive and desperate efforts to regain control of the world. The co-dependent further neglects his or her own needs and can become overtly self-destructive. The anxiety created by changing interpersonal distance can spiral into fear of abandonment or of being overwhelmed by intimacy. All of these factors contribute to relationships being particularly difficult for co-dependents.

Criterion D:

The Person Feels Entangled in Relationships with Chemically Dependent or Other Co-Dependent People

Maintaining direct contact with chemical dependents or co-dependents (or other people with immature defense systems) eventually becomes intolerable—unless one is co-dependent. When confronted with the immature defenses of projection, rationalization and denial, the co-dependent responds by mirroring them.

There are other reasons for this mutual attraction. Criterion A notes the tendency of co-dependents to give others power over their self-esteem. But not everyone wants that sort of power, and those who do usually possess a narcissistic need to be considered special. Chemical dependents who are using drugs (and people with personality disorders) have this need. Thus a complementary situation exists in which the co-dependent and the chemically dependent person can find mutual gratification without ever having to express their needs overtly. They call it "chemistry." They fall in love!

Unfortunately, a chemically dependent person is not the ideal caretaker for one's self-esteem. When the co-dependent's self-esteem is dashed, the co-dependent responds with a pledge to redouble his or her willpower and make it work next time.

Criterion E:

Three or More of the Following

Co-dependence is similar to chemical dependence in a number of ways. Both are diseases of denial, and both exhibit a wide range of symptoms.

Any chemical dependent can point to certain symptoms of dependence which he or she does not display; the unrecovering chemical dependent may then use such "evidence" to shore up his or her faulty denial system. There is a similar range of co-dependent symptoms wide enough so that no individual could have them all. In fact, some of the symptoms even seem contradictory. Co-dependents who are still in denial frequently ignore obvious symptoms while focusing on those symptoms they do not display. Such "negative" evidence is cited as proof that they are not co-dependent. This whole process is further evidence of denial, which is a prime symptom of active co-dependence.

1. Denies Most Problems: People deny co-dependence and deny chemical dependence in the same ways. They cannot consciously and directly control their denial. They are unwilling to have the feelings that would result from acknowledging reality. It is a very active, if unconscious, process, requiring them to constantly scan the environment and quickly put on "blinders" when needed.

Denial may be seen as a flawed way to feel secure. When threatened, narrowing one's awareness can create the appearance of safety. A complete constriction of awareness would be *psychotic* denial; the denial of co-dependence and chemical dependence is more selective, excluding awareness of threatening realities while admitting others.

If a threat can be ignored, then one doesn't have to take any action to avoid it. But one must be constantly vigilant. As a result, the need to deny increases and may eventually overwhelm the psyche.

Co-dependents frequently see the breakdown of their denial system as a sign of their own personal inadequacy, much as chemical dependents view their growing lack of control over their drug use as a sign of personal weakness. Each typically attempts to regain control through renewed applications of willpower.

Paradoxically, the recovering person reacts to a threat in quite the opposite way—by *expanding* his or her awareness. This allows him or her to more accurately assess the level of danger and, if possible, take effective action.

For unrecovering chemical dependents and co-dependents, however, denial continues to give the false impression of security. It is rarely acknowledged and relinquished until the pain and emptiness of their ever narrower and more isolated life becomes too much to bear.

2. Cannot Feel or Express Emotions: Co-dependents frequently view emotions as enemies (or as weapons). Many families in the early stages of treatment mistakenly believe that they must curb their emotions and not allow them to affect their behavior or relationships. This becomes a test of willpower, a way to prove that they are able to maintain at least a semblance of control over their lives.

Typically, the emotions they work hardest to restrict are those normally considered to be immature, dangerous, uncomfortable, or just plain bad: anger, fear, sadness, rage, embarrassment, bitterness, loneliness, etc. Unfortunately, it is impossible to put a lid on such "negative" feelings without also restricting the expression of more positive ones, such as happiness. Co-dependents tend to use perhaps thirty percent of their emotional energy to cage another thirty percent they have deemed undesirable. That leaves only forty percent of their emotional energy available to enjoy a full, rich, and gratifying life.

This effort to control one's feelings is precisely the behavior targeted by the second half of A.A.'s First Step: "We admitted . . . that our lives had become unmanageable." Co-dependents are deeply dedicated to "managing" their lives—a dedication which stems from the same self-importance which leads humans to believe they can improve on nature by exterminating animals or by throwing poison on fields to eliminate "bad" insects. Sooner or later the entire ecosystem reacts to such uses of brute force, and the consequences can come from unexpected directions. The lesson to be learned here is that complex natural systems cannot be "managed" to suit our goals without becoming less healthy.

The meadows of our emotional landscape are equally complex. When one part attempts to "manage" the whole, our general emotional makeup suffers. We cannot improve our lives by stifling undesirable emotions, any more than we can improve nature by eliminating selected elements.

A typical phenomenon in co-dependence is the tendency to

resort to the more extreme mechanisms of dissociation or depersonalization. In a desperate attempt to survive (in other words, not to feel), they will "close down," "shut down," "phase out," or go into a spontaneous trance. This results in a quality of being more present in body than in mind. Clients in therapy can actually be seen to separate themselves from the intensity of the moment. Their facial expressions become fixed, they seem to gaze off into the distance, their breathing grows shallow. These are signs that they have clicked into their "survival mode" and are allowing the world to wash past them. Numbness gives the illusion of safety and control.

Co-dependents may also exhibit symptoms which appear to directly contradict the constriction of feelings: the dramatic outburst and the compulsive exposure of feelings.

When unexperienced feelings have built up over time, the most minor incident can trigger an explosion. An unpleasant feeling will resonate with a backlog of similar feelings, and the effect will be inappropriately intense. For example, a co-dependent who is reluctant to express feelings about a spouse's drinking might blow up at a friend who forgets to send a birthday card. Or a torrent of rage might follow a relatively insignificant act of thoughtlessness on the part of the spouse. In any event, the co-dependent is left feeling "crazy" and "bad."

Note that the outburst is directed at a "safe"—or at least safer—target. It's not the forgetful friend who is the *real* problem, it's the spouse's drinking. Ironically, the very intensity of the outburst will be used as an excuse for discounting it.

The compulsive exposure of feelings is an effective disguise for constricted feelings. Some co-dependents go to great lengths to verbalize *every* feeling as soon as it enters their awareness. They also pressure those around them to continuously expose *their* feelings. While such behavior might appear to be the opposite of the emotional "constipation" so often seen, its purpose is essentially the same: to avoid having to deal with

240

feelings or experience them any longer than necessary.

The essence of co-dependence is to minimize the anxiety and ambiguity of allowing feelings to run their natural course, whether by damming them up or by expelling them as quickly as possible.

3. Feels Depressed: Co-dependents have many reasons to feel depressed: anger turned inward, unresolved grief, the chronic restraint of feelings, being identified more with one's false self than one's true self. Typically, however, they see their depression as inadequacy and the failure to control, and for this reason they usually deny its presence. To acknowledge depression is to acknowledge loss, which challenges the family's shared denial and focuses attention on one's own feelings.

Co-dependents often cite the pressures of children, work, and home life as reasons for not experiencing their personal feelings. ("Too many people depend on me to be there for them.") Admitting that one is depressed means admitting that one has needs, and co-dependents, by definition, always place the needs of others above their own.

For children who spend their developmental years in chemically dependent or co-dependent families, depression stems from actual *deprivation* rather than loss; a bond which never existed cannot be loosened. Children naturally protect themselves from unstable bonds, and those who develop co-dependent traits while their personalities are still forming may be expected to feel depressed. Acknowledging their depression requires that they develop new levels of trust in others—a difficult task since their early experience has taught them that their trust will not be returned or respected.

4. Feels Hypervigilant: The co-dependent's environment is unpredictable, basically incomprehensible, and highly stressful. Drug-using chemical dependents bring chaos into their own lives and family interactions, and those around them can never predict their actions. Decisions that are ninety-five percent made can be randomly reversed or ignored. The only way for the co-dependent to survive is by being ultra-sensitive to subtle shifts in the chemical dependent's behavior and mood.

Such hypervigilance is a recognized symptom of Post Traumatic Stress Disorder, which is most typically seen in combat veterans. By putting his vigilance on automatic pilot, a soldier is always prepared to react. Unfortunately there is seldom an "off" switch. Once a co-dependent starts scanning the environment for signs of impending disaster, a state of free-floating anxiety can be established.

Hypervigilance is also a natural byproduct of investing one's self-esteem in another person's behavior. To feel good about himself or herself, the co-dependent must first attend to everyone else's happiness. The merest hint of dissatisfaction in another signals that one's own behavior needs to be modified. In order to control how others feel and behave—the co-dependent's goal in life—it is essential to stay on one's toes and catch inappropriate behavior in its earliest stages.

Of course, hypervigilance requires a lot of energy. When the strain becomes too much to bear, the co-dependent may suddenly feel overwhelmed and demoralized. Feelings of apathy can alternate with frantic efforts to monitor everything and maintain control.

5. Acts Compulsively: Compulsivity is a primary defense process. A recovering chemical dependent may pass through periods of compulsive eating, compulsive spending, compulsive working, and compulsive relationships after achieving abstinence. Like chemical dependents, co-dependents can only remain active in their disease by disregarding the pain that it brings. *Unlike* chemical dependents, however, co-dependents have no biochemical "booster" for their denial system. For them, compulsions serve the same purpose, whether the compulsion is to eat, to work, to rescue others, to watch television, to read, to seek sex, to gamble, to be religious, whatever. Many co-dependents can describe in detail the subjective experience of sliding gradually into the whirlpool of their compulsivity. There is a surge of adrenaline. An intense buildup of emotions related to the compulsion occurs ("I've *got* to stop eating"), while more threatening emotions ("I feel empty in this marriage") are ignored. A feeling of inevitability takes over. Eventually they stop resisting the compulsion, and this is followed by a temporary sense of relief.

In most cases, the unwanted emotions are avoided while the person is acting compulsively. In order for the emotions to surface, be identified, and be experienced, one must abstain—not act compulsively. This is another way in which the co-dependent and the chemical dependent are similar: to recover, both must choose abstinence.

6. Feels Anxious: The anxiety of co-dependence can take a variety of forms, from free-floating, chronic anxiety to panic attacks, phobias, and existential dread. Some of this anxiety is in response to the random chaos inherent in living with an unrecovering chemical dependent. It becomes free-floating because of the generally high level of denial the co-dependent must maintain. In some cases, that denial blocks the co-dependent from acknowledging that the chemical dependence even exists; in other cases, it protects the co-dependent from having to face a high level of stress. When one is able to ignore that level of stress and its source, the anxiety appears "sourceless" and free-floating and is perceived as still another sign of personal inadequacy.

The deep existential dread that co-dependents experience often goes unrecognized. Co-dependent anxiety reaches this stage for two reasons. First, when one's self-worth must continually be validated by someone else, there is an ever-present risk that one's identity will be thrown into limbo should the relationship come to an end. (As one depressed widow said, "I used to be half of something wonderful. Now I'm half of nothing, and half of nothing *is* nothing.") Second, co-dependents are by nature chameleons. They become whatever their partners want and need them to be. But mirroring the actions and emotions of others means abandoning one's true self in favor of a false self. And even this false self must shift and change according to others' needs.

Gradually the true self becomes less and less real, until the co-dependent's anxiety becomes *anxiety about his or her very existence.* When one devotes more emotional energy to one's false self than one's true self, there is a genuine risk of emotional death. This is what the co-dependent senses, even if he or she can't articulate it.

7. Alcohol or Other Drug Use: Co-dependents can be more likely to become chemically dependent. When one habitually responds to threats by denying that they exist (in other words, by narrowing one's awareness), the use of mind-altering chemicals is a logical next step. Denial is necessary to avoid being overwhelmed by feelings, and drug use serves as a biochemical "booster" for one's crumbling denial. In short, *drug use fits into the personality structure of the co-dependent.*

As noted earlier, co-dependents exhibit a wide range of compulsions, and the use of alcohol or other drugs falls into this category. Traditionally, however, the co-dependent who compulsively uses chemicals for denial is diagnosed as being *chemically dependent.* This is as it should be; when chemical dependence is present, it must always be treated as the primary issue. *But it cannot be seen as the only issue.* Once the chemical dependence has been broken, the co-dependence remains; left untreated, it acts as a barrier to long-term sobriety.

In *I'll Quit Tomorrow,* Vernon Johnson described the "ism" of alcoholism as being the same illness as co-dependence when he wrote, "The only difference between the alcoholic and the spouse, in instances where the latter does not drink, is that one is physically affected by alcohol; otherwise both have all the symptoms."[2] If this "ism" goes untreated in a chemical dependent who stops using alcohol or other drugs, he or she is considered to be "dry." Being dry is a setup for relapse. Similarly, an overwhelmed denial system is a setup for turning to chemical abuse. It is not at all unusual for a co-dependent to become harmfully involved with alcohol or other drugs following a divorce, or the death or recovery of the chemical dependent.

Helping professionals tend to view chemical dependence and co-dependence as two distinct problems and apply different labels to their symptoms. The denial of the chemical dependent is termed "alcoholic thinking," "drug mentality," or "stinking thinking," while the denial of the co-dependent is called "co-dependent thinking" or "co-ing." In fact, these divisions are largely artificial. The disease of chemical dependence and the disease of co-dependence largely overlap, and often the person who has one will have the other as well. While it is probably rash to say that *all* chemical dependents are also co-dependent, we can safely assume that active co-dependence is at least as common among chemical dependents as it is among their family members. (This may be true in part because fully *half* of all chemical dependents have at least one chemically dependent parent they have had to relate to.)

When a co-dependent is also chemically dependent, the latter must be treated first. But the underlying co-dependence must not be ignored.

8. Has Been (Or Is) The Victim of Recurrent Physical or Sexual Abuse: In many chemically dependent families, the threat of physical and/or sexual abuse is always present. Whether it stems from abusive incidents or merely from feeling like a hostage to the angry rantings or depressed ruminations

---

[2] Vernon E. Johnson, *I'll Quit Tomorrow* (New York: Harper & Row, 1973), p. 30.

of an out-of-control spouse or parent, it lodges in the heart like a thorn.

All too often these incidents, rantings, or ruminations occur during a blackout. When the next morning comes, the chemical dependent has no memory of them and, accordingly, feels no guilt. Meanwhile the rest of the family stays caught up in the fear from the night before. They hide their emotions, but for the rest of the day—and often for weeks and months to come—they work anxiously to keep the threat from coming true.

Co-dependents tend to minimize both the amount of violence and the level of stress in their relationships. They do not see themselves as victims of physical or sexual abuse except in the most extreme cases, and even then they frequently take the blame: either they "caused" the abuse or they "deserve" to be treated abusively. Especially if few or no overtly abusive acts have occurred, the co-dependent's denial system prevents him or her from viewing the situation realistically. As one co-dependent said (in all earnestness), "My husband is good to me. Whenever he hits me, he only uses his hand. He never uses a board or anything that could do any real damage."

In extreme cases, co-dependents remain in relationships where they are chronically abused. While it may be difficult to understand how anyone could live this way for any amount of time, it is important to realize that co-dependents perceive their experience from a distorted—and self-reinforcing—point of view. When others are unhappy, they see it as a result of their own inadequacy, and being abused further lowers their self-esteem. As often happens in hostage situations, they begin to identify with their aggressors and empathize with their aggressors' frustrations and disappointments. Their own needs take second place or are not considered at all. In the end, they stop believing that they should be treated with respect. They simply can't conceive of living any differently.

The victims of physical and sexual abuse are usually too

embarrassed to speak freely about it. For co-dependents to speak honestly about being abused, they must develop a high level of trust in a therapist. Telling the truth requires them to "betray" their family, and the resulting sense of guilt may activate the tendency to minimize what they have just said. Or it may release a flood of dammed-up feelings. For a time they may be overwhelmed by grief and rage—feelings which must be fully experienced for the co-dependent to have any chance of seeing how and why the abusive relationship has developed, and how it can be changed.

Physical and sexual abuse take on more ominous dimensions when the victims are children who frequently don't realize that what is happening to them is wrong and *not their fault.* They bring these buried feelings and ancient betrayals with them into adulthood. We now know that many victims of abuse grow up to become abusive themselves. But even those who do not are still damaged. Many co-dependents who become the victims of recurrent abuse are caught up in a forgotten pattern which was established long ago. They never verbalized their feelings then and are reluctant (or unable) to do so as adults, which is why the therapist's role is potentially so important. By taking seriously the client's buried feelings, the CD professional can create the first safe environment the client has ever known in which to explore and deal with them.

Chemical dependence is such a common contributor to physical and sexual abuse that its presence should always be considered. One of the most reliable symptoms of co-dependence is the inability to leave a chronically abusive relationship behind, whether that relationship is ongoing or past.

9. Suffers From Stress-Related Medical Illnesses: Family members of chemical dependents require greater than average amounts of medical care for what are generally considered to be stress-related medical illnesses.

A co-dependent's home life is highly stressful. Compounding this constant exposure to stress is the co-dependent's way of dealing with it: by denying that it exists, or by denying that he or she is affected by it. In the short run, this strategy seems to work. The co-dependent is capable of getting through times that might slow down or stop people with less determination or willpower. This in itself becomes a source of pride, which serves to offset the co-dependent's chronically low self-esteem.

Unfortunately, the body is not so easily fooled. Although the co-dependent may not be aware of the toll that the stress is taking, this does not change the fact that the body is under attack. After a decade (or two, or three), parts start breaking down in ways that can no longer be denied. Conditions that are either created or exacerbated by stress include headaches (tension and migraine), asthma, hypertension, stroke, gastritis, peptic ulcer, spastic colon, rheumatoid arthritis, and sexual dysfunction. The role of stress in a host of other physical conditions is a subject of legitimate debate. While the jury is still out on these, stress-related illnesses *do* exist and are found more frequently in people with dysfunctional reactions to stress, such as co-dependents.

In treating stress-related illnesses, it is common medical practice to prescribe increasingly more powerful medications, or to add tranquilizers. But in many cases co-dependent patients do not respond. In such cases, the most powerful prescription might be a direct referral to Al-Anon. Joining Al-Anon can be the first step toward learning how to respond differently to the stress one is experiencing. By modifying their awareness of when stress is or is not present, co-dependents can often begin responding to treatments which work for other medical patients.

Although co-dependence is not as dramatically or directly life-threatening as chemical dependence, it is potentially just as fatal. The progression into chemical dependence, suicide, violent or accidental death, and death due to untreated stress-related illnesses can all be tied to co-dependence. Since the minimization of one's co-dependence (or the minimization of *oneself*) is a symptom of the disease, it is difficult to get the co-dependent to look honestly at his or her situation. One way to break through this denial is to confront co-dependents with the life-threatening medical consequences of living with stress.

10. Has Remained in a Primary Relationship with an Active Chemical Dependent for At Least Two Years Without Seeking Outside Help: Co-dependents come up with endless reasons for not seeking outside support, and many sound very reasonable. No one likes to admit that their family is incapable of solving its own problems. No one wants to expose their family to the scrutiny of others.

But at some point these reasons become excuses, and the desire to stand on our own two feet becomes martyrdom. When we refuse to seek outside support to avoid having our denial system confronted, our silence has become self-serving. When we are motivated by fear of the chemical dependent, the situation is no longer healthy. When we are blocked by pride, our passivity has become dangerously self-destructive.

How can we tell when we have reached this point? How can we be sure that failure to seek help is a manifestation of active co-dependence, and not simply a normal urge to handle problems in our own way? I propose an arbitrary time period of two years, after which a co-dependent's motives automatically become suspect. Whether this is an appropriate length of time is open to debate. But there *must* come a day when the burden is placed on the co-dependent to prove that his or her actions are not contributing significantly to the problems he or she is trying to hide.

In other words, if a person has lived for two years with an active chemical dependent without initiating his or her own recovery program or doing an intervention, we can assume that person is (actively) co-dependent.

Two years seems long enough for family members to acknowledge the presence of chemical dependence, if they are at all open to facing the truth. It is also long enough to realize the impossibility of trying to live a normal life in the abnormal environment of a chemically dependent family.

Co-Dependent Variants

As noted previously, the symptoms of co-dependence are so comprehensive and diverse that no individual will display every one. There are, however, groups of certain behaviors that are often seen in co-dependents. Co-dependents can often identify with a specific variant more than with the more general diagnosis of co-dependence.

The Martyr

This may be the most common expression of co-dependence. It is probably safe to say that all co-dependents have something of the martyr in them.

Martyrs operate primarily on false pride. They take great pleasure from their capacity to put up with inconvenience, disappointment, even pain. They derive their self-worth from being able to fight the battle as much as from winning or losing. Martyrs deem it more important to be "right" than to be effective.

Many chemical dependents exhibit the equivalent of co-dependent martyrdom: they, too, are committed to solving their problems on their own. Both bear their burdens with a stiff upper lip. In return, they feel that their noble behavior should be respected by others —and, in fact, their family and friends do tend to perceive them as tolerant, long-suffering, and generous (sometimes to a fault).

But behind this impressive front lie some unwelcome truths. Martyrs feel they *they have no choice* in how they live. The alternatives are too frightening to consider: leaving and being on their own, or confronting the situation and being left and on their own. They keep sacrificing themselves in the hope that their investment will eventually pay off, but they cannot be sure that it will.

Martyrs feel empty inside, but they are usually so busy being martyrs that they have little or no time to experience that emptiness and what it means.

The Persecutor

The opposite of the martyr is the persecutor. Persecutors harbor much of the rage and bitterness which martyrs cannot allow themselves to feel. Although their own behavior often seems out of control, they focus on what everyone else is doing wrong. Rather than dealing with their unhappiness, they externalize it and blame it on the actions of others.

While martyrs take full responsibility for feeling miserable, persecutors take no responsibility for theirs. While martyrs push themselves to work harder to feel better, persecutors push *others* to provide them with security and peace of mind.

Both overestimate the impact they have on those around them. Neither knows the difference between what they can and cannot control. The martyr keeps trying to manipulate others by being good; the persecutor keeps trying to manipulate others with anger and guilt.

The Co-Conspirator

Some co-dependents continually undermine chemical dependents' efforts to attain sobriety. Although this seems counterproductive from the outside, it can make sense from within the co-dependent's world.

Co-dependents become attached to the identities they develop within the actively chemically dependent family system. The thought of having to develop a new identity—a requirement for functioning within a recovering family—causes considerable anxiety. Rather than change, they become co-conspirators, or *enablers*.

Enabling behaviors help chemical dependents to deny or conceal their illness. The underlying motives do not matter; it is the end result that counts. The most profound enabling occurs when the co-conspirator continues to deny that the chemical dependence even exists. This denial can be so severe that it goes on long after the chemical dependent has entered treatment.

Most co-conspirators are offended by the mere suggestion that a family member might have a problem. It is a painful irony that many co-conspirators become professionals in the CD field out of concern for the harm that alcohol and other drugs are doing to this country and to family life in general. The words "in general" are key to understanding this phenomenon. Co-conspirators know that chemical dependence is a "bad thing"; they simply aren't willing to recognize its presence close to home.

Some co-conspirators are capable of acknowledging that a family member is chemically dependent, and even of expressing concern about that person. But then they turn around and offer him or her a drink, or volunteer to stop at the store to buy more alcohol! When confronted with the inconsistency of their behavior, they deny that it is contributing to the problem or claim that they can't act any differently. ("What choice do I have? He's going to drink anyway, whether I buy it or he does.")

The Drinking (or Drugging) Partner

As noted earlier, co-dependents are at risk of becoming chemically dependent. Their lifestyle and belief system are already so close to those with chemical dependence that it is easy to slip into addiction. Many co-dependents believe that the best way to "connect" with a chemically dependent family member is by joining in. Eventually they become chemically dependent as well.

Sometimes the co-dependent's eyes are opened when he or she simply can't keep up with the chemical dependent's consumption of alcohol or other drugs. At this point, a healthy person would confront the chemical dependent with this knowledge. For active co-dependents, however, this is too risky. Instead, they reduce their own drug use and bury their heads in the sand, hoping that the chemical dependent will someday do the same.

The Apathetic Co-Dependent

Some co-dependents simply stop caring. They become so thoroughly demoralized that they sink into an emotional stupor, like concentration camp inmates resigned to their fate. Apathy may bring a certain peace or calm, but it is devoid of any sense of hope or meaning in life.

This is especially distressing when there are children in the home. When Dad or Mom gives up, there is no one left to model healthy responses to the chaos and insanity of living with chemical dependence.

For severely apathetic co-dependents, suicide becomes a realistic and acceptable option. They may take their own lives actively and directly, or passively and indirectly—by doing nothing to avoid an accident, for example, or by refusing to see a doctor at the onset of disease.

It is important to realize that co-dependence wears many faces. Doubtless there are variants other than the ones just described. And there are no "rules" determining which ones co-dependents may manifest and when; the martyr may become the persecutor, the co-conspirator may become apathetic, and so on.

Oversimplification of the concept is an ever-present danger, and describing "typical" behaviors or roles is a sure way of falling into that trap. I have presented the most common variants solely as illustrations. The absence of any (or all) of these recognizable variants should not be taken as evidence that co-dependence does not exist.

It is also important to remember that just as there are self-help groups and treatment programs available to help chemical dependents, there are similar groups and programs to assist co-dependents in their search for healthy, happy lives.

Timmen L. Cermak, M.D.

This section is taken from *Diagnosing and Treating Co-Dependence: A Guide for Professionals Who Work With Chemical Dependents, Their Spouses and Children*, published by the Johnson Institute.

CHAPTER THIRTEEN

Recovery Through Detachment

The feelings of anger, shame, and guilt associated with family alcoholism come from the constant confusion, conflict, unpredictability, inconsistency, mistrust, and sense of failure that each member experiences. The family victims seldom learn without outside help that they didn't cause the disease and they can't control it.

Literally, to save and enjoy their lives, *they need to do something positive*, something that will help them focus on their own problems and the treatment they need to get well. They need to shift the focus of their attention from alcohol and the alcoholic to themselves: to their problems, their reactive behavior, and what they can do for themselves in their own recovery from the family disease of alcoholism. To free themselves for these positive steps in their return to a healthy life, these family victims need to separate themselves from their reactive behavior and its causes. How? By developing the skill of *detachment*.

"Detachment" is often a chilling word. It summons images of unfriendly isolation and solitary existence. When we have the word used to describe somebody, we tend to think of a person who's aloof, separated from the rest of the world, self-contained, a bit self-satisfied. But those who have experience in Al-Anon know that detachment doesn't have to be negative.

Furthermore, if we look at its opposite, involvement in a

family where an alcoholic is drinking, detachment is far and away the healthier, happier state to be in.

Detachment Is Building of Self

For many whose lives have become shackled to the life of a drinking alcoholic (one source estimates that every alcoholic affects as many as ten other people), the skill of detachment can mean a new life. Very simply, *detachment is the ability to live one's own life.* It means living a life not centered on someone else's drinking. Any family living with alcoholism needs to learn detachment, even though the skill comes neither easily nor quickly.

Detachment isn't only the way to happiness; it's an *essential ingredient* of any future happiness. Detachment can restore people to healthy thinking in which they feel free to be responsible for themselves, not for the drinker, and to respond to their own needs. Detachment helps people learn that they must work on their own problems, that blaming others for their unhappiness is unrealistic and useless, that they're responsible only for their own behavior, that the most helpful thing they can do for the alcoholic is to put their own lives back in order.

Detachment is simple to talk about, hard to practice. The difficulty in learning how to be detached is to learn that the world doesn't center around us and that we're not really responsible for somebody else's behavior. We have to learn that our agony is self-inflicted, that our desperation is self-imposed. The people who find it difficult to learn detachment are those who are over-conscientious and often extremely moralistic. Most of all, they feel responsible for the alcoholic and his or her drinking. They're committed to an unalterable set of ways they're "supposed to" feel. They reject any suggestion that there are other right ways to think, feel, or behave. They rebel at even the thought of alternatives.

Family Alcoholism and Self-Centeredness

Victimized by their situation, people who live with an alcoholic can become just as self-centered as the drinker.

Notice their language:

"Why are you doing this to *me*?"

"What will people think of *me*?"

"Why are you making *me* suffer?"

"Don't you care about *my* feelings?"

"Don't you love *me*?"

"What am *I* going to do with you?"

Living amid such stress, members of the alcoholic family tend to distort reality. They easily interpret the slightest act, word, or look as a personal attack. The smallest matter can assume earth-shaking importance. Their guilt, despair, sense of inadequacy, futility, and sometimes undue optimism often turn into anger, bitterness, a resolve to try harder, and a desire for revenge on those who they feel have wrecked their lives. They fail to see that they're as sick in their own way as is the alcoholic. In short, they're likely to have become co-dependent. Co-dependence is an illness in itself—an illness that can produce in the spouse (and sometimes in the children as well) emotional and psychological damage often as severe as the alcoholic's. Imprisoned in their self-made cage, family members fail to realize that the prison key is within reach. That key is detachment.

Such people often avoid looking other people in the eye because they fear rejection, because looking someone in the eye takes self-respect. And they don't have much self-respect. Still, their situation is by no means all dark. If nothing else, it often forces them to take the first step in Al-Anon: admitting they're powerless in dealing with alcohol. At the same time, though, they're seldom ready to admit that their own lives are unmanageable.

People living close to alcoholism can have such pain and fear that recommending detachment seems like telling them to admit they can't cope with life. "How can I be detached when I'm in such pain? You tell me detachment means living my own life. But how can I neglect my alcoholic husband (or wife or child or parent)? Look at all the love I've invested!"

These people misunderstand what detachment means. They need to see that detachment means disentangling themselves from the alcoholic they love. What they want for themselves and for everyone involved is an end to the pain. What they need to do is detach themselves from their *victimhood*. That in turn means consciously pursuing alternative ways of looking at the world and at their own lives—a difficult task indeed. But they *can* learn detachment. One stage at a time is the answer. The following pages contain suggestions for developing the difficult but indispensable skill of detachment.

Stages of Detachment

Stage One

If the lifestyle described above resembles the way you live, go back and reread the preceding pages. Does living this way make sense? If it doesn't, why are you doing it? What choices are open to you? Few people who are desperately unhappy take the time to look objectively at their situation. But in being objective, it becomes clear that there are options to every situation. You have a right to explore those options and make a choice of how to live.

There are many possible responses to the challenges in our lives. Do you have a pattern of thinking that dictates only one right answer to every problem? Have you dug a rut? Some familiar ruts:

- Do you consistently make decisions based on the actions and wants of other people in your family?
- Do you consistently react, withdraw, or retaliate when you're hurt?
- Is your behavior so erratic that no one knows what you're going to do next?

Behavior in an alcoholic family seldom is thought out; usually it's only a reaction. Rarely do any family members—the alcoholic or any others—stop to consider the alternatives open to them. Life in a family with the disease of alcoholism is often reduced to a matter of stimulus-response.

Pick a problem in your life—any problem. List at least three possible ways of solving it. Don't worry about being practical, because that limits your vision (and encourages mistaken thinking). You're just opening your mind to new possibilities. At this stage you don't have to do anything about the problem; you're merely exploring possible approaches.

An example of a problem that always exists in an alcoholic home is "Will he come home drunk, or sober?" Or "Will she come home at all?" An example of an all-too-frequent answer is anger, silence, or threats. Almost without a doubt, you've countered this problem with one of these answers. And there probably have been tough moments when you've even faked kindness and consideration.

In this example, those are but a few ways of coping. Seldom have any of these ways worked well because they're not responses that come from an objective appraisal of the situation. They're reactions. What you need to do is find solutions that are objective, solutions that can show that you're responsible to and for yourself and don't perform only as a sounding board to the alcoholic's moody vibrations. Before you begin to list real solutions to the problems of living in an alcoholic family, you need to understand that nothing you can do is by itself going to stop the drinking. If you're living with an active alcoholic, that problem will probably continue if you don't act. And even if you try to do something about it, the problem may continue in spite of your best attempts. That's why so much of your effort in the process of detachment has to do only with yourself. Given the example mentioned above, what would be some appropriate responses?

Recommendations:

1. Make plans for yourself based on your needs. A night out, a weekend away from home. Go, enjoy yourself; leave your troubles for a time.
2. Maybe you'd like to take some night-school courses. Make some arrangements to do it; and go regularly whether or not your spouse arrives home on time.
3. When your spouse doesn't come home, use the time as a gift to do something special for yourself: a manicure, a new hairdo, a movie, a telephone chat with a friend, running, working on the car, the house, the lawn. Read a good book. Go fishing.
4. Instead of being angry about the tardiness, be grateful you can relax for a while. This is extremely difficult, but gratitude for the positive aspects of the problem can change your whole way of looking at it.
5. Do something special and healthy for your children.
6. If separation or divorce is in the back of your mind, look for positive ways to prepare for it.

The important thing to realize in Stage One is that you're only beginning the process of detachment. Whatever ways you act for yourself, make sure that these actions aren't designed to punish yourself or anybody else. You plan for yourself; you don't wait to see whether he or she comes home drunk or sober before you make your plans. You make your plans, either alone or jointly with the other person, then carry them out, no matter what behavior you meet in the other person.

Stage Two

At this early stage it's helpful to take a couple steps back and look at your situation. Open your eyes, see what's going on around you instead of listening to what's being said. As objectively as you can, make a list of the events that take place in your home every day for a month. Make no judgments, no excuses, no exceptions. Keep a journal of everything that happens in your day. Focus only on happenings. Leave out all thoughts and rationalizations. Be scrupulously honest in your account, because it won't be helpful if you soften it or change it.

During this month don't accuse, attack, berate, or belittle the alcoholic. Don't apologize, don't make excuses, and don't mentally agonize about what takes place. Say nothing good or bad about the drinker's behavior. Resist the temptation to control with praise or threats. If it helps, pretend you're an impartial observer reporting on what you see in a stranger's home. In this month concentrate on yourself. Don't focus on self-pitying and fruitless thinking about the past. Open yourself up to a new way of living.

Make a new friend. Indeed, the demands of friendship can make life even more complicated, but you need new people around you. And you need at least one new activity, something you've never tried before. What's important is that you get out of your familiar routine, if only for an hour now and then. If you've been coping in a certain way, look for another approach. Just try it; if it doesn't work, go back to the old way after a while.

It also helps to learn to laugh at yourself, not in mockery but in pleasure. Enjoy your foibles. If you find yourself drowning in the misery of the past, make up a little jingle that can bring you back to the present. You can do it. Try this example.

Help me laugh, help me smile,
Help me feel that I'm worthwhile.
Help me look at life and love it,
Help me see the past but
Leave it in its proper place.

When you catch yourself dreaming about a joy-filled tomorrow, remind yourself that this hour, this day is your reality. There's no guarantee you'll see tomorrow, so relax and enjoy the present. Ask yourself if what you're doing now would be worth doing on your last day of life. Reach out to people, experience life fully, and be grateful for every opportunity for growth. Acknowledge your strengths. Take some time to list your talents. ("No talents," you say? That's what we all say.) List strengths and talents you'd like to develop. What are your weaknesses? List them. How many of these weaknesses on your list are self-imposed? How many are the result of too little effort? How many aren't really weaknesses but only reflections of how exorbitant your demands for perfection are?

Set up a program that will help you reshape your attitudes about yourself. If you catch yourself putting yourself down, balance yourself by taking time to list all your good points. Be committed to feeling good about yourself; stick to your resolve. You'll soon get tired of making the same list fifty times a day. This process can go a long way in helping you break your habit of belittling yourself.

Once in a while let the world be good enough as it is. Don't always try to change the course of human events. When you find yourself jumping in to take over, back off; give up; disconnect. Practice listening to people. Make a resolve to listen to others without being preoccupied with what you're going to say and how you're going to defend yourself. You don't always have to respond with advice or with a story of your own. Listen with both ears, concentrating on what you're hearing. Don't allow yourself to feel obliged to give others anything other than your attention. Even when someone is confiding in you, blaming you, or lecturing you, you needn't give him or her a piece of yourself in response.

Your life is your own. Your mind, your heart, your body, your emotions belong exclusively to you. If others share them, it's only because you choose to let them. It's possible to give love and attention without depleting your whole self. One reason you might feel like a zombie is that you've allowed yourself to be pulled and squeezed into a dozen different shapes. You've twisted yourself into a pretzel trying to please those others, trying to do the right thing. While you were doing this, you may have thought you were living nobly for the sake of others. In actuality you were drowning yourself in a pool of self-will and rigidity.

Stop and consider: Who are you? What are you doing with your life? What's right for you? You have to be your own person if you're going to be any good to yourself or to the others you're trying so hard to help. One good way to start being your own person is to visit an Al-Anon group if you're not now in Al-Anon. Go as many times a week as you can. Discover the relief of living for yourself. The purpose of Al-Anon isn't to teach you how to live with others; it's to teach you how to live with yourself. Take full advantage of this opportunity. Open up your mind and think for yourself. Work for yourself and enjoy life.

Stage Three

Detachment is a learned art, the art of being responsible for your own actions and your own obligations. Some are fortunate to have learned this truth at an early age. Throughout their lives they've been sure of themselves and confident in their relationships. Others go through a great deal of suffering before they realize that detachment doesn't have to be selfishness but can actually be a way to self-preservation. Once you've learned this important distinction, you can practice skills to strengthen your detachment. Detachment isn't a gift; it doesn't come easily or quickly. It's not a sudden illumination. Rather, it's usually learned in little ways, a bit at a time.

Here are some ways to cultivate detachment.

1. When confronted with another's unjust anger, silently refuse to accept it. Smile inwardly and say to yourself, "I hear the words, but they don't speak about my real self. I refuse to treat this anger as justified. Since I don't deserve this anger, I need not validate it by an angry response."

2. When faced with the arrogant, silent treatment of being ignored, don't fight back. Don't give in to the temptation of screaming or using abusive language. Be sure to avoid giving physical punishment. Instead, realize that smirking arrogance is the weapon of an unhealthy mind designed to evoke your emotional response. It's meant to upset you. If you're face to face with such a person, take a deep breath, sing a little song in your mind, whistle a tune, move to another room. As provocative as it can be, sick behavior is never an excuse to act in the same way. When the drinking alcoholic is no longer present, keep your mind occupied with other matters. Spend your efforts on taking care of yourself. Think positively and specifically about what you plan to do today to show your appreciation for yourself.

3. When someone you love is trying to manipulate you with apologies, contrition, begging, tears, and maybe even threats of self-destruction, feel compassion for the pain that person is experiencing. Feel

sympathy for the body that contains the disease causing this type of behavior; but don't be misled into thinking that your forgiveness or sympathy will in any way change the course of the disease of alcoholism. Such people must have outside help, but their first step, as with everyone else, begins with their own personal action of taking responsibility for themselves. Don't allow your inclination to be a Savior to control your actions. Refuse to give in to the temptation to be the Bountiful Giver and Forgiver.

As you listen to the begging, pleading, and conning, repeat silently to yourself, "Detach, . . . detach, . . . detach, . . . detach." You'll survive the session and feel amazingly stronger. How can you react to the conning pleas if you're busy reminding yourself to detach? You're under no obligation to anyone to answer, to make things right, or to give others what they want. You're listening only because you love that person. As your imperviousness to the swindle becomes obvious to the smooth talker, very often contriteness turns to rage. If that happens and you're in physical danger, get away immediately. If you're showered with verbal abuse and you choose to stay around, try to let the words bounce off. Say to yourself, "This person is sick; to preserve my own health, I must let go." If you can come through one of these sessions unruffled, you're on your way to a wonderful feeling of self-worth. Don't allow yourself to relive the argument later. To do so is to court self-doubt and resentment.

These acts of self-protection will improve your feelings even in other relationships. One area of improvement that's especially worth noting: you'll find yourself less willing to be hurt or influenced by those friends and relatives who blame you for the drinker's behavior.

Stage Four

When we stand by and watch someone we love or used to love engage in self-destructive behavior, particularly someone with whom we now have little contact, (alienation is one of the effects of family alcoholism), we should realize that to antagonize, worry, predict improvement, suffer guilt, or inflict sleepless nights on ourselves will only make a bad situation worse.

Often we have to endure the sight of loved ones wreaking havoc on their own lives. Guilt and worry help neither ourselves nor anyone else. Anger doesn't help. Wallowing in self-pity doesn't help. Blaming and retaliation don't help. Useless self-sacrifice doesn't help.

But the practical action of setting up an intervention will help.[1] Intervention takes courage, understanding, insight, and the ability to accept the reality of alcoholism as a disease. The intervention may provide some immediate change for the alcoholic, or it may not. If it does nothing else, it will help you realize that you're taking care of yourself by refusing the role of passive victim. No one, not even the person about whom you're concerned, is inflicting suffering on you. You're inflicting it on yourself. You can change that situation. In a successful intervention the people involved let events take their course. It may not work out the way you want it to, but that's neither your worry nor your need. Intervention is a process, not an event, and typically the only intervention that fails is the one in which the participants demand specific and quick results.

---

[1] Intervention is a process in which a prepared group of significant people in an alcoholic's life present the reality of the alcoholic's situation to him or her in a receivable way. For additional information, read Part Four of this book, or the book *Intervention: How to Help Someone Who Doesn't Want Help*, by Vernon E. Johnson, D.D., published by the Johnson Institute.

Stage Five

By now you should realize that problem drinkers don't drink deliberately to hurt you any more than children misbehave with a plan to show the world their parents aren't doing their job. Other people may encourage you to take the blame for their actions; they may project their self-hatred onto you. Such behavior is standard procedure in the disease of alcoholism. While you need to accept the fact of the disease, you don't have to sit back and go along with all the behavior of the alcoholic. Sick people act in sick ways, but they don't do it to you; they do it in spite of you.

Two actions most difficult to detach from are sneers and mockery. It might be difficult to detach from these because you lack the confidence and self-respect to endure them; or it might be difficult because you may still deeply love the person who's behaving this way. By an offhand gesture, sick people can tell you they think your ideas aren't important. It almost seems that they're sure to regard what you want as ridiculous. You become the court jester. They use you; they don't take you seriously. Such behavior can devastate your self-image. You may mentally, and sometimes physically, crawl into a safe retreat to protect your ego. You may think you're the dumbest human ever.

But if you're so limited, how can you do the many tasks you do every day? The fact that you're reading these words proves you have an idea of what you need and are looking in the right places. Don't waste words on those who laugh at you. Have the courage to change the things you can, and take action. Know that if you make a mistake, it's your mistake. But even in your mistakes you can learn; you can build self-confidence. You weren't born with a tag that reads "Does not make mistakes."

Stage Six

Detachment must apply to all the people in your life—to nonalcoholics as well as to the problem drinker. Detachment is an attitude you practice in living your own life, not a technique for coping with the unexpected from an alcoholic. Specifically regarding the alcoholic and the rest of the family, detachment can be thought of as one form of the willingness to stand back and allow those you love to grow in whatever ways they must. It's not easy to let those around you lead their own lives, but you know it's necessary.

When the people you most care about constantly explain their actions and constantly worry about what you'll say or how you'll feel, they aren't necessarily proving how concerned you are about them. It's more likely that you've turned their world in on yourself. If they must constantly defend their thinking, their behavior, their friends, their life, in your courtroom, these are signs you're thinking about You, the all-powerful You, the One who has all the answers. Make it your policy to let others—even your children—lead their lives. Be convinced of your right to live your life, but allow others the same right. Misshaping yourself to fit into another's lifestyle isn't healthy.

Don't waste precious hours looking for excuses for the people you love. Promise yourself to pass the whole day without asking for explanations from others for their actions—and do it. Give up your futile attempts of trying to figure out what makes others tick. Decide that from this day forward you won't accept the blame for anyone else's attitudes or actions. Resign from your present self-appointment to be judge, jury, and guilty defendant. Insist on your right to care for yourself and to be yourself, realizing, though, that when you let your family members care for themselves, they may feel lost for a while.

The old family patterns, however, will begin to change. You may be frightened at first, for responsibility can be unfamiliar and disconcerting if you haven't exercised it before. A better result of your responsibility will be a new level of love, trust, and self-confidence manifested by other members of the family.

In your zeal to practice your skills of detachment, keep certain cautions in mind. Be careful not to force your new ways onto others. Let them adopt an attitude of detachment in their own time. For the moment concentrate only on yourself. Just as with an alcoholic, it's impossible to force other people to behave the way you'd like them to act. Pressuring them encourages them to lie. They'll become appeasers, telling you what you want to hear. Each person, whether walking before you or traveling miles away, marches as he or she will. You can pace the floor, wring your hands, and tear your hair. Or you can immerse yourself in activities that benefit you. Neither of these responses will have the least bit of influence on what will or won't happen, but one will help you be happy and healthy, and the other won't. Some people will say, "I could never forgive myself if I were having a good time and something tragic happened." Such attitudes simply don't make sense; throw them out.

Stage Seven

Detachment doesn't mean you must repress your emotions. Everyone needs an outlet for emotions. You may be confused at times because you're in the process of learning which emotions are real and appropriate and which are products of your own unhealthy behavior. To discover the difference, use your Al-Anon group and your Al-Anon sponsor. From them you'll learn healthy ways to release your frustrations and how to distinguish between healthy and unhealthy ways of displaying emotions.

When you've learned detachment you'll be able to express anger, not out of self-righteousness, but out of an awareness of self-worth. You'll be able to laugh, not because you're expected to, but because you feel like it. You'll be able to cry, not out of hopelessness, but because it's a relief to cry when you feel sad.

Many dear and loyal friends can be found in Al-Anon. There you'll discover people who listen and share your concerns, who tell you the truth about yourself, who love you for yourself, who provide you with an acceptance you've probably never before experienced. Accept what they give you, revel in it, and pass it on to others who are in pain.

When you begin Al-Anon, stick with the winners. That is, seek out people who don't reflect your own sick thinking. The temptation is to seek out as a friend another newcomer who's as miserable as you are, and then seek to find contentment in mutual miseries. Instead, seek out friends in Al-Anon who show the spirit of growth: those who accept challenge and aren't afraid to challenge you. True friends will refuse to accept excuses for unhealthy behavior. Such people demonstrate tough love by caring enough about you to tell you they see self-pity or self-belittlement taking over in you.

Seek out friends who live healthy lives. Visit their homes and see how their lifestyles contrast with what was the norm for you. A weekend in a healthy home can be a real eye-opener. Beware of friends and family who don't help you change. Accept the fact that learning new approaches to life can be a lonely business. Know that ultimately you're the only person who can change your behavior and your way of thinking. Others can support you, but you must do the work. And it is work. Don't expect any worthwhile change to come easily. Beware of perfectionism. Forgive yourself if you slip in your resolves. Don't condemn yourself for past mistakes; be grateful that today you can see them.

As you go through various stages of detachment, study them. Write down your ideas about new ways to approach your problems. Consider alternatives that occur to you. Try not to give in to the temptation that lures all of us: the temptation to shelve our troubles until we "have more time" to take care of them. If you really want to change your life for the better, you'll need discipline and determination. But avoid rashness, and don't plunge into any type of change so completely that you lose objectivity and balance. Be aware that the most difficult part of any change is making up your mind to do it.

You'll know that you've found detachment when you can feel empathy for the alcoholic's drinking and behavior, when you can accept constructive criticism without the old feeling of failure, and when you can hear impassioned but dishonest pleas without giving in to them. You'll know you've found detachment when you're accused falsely and don't feel guilty, when you can laugh at the funny things in your life, when you can cry and not care who sees it, when you can show anger in a positive way. You've gained detachment when you can truly see that people you love must live their own lives, make their own mistakes, and live with the consequences of their acts— and that they're not doing it to you. Fill yourself with feelings of self-worth, not of self-importance. Put all things into perspective. Practice detachment. It's the key that finally frees us from the strongest of all chains, the bondage of self.

EVELYN LEITE

This section is taken from *Detachment: The Art of Letting Go While Living With An Alcoholic*, published by the Johnson Institute.

PART THREE

Children of Alcoholics

Introduction to Part Three

When a family suffers from the disease of chemical dependence, it is the children in the family that suffer the most. We have learned that these victims can begin their own recovery whether or not their chemically dependent parents ever accept care.

Chapter Fourteen is my effort to gather pertinent information for teenagers who suffer from their parents' use of alcohol or other drugs. It has been my experience that well-informed children are not only capable of helping themselves by changing their enabling behaviors into coping behaviors, but that a great many of them can become effective participants in an intervention with a chemically dependent parent.

Chapter Fifteen is for the millions of adult Americans who grew up in families that were dysfunctional because of parental alcohol or other drug use. These "adult children" carry scars from those years of living in a dysfunctional family, and many of them don't even realize the depth of their pain. Chapter Fifteen will not only help them recognize themselves, but will also discuss the ACOA movement as a route to recovery.

VERNON E. JOHNSON, D.D.

CHAPTER FOURTEEN

What Teenage Children of Alcoholics Need to Know

You'll notice that we use the phrase "alcohol and other drugs" in many places throughout this chapter. We use it to emphasize that *alcohol is a drug*—just like cocaine, marijuana, uppers, downers, or any other mind-altering substance. Too often people talk about "alcohol *and* drugs" or "alcohol *or* drugs," as if alcohol is somehow different from drugs and off by itself. Wrong! Repeat: *Alcohol is a drug*.

If you didn't know that until now, you're not alone. Our culture, our government, even our laws treat alcohol differently than they treat so-called "other drugs" like pot, crack, smack, and so on down the list. As long as you're old enough, you can buy and use alcohol without a prescription. You can get it in a store, a restaurant, or a bar without doing anything illegal. You can give it to your friends (as long as they're old enough). You can even get a license to sell it.

The words *chemical dependence* are often used to describe the condition of being dependent—hooked—on alcohol or other drugs. Some people prefer them to words like "addict," "drunk," "junkie," or "alcoholic," maybe because they sound more scientific or polite. We use them here because they're easier and shorter than saying "alcoholism or dependence on other drugs."

277

In the end, though, it doesn't really matter which words you use. A chemical is a chemical. An addiction is an addiction. A disease is a disease. And pain is pain.

A Questionnaire for Children of Alcoholics

Does someone you love drink too much? Are you starting to think that there's an alcohol or other drug problem at your house? And every time this thought crosses your mind, do you tell yourself, *No, it couldn't be—not MY mom (or dad)?*

Even though you may deny it, deep down inside you want to know the truth. Everyone wants to know the truth. Because the longer we live without it, the harder it is to live.

Here's a short quiz that can help you to come closer to the truth. Take a few moments to read the statements and consider whether they fit you. Each one that does gets a "yes"; each one that doesn't gets a "no."

1. I feel like I get blamed for everything that goes wrong at my house.

   ☐ YES ☐ NO

2. I feel like I take care of everyone and no one takes care of me.

   ☐ YES ☐ NO

3. I often feel afraid when people get angry with me.

   ☐ YES ☐ NO

4. I often feel guilty even when I haven't done anything wrong.

   ☐ YES ☐ NO

5. I worry about my parents' alcohol or other drug use.

   ☐ YES ☐ NO

6. I sometimes pour out bottles of alcohol I find around the house (or add water to them to dilute them.)

☐ YES ☐ NO

7. I daydream almost all the time.

☐ YES ☐ NO

8. I often feel depressed and sad for no apparent reason.

☐ YES ☐ NO

9. I lie about my parents' drug (including alcohol) use.

☐ YES ☐ NO

10. I try hard to do everything right.

☐ YES ☐ NO

11. I often feel lonely and rejected.

☐ YES ☐ NO

12. I have found drugs (or alcohol) that my parents have hidden.

☐ YES ☐ NO

13. I often have trouble concentrating, so my schoolwork suffers.

☐ YES ☐ NO

14. I'm afraid to ride in the car with my parents when they've been drinking or using other drugs.

☐ YES ☐ NO

15. I feel guilty about my parents' drug use—as if it's somehow MY fault.

☐ YES ☐ NO

16. I try to hide the fact that my family seems different from other families.

☐ YES ☐ NO

17. I make excuses for my parents when they've been using drugs.

☐ YES ☐ NO

18. Sometimes I just want to give up.

☐ YES ☐ NO

19. I sometimes get embarrassed by my parents' behavior, especially when they've been drinking or using other drugs.

☐ YES ☐ NO

20. I worry a lot and have trouble sleeping.

☐ YES ☐ NO

21. I sometimes feel ashamed of my family.

☐ YES ☐ NO

22. I hate holidays because my parents always get drunk or high.

☐ YES ☐ NO

23. I don't believe the promises my parents make to me.

☐ YES ☐ NO

24. It scares me to be around my parents when they've been using drugs.

☐ YES ☐ NO

25. I WANT THINGS TO CHANGE!

☐ YES ☐ NO

Did you end up with more yeses than nos? Then you have reason to think that something is wrong at your house. And if one (or both) of your parents drinks a lot or uses other drugs, that something may be a drinking or other drug problem.

Most people, when they first say the words "alcoholic" or "addict" or "chemically dependent," spit them out as if they taste bad. (Say them to yourself to see how they taste to you.) Naturally, no one—absolutely *no one*—wants to use these words to describe their own parents.

It might surprise you to learn that there are worse things in life than having a chemically dependent parent. There are worse things in life than feeling the way you feel right now (even though you might not be able to think of anything). The *very worst thing* is to have a chemically dependent parent and refuse to consider it, refuse to admit it, refuse to accept it. The very worst thing is to deny that a problem exists.

Why? Because as long as you keep denying it, you'll spend your whole life believing that there's something wrong with *you*. Every move you make to find out the truth, every thought you think along those lines, will seem like a betrayal of your family.

Chemical dependence is a disease of the mind, the body, and the spirit. It acts like a contagious disease in that it affects not only the chemical dependent but also anyone who lives or works closely with him or her. This means that if your parents are chemically dependent, *their* disease is affecting *you*.

No wonder you feel rotten so much of the time. No wonder you feel afraid and lonely and confused and rejected and sad so much of the time.

The good news is, *you can feel better*. About yourself.

If you want to feel better, if you *dare* to feel better, this chapter is for you.

There's something strange going on at our house. Not all the time . . . some days are good and on those days I try to forget what happened on the days that weren't so good.

I try to forget about things. I try to look the other way when things don't look right to me. I'm learning how to live with what's going on—but still I wonder if it really has to be like this.

Nobody understands what I'm going through.

If You Are Living With One or More Chemically Dependent Parents, You Are Not Alone

Fact: Approximately twenty million kids under age eighteen are growing up in homes where one or both parents abuse alcohol or other drugs. You're part of a BIG crowd. That may not help you feel better, but it should help you feel less isolated and different from everyone else.

Fact: In a typical classroom of 25 students, somewhere between four and six of them are the children of alcoholic parents. This means that *someone you know* understands *exactly* what you're going through. Because he or she is going through it, too. Someone you know has one or more chemically dependent parents. Someone you know is feeling as confused, guilty, scared, embarrassed, angry, and ashamed as you are.

Our family doesn't seem "normal"—like other families. Yet it's a lot like Barney's family down the block or Connie's family across town. So we must be "normal." . . . Why doesn't it feel that way? Why does my family feel different from everyone else's? Why do I feel different from my friends?

If You Are Living With One or More Chemically Dependent Parents, Your Family Is Special

Chemically dependent people put drugs above everything else in their lives. Not because they *want to*, but because they *have to*. This makes your family special.

Chemically dependent people drink to get drunk or abuse other drugs to get high. Not because it makes them *feel good*, but because it makes them feel *less bad*. This makes your family special.

Chemically dependent homes are scenes of secrecy, despair, turmoil, hidden emotions, lies, broken promises, and shattered dreams. They are also scenes of laughter and good times—sometimes. The trouble is, you never know what to expect! So people learn not to trust one another or count on one another. This makes your family special.

Not necessarily "normal"—but special.

Mom and Dad don't drink all the time. Sometimes they stay sober for a week, a month, even three or six months at a time. But I can always tell when they're about to start drinking again. It hangs there like an invisible something in the air and I get a feeling of dread inside and sure enough, it's drinking time.

I CAN'T STAND IT when they drink. I HATE IT when they drink. I hate THEM when they drink. I hate ME when I hate THEM.

Some Myths and Facts About Chemical Dependence

Myth: An alcoholic or addict is someone who drinks or uses other drugs every day.

Fact: A person can drink or use other mind-altering drugs once a month, once a week, even a few times a year and still be chemically dependent. It's not *how often* people drink or use that really matters. It's *what happens* to them and to others around them when they drink or use that makes the difference.

If the use of alcohol or other drugs causes any continuing disruption in their personal, social, physical, spiritual, and/or economic life, *and they don't stop using,* then they are chemically dependent.

Myth: Someone who uses only a small amount of alcohol or some other drug can't be chemically dependent.

Fact: It's not *how much* people drink or use that really matters. It's *what happens* to them and to others around them when they use that makes the difference. Did you ever see a shy person turn into the life of the party? Did you ever see a nice person turn nasty or a happy person burst into tears for no reason? Did you ever see a quiet person turn into a mile-a-minute talker? These can all be possible signs of the disease of chemical dependence.

Myth: An addict is someone who uses hard drugs, like cocaine or heroin or PCP. You can't be an addict if all you use is marijuana or downers or uppers.

Fact: Marijuana, downers, and uppers are drugs. (By the way, so are caffeine and nicotine.) Therefore, people who use them can become addicted. **A Drug Is A Drug Is A Drug.**

Myth: An alcoholic is someone who drinks hard liquor, like Scotch or whiskey or vodka or gin. You can't be an alcoholic if all you drink is beer or wine.

Fact: Alcohol is a drug. Beer and wine contain alcohol. Therefore, people who drink beer and wine can be alcoholics. **A Drug Is A Drug Is A Drug.**

I learned at school that alcoholism is a disease. Sure it is. I never heard of a disease that forces someone to go to the liquor cabinet and take out a bottle and open it and start guzzling it.

I think I'll catch a few diseases of my own. Like the I-refuse-to-do-my-homework disease. Or I'll-never-pick-up-my-room-again disease. Or the I'm-not-going-to-the-dishes disease.

This whole disease thing sounds like a big excuse to me.

Chemical Dependence Is a Disease

You may not believe this at first, but it's true: people who abuse alcohol or other drugs are sick. The trouble is, they don't know it, won't admit it, and usually won't get help for it. Instead, they will deny that they're sick. They may even blame *you* for their problem.

Have you ever heard your mom or dad say, "If it weren't for you, I wouldn't have to drink"? Or, "If you had come home on time, I wouldn't have gotten high"? Or, "If I didn't have to worry about you, I wouldn't need pills to relax"?

Don't buy it! That's like saying, "If you had done better on your math test, I wouldn't have caught this cold!" It's silly. It's sad. And it simply isn't so.

Chemical dependence is a *primary* disease. That means it isn't the result of some other disease or problem. For a long time, doctors thought it was. They told their patients, "Let's find out what's really wrong with you and then you won't have to drink (or use) anymore." That didn't work. Chemical dependence isn't caused by other diseases. Instead, *it* causes *them*.

Chemical dependence leads to diseases of the liver, stomach, heart, and brain, to name just a few important organs. It also leads to mental and emotional problems like mood swings and memory loss.

If you come from a place where people say bad things about alcoholics and drug addicts, you may be wondering if chemical dependence is really a disease after all. You may be wondering if what they're saying is true: that chemical dependence is a *moral issue*, and that chemically dependent people could change if they tried.

Please read these lines out loud:

> Chemical dependence is a disease.
> Chemical dependence is a disease.
> Chemical dependence is a disease.

It may take a while, but one day you'll believe them. And when you do, you'll start seeing your parents in a brand new light: as sick people who need help.

Maybe it's my fault. Maybe if I were a better person this wouldn't be happening to my family. Maybe if I worked harder, prayed harder, tried to be nicer to my sister, studied more, kept my room clean, didn't talk back as much, or maybe if I was never even born—maybe then my dad wouldn't have to drink.

What Causes The Disease of Chemical Dependence?

No one knows for sure. What we do know is that all kinds of people become chemically dependent. Rich people. Poor people. People of all races and creeds. Professional people and working-class people and unemployed people. Husbands and wives. Fathers and mothers. Grandparents. Even children.

We do know that chemical dependence isn't caused by lack of willpower, or "weakness of character", or "immoral" or "sinful" behavior or outside influences like an unhappy marriage, an unhappy childhood, trouble on the job or peer pressure. Most of all, chemical dependence isn't caused by YOU. If someone you know is chemically dependent, IT ISN'T YOUR FAULT.

Nothing you did caused it. Nothing you are doing keeps it going. Nothing you can do can make it go away. It has nothing to do with you. No matter what your parents may say. No matter what you may think. No matter how you may feel. **You Are Not Responsible.**

I'm so ashamed of my parents. I'm ashamed of the way they look and the way they act and the way they drink. I'm ashamed of them for being alcoholics.

When people get sick, don't they try to get well? Don't they go to the doctor and get medicine? And if there's something that's making them sick, don't they try to stay away from it? If my parents are sick with alcoholism, why don't they stay away from alcohol?

What Happens to People Who Have the Disease of Chemical Dependence?

They always get worse unless they get help. Once they develop the disease, they have it for the rest of their lives. That's because chemical dependence is a permanent disease.

People who have it can be treated. They can stop getting sicker *as long as they stop using alcohol and other drugs.*

If they don't get help, they usually die prematurely—either as a direct result of the disease, or as the result of something else that can be traced back to the disease. According to insurance company statistics, an alcoholic who keeps drinking has an average lifespan *12 years shorter* than the nonalcoholic. Heavy drinkers are *three times* more likely to have fatal strokes than people who don't drink.

I used to laugh when my Dad got drunk and tease him about having a little too much. I used to tiptoe around his hangover and feel sorry for him when he got that shamefaced look in the morning after drinking a lot the night before. I used to have sympathy for him and I wanted to protect him from Mother's nagging and bring him aspirin for his headaches. I even hung around for hours just in case he needed me.

But now I just feel sad or mad and try to ignore him. Sometimes I even get sick of him and wish he'd go away and stay away and then I feel guilty . . and when I feel guilty about not liking him I break my neck to be good to him because I don't really want him to go away, I just want him to stop drinking.

Can The Disease of Chemical Dependence be Cured?
No.

But it CAN be arrested. With help, chemically dependent people can stop getting worse and start getting better.

Help might include joining Alcoholics Anonymous (A.A) or Narcotics Anonymous (N.A.). It might involve going into a treatment center or clinic. It might involve private counseling or therapy. It *always* involves being willing to stop using alcohol and other drugs.

I've tried talking to my mom about my dad's drinking. I know she's hurting—I can see it in her eyes and in the way she acts around him. All I want to do is help. But she won't even admit there's a problem. She keeps making excuses for him. He's tired . . . he had a hard day at work . . . you don't know the pressure he's been under . . . you're too young to understand. . . . What really gets to me is when she tells me I didn't see something when I know I did. I say, "Mom, he could barely walk last night," and she says, "That's not true, dear, your dad was perfectly fine."

Why does she keep covering up for him? And why does it make me feel stupid? And crazy?

Clues to the Presence of Chemical Dependence

How can you tell if your parents are chemically dependent? Read through the following behavior "clues" and decide which sound true to you.

1. They use alcohol or other drugs more now than they used to.
2. They do things while they're using, and later they deny them or say they've forgotten them.
3. They refuse to talk about their using.
4. They make—and break—promises to control or stop their alcohol or other drug use.
5. They lie about their using.
6. Most of their friends are users.
7. They make excuses for their using or try to justify it.
8. Their behavior changes when they're using.
9. They avoid social functions where alcohol isn't served and other drugs aren't available or permitted.
10. They sometimes drive while drunk or under the influence of other drugs.

11. Sometimes after a using episode, they apologize for the way they acted.
12. They hide alcohol or other drugs around the house or in the car or garage.

When I hear Mom or Dad talk on the phone and tell a friend how high they got last night, or apologize for something they said or did, or brag about how they told so-and-so where to get off, I pretend I'm not listening. Sometimes I even close my door and lay on my bed and put my pillow over my head to shut it out.

More Clues to the Presence of Chemical Dependence

Your parents' behaviors don't provide the *only* clues to the existence of chemical dependence. *Your own behaviors and feelings can also be revealing.* Read through the following and decide which sound familiar.

1. I'm afraid to be around them when they're using alcohol or other drugs.
2. I'm suspicious of their promises.
3. I feel anxious and tense around them.
4. I don't trust them.
5. I feel embarrassed when they're using.
6. I feel guilty when they're using.
7. I lie about them to other people.
8. I hate holidays because those are times when they're almost certain to use.
9. I make excuses for them.
10. I'm afraid to ride in the car with them when they've been using.

I've tried talking to my mom and dad about drugs, but they don't listen at all. I try telling them they're ruining their health. Sometimes I even threaten them, saying I'm going to run away from home or kill myself or get even with them someday. I want them to stop. I want them to stop NOW.

How Can You Make Chemically Dependent People Stop Using Alcohol or Other Drugs? You Can't.

You can pour their alcohol down the sink or flush their drugs down the toilet, and it won't make any difference. They'll just get more. You can nag and complain and cry and threaten, and it won't make any difference. They'll keep using until they get help—if that day ever comes.

You can be extra nice and take care of them and your brothers and sisters and the dog and the cat and the house and the yard, and it won't make any difference. In fact, it may make it *easier* for them to use alcohol or other drugs because you'll be freeing them of so many of their responsibilities.

You can bribe them to stop using, and maybe they'll promise that they will. Maybe they'll even quit—for a while. Just to prove to you (and themselves) that they don't have a problem. But unless they get help staying stopped, they'll probably start using again sooner or later.

You didn't make your parents chemically dependent. You can't make them UN-chemically dependent. You can try, and you can keep trying for the rest of your life, but it won't work.

You can, however, take care of yourself. By admitting that the problem is real. By refusing to take the blame for it. And by refusing to cover up for it.

I heard my parents fighting last night, calling each other obscene names, saying foul things about each other. I heard my mother crying and my dad pleading and both of them screaming. They don't know how my gut twisted around in a little ball, squeezing tighter and tighter until I thought I'd puke.

Your Parents' Chemical Dependence Can Make <u>You</u> Sick

Chemical dependence acts like a *contagious disease*. Even if you yourself don't use alcohol or other drugs, just being around someone who is chemically dependent can make *you* sick.

Chemical dependence has been called a "family disease." That's because it affects everyone who lives with, loves, or works with the chemically dependent person. They can become *co-dependents*.

Clues to the Presence of Co-Dependence

Are *you* a co-dependent? Following are some statements that describe the way co-dependents feel and act. See how many describe you.

- Co-dependents often feel trapped, depressed, and alone.
- Co-dependents feel embarrassed by the behavior of their chemically dependent family members—as if it reflects on them.
- Co-dependents are easily hurt by what others say, feel, think, or do.
- Co-dependents let others tell them how to feel, how to dress, and how to act.
- Co-dependents work very hard to keep other people from being upset with them or disappointed in them. They may lie or distort the truth to avoid making others angry.

293

- Co-dependents hide their less-than-perfect behaviors (like making mistakes, swearing, smoking, or overeating) from their family members.
- Co-dependents are afraid to leave home for fear that something will happen to someone they love.
- Co-dependents feel obligated to take care of other people. They feel guilty when they ask for something for themselves. They give up their own wants and wishes to make other people happy. On the other hand, they try to control other people in order to get what they want without having to come right out and ask for it. (If this sounds confusing and complicated, that's because it is!)

I keep the house picked up. I watch my little brother. I do the laundry and make sure dinner gets on the table. I mow the lawn. I answer the phone when it rings and give excuses for why my parents can't talk. I answer the door when someone comes to our house and ask them politely to come back later, and when they come back I do it again.

I take care of everything. And I've stopped expecting anyone to take care of me. Instead of crying and feeling sad, I just work harder. Maybe if I do it long enough someone will start appreciating me.

Co-Dependent Roles

Being co-dependent is hard work. It takes a lot of effort and energy to live with chemically dependent people! Co-dependents are clever, though. They come up with elaborate defenses just so they can make it through the day. These take the form of *roles* they play within their families.

Do any of these describe a role *you* play?

The Super-Responsible Kid. You're VERY organized. You take care of your brothers and sisters, clean the house, fix the meals, and do the laundry. Plus you do well in school. And inside you feel angry.

The Super-Flexible Kid. You go with the flow. Whatever happens, happens. If your parents promise to show up at your school play and don't, you shrug it off. If they tell you one thing in the morning and something else at night, you don't argue. You bend. And inside you feel angry.

The Clown. You see the funny side of everything. You're always good for a joke, a laugh, or a prank. Especially when things get tense at home. You make faces, act silly, and tell hilarious stories. And inside you feel angry.

The Peacemaker. You're always stepping into family fights and trying to stop them. You want everyone to feel better. You want everything to be okay all the time. And you tell yourself it's not nice to feel angry.

The Troublemaker. You're mad at your parents, and you'll show them! They can take their rules and stuff them! You talk back. You skip school. Maybe you even abuse alcohol or drugs yourself. Outside you're angry—and under all the anger is fear.

I can't handle school anymore. What's the point? I go sit in class and read about stuff that doesn't have anything to do with ANY-THING, and learn a bunch of facts, and take a lot of stupid tests.

Besides, I can't think straight. Every day I sit in class reliving last night's fight around the dinner table. What if I hadn't said this, what if I had said that, what if I just kept my mouth shut? Would Mom have stayed sober another hour or another ten minutes? I always say or do the wrong thing. So what if I flunk the math test tomorrow.

Co-Dependent Behaviors and How to Change Them

You can't make your parents less chemically dependent. *But you can make yourself less co-dependent.* You can't change your parents' behaviors. *But you can change your own.* Starting with these:

Protecting Your Parents. You love them, so you lie for them, cover up for them, and make excuses for them. You even lie to your closest friends—and feel guilty and ashamed for doing it.

STOP IT. QUIT IT. CUT IT OUT. Let them experience the consequences of their own actions. By protecting them, you're making it easier for them to stay sick. (Which is NOT the same as MAKING them sick.)

Letting Them Decide How You Will Act And Feel. You get up in the morning and check out your parents before you decide if you'll have a good day. You plan your activities according to what you think *they* want and expect.

STOP IT. QUIT IT. CUT IT OUT. Start making your *own* decisions and live your *own* life.

Withdrawing From the Family and Avoiding Your Parents. You punish them with the silent treatment. You keep your thoughts and feelings to yourself. You stay so busy with school, sports, and work that you hardly have time to think or feel.

STOP IT. QUIT IT. CUT IT OUT. Treating your parents as if they don't exist won't help anyone, least of all you. They may be sick, but they're still human—and chances are they still love you *very much*. They just may not be very good at showing it. Don't cut them out of your life!

Blaming Your Parents For Everything That Goes Wrong In Your Life. You're angry and resentful, and you take it out on them. If you fail a test in school, it's their fault. If your boyfriend or girlfriend dumps you, it's their fault. If you cut your finger peeling potatoes, it's their fault. When you see them hurting or having problems, you feel good—it serves them right.

STOP IT. QUIT IT. CUT IT OUT. Again, your parents are people, and people have feelings. Try not to judge them so harshly.

Feeling Ashamed And Covering It Up By Being Phony. You're ashamed of your parents. You're ashamed of your home. Maybe you don't even let your friends come over. You don't want anyone to know how ashamed you are, so you cover it up with a lot of bragging and showing off. Or you laugh and clown around to cover your shame. Or you shove other people around or do things to hurt them.

STOP IT. QUIT IT. CUT IT OUT. Covering up your shame is like getting on a giant merry-go-round. The more ashamed you feel, the more you try to cover it up; the more you cover it up, the more ashamed you feel. *Your parents are not you.* Stand tall, be yourself, and be proud of who you are.

Joining Your Parents In Using. You've heard the old saying, "If you can't beat 'em, join 'em." You can't "beat" your parents' problem, so why not try some alcohol or other drugs yourself?

STOP IT. QUIT IT. CUT IT OUT. A large percentage of kids who come from chemically dependent homes become chemically dependent themselves, even though they swear that will never happen. *Don't set yourself up for a fall.*

I'm sick of hearing about what a perfect family I have. About what a perfect house we live in. About how lucky I am to have a mom and dad who let me go out as much as I want.

Nobody knows the truth. My parents don't let me go out. They just don't notice when I'm gone.

Share the Secret

Chemical dependence is a disease of deception, denial, cover-ups, and lies. The longer it's kept secret, the worse it becomes, and the more cut off, isolated, and different you feel.

Find someone to talk to. Someone you trust. A minister or priest or rabbi, a teacher or counselor, or friend or neighbor. DON'T FEEL GUILTY for sharing the secret. If your mom or dad had cancer, you'd talk about it, and you'd understand that it wasn't your fault. The same holds true for the disease of chemical dependence.

Give yourself permission to open up to someone who can listen and give you the support you need. You deserve it. You're worth it!

Admit it: you're REALLY ANGRY. Angry at your parents for being chemically dependent. Angry at them for making your life so miserable. Angry at them for not getting the help they need. Angry at them because you feel different, because your family is different, and because you want to be like everyone else.

Let it out! Talk about your anger with someone you trust. Find yourself a punching bag, or a broomstick and a pillow. Give the pillow a few good whacks. Go out in the country and scream your head off. Start running or lifting weights. Dance until you drop.

Be mad at the right thing: the *disease*, not your parents, who are only its victims. Say to yourself, "It's hard to be angry at a disease, but I can do it. I've done lots of hard things in my life, and I can do this, too."

Don't forget the power of prayer. Pray for your family. Pray for your parents. Pray especially for the person you are angriest at—the one who has hurt you the most. Pray that God will help them find health and happiness. It won't be easy. At first, it may be VERY difficult. The words may stick in your throat. Keep trying. One thing you can be sure of: your parents *need* your prayers.

I lied to my parents again today. Actually, I lied to them lots of times. It just seems easier to lie than to tell the truth. I lied about where I went after school. I said I'd gone to Mandy's house when I really went to Jennifer's. What's funny about this is, my Mom wouldn't care if I went to Jennifer's. She likes Jennifer. So why did I lie about it? Habit, I guess.

Give Your Parents What They Deserve

Your parents may give you a hard time. They may embarrass you. They may act stupid. They may run over your feelings until you wonder if you have any left. But they're still your parents.

Treat them with respect and dignity—for your sake as well as theirs. Don't nag, argue, spy on them, dump their liquor or flush their drugs, scream at them or call them names. Think about the respect you give a close friend or teacher, and give the same to your parents.

Be accountable. Don't use your parents as an excuse to avoid your own responsibilities. Be on time, do your homework, be clean, keep your word, strive for honesty, and give yourself a pat on the back every time you do something even halfway right. Why bother? Because you'll feel better about *yourself.*

I can't stand it anymore. I can't stand the scenes and the arguments and the fighting. I can't stand the drinking and the yelling and the broken promises. I can't stand the silent treatment and the false affection and the boozy smelly hugs and the red eyes.

Yesterday I yelled back at my Mom. I said "You should see yourself! You look like hell! And you stink!" She slapped my face. Then she did it again. I guess I deserved it for mouthing off. But I can't stand it anymore.

Plan for Your Personal Safety

Know what's best for your own safety and act on it. When your parents get drunk or stoned, don't argue with them or provoke them in any way. Sometimes it's safest to say nothing. Sometimes it's safest to disappear. Sometimes it's safest to carry on as though everything is normal. Only you can know what's right for you. Try never to put yourself in a situation where you might get hurt—and don't feel guilty because you're protecting yourself. Feel wise instead!

Living with chemically dependent parents can be a nightmare. Not all chemically dependent people are abusive, but some of them are. What can you do if your parents are abusive? Avoid getting into arguments with them. Don't let them trick you into fighting with them. Don't believe what they say when they call you names or say terrible things about you. And if it looks as though one of them could hurt you, LEAVE THE HOUSE AND CALL FOR HELP.

If one of your fears is that your parents will set the house on fire by passing out with a cigarette in hand, *be ready* in the awful event it ever happens. Locate the fire escapes. Make sure that your house has at least one smoke alarm, and that it's working. Plan for ways to alert others in the house. Then sleep soundly, knowing that you've done all you can do.

Planning for your personal safety isn't silly, and it isn't a

300

betrayal of your family. It's just good sense, and it will give you peace of mind—which you deserve. It's not easy to be practical about matters like these, but you're used to doing hard things. You do them all the time.

*All I ever wanted was a normal family. A family who had normal arguments and normal good times together and normal problems. I look around our house and everything **seems** normal. We have furniture just like other families. We have a dog and a cat. We have neighbors and a yard and a garden.*

So why am I so torn up inside? Why am I always angry and upset and edgy? Why am I failing in school? Why don't I have any friends? There are eight million WHYS and no BECAUSES.

All I ever wanted was a normal family. Is that too much to ask?

You Have Rights!

YOU HAVE THE RIGHT to be yourself and like who you are.

YOU HAVE THE RIGHT to refuse requests without feeling selfish or guilty.

YOU HAVE THE RIGHT to be competent and proud of your accomplishments.

YOU HAVE THE RIGHT to feel and express anger.

YOU HAVE THE RIGHT to ask for affection and help.

YOU HAVE THE RIGHT to be respected as a human being with feelings.

YOU HAVE THE RIGHT to be illogical in making decisions.

YOU HAVE THE RIGHT to make mistakes—and be responsible for them.

YOU HAVE THE RIGHT to change your mind.

YOU HAVE THE RIGHT to say, "I don't know!"

YOU HAVE THE RIGHT to say, "I don't agree!"

YOU HAVE THE RIGHT to say, "I don't understand!"

YOU HAVE THE RIGHT to say, "I want more!"

YOU HAVE THE RIGHT to offer no reasons or excuses for anyone else's behavior.

YOU HAVE THE RIGHT to have your opinions respected.

YOU HAVE THE RIGHT to have your needs be as important as other people's.

YOU HAVE THE RIGHT to be listened to AND understood.

YOU HAVE THE RIGHT to take pride in your body and define attractiveness in your own terms.

YOU HAVE THE RIGHT to grow, learn, change, and value your own experience.

And sometimes to make demands on others. . . .

Don't hide behind a wall of silence; it will destroy you. Know that you don't have to talk about your parents to anyone if you don't want to—only about yourself and your own dreams.

Inside of you is a spark that tells you when something feels right or wrong. Watch for that spark, nuture it, trust it. It's your God's center and it will protect you.

EVELYN LEITE AND PAMELA ESPELAND

This section is taken from *Different Like Me: A Book for Teens Who Worry About Their Parents' Use of Alcohol/Drugs,* published by the Johnson Institute.

CHAPTER FIFTEEN

What Adult Children of Alcoholics Need to Know

> My name is Sheila and I am the child of an alcoholic.
> My mother always drank. I could see it, smell it and
> I had to deal with it constantly, but I couldn't really
> **know it until now.**

Sheila is one of an estimated 28 million adults and young children who grew up in a family with one or two alcoholic parents. She is what is called today an adult child of an alcoholic (ACOA). As Sheila said, her mother always drank, but it wasn't until Sheila read about parental alcoholism and heard the term ACOA that she could finally allow herself to know the painful reality that she'd lived with all her life. In this chapter we'll look at what it means to be an ACOA: how the idea was born, how the alcoholic family works, what it's like growing up, how kids cope and what happens in recovery.

The Birth of a Concept

Knowledge about alcoholism, or chemical dependence, has undergone tremendous change over the last ten years. Today, it's hard to conceive of a time when the notion "children of alcoholics" or "adult children of alcoholics" didn't exist. It's hard to believe that just fifteen years ago there wasn't such a thing. ACOAs existed of course, but they weren't known or named. There was no recognition that some people had common childhood experiences and adult problems that could be related to growing up in a family with one or more alcoholic parents.

The groundwork for acknowledging ACOAs as a legitimate treatment population was laid back in the 1950s with the birth of Al-Anon, the autonomous arm of Alcoholics Anonymous (A.A.) designed for the spouse of an alcoholic. Al-Anon provided the first official recognition that alcoholism has an impact on others. Until this time, all attention had been on the drinking alcoholic, as if that individual and the alcoholism existed in a vacuum.

Joan Jackson, a prominent researcher, dramatically altered this single vision when she outlined stages in a developing process of alcoholism for the spouse, similar to the stages of the disease process defined for the alcoholic by Jellinek. Like A.A., the focus of Al-Anon was on the individual, but it was clearly the individual in an interpersonal, familial context. People joining Al-Anon learned that they too could tell the truth, saying what it was like, what happened and what it was like now that denial of a partner's alcoholism had been broken.

Following Jackson's work and the growth of Al-Anon, the concept of "family disease" or "alcoholic family" was born. The focus was not primarily on the alcoholic, but rather on the interactions, adjustments and development of the family with an alcoholic member.

Young children of alcoholics had been identified as a separate population since the 1940s and by the self-help movement since the late 1950s when Alateen was born. By the mid-1970s, the time was ripe for extending the idea of children of alcoholics to adults.

In 1979 Newsweek published a one-page article in its Lifestyle section describing the work of Claudia Black and Stephanie Brown, targeted specifically toward children and adult children of alcoholics. Others around the country were also beginning to recognize this group and a national social movement was launched. The National Association of Children of Alcoholics (NACOA) was formed in 1983, and the Children of Alcoholics Foundation was started to provide support for research, education and public awareness. Over the next ten years this large population was defined, developed and granted legitimacy by the popular media.

It has been a social movement of profound significance and impact. It is probably the first time in history that a treatment population has been defined by the media to such a degree that the concept ACOA has challenged traditional theory and practice in all the health fields, including chemical dependence.

How? First, there is an entirely new treatment population, this group called "adult children." There never has been such a thing as an "adult child," either as a patient or a diagnosis. If there are suddenly 20 million or so new patients, what do we do with them? And, which of our traditional theories fit and which do not? Is this an individual diagnosis or a family problem? Who should get treatment and who will pay for it? None of these questions yet have answers. ACOAs have come on the scene, announced themselves and the professional world is trying to catch up.

The social movement broke denial, named reality and, through the label ACOA, provided a new framework that has allowed adults to literally rewrite their childhood and family histories to include the reality of parental alcoholism, a reality that profoundly shaped and influenced their development, but could not be named or understood until now.

What's different about this framework? It is a systems designation which connects child to parent and vice versa and names alcoholism as the central organizing principle for both.

305

What Do We Know?

Ten years later, we know a great deal about the kinds of things that happen in an alcoholic home, what it's like to live in this environment, how children cope and what the costs are for coping. We've got a well-documented portrait of the environment. And we are just beginning to understand that there's more to being an ACOA than understanding the environment. We must also understand the workings of the alcoholic system and its impact on the family's stability and development. We need to know what happens to the normal tasks of individual development for a child growing up in this environment and this unhealthy family system in order to know what it really means.

While being an ACOA is an individual experience and it is up to each person to give it meaning, we can examine the communalities in both experience and consequences in the family system, the environment, and the impact on individual development.

The Alcoholic Family System

If you and I were to go home, back to childhood, to your family, what would we see? How did your family work? Jack recalls:

> You'd see a family with alcohol at the head of the table, so to speak. My father's alcoholism organized everything about our family, but everyone would tell you it wasn't so. My father was drunk every night, but no one could talk about it. We knew that drinking provided relief from the stresses of Dad's difficult job, but we couldn't know or talk about the fact that the drinking itself was a problem.

As Jack illustrates, the alcoholic family becomes dominated by the presence of alcoholism and its denial. Maintaining this secret—the reality of alcoholism—while denying it at the same time, becomes the central focus around which the family is organized, what theorists call the "central organizing principle" of family life.

Family systems theorists tell us that all groups, organizations, or systems naturally strive toward achieving and maintaining a sense of internal balance. In an alcoholic home, this stability is maintained by covering up and denying what is most visible, central and problematic **and** explaining it as something else. As Patti says:

> We all knew there was no alcoholism in our family. We also knew we weren't supposed to talk about it. Dad drank, but he didn't have a problem and the reason he drank as much as he did, which was a lot, was because he had such a hard time at work. We grew up blaming my father's job for all our problems.

Sometimes the children learn that they are part of the excuse, as Toni notes:

> My parents drank a lot everyday. We kids tried to stay out of the way but always got pulled in, especially when they started fighting. By the time it ended, one of us got the blame for the whole mess—"If we'd get better grades, or stop arguing with each other, Mom and Dad wouldn't need to drink." We grew up knowing we'd cause some major problem today, but we couldn't predict what, when, how or whose turn it would be.

The alcoholic family maintains its stability by relying on denial and rationalization. Denial simply says "It isn't so." Rationalization says why it IS so in a way that lets everyone feel okay about it.

> In our family, we knew my parents drank and it was okay to talk about it. What really counted was proving that they didn't drink too much. They were always reassuring each other that they didn't drink anymore than Aunt Olive or Dr. Thompson so they couldn't possibly have a problem.

Why would anyone go along with this kind of blatant denial or even subtle distortion? We know from experts in child development that all children need a very close human bond, a primary attachment, in order to survive. Usually a parent fulfills this role. We also know that the preservation of that bond is of utmost importance to the developing child. Any threat of disruption in the parent-child bond will cause tremendous fear and anxiety in the child. And challenge of the family's denial about parental alcoholism is seen as serious threat to family attachment and solidarity. So, children will readily accept the secret-keeping, joining the adults in the denial and distortion, in order to maintain family ties. Everyone in the family fears that telling the truth about drinking will result in loss of love, abandonment and perhaps the break-up of the family.

Children must join in the denial or risk betraying the family. They learn not to trust their own perceptions of reality, not to say what they see, but rather to view the family experience through an alcoholic perspective modeled by both parents. At the same time that they learn not to trust their own perceptions, they also learn not to test reality because it will not be congruent with their parents' reality. In this atmosphere the child's needs, feelings, and behavior are dictated by the unpredictable state of the alcoholic. All members of the family assume responsibility for maintaining stability in the system, struggling to find ways of controlling a situation that cannot be controlled.

We've looked at how the alcoholic family works and how everyone gears their perception and behavior toward maintaining the family secret. Now, let's see what's actually happening in the alcoholic environment.

The Alcoholic Environment

Let's say you take me home again—what would I see? What's going on and how would it feel? What's the tone, the mood, the atmosphere? Jack recalls:

> In my family there was an atmosphere of dark and gloom that hung around like a cloud. I'd be happy outside, enjoy school and sports, but as I headed home, I was overwhelmed by a feeling of discouragement and hopelessness. Walking into that home meant trouble. There was just this overriding sense of impending doom.

Many authors suggest that the alcoholic family lives in an atmosphere characterized by chaos, inconsistency, unclear roles, unpredictability, arbitrariness, changing limits, repetition, illogical arguments, and perhaps violence and incest.

Chaos may be overt or covert. It reflects the predominant control the alcoholic exercises over the family and the constant feeling by all family members that things are or soon will be out of control. Since stable routines may be disrupted at any time during a drinking bout, the potential for instability is constant. As families adjust to the reality of chaos, inconsistency may ironically become a stable and predictable feature of the family environment. A permission granted by an alcoholic parent on one day is rescinded arbitrarily the next. The complex pattern of rationalizations necessary to sustain family denial also may lead to inconsistent explanations for behavior and events. What explains behavior one day is contradicted the next.

Inconsistency is also evidenced in unclear parental roles. One parent may take over the role of both mother and father, or a child may substitute for one or both. This pattern may be stable or constantly affected by the drinking behavior of the alcoholic or the inconsistent and unpredictable response of the partner.

There is an increasing recognition of the relationship of alcohol to family violence and incest. Several researchers note that most of the communication in an alcoholic family is seen as hostile and angry by the children, who are disturbed and frightened by parental arguments.

Alcoholic family environments are not all the same, anymore than the kind of denial relied upon or the particular systems dynamics that maintain the family's balance. One family may feel dark and depressing, like Jack described, while others may be characterized by an atmosphere of anger, isolation and withdrawal, or perhaps a feeling of false happiness and good will.

Still, there are many experiences held in common. Most ACOAs can recall the painful memories of a holiday ruined by drinking or the agonizing compulsory ritual of dinnertime. Held captive at the table, children are both witness and victim to the nightly drama of alcoholism.

Individual Development

For many years, it was believed that children of alcoholics were not affected by the alcoholism of a parent. But we know now that parental alcoholism and the reaction of the non-alcoholic parent (what is called co-dependence) have profound consequences on children's development. The problems in the alcoholic environment discussed above contribute to an overall lack of stability and uncertainty in the environment as well as severe emotional trauma. Because of the nature of the environment, members of the family expend enormous amounts of energy just to cope with their external family world. So much effort goes into denial and coping with the chaotic reality that there is little energy left over for internal development. Early on, individuals develop overt problems with trust and issues of control. They are guarded and suffer from low esteem and a deepening sense of family isolation.

In many alcoholic families, individual development is overshadowed by the emphasis on alcoholism and the need for defense. As Carla notes:

> All my energy went into coping. I can't remember thinking about what I wanted to be or what I hoped for.

Because of the strength of denial and the threat of its disruption, the alcoholic family is constantly on guard, defending its view of reality and adapting itself to cope with that same reality: parental alcoholism that dominates and organizes the family, but which must be denied and explained as something else. There is little room for autonomous individual development. Instead, the family emphasis is on defending, coping and adapting to the alcoholic reality.

Susan Beletsis and Stephanie Brown, using developmental theorist Erik Erikson's model, suggest that this emphasis on defensive coping seriously interferes with the child's ability to progress through the stages of normal childhood development. In Erikson's theory, children move through three early stages: trust, autonomy and initiative. If all goes well for children, these early stages prepare them for the ongoing tasks of identification and separation from the close emotional bonds of attachment with parents. But in an alcoholic family, all does not go well. The child's fundamental sense of attachment is based on sharing the distorted family beliefs, that is, the particular "family story" that holds the family system together.

For example, an infant whose parents are preoccupied with

drinking will have difficulties establishing basic trust, the first stage and the foundation of healthy development. The parents are simply too involved with their own needs to provide the predictable responsiveness and attention required to give the child a deep experience of safety and security.

Erikson's second stage, autonomy versus shame and doubt, is a time of experimentation with issues of "holding on" and "letting go," negotiating closeness and distance. The toddler in an alcoholic family may be quite confused and frightened because parents are struggling so unsuccessfully with issues of control themselves. Children may also experience mixed messages from parents. At one time, parents encourage independence, or even push a child away, while at another they may thwart autonomous efforts of the child because of their own needs and insecurities.

The same process interferes with the next stage of initiative versus guilt, which is the focus for pre-school children. By now, the child in an alcoholic family is geared, like the parent, to defense and can't risk the experimentation necessary to develop feelings of competence and mastery. Many children with alcoholic parents grow up with a chronic deep feeling of fear and are capable of experiencing themselves only as reactors and never initiators.

As children from alcoholic families move toward adulthood unable to challenge the family's beliefs or identity, they will acquire and develop their own "personal identities" by imitating and modeling the beliefs and behavior of their parents. They are thus in a position to "do it all over again," which is exactly what happens for many. ACOAs may marry an alcoholic or become alcoholic themselves, replicating the family pattern centered on parental alcoholism.

Or, they may remain in an arrested state of development, frightened of becoming an adult because it equals acting out an identification with out-of-control parents. Only when there are

312

healthier models available (which there may be in many alcoholic families), or when it becomes safe to break denial, can the impact of parental alcoholism be interrupted.

How Children Cope

In their pioneer studies, therapists Claudia Black and Sharon Wegsheider describe particular roles that kids develop in response to the requirements of the alcoholic family system and the environment. Kids learn who they are and how to behave in a way that allows them to maintain the critical bond of attachment with their parents. Again, there are lots of differences as well as similarities. It's very important to understand that a particular role may serve one child very well in an adaptive sense and not work well at all for another. It's also important to realize that a particular role may be very adaptive during childhood, but terribly restrictive and maladaptive for the adult outside the family. In fact, it is this horrible recognition by adults—that what worked inside the family doesn't work outside—that brings many to treatment.

Children may also cope by growing up fast, focusing on a too-narrow pattern of achievement, or becoming sexually active or delinquent at a young age. Many children experience role reversal, assuming the a task of parenting their parents. Sheila illustrates:

> My mother would often feel guilty and remorseful about her drinking. It was my job to make her feel good. I needed to constantly reassure her that she was a good parent.

With parental role reversal, children also may develop a strong need for self-reliance. Many come to believe that the way to make it in the world is not to ever trust or rely on anyone. While adaptive at home, this kind of belief creates major difficulties in establishing and building intimate relationships outside the family.

In addition to self-reliance, ACOAs also develop other deeply held core beliefs about themselves that ensure the maintenance of attachment to parents and the balance of the family system. But these beliefs are often negative and the costs exorbitant. Some examples:

> If there was no problem with alcohol, but there was a problem, I knew it had to be me. I always believed that I was bad, that I caused all the difficulties.

> or,

> I spent my childhood years trying to figure out how to get my mother's attention. If I could just be a good enough kid, she'd notice and love me. It didn't happen. I've always felt like a complete failure.

> or,

> I loved and admired my parents even with all the drama of the alcoholism. I wanted to be just like them and I was. Now that I've done the same kind of damage, I'm afraid of myself. I deeply believe that others need protection from me.

These kinds of core beliefs are created by the child as a result of traumatic experiences in the alcoholic family. They are adaptive for the time because they allow the child to make sense of a confusing, painful reality and to maintain attachments. These beliefs also permit the child to sustain an idealized image of the parent which counters severe depression and fear that would result from recognizing the reality of the parent's condition. Finally, these beliefs offer a false illusion of hope, as Sheila recalls:

> I always thought if I caused it, I could fix it. So I never stopped trying to make it better for my parents.

Defensive Traits

In addition to negative core beliefs, children also develop defensive traits which serve them well for survival in the alcoholic family, but eventually cause trouble.

The first is an overriding emphasis on control. The ACOA is constantly on guard, vigilant for signs of impending catastrophe, which often means a loss of control by the ACOA or someone else. The ACOA is constantly assessing "Who's in charge here? Am I in control? Am I being controlled? Or, who's about to lose control?" This emphasis on control dominates interpersonal relationships and leads to severe problems establishing trust. It also interferes with the ability to establish mature partnerships based on reciprocity and interdependence.

The second ACOA defense is the emphasis on denial. The ACOA learns that most reality—feelings, perceptions, behaviors—can't be known or talked about. The world is a dangerous place, with the only protection resting in denial. These individuals often feel confused, uncertain and frightened.

The third defensive characteristic is an overwhelming sense of responsibility for everything and everybody. This characteristic frequently stems from role reversal, but also evolves from a normal sense of childhood omnipotence—i.e., the child's egocentric view of self at the center of the universe. Again, such a sense of responsibility may help counteract tremendous fear and depression in a child who recognizes the absence or loss of a parent to alcohol.

The final characteristic is all-or-none thinking, a primitive, rigid framework for interpreting the world that rests on dichotomous categories. There are all-rights and all-wrongs in the world with no grey to mess things up. The trick is to find and side with the right. For many ACOAs, the wrong and the bad equal alcoholism. They set about to do it differently.

Consequences

It is now recognized that the alcoholic family is an environment frequently characterized by chronic trauma. Simply living with the realities of alcoholism constitutes the trauma. There may be additional episodes of acute trauma, such as a particularly frightening argument, physical abuse, molestation or incest.

The mental health field now recognizes that exposure to trauma has serious consequences. Many children have nightmares and sleep disturbances, some are aggressive and have school or social problems and others become passive and withdrawn. Children growing up in this traumatic kind of home are robbed of critically important experiences and relationships necessary for healthy development. As a result, they reach adulthood unable and unprepared to cope with the demands of maturity.

Adults from alcoholic families emphasize the damaging consequences of the traumatic environment, including their parent's behavior and distorted logic. Many trace their problems with trust and their guarded, suspicious stance as adults to this childhood environment in which a disaster was always imminent.

The repetitious and illogical explanations and arguments also have a profound impact. Adults report severe difficulties trusting their perceptions about events and their relationships with others, believing that they do not see things accurately. Many relate this belief back to childhood when they were told by a parent that what they saw (i.e., a drunken parent) was not what they saw.

Many ACOAs suffer from depression, anxiety and chronic fear. They are terrified of becoming like their parents—alcoholic or addictive, abusive, emotionally unavailable, and destructive to themselves and to their own spouses and children.

ACOAs also report difficulties feeling or expressing anger and a tendency to experience substantial guilt, embarrassment and shame, often unconnected or inappropriately connected to any real situation in the present. A common feeling carried long into adulthood by many is survivor guilt, the painful awareness that one has emerged, or could emerge, somehow better off than parents and family.

The ACOA may also feel a profound sense of sadness at the notion of emerging at all, leaving behind parents who need help or giving up the hope of ever having competent parents to care for them. Sheila explains:

> I used to dream about getting out and how I'd do it better. But that was just a dream. How could I leave them all behind, desperate and suffering? If I could figure out how to help them, I could have a life of my own.

Indeed, many ACOAs don't make it out of the family, emotionally or physically. Many symbolically "stay home," becoming just like their parents and replaying the whole family drama over again. Some have trouble leaving their families because they haven't learned what they need to learn to make it in the world away from home. If anything, they've learned the wrong things. ACOAs develop a sense of self based on the distorted logic, roles, behavior and defensive traits required to belong and maintain the family's balance. They are often skilled reactors, acutely sensitive to pleasing others and on the lookout for approval.

Finally, many ACOAs have great difficulty establishing and maintaining close intimate relationships, in part because they had no models and because their development was so dominated by the family's defensive focus. Their own needs and motives had to be stifled or disguised so there was little or no chance to develop an independent sense of self. Opportunities for individual development that would have given them the foundation for making a healthy separation and forming healthy relationships outside the family were overshadowed and influenced by the alcoholism.

Many ACOAs reach adulthood unprepared to cope with the realities and complexities of life in a healthy or adaptive way. They often seek treatment precisely because they are not coping or not making it. The process of treatment and recovery takes the ACOA back home again, but this time to break out and away by challenging denial, naming the reality and rewriting family history to include the realities of parental alcoholism.

The Process of Recovery

Denial

The process of recovery occurs in stages, similar to what the alcoholic in A.A. experiences. In the first stage, the alcoholic is still drinking and denying that there are any problems. The ACOA in the first stage is also denying that a parent has any problem with alcohol. The individual may be experiencing difficulties as an adult that can be traced back to childhood and the alcoholic home environment, but this ACOA doesn't know it yet.

Transition

The alcoholic in transition is moving from drinking into abstinence. The individual makes this shift only when denial about the drinking begins to crack. The alcoholic comes to recognize that drinking is indeed a problem that is out of control, identifies as an alcoholic, and stops drinking.

Similarly, the first step for the ACOA moving into recovery

is to break denial. The adult comes to realize that his or her parent(s) was alcoholic and begins to make sense of childhood family life in a new way. What couldn't be known or talked about before is now acknowledged and eventually reported to someone else.

Early Recovery

The alcoholic in early recovery is learning new behaviors that support abstinence and beginning to construct a new personal "story," what is called in A.A. a drunkalog. If ACOAs are attending Al-Anon or another Twelve Step program, they will be hearing about detachment and disengagement. This means they must begin to alter their own reactions to the alcoholic parent and perhaps the alcoholic family. They must start to change old ideas and patterns of behavior that supported denial. Like the alcoholic, they too begin constructing their own new "stories" about childhood that include the reality of parental alcoholism. Making the past real and understanding its influence on the present is the heart of recovery. Defenses which protected the child from seeing or feeling reality must be challenged. The adult will then look underneath, at a range of feelings and strivings, including anger, loss, sorrow, or deep need that could not previously be acknowledged or accepted as one's own.

Ongoing Recovery

The alcoholic in ongoing recovery continues to follow the new behaviors of abstinence and to learn more about what it means to be an alcoholic: what I really did and what really happened. Sobriety is now stable. The alcoholic can pay more attention to working the Twelve Steps of A.A.

The ACOA in ongoing recovery is working toward achieving an emotional separation from the unhealthy patterns of family relationship. The individual can now pay attention to developing the self, or toward developing mature, healthy relationships with others.

The whole process of recovery for the ACOA is oriented toward separation from the first family. It might well be called "growing up, growing out and coming home." It takes a long time. Opening up the past to look at what really happened, what it was like, and what deep, but faulty beliefs and coping skills were developed is a painful process because it threatens to disrupt the very bonds that were so necessary for childhood survival. But that's exactly what happens. The adult accepts a new identity as an ACOA and begins a new process of development, this time based on healthier premises.

This developmental process is nothing short of "starting over" for many because so much old must be unlearned and so much new must be learned from scratch. It is not just a process of uncovering the past or understanding that current problems are closely related to family history. The individual also learns that there are no simple cut-and-paste solutions that will reverse these deep beliefs and defensive patterns. By coming to see that they took an active role in developing and maintaining these ways of living, ACOAs are empowered to change. Recovery is a complicated process that takes time and requires help. It is very similar to what the alcoholic in recovery in A.A. experiences: growing up all over again with a much sounder foundation.

What About You?

Like many thousands of adults, you may be breaking your denial of parental alcoholism and beginning your own process of recovery. No doubt, you've got many questions. Which ACOA group should I belong to? Should I go to Al-Anon? Should I seek professional treatment and, if so, what kind? And, if I'm newly recovering from my own addictions, when should I begin exploring ACOA issues?

There are no quick and easy answers to these or any of the other questions you may have because recovery is an individual process. One newly recovering alcoholic might do well to table ACOA issues for a time, while another must tackle them head on in order to maintain sobriety. The right treatment choice and the timing for one person are not necessarily right for another. Unfortunately, often it's not clear what the best choices are, so it's useful to seek professional help and follow some general guidelines.

ACOA self-help groups affiliated with Al-Anon are now available all over the country. Large and small, these groups offer support and education through the sharing of personal experience. The Al-Anon group is a good choice for anyone just starting to look at the painful reality. There are also ACOA Twelve Step meetings all over the country modeled after, but independent of Al-Anon. It's best to look around, ask questions and check local referral resources for the best program for you.

A wide range of treatment options such as lectures and short-term educational services is now available in most communities, as well as counseling for individuals, couples and families. Many books are also available, outlining the childhood reality and the path to recovery. The local affiliate of the National Council on Alcoholism or a community referral agency can provide a list of resources. The National Association of Children of Alcoholics is open to public membership. Dedicated to education and prevention, it provides a newsletter, updated information on ACOAs and conference listings. The address and phone number for this and other national organizations can be found at the end of this book.

Is recovery ever complete? We really don't know that yet, but probably not, anymore than any process of development and learning is ever really finished. But does it get better? And, is change really possible? We don't know these answers yet either, except what ACOAs in treatment and recovery tell us. What they say is yes, it does get better, but not without seriously challenging the past and the present; not without taking off the blinders to see what couldn't be seen and to know what couldn't be known.

STEPHANIE BROWN, PH.D.

Intervention,
or How You Can Help Someone
Who Doesn't Want Help

Introduction to Part Four

This section is designed to give a positive response to the question: "Why do chemical dependents suffer so long?" Chemical dependence differs from any other deadly disease because its very nature renders its victims **incapable** of spontaneously recognizing their problem. They are not just unwilling, they are delusional—out of touch with reality. They are not just victims of a drug, but of their defenses run amok and their grossly distorted memories.

That is why it is necessary, if the chemically dependent person is to survive, for meaningful people around him or her to present reality in a receivable way. This process of intervention, described in the following chapters, has been successfully practiced at virtually every economic and social level in the United States.

Chapters Sixteen and Seventeen, from my book on intervention, detail the five basic principles of intervention: (1) how to gather the meaningful people needed for this process, (2) what specific information they need to collect, (3) when professional help should be obtained, (4) how to select a professional interventionist, and (5) how to rehearse the intervention.

The material in Chapter Eighteen was selected to address unique aspects of intervening when the chemically dependent person is a teenager. Because teenagers live different lives than adults and because in some ways chemical dependence is different for them, some aspects of the intervention process must be modified. But the principle remains the same: meaningful people must care enough to act.

325

Typically those living with chemical dependents are immo-bilized for a variety of reasons including fear, shame, and ignorance. It is my hope that the information provided in this section will move them to life-saving action. I know that inter-vention changes lives: One day in a crowded passageway in LaGuardia Airport, a stranger stopped me to say, "You don't know me, of course, but I know you and a certain book. My wife is now three years dry! Thank you very much!" Could there be a better "payday"?

VERNON E. JOHNSON, D.D.

CHAPTER SIXTEEN

Preparing for the Intervention

You are probably reading this because you suspect that someone you care about is chemically dependent. That someone may be a spouse or a child, a parent or a cousin, a co-worker or a neighbor or a friend. The drug of choice may be alcohol, marijuana, cocaine, amphetamines ("uppers"), barbiturates ("downers"), or some combination of these. What it is does not matter; what matters is that the person is abusing or misusing it, and that this is causing problems for him or her *and for you.*

These problems may range all the way from mildly erratic behaviors on the individual's part to major personality changes and physical deterioration. Maybe the individual is performing poorly at work. Maybe there's been one or more DWIs (driving while intoxicated) or DUIs (driving under the influence). Maybe things are tense around the house (or office). Maybe you have caught the person telling lies, breaking promises, or making excuses that are directly related to using. Maybe there have been occasions when the person has been hospitalized, or taken to detox, or jailed. Or maybe you simply have the uneasy feeling that something is wrong somewhere, and chemical dependence could be the cause.

Fortunately for that person, *you want to help.* At the moment, though, you are not sure how to go about it. Furthermore, the person does not seem willing to accept help from you or anyone else. In fact, he or she may loudly deny that a problem exists, or even blame it on you!

If you are like most people, you may believe that there is nothing you can do except wait for the person to "hit bottom" and then try to pick up the pieces. For the past 20 years, our task at the Johnson Institute has been to prove that just the opposite is true. Waiting is too dangerous. It is also cruel. It allows an already bad situation to get worse. If a friend wanted to jump off a bridge, would you let him do it before you reached out a hand to stop him? Of course not; and neither must you stand by and watch the chemically dependent person plumb the depths of suffering and despair before doing something about it. You don't have to bide your time until your family breaks up, or the person is fired from his or her job—or kills someone in a car accident. You can reach out *now*.

You may also believe that only the experts—physicians, psychiatrists, chemical dependence counselors—are equipped and able to help the chemically dependent person. That is not necessarily the case. Another thing we have learned at the Johnson Institute is that *anyone who sincerely wants to help, can help.* You do not need a clinical background or special expertise. You should, however, have some understanding of what chemical dependence is and how it affects its victims. With this information in hand, you may then decide whether to seek help from one of the many capable professionals with experience in this field.

The important thing is to *take action*—and soon. By definition, a chemically dependent person is out of touch with reality. Through a process called *intervention*, you can play an important role in moving the person you care about back toward reality, recovery, and a richer, fuller, longer life. Thousands of concerned people like you have done it for their relatives and friends; thousands of chemically dependent people are alive and well today as proof that it works. In this chapter and the next we describe the process of intervention and the steps involved in preparing for it, initiating it, and seeing it through.

Beginning the Process

Intervention is a process by which the harmful, progressive, and destructive effects of chemical dependence are interrupted and the chemically dependent person is helped to stop using mind-altering chemicals and to develop new, healthier ways of coping with his or her needs and problems. It implies that the person need not be an emotional or physical wreck (or "hit bottom") before such help can be given.

There is a shorter, simpler way to define intervention: *presenting reality to a person out of touch with it in a receivable way.* In Part One of this book, we explored the delusional system which the chemically dependent person uses as a shield against the painful and debilitating reality of the disease and its effects. The goal of the intervention is to break down those defenses so that reality can shine through long enough for the person to accept it.

By "presenting reality," we mean presenting *specific facts* about the person's behavior and the things that have happened because of it. "A receivable way" is one that the person cannot resist because it is *objective, unequivocal, nonjudgmental,* and *caring.*

An intervention is a confrontation, but it differs in some very important respects from the sort of confrontation with which most people are familiar—and which have little or no positive effect.

In an intervention, confrontation means compelling the person to face the facts about his or her chemical dependence. It is not a punishment. It is not an opportunity for others to clobber him or her verbally. It is an attack upon the victim's wall of defenses, not upon the victim as a person.

Similarly, an intervention is an act of *empathy* rather than sympathy. You agree to take part in it out of the deep concern you feel for the chemically dependent person. You stop *caring for* the alcoholic or drug addict—and start proving how very much you *care about* him or her.

For the chemically dependent person, the intervention is the "moment of truth." He or she experiences it as a crisis, a discrete event. In fact, it takes days, even weeks, of advance preparation. *The better prepared you are, the more smoothly the intervention will go.* The only "surprises" during the process should be those the victim experiences when finally met head-on with the realities of his or her disease.

Conquering Your Own Reluctance

You may need to start by convincing *yourself* that intervention is the best approach, and the best time to begin the process is *now*.

It is normal to approach intervention with reluctance or even fear. You may worry that it will only make things worse. You may feel despondent, as if nothing will help and nothing will ever change. You may feel angry and resentful. You may be so weary of the whole situation that you're not that interested in helping.

Following are some questions you may be asking yourself—and some answers that should motivate you to take action.

"Why Now?"

The longer you delay, the longer the person will suffer—and the more life-threatening the disease will become. Permanent disability (including brain damage) and even premature death are inevitable unless the destructive process is successfully interrupted. The sooner this happens, the more likely it is that the person will recover.

Studies indicate that those alcoholics whose illnesses resulted in the more severe physical, economic, and social disorders had more difficult and prolonged recoveries. On the other hand, there's evidence that where physical health has *not* been broken, jobs have *not* been lost, and families have remained intact, alcoholics have tended to recover more often and more quickly.

"Why me?"

If you have read the first part of this book, you know quite a bit about chemical dependence—probably a great deal more than most of the other people surrounding the person. As a result, you can play an especially important role in the process by educating others about the disease.

Besides, if not you, then who else? Has anyone approached you about the need to intervene with the person? If not, it may be due to their own entrapment within the delusional system. It is possible that they can no longer see the disease for what it is, if indeed they ever could. Or they may be waiting for "something to happen" to change the situation.

You are aware of how dangerous it is to wait. If nobody else is taking action, and if you truly care about the person, then you *must* take immediate steps to halt the progress of the disease.

"I've heard of people who simply turned themselves in for treatment. They seemed to realize all at once that they had a problem. Can't that happen to the person I know?"

It's possible, but not probable. What you're wondering about is something we call *spontaneous insight*, which isn't really spontaneous at all.

The emotional syndrome and the delusional system of chemical dependence combine to make it virtually impossible for the chemically dependent person to admit or even recognize that he or she has a problem. Once in a while, and this is *very* rare, so many things will go wrong at the same time that a piece of reality slips through the wall of defenses. (In retrospect, the recovering person will claim that "Everything went to hell in a handbasket.") These *fortuitous groupings of crises* prove so overwhelming that the person practically flees into treatment. Life reaches such a critical point that he or she may pick up the phone and call for help, or go to detox, or join A.A.

But this doesn't always happen, and you can't afford to gamble on it. Remember that we are talking about *certain premature death* if the disease is not arrested.

People who reach this point—those who have been saved by fortuitous groupings of crises—are those who have gotten the sickest. At the Johnson Institute, our goal is to reach the "up and outers," not only the "down and outers." Early intervention is the way to accomplish this.

"I'm not married to the person—we're just friends. Won't intervention look like interference in his or her private life?"

This is a genuine concern for some people. Most of us were raised to be polite, to respect others' privacy, and to mind our own business. We hesitate to be rude, or cruel—both of which intervention seems to require.

It is not rude to help a sick person; it is not cruel to save someone's life. In fact, intervention is a profound act of caring.

"Intervention seems so secretive—even sneaky. I don't like the idea of going behind someone's back."

Intervention is the opposite of secretive. In truth, it helps everyone—from each concerned person who participates, to the chemically dependent person himself or herself—finally to break the "rule of silence" under which they have all been living.

It's a great relief for the spouse or child or neighbor or co-worker to be able to talk about what he or she has seen and experienced. At last, everyone can tell it like it is!

First, however, certain preparations must be made. The group must be organized into a process. Where, when, and how the chemically dependent person will be approached must be decided. All of this must take place without unnecessarily arousing the person's defense systems, which are already pathological. The overriding goal is to reach the person when he or she is most likely to listen, *and to hear.*

Revealing the nature of these preparations should be part of the intervention. On that occasion, you might say something like this: "We've all been having a tough time for the past few weeks. We've been meeting about you, and we've wanted to take you into our confidence, but we couldn't just yet. Finally, today, we can." Or: "We're going to share everything with you now. We haven't been going behind your back; instead, we've been getting it all together so we can share it appropriately and usefully."

If you are concerned that the person might become angry or defensive, keep this in mind: Countless numbers of recovering alcoholics have later said, "Thank God someone knew enough and cared enough to do this for me!"

Gathering the Intervention Team

The intervention should be conducted by a team comprised of two or more people who are close to the dependent person and have witnessed his or her behavior while under the influence. The chemically dependent person's defense systems are far too highly developed to be breached by one person acting alone.

There are many advantages to doing it in a group. First, the dependent person immediately realizes that the situation is serious when he or she is faced by several people all saying essentially the same things. It is fairly easy to discount or dismiss the claims of one person (especially if that person has tried before to introduce the subject of the drinking or drug use); it becomes harder when these claims are made by a chorus. A group carries the necessary weight to break through to reality.

As the old saying goes, "He will laugh if one person tells him he has a tail. If three people tell him, he may turn around to look!"

Second, it can be reassuring and strengthening for *you* to have supportive company during this potentially painful event. The chemically dependent person is bound to react with a variety of negative responses, and it's best if you don't have to bear their weight by yourself. And third, more people can present more evidence that a problem exists. Unless you have been with the victim during every second of the disease, you haven't seen it all!

Thus the intervention process begins by gathering a team of people who, like you, sincerely want to help.

Step 1: Make a list of meaningful people other than yourself who surround the chemically dependent person

The key word here is *meaningful*. These should be people with whom the victim has a fairly close relationship, whether by necessity or by choice. They should exert a strong influence upon the victim, since his or her denial will sweep aside the efforts of others.

They should *not* be chemically dependent themselves. People who have not come to terms with their own disease are unlikely to want to point out the symptoms in someone else, even if they are capable. And the chemically dependent person is not likely to stand for the pot calling the kettle black!

If the person is married and you are not the spouse, then the spouse (or significant other) should be at the top of your list. He or she can help you to determine other potential group members from among the following:

The chemically dependent person's employer or immediate supervisor: It can be *extremely* helpful to have the employer or supervisor as part of the intervention team. In our society, people's identities center around their jobs. Chemical dependents often cling to their job performance as the last bastion of respectability as the disease brings the rest of the world crashing down around their ears. They use it as "proof" that they can't have a problem: "I've never missed a day's work in my life because of drinking." (An honest look at their performance usually destroys this myth!) Sometimes the employer is a more effective intervener than a family member or a friend, simply because he or she holds such an important card.

The chemically dependent person's parents: It is most convenient if they live in the area. Even if they do not, however, you may want to consider getting them involved. Siblings are other good possibilities, again depending on geography.

The chemically dependent person's children: Children can be a valuable part of the intervention team; in most cases, they are well aware that a problem exists. As a very *general* guideline, we recommend that the children asked to participate be at least eight years old. They should be able to verbalize their feelings and describe the behaviors they have seen (and the disappointments they have experienced).

Adults often wonder if children will be frightened or upset by the intervention. Chances are that they have already been touched by the effects of the disease on their parent. In the intervention setting, they will finally have the opportunity to speak out and be supported by other adults. This can be a great relief, especially if they have been covering up their own feelings of fear, confusion, rejection, and hurt.

There is another way in which children tend to benefit from an intervention: Educating them about the disease can help them to understand it better, and this in turn can actually strengthen the relationship between them and the victim.

Close friends or neighbors of the chemically dependent person: While the chemically dependent person may socialize primarily with a group of "drinking buddies" or drug users, there may still be old friends "left over" from the pre-disease days, or new friends who are not heavy drinkers or users. These two criteria will help you to decide which to invite into the group; 1) Does the person listen to them and respect their opinions and viewpoints? 2) Have they been around the person during drinking or using episodes, and have they witnessed instances of bizarre or unusual behavior? In other words, do they have firsthand knowledge of how the disease is affecting the person?

The victim's self-delusion can usually be penetrated only by those whose approval or esteem are essential to his or her self-image. On an emotional level, this most often means members of the immediate family and the employer. Often, however, friends may be especially effective in helping the person to face his or her behavior. He or she may have been able to rationalize that the drinking is only the symptom of a family problem. Hearing from an observer who is outside the family circle may help to destroy this rationalization.

Co-workers: These should be people with whom the dependent person works on a regular basis; perhaps they share the same office or have cooperated on a long-term project. Again, the dependent person should respect them, and they should have firsthand knowledge of the situation.

A member of the clergy: If the dependent person attends a church or synagogue, the pastor, priest, or rabbi can be a vital part of the team, as long as he or she personally possesses useful information. This can either by firsthand knowledge of the victim's behavior, or extensive experience in working with other chemically dependent people.

Step 2: Form the Intervention Team

Now you must contact the people on your list and ask them to participate in the intervention. (If your list has turned out to be quite long, you may want to narrow it down. A large group can be unwieldy. In fact, our experience has shown that groups of three to five seem most effective.)

The best team members are those who *know something about chemical dependence, are willing to risk their relationship with the dependent person, and are emotionally adequate* to be interveners.

The friend or co-worker who insists that alcoholism or drug addiction is a sign of "moral weakness" will not be much help during the intervention. Each member of the team should have sufficient knowledge about or insight into chemical dependence to:

- accept the definition of addiction as a disease in which "normal" willpower is inadequate to control the use of the chemical

- realize that the effect of the chemical itself further reduces the strength of even "normal" willpower
- realize that the dependent person, because of the need to explain away his or her behavior, has developed a defense system so effective that it results in a high degree of self-delusion—including the inability to recognize the true nature of the disease
- understand that because of this degree of self-delusion, the dependent person is *absolutely unable* to look at his or her behavior with a clear eye, which is why help must come from the outside
- realize that chemical dependence isn't just a bad habit— and that the dependent person is going to live or die based on what happens during the intervention and afterward

You may find yourself doing some educating. Simply by reading the first part of this book, you have learned a great deal about chemical dependence. Share this information with prospective team members.

Expect some resistance, especially when it comes to making the commitment to play a active role in the intervention. People will be glad to talk to *you* about the person's drinking or using and how they feel about it (especially if they feel personally affronted or wounded by it), but it's another matter entirely to put their relationship with the victim on the line. That can be frightening.

A spouse will say, "I agree, my husband has a problem, but if I do what you're asking he'll divorce me!" A friend will say, "She'll never speak to me again. I'll lose her friendship for sure." A child will say, "Daddy gets mad when I talk about his drinking." A supervisor will say, "We're so busy that I don't know if I can afford to rock the boat. And what if she turns around and claims discrimination or some such thing, and raises the roof with my boss?"

You can counter each of these arguments in various ways. For example, with a young child, it's often enough to explain that Daddy (or Mommy) is very sick and needs help *soon*. Many companies today have at least some insight into the widespread problem of chemical dependence; some even have counselors on staff to assist employees.

But the ultimate argument is the simplest. *If they do nothing, the chemically dependent person will die prematurely.* It all boils down to two choices: They can intervene, thereby risking their relationship with the person (which is already deteriorating as a result of the disease), or they can do nothing and watch him or her continue to die slowly but surely.

The final criterion is emotional adequacy. Intervention should not be attempted by people who are so distressed that they might harm themselves or disrupt the process. Similarly, it should not be attempted by those who are immobilized by fear, or so full of rage toward the sick person that they cannot see beyond it.

Gathering the Data

There are two types of data you should compile in preparation for the intervention: facts about the dependent person's drinking or using behavior, and information about treatment options.

Step 1: Make written lists of specific incidents or conditions related to the dependent person's drinking or drug use that legitimatize your concern

This is something that *each* member of the intervention team should do. Even children can write out lists or ask adults for assistance in putting what they have experienced into their own words.

These lists should be written in the second person, since they will be read aloud to the person during the intervention. ("*You* did so-and-so," not "*My husband* did so-and-so.") And they should be *very* specific. Generalizations—"You drink too much," "You have to stop drinking," "Your drinking is getting worse," "You're away all the time"—are useless and even harmful, since they are felt as personal attacks.

Each item should explicitly describe a particular incident, preferably one that the writer observed firsthand. Here are some examples:

- "Last Thursday night at eight o'clock you came in slurring your words and knocked over and broke the lamp on our living room table. Perhaps you do not remember that because you had obviously been drinking."
- "On Monday, when I went to do the laundry, I found another empty bottle in the basement clothes hamper."
- "Last month we had to break a dinner engagement three times in a row because you had been drinking so much during the days."
- "Jim talked to me after the meeting on Friday and told me how concerned he's getting about your drinking. You insulted the speaker and several guests, and he had to drive you home."
- "Our neighbors mentioned this morning that they've noticed how withdrawn you've become this year. They wonder if there's any way they can help."
- "Do you remember falling down in the bathroom at two a.m. last Saturday morning? When I went to see what all the noise was about, I found you sprawled on the floor. There was liquor on your breath."
- "On Monday night I looked out my window and saw you passed out on your front lawn. It was 20 degrees outside, and I was worried about you."

- "Last month you charged $300 worth of liquor on our credit card."
- "A week ago you stayed home from work for three days in a row, claiming you had the flu. But it was really because you were too hung over to get out of bed."
- "On Monday night you told me you'd come straight home from work. Instead, you came in at one a.m. and slept in your clothes, which smelled of alcohol."
- "Last week I came home to find the children outside by themselves. You were asleep on the couch, and there was an empty liquor bottle on the floor beside you. The children were hungry and frightened. Susie said she'd tried to wake you up and couldn't."
- "You lost the car twice last month after you'd been out drinking. I had to drive around parking lots trying to find where you'd left it."
- "When you picked us up from school, you drove so fast that I and my friends were scared. And you said a lot of things that didn't make sense."
- "You promised to come to my class play, and then you got sick again. I was really disappointed."
- "Sam had to cover for you on Tuesday when you didn't get back from lunch until three in the afternoon. When you did arrive, you were slurring your words."
- "At the office party, you had four drinks in a row and then spilled your fifth all over somebody. I was embarrassed for you and worried that you might lose your job."

Each incident should be described in unsparing detail. The more incidents that each group member can list, the better.

The age of technology may have brought us the ultimate intervention tool: the camcorder (video camera). As these are becoming more affordable, more families are buying them. Nothing has quite as much shock value—and is harder to deny—than a full-color, stereo videotape of the alcoholic weaving around, slurring his or her words, and generally behaving inappropriately. If you have a camcorder, use it!

Step 2: Find out About Treatment Options in Your Area

The ultimate goal of the intervention process is to get the person into treatment or some other form of continuing care. You should be prepared to suggest this at the intervention itself—and to offer specific recommendations. It is wise to make an advance reservation at a treatment center or clinic; if the wall of defenses crumbles, the victim may be willing to go then and there.

There are several sources to consult. You may want to start by calling your family doctor for advice. Or visit your local library. One book you may find useful is *Roads to Recovery*, edited by Jean Moore (New York: Macmillan, 1985); she lists several hundred residential treatment facilities nationwide and provides brief descriptions of each.

Or check the White Pages of your telephone directory for the following:
- Alcoholics Anonymous (A.A.)
- (Your city, county, or region) Committee on Alcoholism or Council on Alcoholism
- Division on Alcoholism, Public Health Department
- Division on Alcoholism, State Health Department
- (Your state) Department of Mental Health
- (Your state, city, or county) Medical Society

In the Yellow Pages, look under "Alcoholism Information and Treatment Centers," "Family Service Organizations," and "Mental Health Clinics." Addresses and phone numbers for national organizations that can help can be found at the end of this book.

Once you have a list of possibilities, *find out more.* Request copies of brochures or other publications. Ask for complete program descriptions. Do they have an aftercare program? What percentage of their patients are still recovering after one year? Two years? Ten years? Does the program stress treatment of the entire family through A.A., Al-Anon, Alateen, Narcotics Anonymous, or a similar group that integrates the principles of the Twelve Steps? And—importantly—does the program consider intervention a viable and worthwhile approach? Some do not.

Don't rest until you have at least one treatment option that seems workable. *You are not ready to do the intervention until you have performed this critical task.* When interventions do not result in victims accepting care, it's because the intervention team is unprepared in this area. If the chemically dependent person does express willingness to go into treatment and you can't respond with a name, address, and telephone number, then the wall of defenses may well rise up again, stronger than before. And your other efforts will have been in vain.

Rehearsing the Intervention

It is recommended that you conduct one or two "rehearsals"—practice sessions—prior to the actual intervention. These should be attended by everyone who will be at the intervention, with the exception of the chemically dependent person. Each member of the intervention team should come prepared with his or her written list of facts about the chemically dependent person's behavior.

Rehearsals perform several functions in addition to the obvious one of preparing team members for the intervention.
* They help family members and other concerned people to realize that they are not alone—that others have been affected, too.

- They provide a forum for mutual support and understanding.
- They alleviate tension and fear and reduce the likelihood that people will say unclear or unfocused things, or things they never really meant to say.
- They require team members to focus on their choices and the possible outcomes of those choices.
- They establish a climate for change and inspire the belief that it *is* possible to do something about the problem.

You may want to devote part (or all) of your first rehearsal to reviewing the characteristics of the disease of chemical dependence. Give people a chance to ask questions and share what they know.

When you are reasonably sure that all team members have some understanding of the disease and its effects, you are ready to move on.

Step 1: Designate a chairperson

Team members should agree on one person to "direct" the rehearsals and the intervention itself. If the victim's employer or immediate supervisor is part of the team, there are two good reasons why he or she might be your first choice: his or her management experience, and the fact that he or she is *not* a family member. Spouses and adult children who have suffered a great deal of emotional pain as a result of living with the chemically dependent person are usually not suited for this role.

The chairperson's primary responsibility will be ensuring that the intervention does not turn into just another family row. Thus, team members should also agree to follow his or her direction. When the chairperson says, "All right, Mary, it's time to let Fred have his say," then Mary should give the floor to Fred.

Step 2: Go over each item on the written lists that team members have prepared

Team members should read their lists aloud, one item at a time, and each item should be either approved by the team or revised as necessary.

Remember that these should be *specific* descriptions of incidents or behaviors that are related to the chemically dependent person's use of alcohol or drugs. They should be totally honest and as detailed as possible. They should be devoid of value judgments, generalizations, and subjective opinions.

Be alert to overtones of self-pity or hostility—emotions that can block communication and turn the intervention into a shouting match or a stalemate. The *only* emotion present in these statements should be one of genuine concern.

If children need to be coached in reading their lines, take this opportunity to help them. Resist the urge to put words in their mouths; it's preferable if they say things in their own way and don't sound as if they're parroting the adults on the team.

Reviewing team members' lists is important for two reasons. First, it gives people the chance to "get their stories straight"—to figure out exactly what they want to say and how they want to say it. And second, it works to break the "rule of silence."

There is a pattern that is typical of almost every chemically dependent situation, whether at home or on the job. As the victim moves into increasingly bizarre or destructive behaviors, there are usually several witnesses. But they tend not to share what they know with one another. They are afraid that doing so will hurt the victim, or they hesitate to speak out because of some kind of misplaced loyalty to him or her. Whatever the reason for their silence, it works to support the sickness—to enable it to progress and worsen.

Many an intervention rehearsal has been interrupted by cries of "I didn't know you knew that!" or "I thought I was the only person who noticed that!" Some secrets turn out not to be so secret after all. Others, revealed at last, work to strengthen team members' sense of commitment. As more than one person has said, "If I had known even half of what I've heard tonight, I would have done this sooner!"

Step 3: Determine the order in which team members will read their lists during the intervention

Someone will have to go first! And second . . . and third. Determining the order ahead of time will prevent awkward pauses and keep the victim from interrupting or sabotaging the process.

It is best to start with someone who has a close and influential relationship with the chemically dependent person and stands the greatest chance of breaking through the wall of defenses. Often the best choice is his or her employer or supervisor.

Don't rely on memory for this step; the chairperson should write down the order and bring this record to the intervention, prepared to remind people as necessary that their turn has come.

Step 4: Choose someone to play the role of the chemically dependent person during the rehearsals

Although this is not required, it can be extremely helpful. One purpose of the rehearsals is to give team members a feel for what the real intervention will be like—all the way down to the probable objections, denials, excuses, and outbursts from the person for whose benefit the intervention is being done.

You may want to pass this role along from one team member to the next, giving everyone a chance to voice the objections, denials, excuses, and outbursts he or she may already have heard from the chemically dependent person. The point is to be aware of these and prepared to respond to them. It is highly unlikely that the victim will sit through the entire intervention without saying a word; it's best, therefore, to anticipate what he or she will say and decide ahead of time precisely how to respond. This leads us to the next preparatory step.

Step 5: Determine the responses that team members will make to the chemically dependent person

The decisions to take part in the intervention represents only part of the commitment that each team member must make. Now is the time to discover just how far people are willing to go and what they are willing to do to convince the victim to accept help.

A wife may say, "I've had it with him. If he doesn't get help, he can move out—or I'll take the kids and go." Does she mean it? *Will* she take the kids and go? Does she have somewhere to go to? Has she said all this before, and let it pass?

A supervisor may say, "Her production is way down, and she's having a harmful effect on her co-workers. They've been complaining to me about their extra workload. If she doesn't enter treatment, I'll have to fire her." Can he do this? Will he?

A neighbor may say, "I've put him up on my living-room couch for the last time. Unless he gets help, my door stays closed." Does he mean it? The next time the victim shows up and pleads for a place to sleep, will the neighbor turn him away?

A child may say, "I'm not getting in the car anymore when

Mom is driving. She scares me when she's drunk. From now on, I'll get rides from my friends' parents, or I'll stay home." Will she stick to it? Are there friends she can call for rides? What if she can't find anyone to drive her someplace she desperately wants to go?

Most people involved with the chemically dependent person will be accustomed to giving ultimatums—and equally accustomed to backing down. That process must come to an end.

Responses must be both *realistic* and *firm*. If the wife isn't genuinely prepared to take the kids and leave, she shouldn't say that this is what she plans to do. The supervisor should find out precisely what his company's policy is on chemical dependence, determine an action (or series of actions), and be ready to follow through.

What if the victim stands up and threatens to walk out during the intervention? Someone must be prepared to say, "Please sit down and hear us out." What if he or she verbally attacks a team member midway? That person must be prepared to continue reading his or her list anyway, all the way to the end. What if the victim bursts into tears and vows to reform? While it's tempting to accept such a vow on face value and stop the intervention then and there, it isn't at all wise to do so. The team should be prepared to move on to the conclusion—the point at which everyone has had his or her say, and the chemically dependent person is told that he or she must accept help of some kind.

Each action on the part of the chemically dependent person must be met with a reaction that is in keeping with the tone and purpose of the intervention. If the most appropriate reaction is an ultimatum, the person who delivers it must be ready to carry it out.

Step 6: Conduct the rehearsal

The rehearsal—and the intervention itself—should begin with a simple and empathic introductory statement from the chairperson. It might go something like this:

> "_____ (the name of the chemically dependent person), we're all here because we care about you and want to help. This is going to be difficult for you and for us, but one of the requests I have to start out with is that you give us the chance to talk and promise to listen, however hard that may be. We know it's not going to be easy for the next little while. . . . Would you help us by just listening?"

Notice that this statement clearly establishes the chemically dependent person's role as *listener*—and the intent of the group to keep him or her in that role.

Next, the team member chosen to go first should read through his or her written list. The person who is playing the part of the chemically dependent person may now bring his or her acting skills to the fore. What is he or she likely to say? How is he or she likely to behave? Most team members already will have had some sort of confrontation with the chemically dependent person; they may even be able to quote him or her. ("What do you mean, I have a problem? *You're* the one with the problem. If you'd quit nagging me, I'd quit drinking!") Practice responding with, "Please listen to what I have to say . . .," followed by more from the lists.

Each team member should have the opportunity to read through his or her lines and predict how the chemically dependent person may react. Meanwhile, the chairperson should serve his or her primary function of keeping team members on track. A rehearsal can be awesomely true-to-life; it is not unusual for team members to revert to accusations or generalizations, or to get carried away by their emotions. That is why each person should also practice expressing his or her caring and concern for the victim of the disease.

Try preceding each complaint with a positive statement: "Honey, you've always been a great husband, but I'm worried about you. Last week, when you'd been drinking, you drove right through the garage door...." "Mom, I really appreciated all the effort you put into my birthday party. But I was really embarrassed when you feel over the chair. I knew you were drinking wine instead of punch...." "Howard, your co-workers like you a lot. Everyone says that you're always willing to help out in a pinch. But you've been coming back from lunch later and later with alcohol on your breath, and last week I saw you sleeping at your desk."

The intervention process assumes that reality will break through somewhere along the line. At some point, the chemically dependent person will "see" his or her life *as it really is*—perhaps for the first time in years. Those who have participated in interventions describe the remarkable changes that take place. The room is permeated with a feeling of relief, and often of love. Team members are simultaneously exhausted and filled with hope. Any anger the victim may have been feeling is replaced by shock and anguish, and sometimes profound embarrassment. More than one has looked around the room and said, "My God, I didn't realize I had hurt you all so much. I'm sorry!"

While this may feel like the end of the intervention, it is only the end of the *first stage*. It is equally important to rehearse what comes next: insisting that the victim agree to accept help, and presenting the available options. The options, which you will have carefully researched, should be narrowed down to *this* hospital, *that* treatment center, or, in some cases, outpatient counseling and A.A. Allowing the victim to choose from among them will help to restore some measure of his or her dignity.

Of course, there is always the possibility that he or she will insist that treatment is unnecessary because a decision to stop drinking has been made from the heart. You know that it can't last, so you should be prepared to try an alternate approach. (We call it the "What If" response.) "You've made that decision before. Go ahead and try. But *what if* you take even one more drink? Will you agree to accept help then?"

In all probability, the victim will make a sincere effort to stop drinking on his or her own. But *just because a person stops drinking does not mean that he or she starts recovering.* The disease—including the emotional syndrome—is still present and as virulent as ever. This results in what is commonly called the "dry drunk."

What are the signs of a dry drunk? Irritability, anxiety, nervousness, resentment, and self-pity, to name a few. The person may overreact to simple frustrations, be hypersensitive or hypercritical, and generally behave unpredictably. Often the people around him or her will yearn for the good old drinking days, when the person was easier to live with!

In other words, while abstinence is an important goal, it is not the *only* goal. In truth, it is a single step, albeit a significant one, on the road to leading a full and fulfilling life once more. Stopping drinking by itself creates a vacuum, and living in that vacuum can be pure hell.

The central goal of recovery—and of the kinds of care that promote it—is the restoration of the victim's ego strength. The *whole person* must be treated, and that includes the mind *and* the body. The chemically dependent person suffers emotionally, mentally, and spiritually as well as physically. The best treatment programs available today recognize this, and they make use of interdisciplinary teams that include psychologists, psychiatrists, chemical dependence counselors, social workers, members of the clergy, physicians, and nurses.

Thus the second stage of the intervention—which you should practice as thoroughly as the first—involves eliciting a firm agreement from the victim to accept help. You *must* be

351

prepared with one or more concrete suggestions: "You have an appointment to see Dr. so-and-so right after we're through here; I'll drive you." Or: "We've reserved space for you in such-and-such a hospital. I already have your plane ticket, and your bag is packed and waiting in the car."

Try to anticipate as many objections, excuses, and well-meaning promises as you can—and prepare a firm response to each.

With so much work to do prior to the actual intervention, it's easy to see the necessity for one or more rehearsals. In fact, you may conduct as many as you wish; the more prepared you are, the more able you will be to deal with the realities of the situation. Just remember that time is of the essence. The sooner you arrest the progress of the disease, the sooner the victim can begin the process of recovery.

Finalizing the Details

When will the intervention be held? Schedule it for a time during which the chemically dependent person is likely to be sober. It's best if this is also a time soon after a drinking or using episode—for example, a Saturday morning following a regularly scheduled Friday night out. If the person is feeling under the weather as a result, that could work to your advantage, since his or her defenses will be proportionally weakened.

Where will the intervention be held? Choose a place that won't arouse too much anxiety in the victim, since you do not want to raise his or her defenses. It should also be a place where there will be no interruptions.

Who will be responsible for ensuring that the chemically dependent person arrives at the intervention site? That person should say only what is necessary to cause the person to attend.

Will anyone else need help getting there? Who will call the others to remind them of the time and place?

Which team member will ask the chemically dependent person for the commitment to listen to what the team has to say? Who will make the necessary arrangements for the person to go into treatment, provided that he or she agrees to accept help immediately? Who will explain the treatment and recovery plan?

Leave nothing to chance—not even the most minute detail. You will never again have the element of surprise so completely on your side. Use it!

Should You Seek Professional Help?

The introduction to this chapter expresses the Johnson Institute philosophy that *anyone who sincerely wants to help, can help.* Chances are you're quite capable of doing an intervention without the assistance of a qualified professional. However, *if you feel the need for such assistance, you should seek it.*

It is recommended that you conduct an initial face-to-face interview with any professional with whom you are considering working. Find out the following:

- Does he or she recognize chemical dependence as a disease?
- Does he or she support and believe in the intervention process? (Those who do will forego the classic counseling approach—"Do you think you could get the person in to see me?"—and focus instead on assisting those people who can intervene more effectively.)
- Has he or she had firsthand experience with intervention?

If the answer to all three questions is yes, you are on your way toward a productive relationship.

There are many excellent reasons to enlist the aid of a professional counselor, especially one who will commit to the entire process. To begin with, a counselor's position outside the circle of those who are directly involved with the chemically dependent person can ensure objectivity. A counselor makes a good chairperson and may also be skilled at playing the part of the chemically dependent person during rehearsals; he or she has probably seen and heard all (or most) of what you will witness during the intervention.

A counselor can provide valuable input during the gathering of data, ranging from going over team members' lists to recommending available treatment options. He or she will also be trained to alleviate team members' fears and anxieties about the intervention.

Finally, the counselor can help you and the other team members to understand how living, working, or closely associating with a chemically dependent person can lead to the parallel symptoms of co-dependence. He or she can also help you to understand and come to terms with your own enabling behaviors—and identify your own needs for treatment and recovery.

A few words of caution: At the Johnson Institute, we have grown concerned in recent years over the tendency of some counselors to prolong the intervention process. While they conduct one preliminary meeting after another with the chemically dependent person's family members and friends, the disease rages on unabated. Two to three educational and practice sessions are acceptable and even advisable, but there is seldom a need to undergo several months of counseling or preparation prior to the intervention. Afterward, perhaps, but not before. Your most pressing goal should be that of arresting the disease, and the best time to do that is as soon as possible. Your counselor should have the same goal and the same sense of urgency.

VERNON E. JOHNSON, D.D.

This section is taken from *Intervention: How to Help Someone Who Doesn't Want Help*, published by the Johnson Institute.

CHAPTER SEVENTEEN

Initiating the Intervention

It's time to act. You now have the ability and the resources to arrest the disease of chemical dependence and help the person you care about to start on the road to recovery.

You may be nervous. You may be fearful. You may be worried about the unpleasant scene you suspect will ensue. But your overriding feelings at this point should be those of commitment and genuine concern.

As you prepare to walk through the door to wherever the intervention is to be held, take a moment to congratulate yourself for going as far as you have. You have made the effort to learn about the disease and how it is affecting you; you have undertaken the arduous and painful task of looking back at the person's behaviors and seeing them for what they are; and you are willing to put your own relationship with him or her on the line. The Good Samaritan himself could have done no more.

An Intervention Scenario

No one can tell you precisely how to conduct your intervention. There are simply too many variables: the condition of the chemically dependent person, the stage to which the disease has progressed, the personalities of the team members, the dynamics of the interpersonal relationships, how much the team members know about chemical dependence, the presence (or absence) of a trained professional, the treatment options available, and so on.[1]

We can, however, walk you through a scenario that represents some of the events that may occur during an intervention. While no intervention is "typical," the following should be fairly representative of what goes on.

The person about to be intervened upon is our old friend from Chapter Two, Ed. His wife, Caroline, has spent the past several weeks learning about chemical dependence—reading books and articles and talking with friends who have chemically dependent loved ones. She had an especially long conversation with her sister in another city, whose husband has been recovering for five years.

She also had a private meeting with Ed's supervisor, Bob. After reviewing company policy, Bob has agreed to take a hard line with Ed and insist that he accept treatment. The company's

---

[1] There are some very special circumstances when a team comprised of laypersons should *not* attempt to do an intervention.

It is strongly recommended that you seek professional help before proceeding should any of the following apply:
- The chemically dependent person has a history of mental illness
- His or her behavior has been violent, abusive, or extremely erratic
- He or she has been profoundly depressed for a period of time
- You suspect polydrug abuse but lack sufficient information or eyewitness accounts of the victim's actual usage

We have noted that the person must be sober during the intervention. But while it is fairly easy to recognize the signs of alcohol consumption, the presence of other drugs or combinations of drugs may not be as obvious. Some have been known to produce psychotic or near-psychotic states. *If you cannot be certain that the individual is chemically free at the time the intervention is scheduled, wait and seek professional help before trying again.*

insurance will cover it, and Ed's job will be waiting for him when he returns.

This is the intervention team that Caroline has gathered:
- Bob, who will serve as chairperson
- Melanie, Ed and Caroline's 24-year-old daughter
- Tom, their 16-year-old son
- Howard, a neighbor and close friend to Ed

The intervention is scheduled for ten o'clock on Saturday morning in Bob's office. Bob has asked Ed to come in to prepare for a report that is due to a client on Monday. He will arrive at ten, and Caroline, Melanie, Tom, and Howard will walk through the door together at 10:15. The team has met twice before to rehearse the intervention and finalize their lists.

Promptly at 10:15, Ed looks up to see Caroline, Melanie, Tom, and Howard enter Bob's office.

Ed: "What's going on?"

Bob: "I'll tell you in a minute, Ed. Caroline, come on in and help the others get situated. Melanie and Tom, it's nice to see you again."

Ed: "I'd think it was my birthday, except that everyone has such a long face. Come on, someone, clear up the mystery."

The team members are seated and ready to begin. As chairperson, Bob begins.

Bob: "Ed, I want you to know that this is going to be tough for all of us. I did want to talk about the report, but the more important reason for this meeting is the one that brought your family here. I'm relieved that we can finally bring it out into the open. None of us had any desire to withhold anything from you, and in fact we were uncomfortable doing so. But we wanted to be sure to do this right.

"Now I'm going to ask you to do something for us, and that's to give us a chance to talk. Promise to listen, however difficult that may be. We know it's not going to be easy for you. . . . Would you help us by just listening?"

Ed: "What's this all about?"

Bob: "We've been getting together over the past few weeks because we all care about you and are deeply concerned about what's been happening to you. If you'll hear us out, I'm sure you'll understand why we feel as we do. We're here to talk about your drinking, and all we ask is that you hear us out. Will you do that?"

Ed (glaring): "I can't believe this. I thought you wanted me here to work on that report."

Bob: "We're going to table that for right now, because this is really more important."

Ed (turning to face Caroline): "I suppose you're behind this. You've been after me for years about my drinking."

Caroline: "We're all here together because we all care about you, Ed. Melanie and Tom and Bob and Howard and I all care about you very much."

Bob: "Ed, this is really quite serious. I understand that you might be feeling angry right now, but if you decide not to participate, or to keep interrupting, then there could be serious consequences."

Ed: "Are you telling me that my job is at stake?"

Bob (nodding): "It could come to that. But I don't want to talk about that now. Instead, let's all listen to what Melanie has to say."

Ed: "All right, I'll listen. I won't promise to like it, but I'll listen."

Bob: "That's all we ask. Go ahead, Melanie."

Melanie reaches into her purse and takes out her list. She looks nervously at her father before beginning.

Melanie: "Dad, you know that I've always loved you. Nobody could have had a better or more considerate father. I remember all the time we spent together when I was little—especially the camping trip you arranged for the two of us when I was nine.

"But lately I've been really worried about you. Whenever

Mom invites me over for dinner, you never make it through the meal without several drinks. And then it seems we always get in an argument. Last Sunday you almost threw a glass at me. That's not like you, Dad. You never raised a hand to me before you started drinking."

Ed: "Melanie, I was just kidding. . . ."

Melanie: "I was frightened. Remember I left early? That was why."

Ed: "Well, if that's all. . . ."

Melanie: "It isn't. Last month I brought Sam, a new guy I was dating, over to meet you and Mom. It was obvious that you had already been drinking, but you got out the liquor and started mixing cocktails anyway. Before long you were stumbling around and slurring your words. I was very embarrassed, Dad. And after that I didn't hear from Sam again."

Ed: "Surely you don't think that's my fault!"

Melanie: "Then there was last Christmas eve. I was singing a solo in the church choir, and you and Mom were supposed to come to hear me. She showed up by herself and said that you had the flu. The truth was, you were passed out on the couch. You'd been drinking since early afternoon."

And so it goes, item after item. By the time Melanie has finished reading, Ed is sitting in stony silence. Then Howard begins.

Howard: "Ed, you're the best bridge partner I've ever had. And you've been a good friend for years. But I'm concerned about your drinking, too."

Ed (sarcastically): "Well, Howard, we've tipped a few together, as I recall. Besides, weren't you the one who taught me how to mix the perfect martini?"

Howard: "Ed, the last time we got together for a game you arrived intoxicated. It was obvious to everyone there. Then you proceeded to fix yourself another few drinks over the next hour or so. You couldn't concentrate on the game, and you started telling some long involved story that went nowhere.

You played out of turn and finally we had to call it quits."

Ed: "Okay, so I got distracted. There's been a lot on my mind lately."

Howard: "Two weeks ago, when you asked to borrow my car because yours was at the station being serviced, I had to say no. That's because the last time I let you have it, you left it in a parking lot downtown overnight. And you didn't even remember *which* parking lot. Caroline told me that you came home in a cab and that you had been drinking."

Ed: "I found your car the next day, didn't I? Besides, I thought Caroline and I agreed to keep that between the two of us. So much for secrets!"

Howard: "Remember the last time you were invited to Stan's for a party? You not only threw a pass at Elizabeth, you were rude to my wife, too. She decided to brush it off, but she was really upset.

"I had seen you making yourself a drink earlier. You poured a whole glass of bourbon and drank it, and then you mixed yourself another. I know you didn't see me watching. I'm really concerned about you."

Ed: "Great. Now people are spying on me. Are we almost through here?"

Bob: "Ed, please hear us out. We know it isn't easy. It's tough on all of us."

Ed folds his hands across his chest and stares at the ceiling. He is still staring at the ceiling when Howard finishes reading and the turn passes to Tom.

Tom: "Dad, this is hard for me. I'm afraid that you're going to get mad at me. We've already had our share of problems. But I love you, Dad. And I can't sit back and watch you do this to yourself and Mom and me and Melanie."

He takes a deep breath before beginning to read.

Tom: "Dad, remember last summer when we took that camping trip? You kept getting out of the car, supposedly to check the trunk and find out what was rolling around in it. I knew that it was a bottle, and that every time you stopped you were sneaking a drink. By the time we got to the campsite, you were loaded."

Ed: "Tom, that's not fair. I thought we had a great time."

Tom: "Well, we didn't. At least, I didn't. I spent the whole weekend worrying if you were going to tumble into the campfire or get lost in the woods. You were drunk most of the time, Dad. I couldn't wait to get back home."

Ed: "You just wanted to be back here with your friends. I know it's hard for a teenager to spend a weekend with his old man."

Tom: "That's not true! But Dad, it's not any fun when you're drinking. Can't you see what your drinking is doing to all of us? Melanie and Mom and me?"

Bob: "Tom, please keep reading from your list. What's next on your list, Tom?"

Tom is visibly upset. In a moment, he takes another deep breath and starts reading again.

Tom: "Okay. Here goes. A couple of weeks ago I came home late and brought two friends into the house. I admit we made too much noise. Anyway, the next thing I knew you were standing in the kitchen in your pajamas. And you were shouting at me, and swearing at me, in front of my friends. Everyone could tell you were drunk. You were drunk in front of my friends!"

As Tom goes on reading, Ed pretends not to listen. He shifts in his chair, looks at his watch, reties his shoelaces. He avoids the eyes of everyone in the room.

When Tom finishes, Bob pulls his list from his pocket. He lays it on the table in front of him and starts to read from it.

Bob: "Ed, you've always been a terrific employee. During the first five years you were here, sales soared and you were largely responsible. But that's not the case anymore. For the past several months your performance has gone way down."

Ed: "Bob, be realistic. Our whole industry is in trouble."

Bob: "Perhaps, but the only department in our company that's in trouble is yours. Your co-workers are complaining that you're not carrying your share of the workload. Your reports aren't up to snuff. When we lost the Martin account, and I asked Stu Martin why, he told me that he couldn't work with you anymore. He didn't want to say anything against you, but I have suspected for a long time that that account was in trouble because of your drinking."

Ed: " Did he also tell you how much grief he gave me when I was only a week late with his order?"

Bob: "Last Monday you came in from a two-hour lunch reeking of alcohol. You refused to take calls for the rest of the afternoon."

Ed: "I've seen you have a drink during lunch yourself."

Bob: "I don't do it every day. You do. Even when you eat in the cafeteria, you somehow manage to smell of liquor by the middle of the afternoon."

Ed stands up.

Ed: "All right. Wait here. I'll show you."

He leaves the room, and in less than a minute he's back — carrying a bottle. He puts it down in front of Bob.

Ed: "I'll admit, I had it in my desk. Maybe I have an occasional pick-me-up during the day. But that's all over. I'll never do it again, I promise."

Bob: "That's great, Ed, and I'm sure you mean it. But the rest of the group and I have decided that you need help sticking to that kind of decision."

Ed: "What do you mean, help? Are you talking about detox or something?"

Bob: "Let's listen to what Caroline has to say, and then we'll let you decide. Ready, Caroline?"

Caroline stares down at her list as if trying to memorize it.

Everyone waits quietly. Finally she looks up and at her husband.

Caroline: "Ed, I married you because I loved you, and I still love you. But I'm at the end of my rope. Lately I've been tempted to ask you to move out, to leave Tom and me alone. I'm scared when you drink, and I'm afraid that you might hurt us.

"Two weeks ago you didn't get home from work until ten o'clock. When I asked you where you'd been, you hit me and told me to mind my own business. In all the years we've been together, nothing like that has ever happened."

Tom (shocked): "Mom! You never said anything about that in our other meetings."

Caroline: "I wanted to say it to your father first. I wanted to let him know that for the first time in more than 25 years of marriage, he frightens me."

Ed looks down from the ceiling at Caroline, and some of the defensiveness goes out of his posture.

Ed: "Honey, I'm really sorry. I don't know what got into me. I swear it will never happen again."

Caroline: "I just want you to get better, so things can be the way they used to be. Ed, I've been handling the checkbook for months now. I've been covering your bad checks, and sorting out your financial messes, and taking money out of our savings to make up for the overdrafts. Last month you overdrew more than $500 and never even realized it. The more you drink, the more the money seems to disappear. You used to keep track of every penny you spent."

Ed: "I make a good salary. I don't have to keep track of every penny anymore. We have plenty to live on."

Caroline: "Last month you left your wallet in a bar. You didn't even notice until three days later. I was on the phone immediately to department stores and bank card companies, but whoever took your wallet had three whole days to use your cards. I told our creditors some made-up story about where you'd lost it because I was ashamed to tell the truth."

Ed squirms in his chair. Caroline continues reading.

Caroline: "Last week, when we went out to dinner, I had to sneak the car keys out of your jacket and hide them in my purse so you wouldn't insist on driving. You had finished off a bottle and a half of wine all by yourself. I wasn't about to get in the passenger seat."

Ed: "I'm a safe driver. Have I ever had an accident?"

Caroline (speaking very softly): "Not yet. But three weeks ago you came awfully close. Remember when that little boy ran out from between the parked cars? I had to grab the wheel. You'd been drinking that afternoon—even though you hid the bottle in the garbage, I knew you'd been drinking—and if I hadn't reacted as quickly as I had, you would have hit that little boy. And you might have killed him."

For the first time, Ed has nothing to say.

Caroline: "I'm not going to cover for you anymore. I'm not going to tell people like Melanie that you have the flu when you're really sleeping off a drunk. I'm not going to call Bob and make excuses for your tardiness. And I'm not going to stick around and wait until you really do hurt me or Tom. It has to stop, Ed."

By now Ed is looking down at the floor.

Bob: "We're almost through, Ed. I know this is painful, but we're almost through. Everyone has one or two more things to say to you. When they're finished, we can all talk."

Melanie: "Dad, I hardly know how to say this, but I don't even like coming home anymore. I never know what condition I'm going to find you in. It used to be such a happy house, and now there's so much tension. It makes me want to stay away."

Howard: "Ed, I value your friendship, and I can't stand to see this happening. And I can't have you over to our house anymore until things change. Linda cares about you, too, but she feels protective of the kids. She doesn't want you around them when you've been drinking."

Caroline: "Ed, I can't go on this way any longer. Your drinking is affecting me, too. Sometimes I think I'm going crazy. We don't talk anymore, we don't do things together like we used to, and I feel that I have to watch over you every second. One thing I've learned in these past few weeks is that I'm as sick as you are. We *all* need help, Ed."

Melanie: "Mom is right, Dad. What you've got is a disease called chemical dependence, and it's catching. We've got it, too, Tom and Mom and I, in our own way."

"But you don't have to stay sick, and neither do we. You can get better. You can get better. We can all get better, but we have to stick together."

Tom: "Dad, please say yes. I love you, Dad. We all love you, and we don't like to see you like this. You're not the same person I used to know. I'm ashamed to ask people over to the house because I never know what shape you're going to be in. I feel like I don't have a father anymore."

Bob: "I mean what I said earlier, Ed. You've got to get your performance back up. But I don't think you can until you accept some help for your drinking problem."

Ed covers his face with his hands. After a moment or two, he looks up and into the faces of everyone in the room. When he speaks, it is barely a whisper.

Ed: "Good Lord, is it possible that everything you're saying is true? Have I really been such a jerk?"

Caroline: "We're not here to call you a jerk or to blame you for anything, but to get all of us some help. I know I need it as much as you do."

Ed: "Well, just what is it you want me to do? Do you want me to pack my things and move out? Is that what you want?"

Caroline: "No, it's not what we want. We want you to get better."

Bob: "Ed, alcoholism is a disease. With help, you can get well again."

365

Ed: "I don't understand. What do you mean, a disease? I can stop drinking whenever I want to. And I will, starting today. You'll see!"

Bob: "The people who will help you can tell you more about the disease. Quitting drinking is a lot harder than you think. Besides, there's more to it than that."

Ed (resolutely): "Bob, you know that when I make up my mind to do something, I do it. I mean what I'm saying: I'll never take another drink in my life."

Bob (looking Ed straight in the eye): "We're not here to have you promise you'll quit again. We're here to have you agree to accept help. It's time to try something new and different."

Ed: "What are you talking about—Alcoholics Anonymous or something like that? Some club for drunks and derelicts?"

Bob: "I think you'd be surprised by the kinds of people who go to A.A. But that's not where we want you to start. You can go to Park City Hospital, or you can go to North Treatment Center. They're expecting you at either place today."

Ed (obviously stunned): "Today? Wait just a minute. We have to talk about this some more. Besides, I can't go today. That report is due on Monday."

Bob: "We'll take care of it here. We can manage for a month without you. Besides, when you get back, you'll be so much better that you'll probably be twice as productive."

Ed: "A *month*? Did I hear you say a month?"

Bob: "That's how long the treatment program lasts. You go in today, and you come out 30 days from now."

Ed turns to Caroline.

Ed: "I can't leave you and Tom for a month."

Caroline: "I'll visit as soon as they'll let me. And I'll be there every day during Family Week."

Ed: "But it will take time to get ready and pack, and you probably have to make a reservation or something. . . Can't it wait until Monday?"

Caroline: "Your suitcase is already packed and ready to go. It's in the trunk of my car. If you need any other clothes, I'll make sure you get them."

Bob: "And if you go today, your job will be waiting for you when you return."

Ed: "And if I don't?"

Bob: "That's the only alternative you have, friend. I can't accept any other."

By now Ed is crying softly. Melanie moves to stand behind him and puts her arms around him.

Melanie: "Dad, this is going to help us all. You'll get better, and we'll get better too. Mom and I are going to our first Al-Anon meeting tonight."

Ed: "I can't believe this is happening. Why didn't anybody say anything about this earlier? Why didn't anybody tell me what I was doing to you?"

Caroline: "We all tried, but you didn't believe us. I understand now why that was. You couldn't see how sick you were. You didn't know. It's all right, Ed."

Bob: "Now we've got a decision to make. Which will it be, Ed? Park City or North?"

Early that afternoon, Ed checks into North Treatment Center. His wife and children are there for support. The intervention has been a success: Ed will get the help he needs.

The intervention described above proceeded exactly according to plan. That plan can be summarized by what we call the Five Principles of Intervention:

1. Meaningful people in the life of the chemically dependent person are involved.
2. All of the meaningful people write down specific data about the events and behaviors involving the dependent person's chemical use which legitimatize their concern.

3. All of the meaningful people tell the dependent person how they feel about what has been happening in their lives, and they do it in a nonjudgmental way.

4. The dependent person is offered specific choices—*this* treatment center or *that* hospital.

   Had Ed absolutely refused to consider either of these choices and vowed to quit drinking on his own, then the team would have presented the "What-If" question: "What if you do start drinking again? What if you have just one more drink?" They would have made an agreement with Ed that *if* he began using again, he would accept help. And they would have made him stick to it!

5. When the victim agrees to accept help, it is made available immediately.

At the Johnson Institute, we have learned that *if a team sticks to this plan, its chances of succeeding are eight in ten.* In my personal experience, I have expected it to work every time—and it has. A crack appears in the victim's wall of defenses and he or she agrees to accept some form of help.

What If the Intervention Doesn't Work?

What if the victim doesn't agree to accept help then and there? *Keep trying.* Don't give up! Remember that the victim's life depends on your continuing commitment.

We have found that intervention tends to have a cumulative effect. If the initial session doesn't propel the person into treatment, the second probably will—or the third. Sometimes it takes even more effort on the part of the team members to break down the victim's defense system. Rationalization, projection, denial, repression, and self-delusion combine to create a barrier to self-awareness that rivals the Great Wall of China.

But what of the truly "incorrigible" drinker, or the one who walks out of the intervention and never comes back, or the one who really is "too far gone" for help? If that person continues drinking and never enters treatment, has the intervention been a failure?

No, it has not. *Properly done*, intervention works every time. *Properly done*, there are no failures. Here are the reasons why:

- The people who do the intervening — the team members — are forever changed. They know that they are not alone. They know that help and support are available to them. Their lives are never the same afterward.
- The family unit is also changed — from the immobilized, fearful, guilty, shame-ridden group they once were to an entirely new dynamic. They know what chemical dependence is. They see its symptoms *in themselves*, and they seek help *for themselves*. They come to see that the chemically dependent person's sickness is *not their fault*. What a liberating realization this is!
- Finally, the victim is changed in relation to the drug. The crack in the wall of defenses has admitted knowledge that he or she will never again be able to fully deny. (As one spouse remarked, "At least we spoiled his drinking!")

In sum, intervention always has *some* effect, and that effect is invariably positive. There is no way it can ever make things worse. At the very least, it offers a chance for recovery where before none existed; at the most, it starts the whole family on the path toward fully living again.

It is to be hoped that these observations will move you to try yet one more time, if your first intervention does not result in the victim immediately accepting treatment.

VERNON E. JOHNSON, D.D.

This section is taken from *Intervention: How to Help Someone Who Doesn't Want Help*, published by the Johnson Institute.

CHAPTER EIGHTEEN

When A Teenager Needs Intervention

You have reason to believe that a teenager you know—your son or daughter, a student, an employee or a friend—is using alcohol or other drugs. You think you should do something because you feel responsible for him or her.

Wrong! You are not responsible *for* others, but *to* them. This is the first basic principle of intervention. Believing it will free you to exercise your responsibility in ways that work.

- "You are not responsible for others" means that you cannot control another person's behavior, feelings, or decisions.
- "You are responsible to others" means that you can control these two things: yourself and your environment.

You can control your own behavior toward, feelings about, and decisions concerning others. You can control the environment that is under your care—the home, the school, or wherever else you come into contact with teenagers as a person in authority.

This principle is easier to understand if we apply it to our interactions with little children. Picture, for example, a scene we've all witnessed more than once: a grocery store, a set of parents, and a three year old throwing a temper tantrum.

How do parents handle this situation? Some shout at the child. Some threaten the child. Some buy the child anything he or she wants, just to get a few moments of peace and quiet. Some hit the child.

In other words, the parents try to control the child's behavior. A far better approach is to ignore the child's behavior and control their own by not shouting, threatening, giving in, or hitting. If this doesn't get results, they can move on to controlling the environment: They can take the child out of the store.

That makes sense, you say. But what about the teenager who comes in two hours late, obviously intoxicated, loud and argumentative? (And he—or she—drove your car home!) Some behaviors can't be ignored. How do you control the environment? Do you remove the teenager from the premises, or is that even the thing to do? Do you yell and accuse and complain? Or do you look the other way, telling yourself that "kids will be kids"?

Now we're talking about the need for a whole new strategy, *but the principle is the same.* You can't control your teenager's behavior. You can't control his or her feelings. You can't make his or her decisions. But you *can* control how you yourself react to the situation, and you *can* control the environment to set the stage for positive change.

When you try to control the behavior of someone who uses alcohol or other drugs, you become what chemical dependence professionals call an *enabler.* Enablers are people—usually family or friends—who take responsibility for the behaviors, feelings, and decisions of the user. Out of love, concern, fear, or a combination of these, they react and behave in ways that shield the user from experiencing the consequences of drug use. They mean well, but *the effect of their actions is to make it easier for the user to keep using.*

Let's look at some examples of enabling behaviors. We'll take the scenario of the teenager (a boy, for the sake of convenience) coming home drunk. He stumbles into the house, where Mom and Dad are anxiously waiting.

Dad says: "You're drunk!" (*Accusing behavior.*) "You know our rules about drinking alcohol. You are NOT allowed to drink, and that's that." (*Laying-down-the-law behavior.*)

Mom says: "What's wrong with you? You know better than to drink and drive! Have you lost every bit of common sense?" (*Provoking behavior.*) "I'll bet it's those friends you've been hanging around with; I knew they were no good!" (*Laying-the-blame-else-where behavior.*)

Dad says: "It had better not happen again, or else!" (*Threatening behavior.*)

Mom says: "How could you do this to us? Don't you know how much we love you, and how hard we've worked to give you a good home?" (*Guilt-inducing behavior.*)

Dad says: (to Mom and himself) "I'm at my wits' end with this kid. If it isn't one thing, it's another. He never listens to us anymore." (*Feelings-of-helplessness behavior.*)

Mom says: "I can see that this conversation isn't doing any of us any good. And Frank (the son) looks terrible. Maybe this isn't the time to talk. Honey, why don't you go get ready for bed, and I'll come and tuck you in." (*Caretaking behavior.*)

Dad (grumbling) says: "And I'll go make sure the car is in the garage." (*Taking-responsibility-for behavior.*)

Both say: "Well, I guess it's no big deal . . . after all, boys will be boys." (*Making-excuses-for behavior.*)

What's happened here? The parents have let their son off the hook. They have helped him to avoid the consequences of his behavior. They have taken those consequences upon themselves and *enabled* him to keep using.

Intervention demands that one stop enabling (being responsible for) and start really caring (being responsible to). This is the first thing we teach people who live with drug abusers: *Stop trying to control them.*

My Aunt Liz, who died recently at age 93, had a saying she used when I was going through some tough times as a teenager: "You sat on the burner, baby . . . you sit on the blisters." What she meant was, "You made your choices . . . now you take the consequences." She never said, "Here, let me suffer for you; let *me* sit on your blisters." She was too smart for that!

Who sits on the blisters of the three year old throwing the tantrum in the frozen-foods aisle? The parents who shout, hit, or hand over the candy bar. Who sits on the blisters of the teenager who comes in drunk at 2 a.m.? The parents who yell, accuse, and complain or dismiss the whole thing as "normal teenage behavior" or "sowing wild oats."

Teenagers who use drugs are pros at getting others to sit on their blisters. Every time adults react to their behavior by showing anger, guilt, or hurt feelings, the adults are sitting on their blisters. And if others are willing to experience their pain, why should they change?

The second basic principle of intervention concerns the need for a "connector"—a significant other big person outside of the immediate family whom the teenager can trust and relate to. This person is called the "connector" because he or she "connects" with the teenager through unconditional acceptance.

He or she cares for the teenager *no matter what*, and there are no strings attached to that caring. (Another name for the connector is the "cookie person"—someone who gives out chocolate-chip cookies without reminding you to brush your teeth.) Everyone needs a connector; everyone needs the experience of being accepted unconditionally. Parents can't play this role because it's impossible to do that *and* fulfill one's responsibilities as parents.

So who can? That's a hard question nowadays. Prior to World War II, America was full of extended families. It was not uncommon to find grandparents, parents, aunts and uncles living under the same roof. Some of them were natural "connectors" or "cookie people." In most families today, however, both parents work or one parent is absent and the other relatives live somewhere else—across town or across the country.

We parents need help! We can't raise our children by ourselves. We can't love them unconditionally while at the same time making and enforcing the rules that will help them to grow into decent, responsible people. We need to find the "connectors" in their lives. Start thinking now about some possible "connectors" in the lives of the teenager(s) you know.

The third basic principle of intervention has to do with the need for a *network* of people willing and able to confront the teenager about his or her drug use. No one should attempt such a confrontation alone.

Chemical dependence has been called a "system illness." The chemically dependent teenager is trapped within a *delusional system* supported by many people. *It takes a system to crack a system.*

Successful intervention consists of people working together to confront the teenager's delusional system. They must present a united front. The teenager must hear the same message from all of them: "You are responsible for your own behaviors and feelings and decisions." You sat on the burner, baby ... you sit on the blisters.

Teenagers in trouble always manage to find the weak link—whether at home (parent against parent), at school (teachers against teachers or administrators), or in the community (courts against treatment programs or the schools). They always find a way to slip between the cracks. *If we really want to do something about adolescent alcohol or other drug use, we adults must work together.*

How Intervening With Teens Differs From Intervening With Adults

Intervening with teenagers is different in a number of important ways, and we need to understand these differences before we continue.

1. **Intervention with adults usually involves family members and employers; intervention with teenagers usually involves more "outside" people.**

A professional caregiver or other concerned person may not be able to count on the parents' support. A large percentage of young people in trouble with drugs have a chemically dependent parent. The parents may be so involved with their own problems that they simply can't help.

Some are rendered so psychologically and emotionally dysfunctional by their relationship with the chemically dependent person that they can't stop enabling long enough to help. They are *co-dependent* and are as deluded about addiction as the chemical dependent is.

We cannot wait for parents to recover before intervening with teenagers. We can, however, turn to the school, the court, and treatment centers for the help we need. Because chemical use has legal implications for adolescents, it's possible for schools or courts to require that intervention be done with or without the parents' involvement.

2. **Intervention with adults makes use of existing contracts; intervention with teenagers makes use of contracts developed especially for that purpose.**

Adults have marriage and employment contracts that can be put on the line during intervention. But most teenagers aren't married and don't have jobs (at least, not permanent ones), so these contracts don't exist for them. Special contracts must be developed for intervention purposes. These will be explained later in this chapter.

3. **Intervention with adults may require one session, or several; intervention with teenagers always requires more than one session.**

Since intervention with teenagers involves developing contracts, successful intervention will require more than one session. Usually, a series of contracts or agreements is developed, starting with the least restrictive and moving toward the most restrictive.

4. **Intervention with teenagers requires a more extensive network of significant people than intervention with adults.**

Intervention with adults usually involves the family, a boss, a friend, and maybe the court. Intervention with teenagers may involve the family, the school, the court, a treatment center, the church or temple, a hospital, a recreation center, and friends.

5. There are more support and aftercare programs for adults than for teenagers.

Adults coming out of treatment are encouraged to attend A.A. meetings and weekly support groups. Teenagers are encouraged to attend similar groups. But where do we send them after treatment? Back to school—and back to their using friends.

There is a pressing need for more support and aftercare programs in the school setting; for Alcoholics Anonymous, Narcotics Anonymous, and Cocaine Anonymous groups for teenagers; for aftercare groups in treatment programs; for nonchemical recreational activities; and for recovering teenagers who can serve as models for peers who have just gone through intervention. Unfortunately, many communities don't yet have such resources.

As a result, we must rely on intervention itself to do the job. That is one reason why intervention with teenagers always requires more than one session and is more of an ongoing process than intervention with adults.

6. Teenagers require different kinds of treatment than adults.

Adults usually respond to "therapy groups," such as A.A. groups. Teenagers need more experiential groups that include assertiveness training and classes that build self-esteem. They also need recreational and occupational therapy, tutoring in school subjects, and help in dealing with sexuality issues, grief issues, and children-of-alcoholics issues. In short, teenagers need more help in developing lifeskills.

Adult children of alcoholics who undergo treatment are encouraged to wait for six months to a year before tackling grief issues stemming from their childhood. If they were sexually abused as children, an even longer period of sobriety is recommended before starting to work on those issues.

Adults can afford to take their time because these are generally issues that relate to the past. For teenagers with alcoholic or abusive parents, these issues are very much in the present and cannot be set aside to be dealt with later. Support groups are essential during treatment, and child protection services must often be brought into the circle.

Why We Must Intervene

It's a terrible thing to discover that a teenager is dependent on alcohol or other drugs. And given the harmful effects that addiction has on one's life, it's natural to wonder, "Why doesn't he or she just QUIT?"

The answer is simple: Because he or she can't.

Chemically dependent people don't know that they have a problem. They can't see what's happening to them. They are *out of touch with reality*—delusional. Chemically dependent people are the last to realize that they have a disease, much less admit it—and much less do something about it.

That is why intervention is necessary. During intervention, people who *can* see what's happening present reality to the person who can't in a *receivable* way. As Vernon Johnson explains in Chapter 16, "By 'presenting reality,' we mean presenting *specific facts* about the person's behavior and the things that have happened because of it. 'A receivable way' is one that the person cannot resist because it is *objective, unequivocal, nonjudgmental,* and *caring*."

The object of intervention is to break through the delusional system in such a way that the chemically dependent person will accept the help he or she needs to arrest the disease and start recovering from it.

But intervention isn't just for the teenager who is harmfully dependent on chemicals (described as Level 4 in Chapter 4). It isn't just for the individual who has "hit bottom" and been expelled from school, kicked out of the house, arrested and jailed, or hospitalized after a suicide attempt. Intervention can "raise the bottom" for *any* teenager at *any* stage of the addiction process. In other words, *you don't have to wait until it seems too late.*

Successful intervention consists of three stages: *disengagement*, when you prepare for the intervention, *confrontation*, when you do the intervention, and *reintegration*, when you follow-up the intervention by helping the teenager live without chemicals.

Stage One — Disengagement

The first stage of intervention calls for you to break through the delusional system and *stop enabling*. To put some space between you and the teenager's power plays. TO BACK OFF.

The theme for this stage is *Take Care of Yourself*. This can be especially difficult for parents. We have been programmed to put our children first; anything else seems selfish. But if we really want to help our children, we must to put ourselves first.

Scripture teaches, "Love your neighbor as yourself." When we are busy enabling, we lose our ability to love ourselves. Our self-esteem suffers because we are trapped in a role doomed to failure: trying to control another person's behaviors, feelings and decisions. Disengagement allows you to step out of this role and start shoring up your battered self-esteem.

There are three steps to disengagement: *getting support for yourself, forming a network of people willing to help,* and *learning ignoring skills.*

Step One: Getting Support for Yourself

This is something you can do right away. You don't have to wait for others to change their behaviors first. You can start *now*. Here's how:

Learn about the disease of chemical dependence and how it affects teenagers. Read Chapter 4 of this book, if you haven't already. You should have a basic understanding of the addiction process, the feeling disease, and what alcohol and other drug use does to teenagers.

Join a support group of parents with troubled teenagers. Begun in 1971 by parents in southern California, Families Anonymous is a self-help program for families whose children exhibit destructive behaviors including alcohol or other drug use, truancy, running away, dropping out, sexual promiscuity, and more. It is based on the Twelve Steps of Alcoholics Anonymous (A.A.) and Al-Anon—proven programs of recovery for chemically dependent people and their families.

Both Families Anonymous and Al-Anon have chapters throughout the United States and Canada. You can find the addresses and phone numbers for these and other national organizations at the end of this book. Or consult the White Pages of your local telephone directory to find a group near you. You'll meet other parents who are struggling with problems just like yours. You'll discover that *you are not alone*. You'll be accepted unconditionally, with no questions asked, and this will make it easier to start loving yourself. And, you'll learn to accept the things you can't change and change the things you can—namely, yourself and your environment.

Make time for your own needs. Take more time to do less. The enabling triangle is a tiring place to be. Provoking, rescuing, and being a victim consumes a lot of time and energy. When you do succeed in backing off from trying to control other people's behaviors, feelings, and decisions, you'll find yourself with extra time on your hands. Fill it with things you want to do. Take "minute vacations" throughout the day as needed. Pick some flowers, listen to the rain, watch a sunrise, look for rainbows, gaze at the stars.

Set aside time each day for meditation. It might include prayer, scripture reading, reading poetry, listening to music, reading a good book, or just reflecting and relaxing your body. You'll have time to reexamine your expectations of yourself—as a parent, a spouse, a worker, a friend. Ask yourself how realistic they are, then lower them accordingly. Too often we parents set too-high goals for ourselves and our children.

Start listening to others. What are they saying? What do they mean? Start listening to yourself. What is your body saying? What do *you* want and need?

Start gathering data on your teenager's behaviors. Getting support for yourself also means determining that you haven't been imagining things—that your teenager really *does* have a problem and really *does* need help.

- Keep a daily journal of the troubling behaviors your teenager is exhibiting. It will help to convince you that you're not crazy. It will also help you to assess where your teenager is in the addiction process. And third, it will provide you with specific facts to present during the confrontation stage.
- Record behaviors you have observed *firsthand* that relate to your teenager's alcohol or other drug use. Avoid rumors and hearsay; these can always be dismissed or denied. To break through the layers of the delusional system, you will need to arm yourself with *objective facts*—not opinions, not judgements, but *facts*.
- Make your descriptions as specific as possible. For each incident you record, note when it happened, where it happened, what was said, what was done, who else was there to witness it, and how you felt about it. You can

never be too specific when describing behaviors connected with your teenager's drug use. Some parents have used tape recorders to capture the slurred speech, mumblings, or grandiose claims of their drunk or high teenagers. Some have even used video cameras.

Find out about resources in your community—places you can turn to for information, help, and support. You'll probably be surprised at how much is available in your area.

- Start by making a list of crisis numbers and putting it near your telephone. This should include emergency numbers (police, hospital emergency room, ambulance, your family physician) as well as the number of the local suicide hotline, detoxification center, treatment center, and juvenile court. Also list family members and friends you can count on to be there for you.
- Check the White Pages of your telephone directory for:
  —self-help groups (Alcoholics Anonymous, Narcotics Anonymous, Cocaine Anonymous, Families Anonymous, Al-Anon)
  —your county Social Services office
  —The Division of Alcoholism and Drug Abuse (you'll find this in either the Public Health Department or State Health Department or both)
- Check the Yellow Pages for:
  —Alcoholism Information and Treatment Centers
  —Drug Abuse Information and Treatment Centers
  —Mental Health Services
  —Human Services centers
  —Family Services organizations
- Contact national organizations for information on alcohol or other drug abuse; self-help groups for addicts, family members, and parents; and alcohol or other drug abuse prevention and education. Addresses and phone numbers can be found at the end of this book.

Seek professional help. You should *not* try to intervene by yourself. Successful intervention with teenagers requires a network of significant people working closely together. It's too easy for a teenager to discount what one person has to say—and it's too easy for one person to fall back into enabling behaviors. There are many experienced and capable professional caregivers who are ready and willing to assist you.

Start with your teenager's school. More and more school personnel (teachers, counselors, administrators) are being trained in intervention techniques. Check out the juvenile court outpatient and inpatient treatment centers, mental health clinics, county social services, recreational centers, and your church or temple. *Don't stop looking until you have found someone.* Interview each "prospective" by finding out the following:

- Does he or she recognize chemical dependence as a disease?
- Does he or she support and believe in the intervention process?
- Has he or she had firsthand experience in intervening with teenagers?

The person who meets all three requirements is the person you want at your side as you continue through the next two stages of intervention.

Step Two: Forming a Network of People Willing to Help

Once you find a professional caregiver, you can begin to develop the rest of your network of significant others. To create a united front, work with the caregiver to identify key people around the teenager. Who are the significant people in his or her life? Look to the immediate family (parents, siblings) and other relatives (grandparents, aunts and uncles). Does the teenager have any straight (non-using) friends who are concerned about his or her drug use?

Who are the connectors—the "cookie people"? Look to the school (teachers, coaches, counselors, outreach workers), the legal system (police, probation officers, judges), your church or temple (ministers, priests, or rabbis, lay volunteers), and treatment centers (mental health professionals, counselors, group leaders).

Contact these key people, explain the situation, and find out if they are willing to help. Then set up a meeting with the professional caregiver and the key people. This does not have to be a large group; five to seven people are usually enough. Try to get at least one representative from each agency the teenager is involved in (school, church or temple, legal). Friends can be important *as long as they are straight.*

Arrange to meet with a professional caregiver in his or her office. The caregiver will want to determine how much each key person knows about the disease of chemical dependence and evaluate their emotional capacity to disengage. The professional will then ask each person for specific, firsthand observations of the teenager's drug use. Finally, the professional should be able to provide you with information on various intervention, program, and treatment options.

Step Three: Learning Ignoring Skills

Teenagers are pros at baiting their parents. We *mean* to keep our cool, we *mean* to keep our voices down, but a well-placed word or phrase from the mouth of a teenager can have us off and running before we know it. It's not easy to disengage ourselves from these verbal power plays, but *it can be done.* We can learn to ignore them and not get hooked by them.

Author, counsellor, teacher, and lecturer Tom Alibrandi has come up with five words and phrases you can use whenever your teenager starts playing verbal games. They're short, easy to remember, and amazingly effective. They are: "Yes." "No." "Oh, really?" "Wow." and "Whatever."

Eight Tips to Help You Disengage

When you start disengaging from your role as enabler, your teenager can't help but notice. Until now, he or she has been able to count on you to play Provoker, Victim, and Rescuer roles. Their sudden absence signals a change in your relationship your teenager is bound to resist. He or she is liable to get very angry with you.

1. Don't take that anger personally. It's like standing still while your teenager throws garbage at you. Instead, get out of the way and let it hit the wall! You'll probably get angry in return; that's perfectly normal under the circumstances. BUT. . .

2. Don't confront your teenager when you're angry. Let him or her know how you feel, and explain that you need a cooling-off period. Set a time to talk later.

3. Avoid saying things you don't mean ("I wish you had never been born!) or can't enforce ("You're grounded for a 100 years!")

4. NEVER use violence, physical or verbal. Count to ten, count to 100, count to 1000—whatever it takes.

5. Don't nag your teenager or constantly remind him or her of the effects of alcohol or other drug use. Take a stand, talk about your concerns, keep the lines of communication open, and express your feelings at appropriate times—but don't nag. Remember, nagging equals provoking, and provoking equals enabling.

6. Don't clean up your teenager's messes. Allow him or her to take responsibility for his or her own predicaments.

7. Don't make excuses to family or friends about your teenager's drug use. Especially don't write excuses to the school for hangovers or absence or tardiness. Taking on your teenager's responsibilities equals rescuing and rescuing equals enabling.
8. Keep reminding yourself that chemical dependence is a disease. Your teenager isn't weak, lacking in will power, or a failure as a person; your teenager is sick. And it is not your fault. Repeat this until you believe it; it's true.

Stage Two — Confrontation

The second stage of intervention calls for you to *present reality to your teenager in a receivable way*. To help him or her accept that reality by SETTING LIMITS. To control the environments—home and school—where your teenager spends the most time.

Your job right now is to work with the other key people you have identified to let the teenager know that you're dead serious. If your teenager is chemically dependent, setting limits will give the sense of security he or she has lost to drugs.

The theme for this stage is *Take Back Your Environment*. Teenagers on alcohol or other drugs tend to control their environments. Parents feel like prisoners in their own homes. Teachers feel trapped in their own classrooms. Confrontation allows you to regain the control you have lost.

Before teenagers can accept the reality of how alcohol or other drugs are affecting them, *they must be straight*—they must stop using mind-altering chemicals. Getting them to stop isn't easy. This is why the united front is so important. Significant people in a teenager's life must work together to send this message:

Chemicals have affected your living at home, your progress at school, and your behavior in the community. They have affected you at all levels of your life: physical, mental, emotional, and spiritual. Since we cannot control your decision to use or not to use, we will control the environment by setting limits. Your behavior will tell us what limits to set. These limits will protect you while you regain control over your own life.

Of course the teenager will resist your efforts. You will be tempted to start enabling again, which is why it is critical for you not to attempt confrontation alone. You will need the support of other concerned people, and you will need the help of a professional caregiver.

Learning the "4 C's" of Confrontation

There are four essential parts to confrontation: *choices, consequences, contracts,* and *control.*

1. Choices: Confrontation is not punishment. It does not use violence, threats, shouting, judging, moralizing, or humiliation. It is based on respect and done in such a way that the teenager can receive the information you are presenting without losing face or feeling put down. It elicits the teenager's cooperation and involvement in the intervention process.

Never put a teenager in a corner without a way out. Always be prepared to offer choices. This gives the teenager a sense of dignity and control over his or her life.

There are three situations in which you should be prepared to offer choices to your teenager.

- When you are addressing a specific behavior. Your teenager is watching TV and hasn't done his homework. You say, "You can do your homework now and be free to go out after dinner, or you can wait until after we eat and stay in to do it. What do you want to do?"
- When you are determining consequences. Your teen-

ager breaks curfew by two hours. You say, "You have to come in two hours earlier next Friday night, or stay in for the next two nights. What do you want to do?"
- When you are enforcing consequences. Your teenager is caught with drugs at home, and your spouse doesn't know it yet. You say, "I can tell your father (or mother), or you can. How do you want to do it?"

2. Consequences: Although confrontation is not punishment, this doesn't mean it's permissive. Instead, it involves well-defined rules and consequences for breaking those rules. Rules set limits and perimeters to a teenager's environment. An effective rule is *specific* ("Your curfew on weeknights is 9:30"), *reasonable* ("That gives you time to spend with your friends and also get enough sleep"), and *enforceable* " (it's your home). Apply the same three criteria to rules about drug use. Make them *specific* ("NO USE whatsoever"), *reasonable* ("It's against the law"), and *enforceable* (again, it's your home).

Consequences can be either *natural* or *logical*. Natural consequences are those that happen on their own, with no action on your part. For teens who use drugs, a natural consequence might be a hangover. Logical consequences require some action on your part to help the teenager experience the full impact of his or her behavior. An effective logical consequence is *related* to the incident ("You were drinking in your car, so I'm going to take your keys away"), *reasonable* ("I'm going to keep them for a month"), and *set up in advance* with the teenager's knowledge ("We agreed earlier that if you drank in your car, you'd lose your keys for a month, so what I'm doing now is holding you to that agreement"). They must also be enforced calmly, with respect, and without anger.

Your professional caregiver can help you to determine other logical consequences. In addition, some may be set up by the school or the court. These might include:
- Detention in school for skipping classes
- Suspension from school for alcohol/drug possession

- Spending time in jail for DUI, illegal acts, or violent acts
- Required evaluations or attendance at information sessions about the effects of chemicals

3. Contracts: Confrontation isn't "snoopervision." It doesn't involve smelling your teenager's breath whenever he or she comes home, doing urine analyses, opening lockers to look for drugs, searching bedrooms, reading diaries, or listening in on phone conversations. These actions are required only in extreme cases—such as when a teenager is exhibiting suicidal tendencies.

Rather, confrontation involves the *supervision* and monitoring of behaviors at home, at school, and in the community. These behaviors are set out clearly in contracts drawn up with the teenager. So, too, are the consequences for not abiding by those behaviors.

Contracts perform a number of important functions:
- Helping teenagers take responsibility for themselves
- Giving teenagers some control over their environment
- Helping teens make choices—the consequences include choices
- Helping them to develop trust—the consequences are always consistent
- Letting them know in advance what will happen if they break the rules—the consequences are spelled out ahead of time
- Allowing teenagers to prove that they are not chemically dependent—by abiding by the rules
- Helping to determine when a teenager should be placed in another environment

There are three types of contracts that can be used in the confrontation stage:

The Simple Contract is a written agreement that includes basic non-negotiable rules: no alcohol or other drug use, no violence (physical or verbal), and no skipping of classes or information group sessions. Consequences for breaking this contract include the choice between a chemical dependent *evaluation* in an outpatient setting, or one in an inpatient setting.

The Turf Contract is a written agreement that includes all the rules of the Simple Contract and outlines specific behaviors required for the teenager to earn certain privileges at home (curfews, use of the car or telephone) or at school (participation in activities or sports). These behaviors might include negotiable tasks regarding school performance, personal cleanliness, curfew hours, and chores at home. Consequences for breaking this contract include the choice between treatment in an outpatient setting, or in an inpatient setting.

The Bottom-Line Contract is a written agreement that outlines specific behaviors required for the teenager to retain the privileges of living at home and staying in school. They may include all the elements of both the Simple Contact and the Turf Contract. Consequences for breaking this contract include the choice between two available and reputable inpatient treatment centers.

4. Control: By setting rules, determining consequences, and spelling them all out in contracts, you are *Taking Back Your Environment.* You are re-establishing your control over what goes on in it. You are not controlling your teenager's behaviors, feelings, and decisions. You are saying, in effect, "If you choose to break the rules of the contract, this is how I will change the environment."

How you change the environment depends on the teenager's needs, which are evidenced in his or her behaviors. These may indicate a need for an educational program, an evaluation, outpatient treatment, or inpatient treatment. In some cases it may become necessary to change the environment immediately—calling an ambulance for a teenager who has overdosed, calling the police for a teenager who has become violent, calling a mental health worker or psychiatrist for a teenager who is suicidal.

It may also become necessary to remove the teenager from the home or school to a more protective environment for a period of time. This isn't the same as abandoning the teenager or turning your back; rather it's another way of being responsible to the teenager who can no longer be responsible for himself or herself.

Using the "4 C's" of Confrontation

The confrontation stage of intervening with teenagers takes time. It will probably take at least two sessions and maybe more before you can break through the delusional system. You won't get a teenager to "receive reality" by confronting him or her with facts you have written on a list or by just sharing your feelings and concerns. Instead, you must remind the teenager that he or she has not behaved according to mutually agreed upon rules of behavior, and that mutually agreed upon consequences will now take effect because those rules of behavior were not followed.

The movement in the confrontation stage is from the least restrictive agreement (the verbal "No Use" agreement) through more restrictive agreements (the Simple Contract, the Turf Contract) to the most restrictive agreement (the Bottom-Line Contract). The teenager's ability to abide by these agreements will tell you what level of usage he or she is at and how much more help he or she needs.

There are four levels of confrontation that correspond to four phases of the disease of chemical dependence.

1. The "No Use" Rule. If you discover your teenager is using alcohol or other drugs, you should immediately set up a "No Use" Rule. We are not talking about responsible use at a meal, in the liturgy, or for medical reasons. We are referring to experimental and other uses outside the home, or inside the home without your

knowledge. As soon as you learn that this is going on, you need to take a stand.

2. The Simple Contract. A teenager in the second phase of the disease seeks the mood swing and has been using drugs with some regularity. He or she has been breaking the law. Schoolwork has been affected. The teenager may have been arrested for using at a party or in a car and charged with Minor In Possession, or he or she may have been caught coming to a school function intoxicated or high. In either case, you have been notified. Consequences for breaking the law might include jail time and probation. Consequences for breaking school rules might include suspension from activities and maybe even school itself. At this level, the teenager is put on a Simple Contract.

3. The Turf Contract. A teenager in the third phase is preoccupied with alcohol or other drugs. More laws have probably been broken, truancy has increased, grades have dropped, curfew has been violated repeatedly, and most friends also use drugs. The teenager is very defensive when confronted. It is necessary to move on to a more restrictive environment, and a Turf Contract is established in addition to evaluation by a chemical dependence counselor and attendance at a second-phase intervention group.

4. The Bottom-Line Contract. When a teenager is harmfully dependent on alcohol or other drugs, he or she has lost both control and choice. The drug use has become compulsive. The chemicals are primary in his or her life. The symptoms are progressive and chronic. Without intervention, the teenager will probably die prematurely. Intervention at this stage involves the Bottom-Line Contract, where the choice isn't whether the teenager will go into treatment, but where.

Learning Confrontation Skills

When you put a teenager on a contract you must be willing to monitor and record behavior. One way to approach this is by making an "X" under the day when the behavior or task on the contract is scheduled to be done. Then all you have to do is circle the "X" when the teenager does it.

Monitoring behaviors in this way keeps you from enabling. You don't have to nag or threaten; all you have to do is circle and add points. You are not responsible for the behaviors—the teenager is. It also keeps you from "snoopervision." Monitoring is easy, once you form the habit. *Be sure to do it daily.* Record behaviors as they are performed. Don't rely on your memory; the teenager and you must be able to trust what's on the contract as true and reliable information.

When you put a teenager on a contract you must also be willing to give feedback on what you learn from monitoring and recording behaviors. At the end of each week, tell your teenager how many points he or she earned. Based on these points, you can then tell the teenager whether he or she kept the contract and earned the privileges described in it. The contract makes this a simple matter of adding up the points and comparing the total to the minimums required. "Bill, you have 270 points out of 300 points this week. You needed 285 to use the car." Also describe the behaviors you observed. "You came in late on Thursday night, you were verbally abusive to your father, and you skipped school on Friday. That cost you 30 points."

Eight Tips to Help You Confront

Confrontation isn't easy. It may be the hardest thing you ever do, especially if you have to go all the way to a structured intervention and a Bottom-Line Contract. But it may also be the most important thing you ever do. You're playing for high stakes: your child's life.

1. Never humiliate your teenager. Always confront with respect. Offer choices; this lets your teenager save face.

2. Let your teenager experience his or her own pain. Don't rob your teenager of the right to struggle through it. Be there and be supportive, but don't try to ease the pain or take it on yourself.

3. NEVER confront your teenager while he or she is under the influence of alcohol or other drugs. Wait until your teenager is sober or (even better) suffering from a hangover.

4. Don't be permissive. Set up a "No Use" Rule, then stick to it. Take a stand.

5. Don't "snoopervise." Respect your teenager's privacy. Monitor behaviors, but don't go on spy missions through your teenager's room or belongings unless his or her behavior becomes self-destructive. Then do whatever is necessary to help.

6. Don't make threats you can't enforce. Instead, establish consequences that you're willing and able to enforce. Keep them logical and natural. Get your teenager involved in setting rules for his or her behavior at home.

7. Try not to see your teenager as a "monster" or a "bum"— even though it may be tempting at times. Instead, give encouragement and lots of love.

8. Don't try to go it alone. Seek information and support from outside resources. Find out what's available in your community, then make use of it. Among adolescents, chemical dependence is a system disease; it takes a system to crack a system.

Stage Three — Reintegration

Your teenager has stopped using alcohol or other drugs— either because he or she has been able to follow the terms of the "No Use" rule or one of the contracts, or because he or she has gone through treatment. Now it's time to support the reality of living without chemicals.

During reintegration, the teenager learns to work through the painful feelings of being an adolescent. With your help and the support of other caring people, he or she enters the process of being "habilitated"—learning to handle the tasks of adolescence. During reintegration, you and all other members of your family start to reclaim the power you lost or gave away while your teenager was using alcohol or other drugs.

The theme for this stage is *Let Go*. You will continue doing what you began during disengagement—letting go of trying to control your teenager's behaviors, feelings, and decisions. *You will also let go of your expectations for your teenager.* This is hard enough to do with a teenager who has never been in trouble with drugs. For the teenager coming out of treatment, it is even more difficult.

After going through disengagement and confrontation, it's tempting to think that you're home free. It seems reasonable to expect your teenager to shed all of the objectionable and rebellious behaviors he or she exhibited while using. The using has stopped, and so should the behaviors—or so you believe. Wrong! Objectionable and rebellious behaviors are *normal* for adolescence. Even those that were directly related to the using may be hard to shake off or change, and you can bet that they will be replaced by some others you may not like or understand. *Don't expect your teenager to be perfect.*

It also seems reasonable to expect your teenager to stay straight. You spent a lot of time and energy getting him or her into treatment; he or she spent a lot of time and energy in treatment. The truth is, treatment doesn't always solve the problem the first time around.

Some teenagers have to go back once, twice, and even more before they can really start recovering. They will certainly need to be involved in a structured aftercare or support group for at least one to two years. Attendance at A.A., N.A., or C.A. is also strongly recommended.

You just can't control when and where a teenager will accept reality and see the light. All you can do is keep controlling yourself and the environment. You may be discouraged if your teenager starts drinking or using again after returning home from treatment. *Don't take it personally*. Remember that intervention is a process. Keep the Bottom-Line Contract in effect for the first two weeks. Keep enforcing the "No Use" Rule. Let your teenager know that the consequences of breaking the contract will mean treatment again—and again and again, for as long as it takes.

Remember to keep supporting yourself. Continue with the activities you began during disengagement.

A chemically dependent teenager who emerges from treatment straight and sober is a changed person. Support your teenager in staying sober by welcoming him or her into a creative home environment. By "creative" we mean one in which people *encourage* one another, *listen* to one another, and know how to *problem-solve*.

Giving Encouragement

Teenagers need praise and encouragement—especially if chemical dependence has robbed them of their self-esteem for months or years. Be positive with your teenager. Be supportive. Smile!

Praise recognizes the thing accomplished ("Good job!")

and is conditional and specific ("I like the way you did the dishes." "I respect the way you've been concentrating on your homework." "I appreciate your mowing the lawn."). Encouragement recognizes the effort put into the thing accomplished ("Tell me how you did that!") and is unconditional and less specific ("You are special." "I like you a lot.").

Giving encouragement taps the teenager's inner courage to grow from within, where the real power is (clearness, closeness, curiosity, creativity). It helps the teenager learn to do internal evaluations ("I am good at studying; I am a caring person.") It builds self-esteem and feelings of worth ("I am somebody; I do belong; I am unique.")

Remember that the recovering teenager must meet his or her self-esteem needs *without chemicals*—a new and intimidating task. He or she needs support from you, other family members, teachers, friends, and whoever else can offer it.

Listening

Start tuning in to what your teenager is trying to say. Stay in the "here and now" and also pay attention to what the teenager is not saying. This takes time, concentration, and the willingness to admit you don't always have the answers. ("It sounds to me like you're having trouble making new friends. That can be scary and hard to do, and I can't tell you how to do it. None of us is real experts at it!" Or: "You look sad today. Is it because your old friends are still using?")

When you really listen to your children, you are telling them they are worthwhile because you are spending time with them. You are telling them they are special because you are paying attention to them. You are letting them know you care.

Problem-Solving

This is a learned skill that takes practice. It's the skill you will use as you continue to make rules and set up contracts. It's a skill that all of your children will carry with them for life—if you teach them. And it's essential for the teenager in recovery.

What's important in problem-solving isn't the end result, but the process of getting there. Simply by taking the time to identify a problem, generate alternatives and solutions, and evaluate each one according to its merits, you'll be giving your teenager skills that will last forever.

You can use your encouraging, listening, and problem-solving skills at the same time within the context of a family meeting. It's a good idea to hold family meetings when planning activities and addressing concerns. Meet on a weekly basis. Choose a time when everyone in the family can be there, then ask them to commit to it.

Family meetings, if held regularly, help to produce creative environments. They also give support to recovering teenagers who are struggling to meet and address their sobriety issues.

Finally, they challenge all family members to discover and explore their own inner qualities. Children and adults who are encouraged and praised, listened to, respected, and valued for themselves are free to find out what it means to be oneself. They are free to become whoever they are and develop fully as human beings.

As you struggle with your teenager—to determine whether he or she is using alcohol or other drugs, to break through the delusion system, to confront and confront until your teenager gets the message and chooses to change—please be assured of our deep concern, our prayers, and our belief that *you can do it*. Thousands of parents already have; thousands of teenagers today are recovering because their parents cared enough to act, and professionals cared enough to help.

DICK SCHAEFER

This section is taken from *Choices and Consequences: What To Do When A Teenager Uses Alcohol/Drugs*, published by the Johnson Institute.

PART FIVE

How Parents Can Prevent Chemical Dependence in Their Children

Introduction to Part Five

Chemical dependence always involves the emotions—indeed to the point that it has been called the "feeling disease." As a chemical dependent's behavior becomes more compulsive, painful, and shameful, ego strength ebbs, and shame and remorse lead to chronic feelings of utter despair. This, in turn, drives the chemical dependent more strongly to the drug. It is, therefore, crucial that we do all we can during our children's formative years to help them build strong egos, to give them every aid as they struggle to discover themselves.

This last section tells parents how they can help prevent chemical dependence in their children. I stress the word "help," since it has been my experience in the last thirty years that many young chemical dependents have had exemplary and devoted parents. Why youths from such homes should become chemically dependent simply defies explanation. Until we know much more about what really causes this disease we can only work toward developing environments where it would seem least likely to occur.

Scholars in the field seem to be in general agreement that chemical dependence is less likely to occur in families that are truly nurturing and provide structured, supportive opportunities for children's personalities to emerge. Chapter Nineteen outlines a job description for parents designed to help them create these kinds of family environments.

Chapter Twenty points out that creating a supportive home environment is only part of a parent's job—parents must also

403

teach their children essential lifeskills. This chapter explains and offers tips on teaching six of these essential lifeskills: feeling-processing skills, decision-making skills, skills for establishing positive behavior, mood-maintenance skills, communications skills, and refusal skills.

The last two chapters address some special concerns for parents. Chapter Twenty-One looks at alcohol and other drug use by parents and what messages parents send their children if they drink occasionally, drink excessively, or take other drugs either occasionally or excessively. Chapter Twenty-Two tells the parents in recovery from their own chemical dependence how they can also help their children start healing the pain caused by the family disease of chemical dependence.

VERNON E. JOHNSON, D.D.

CHAPTER NINETEEN

A Job Description for Parents

Larry came from a family known for strict discipline. Rules were numerous and never bent; punishments were harsh. Kids were "seen but not heard." Family members seldom openly expressed their feelings, whether of anger, enthusiasm, or affection. Anne came from a family where parenting was the polar opposite of what Larry grew up with. The kids practically raised themselves. There were almost no rules, and the few they did have were seldom enforced, or were enforced inconsistently. Family members were quite open about expressing their feelings, whether that meant showing anger or sharing affection with hugs and words of praise.

When Anne and Larry's first child, Matt, was eighteen months old and began asserting himself, their vastly different views on parenting also asserted themselves. Larry typically responded to Matt's tantrums with punishment that went on until the child gave in. Anne typically ignored Matt's outbursts with "He'll get over it" and would simply try to wait out the storm.

These opposite views made for greater and greater problems as Matt grew up. When he was in the sixth grade his temper tantrums and angry outbursts became common, and he often skipped school and ignored curfew. Larry's complaint to Anne was "If you'd just support me in setting up some rules and enforcing them with punishment, he'd know what's expected of him and he'd shape up. He *needs* that kind of control. We've got to show him who's boss." Anne's answer was "Matt needs room to breathe. You're on him all the time. I think he skips school because he needs relief from all this tension. You just don't know how to let go; after all, he's no infant."

The story of Anne and Larry illustrates a crucial problem that all parents must face: Do we "take charge" or do we "let go"? As you might expect, the answer isn't simple, but the question can be answered sensibly, and that's what this chapter is about. What is immediately clear is that parents **must** agree on their basic approach to parenting and then on some clear guidelines for implementing their approach. Such an agreement is indispensable because it gives our kids a secure environment—secure because it's *consistent* and therefore *predictable.* You needn't be afraid that these guidelines will straitjacket you, though; if you hold onto them, you can easily work out many variations that suit your own family, as countless other successful parents have done and continue to do.

I'm calling these guidelines **a job description for parents**. Once you've learned these guidelines and how to use them, you'll be more at ease as parents, and your kids will be more at ease, too, because they'll be living in a well-balanced, happy family, in an environment that gives them both the security and the freedom they need—security and freedom that result when parents learn to both "take charge" and "let go."

As you apply these guidelines to your own family, I urge you to keep checking your progress in light of two basic principles:

- Our primary goal in parenting is to prepare our children for dealing with the real world.
- The methods we use to prepare them for that real world must always be evaluated in terms of how well they meet our children's deepest human needs such as

self-esteem, self-respect, self-reliance, and deeply satisfying relationships with others.

All good parenting must pass that double test.

Let's start this job description for parents by discussing a duty that has perhaps been somewhat neglected in recent years, setting limits for children.

Setting Limits

Even the smallest infants are geared to exploring the big, mysterious world around them, and of course parents should encourage what will become a lifelong quest. Experiencing colors, sounds, shapes, textures, and smells, crawling to new, wonderful places—all this is part of the adventure of growing up. But always the parents have to set limits. We don't let the baby put its hand on a hot stove to learn what heat means; we don't let it crawl outside in zero weather to learn what cold is. We set limits. Inevitably, youngsters test those limits, and more and more so as they come into adolescence and reach for true independence. To an adolescent, limits exist to be tested. How serious are Mom and Dad about the jobs they give me around the house and yard, about how much money I can spend, what I can or can't eat, what time I have to be in at night, about using the car, about my using drugs? How far can I really go? And what happens if I go too far? But no matter how much adolescents question or test the limits we set, we must indeed set them. The real world we all have to face is hemmed in with limits of all kinds. The adolescent who hasn't learned to accept reasonable limits in everyday home life isn't likely to accept them in dealing with decisions about alcohol or other drugs either, because the unspoken principle has been "Do whatever you like."

But *how* do we set limits? I suggest these criteria: set limits that are clear and appropriate, expect kids to test them, and enforce them.

Set Clear Limits

The adolescent who for some reason can't distinguish what's appropriate dress for the beach from what's appropriate for church or synagogue can suddenly turn into a razor-sharp attorney when parents establish limits that are open to even the slightest ambiguity. ("I know I'm supposed to finish my homework before I watch TV. But does that mean I can *never* watch before I finish it? *Never*? You didn't say *never*. I figured you must have meant *usually*, and this isn't a usual night; there's a playoff game.")

To tell the truth, parental limits sometimes *are* unclear because parents themselves haven't agreed on them. Parental agreement must come first. But then parents must express the limits in absolutely clear, specific terms that the youngster can understand. To test yourselves and your child, *write down* the limits, *discuss* them until the child agrees they're clear and can, if asked, *rephrase* them in his or her own words. ("Coming home an hour after the game is over" doesn't mean *starting* for home; it means *arriving there*. So we reword it to "arriving." "After the game is over" doesn't mean chatting in the gym for a half hour and then starting to count; it means being home an hour after the final buzzer.)

For additional insurance of clear communication, *post the limits* in a place where you and your child can easily review them, such as on the refrigerator, family bulletin board, or any other easily accessible place frequently used by all.

Set Appropriate Limits

Since no two kids are alike, limits must reflect your child's unique needs and capacities. Here are some areas to consider in deciding what's appropriate.

- **Age:** Kids often complain it isn't fair if they're not given the same freedom that an older brother or sister has. But parents shouldn't be swayed by that argument. Just explain that their time hasn't come but that it will—as they continue to prove they can handle greater freedom by showing maturity and a growing sense of responsibility in handling the privileges they already enjoy.
- **Trust earned:** We need to explain two points about trust to our kids. First, they must **earn** our trust. When we trust people we somehow put ourselves in their hands, rely on them to do what's right. Before we do that, it only makes sense that they show us they're worthy of our trust. Now, young children typically haven't had many opportunities to prove they're trustworthy. We hope they'll prove trustworthy, of course, and in the meantime, we'll be happy to trust them more and more as they earn our trust by doing their chores without being told, by coming home on time, etc. Second, so our kids won't think that's a harsh view of them, we need to explain that **trusting them and loving them are two different things.** Loving them is a commitment we made from the start, and we'll continue to love them no matter what they do. They don't have to earn our love; they already have it.
- **Basic needs:** Strangely enough, in dealing with youngsters we sometimes forget the obvious truth that their basic human needs are the same as those of adults—such necessities as privacy, socialization, work, independence, and the opportunity to take reasonable risks.

If we set limits at a place to prevent kids from meeting their basic needs, we can expect problems. For instance, if our limits for a fourteen year old are so restrictive as not to allow her the opportunity to socialize with kids after school, we can expect that she will either violate the limits or abide by the limits, and miss out on achieving important developmental tasks that being with friends provide. So, in failing to respect her needs, we're encouraging either disobedience or immaturity. But showing respect for her basic needs helps her to respect herself—and kids with healthy self-respect are less likely to get involved in drug problems.

Expect Kids to Test Limits

Sometimes we set limits at a place that seems so reasonable to us that we think our kids won't even be tempted to test them. Wrong. I've learned from long experience that no matter how reasonable a limit looks to parents, kids—especially adolescents—will try it, test it, push it. So expect it; it's part of their growing up; they learn by experience.

Fortunately, kids usually test limits by overstepping just one or two steps. If ten o'clock is the limit, they'll probably try ten-thirty, say, but usually not three a.m. for starters. This gives us a clue. Try to set limits in such a way that if they do overstep them a bit, they won't be in deep trouble. To teach a two year old to look both ways before crossing the street, don't start out on a busy thoroughfare. Or if the police strictly enforce an 11:00 p.m. curfew, tell your kids to be home by 10:30 p.m.

When it comes to setting limits regarding alcohol and other drugs, though, allowing ANY use is too dangerous as well as illegal; we must make it clear that we expect total abstinence. We might expect kids to test this limit, too, but if we allow any use at all our kids will believe

410

we're condoning their use of drugs. (An obvious exception is the taking of a small portion of wine at a religious service in one's church, synagogue, or home.)

Do kids pay any real attention when parents discuss the dangers of drugs and make it clear that they're to avoid them completely? Surprisingly, the answer is *yes.* All respectable research tells us that when kids make their decisions about alcohol and other drugs, one of the most important factors in that decision is *what their parents think.* So don't give up just because kids keep testing limits you set. Kids *do* pay attention to what you're saying and doing; your efforts *will* pay off.

Enforce Limits

Once we've established clear, specific limits, we have to demonstrate that they mean something—that we're serious. This includes several points.

- We must **model** our respect for the limit if it's the sort of limit that should apply to us, too. If parents agree that we all should keep our feet off the furniture but Dad keeps putting his number twelves on the coffee table while watching TV, the kids aren't apt to take the rule very seriously.
- We must **check** observance or nonobservance. If the video arcade is off limits but our kids know we never take the trouble to check compliance, we might as well forget the rule. Constant suspicion and constant checking into every detail are quite a different matter. When our kids say they're going to practice after school for the class play, we need to have some idea of when practice starts and ends, and occasionally we need to check with the person in charge to see if they've attended. However, to call the teacher daily, to call our kids' friends to

check, or to spy on their activities is going too far. It conveys a lack of trust that will eventually erode our relationship with our children.

- We must follow through with **definite consequences** when kids violate the limits. If Michael breaks his curfew, he must know that certain clear consequences will follow.

Setting Consequences

Perhaps no other item in our job description for parents fits in so clearly and powerfully with parents' overall goal of preparing their kids to deal with the real world as this one does. When parents prepare a reasonable, clear set of consequences that will predictably follow when kids act inappropriately, their kids can learn in a loving, supportive environment a lesson that the world outside often teaches in a harsh, unforgiving, even shattering way: that actions have consequences. When kids have learned at home that actions have consequences, they're more likely to consider what effects their decisions will have on themselves and on those they love.

Setting Up Effective Consequences

The guiding principle here is to *set up consequences that most effectively help our kids experience the full impact of their behavior.* Now, we should of course reward good behavior in such a way as to show that it brings pleasant consequences. Kids who prove they're trustworthy should be praised for it and allowed more free time and opportunity to exercise their growing sense of responsibility and judgment. That being said, and sincerely said, the fact is that most parents have a more difficult time knowing how to respond when kids have violated limits. So that will be our focus in this section.

Here are important qualities of effective consequences:

- **They're related to the incident:** "You didn't come home on time, so you're going to lose some free time."

- **They're reasonable:** "You were an hour late, so you'll lose two hours of your free time tomorrow night." It's reasonable that consequences usually exceed the violation; otherwise kids feel only a minimal impact.

- **They're set up in advance and clearly understood:** "We agreed that if you were late, you'd lose double that amount of free time on your next evening out. I'm just holding you to that agreement."

- **They're timely:** The sooner the consequence follows the behavior, the more likely it is to be a learning experience. The fourteen-year-old boy who skips school on Thursday and has to stay home from a long-awaited Friday night party experiences strong connections between action and consequences.

- **They're not too elaborate:** It's a mistake to try to develop a system that covers every tiny bit of behavior and spells out an exact consequence for it. Such a complex system backfires because the child sees it as impossible to observe and will often end up blaming the parents for failings that are clearly the child's own fault. When we develop an overly elaborate system of consequences, it teaches our kids the false message that the world will always respond to them in a prescribed, totally predictable way. Unfortunately, it also teaches them that the primary reason for being responsible is to avoid punishment. While it's important for kids to understand that consequences naturally follow behavior, it's equally important for them to begin developing a more mature level of morality. As kids mature they need to experience the internal satisfaction that goes hand-in-hand with being responsible.

- **They escalate in force:** One of the more important things youngsters must learn is that *patterns* of behavior are more important than isolated behaviors. Being late for a job once may result in little consequence for an adult; being late every other day for two weeks may result in very serious consequences. Consequences must increase in force for youngsters as well. Let's say a ten year old is told he must come home directly after school and do his chores before he goes out to play. The first time he neglects his responsibilities, we talk about how one earns privileges only by first taking care of responsibilities. The second time, he loses the privilege of going out to play the next afternoon. The third time, he loses the privilege for a week. The message registers that his parents mean business: Enjoying privileges means accepting responsibility.

  As kids begin linking privileges with responsibility, they begin to associate responsibility with other more internal rewards such as pride, satisfaction, and being a contributing member of the family and of society. Kids who develop an internal set of reasons for being responsible are much less likely to become involved with drugs.

- **They're applied consistently:** No matter how good the system is in other respects, if parents don't apply it consistently, it fails. Being overly strict one day and overly permissive the next makes it impossible for kids to learn from their mistakes, because we establish no clear, predictable connection between their behavior and its consequences—the very opposite of what we want to teach them.

- **They're enforced calmly, respectfully, without anger:** The spirit is "I'm sorry, but I'm sure you know it's the only thing we can do. You're a sweetheart and we love you, but you have to learn to take responsibility for what you do."

By now it should be clear how this whole practice of setting consequences is connected with the theme of parenting that prevents our kids from ever getting involved with drugs. Kids whose parents have calmly, over many years, helped them absorb and live by the basic truth that actions do have consequences will be in a stronger position when the time comes to make crucial decisions about using or not using drugs. They'll have developed the habit of thinking about the connection between behavior and its consequences, and so when they consider whether to use drugs they'll be realists. They'll see short-term consequences such as feeling guilty, getting caught by parents, school officials, or police, or being injured in a car accident. They'll see long-term consequences such as failing their studies, wrecking career plans, losing their good name, becoming alienated from family and friends, and eventually losing their health and life itself. With such a background, their choices will be immeasurably easier to make.

Setting reasonable consequences and discussing them with our children is a legitimate and important part of parenting. But it's only one part of parenting. If dealing with consequences becomes a primary parenting activity, if we become mere monitors of our children's behavior, it may be a signal of deeper family problems that we need to look into.

Creating Family Spirit and Building Structures

One of life's most beautiful experiences is to live in a close-knit family where the members truly think, feel and act like a family. In such a family we sense a spirit of unity, togetherness.

Each of the family members is loved and respected as a distinct, unique person, but at the same time there's a sense of common purpose and sharing as they all work out their destiny together.

In bygone ages, when society wasn't so complex and so hurried, it seemed a lot easier to build such a family. Today, many families have to try to cope with four or five different work schedules, numerous extracurricular activities, and loaded social calendars of parents and children alike. What we too often see, instead of a united family, is a group of individuals living in the same house but all pursuing their own private and isolated agendas.

Consider the Andersons. Jim and Sharon, the parents, both have full-time jobs and are also active in their church and in PTA; besides that, Jim belongs to the Rotary Club and likes to golf, and Sharon belongs to a bridge club and likes to bowl. To cap it off, Jim's company has just told him he'll have to travel out of town six or seven days a month. Meanwhile, Joan, age 14, and Jeffrey, age 11, both play in the band, participate in several sports, and lead an active social life after school and on many evenings.

Families like the Andersons (and many families with more complicated schedules) have little unity or togetherness; what they really know is fragmentation, loneliness, isolation. I've known families who haven't eaten one meal together in months. And in my experience, that's exactly the kind of family whose kids are having problems with alcohol or other drugs. Lacking a family spirit of love and togetherness and mutual support, the kids look for it elsewhere, and far too often they find it in the fake good fellowship and high feelings they experience when they go along with the drug crowd.

Yet, I'm confident that we can build close-knit, united, loving families. In dealing with hundreds of such families I've learned a number of techniques they've used. If you'll study them, think them over, and adapt them sensibly to your own

416

situation, I know they'll work for you, too.

- **Family schedules:** Set up a weekly calendar outlining where everyone is and when they'll be home, with family activities and events highlighted.
- **Family activities:** Schedule family activities that occur regularly and that all family members are expected to attend—for example, weekday dinner, Sunday brunch, weekly worship.
- **Family events:** Plan special activities such as a visit to the zoo, amusement park, or nursing home; outings, vacations.
- **Family community meetings:** Hold weekly meetings to air feelings or concerns, review events, activities, and schedules of family members. Set aside time to discuss both problems and successes.
- **Home-utilization plan:** Make up a schedule for high-use areas of the house, such as bathrooms in the morning, family room in the evening, laundry room on Saturday. These plans spell out both when such areas of the house are to be used and any special rules governing those areas. Oftentimes kids can contribute nicely to these plans at the weekly community meeting.
- **Work schedule:** Line up household and yard duties and make it clear that everyone in the family is expected to do certain daily chores without expecting remuneration. Kids learn to contribute to the larger society by contributing at home. To understand the importance of giving, kids must experience it first in their own family.

Family practices like these help counter the chaos that does characterize some families today. They give our families reasonable structure, regularity and order, without turning them into rigid military units. Ultimately, by bringing the family together frequently in a relaxed, pleasant atmosphere they help us create a true family spirit: a spirit of togetherness, mutual respect, sharing, and love that lessens the probability that kids will turn to drugs.

Handling Our Own Mistakes and Problems

An important duty of parents is that of presenting a human image to the children. Like all other mortals, parents make mistakes and have to face problems. Handling those mistakes and problems sensibly is important, because how we do it has profound effects on our kids. We need to admit our mistakes and problems, avoid blaming them on our kids, and be willing to get help when we need it.

When we handle our mistakes and problems honestly and calmly, we're teaching our kids a great deal about how to face the realities of everyday life. They need such role models. When they make their own mistakes and get into their own difficulties, they'll have healthy attitudes, and they'll also know they can come to us for understanding and practical help.

Team Parenting

Team parenting is one of the best insurance policies against our kids' use of alcohol or other drugs. But it's often difficult to achieve because "opposites attract," as the old saying reminds us. Sometimes it's almost as though we select our spouse to complement our own strengths and weaknesses but then spend a fair amount of our lives refusing to cooperate with him or her. It's not unusual for a parent who believes in strict discipline to find that the other tends to be quite lenient. Marriages that reflect such totally opposite approaches often get into trouble and end in divorce. But opposite styles can be incorporated into a unified approach if parents learn to work as a team. In fact, the strongest teams are made up of couples who bring together a diversity of perspectives and skills as long as they avoid faulty ideas and use team strategy.

Faulty Ideas About Team Parenting

- **"I'll parent them when they're good; you parent them when they're bad."** The problem with this is that one parent is the good guy and the other is the bad guy. Usually Mom is the sweet Rewarder and Dad the villainous Enforcer. This setup creates problems for both parents. To get out of the pattern, both parents need to set and enforce consequences and both need to establish other bases for their relationships with their kids.
- **"I'll parent the boys; you parent the girls."** Some couples believe that boys need fathers to set limits and girls need mothers to set limits. The unspoken assumption behind this view seems to be that women are by nature loving and nurturing but weak, and that men are by nature strong but harsh, so children can learn only from the respective parent how to be a **real** woman or a **real** man. Fortunately, these stereotypes that have little basis in reality are disappearing in our time. But the stereotypes are by no means dead, so we need to abandon exclusive same-sex parenting and allow both the parents and the children to become whole persons.
- **"I'll parent them when they're babies, you parent them when they're in grade school, and we'll both quit parenting when they're teenagers."** Many parents prefer to deal with kids at one particular stage of their development. But children need us at every stage. It's important for us to go through each of these stages with them, to share their good times and their bad times.

Tips For Team Strategy Parenting

- **Kids need consistency.** Even though our parenting styles can be polar opposites, we simply have to reach a workable agreement on the basics of limits, consequences, and family spirit and structures. Otherwise it's chaos. Becoming consistent takes work. It's important to sit down with our spouse, take out a paper and pencil, and list areas where we've noticed differences in how we handle things. Then we can discuss how those differences are affecting us and the kids. Some differences are nothing more than stylistic issues that really cause no one any harm. Other differences can be much more substantial and cause continual parental struggles. If you and your spouse find that problems with consistency continue to plague your parenting, it may signal other underlying problems. If so, it's important to seek outside counseling as a couple. To neglect resolving these underlying issues leaves your kids trapped in marital dynamics that can be debilitating for them. My clinical experience indicates that kids who get trapped in these adult marital disagreements end up taking on stress that they can do nothing about and that they're significantly more vulnerable to using drugs to relieve that stress.
- **Parents can learn from each other.** Perhaps the reason why opposites attract is that the fusion gives balance and complementary strengths. One parent may be highly organized and therefore loves to plan things thoroughly, down to the last detail of written lists. The other may be spontaneous and therefore loves to do things on the spur of the moment. It's good to expose kids to both these approaches to structure and planning, provided we don't spend our time and energy

disagreeing. If we reach a sensible accommodation that capitalizes on the strengths of both approaches, we demonstrate to our kids the beauty of diversity, and they begin to absorb lifeskills relating to compromise, cooperation, and appreciating differences in people.

- **Strategize away from the kids.** Professional parents such as foster parents or group-home parents make it a practice to get away form their kids regularly to meet with a clinical supervisor who gives them expert help on parenting. It's important that ordinary parents also get away at times so they can work out a consistent parenting approach, especially to discuss volatile issues that arouse strong emotions—emotions that might get out of hand if the kids were around. Parents who feel, for example, that their kids are deliberately playing them against each other or against the school system often get so angry that they want to lash out at the kids in the heat of anger. If an objective third party such as a counselor, school professional, or trusted friend is available, so much the better. Seminars and parent-education classes can also give parents new ideas about working together.

Providing a Safe Home Environment

A safe home environment is one where the kids feel emotionally secure and physically safe. This environment provides for the daily needs of the individual: adequate sleep, food, shelter, privacy, dignity and respect, order, structure, and stability. In a safe environment these basic needs are never questioned or never taken away as a consequence or as a punishment, no matter what the behavior.

Whenever these basic necessities are taken away or threatened, most of us experience extreme insecurity, especially when we feel powerless to control the situation. We must remember that our kids live in an environment where they're never in charge, where they're habitually vulnerable because we're their parents. Because our kids are so vulnerable, both they and our society interpret any violation of their basic needs as abuse.

Three types of abuse occur in our homes more frequently than most of us like to admit. Exposure to any of these abuse patterns will multiply a child's chances of developing alcohol or other drug problems, for reasons we'll mention in a moment.

Emotional Abuse

Neglect, abandonment, humiliation, shame, and being made to feel unneeded, unwanted, or unimportant do untold damage to a child's self-esteem. When, for instance, we're angry with our kids for violating limits in a way that makes us feel personally attacked or offended, it's easy to lash out at them in ways that make them feel unwanted. "I wish I'd never had you," "Life would be so much easier without you," or "I wish you'd just go away" can sometimes roll out of our mouth without our comprehending the impact it may have on our kids. We know we love our kids, and so we assume they'll interpret our behavior in light of that overarching truth. But kids often can't distinguish how we feel at one particular moment from how we habitually feel about them. So we must be very conscious of the messages we give them. When we're confronting them on negative behavior we must be sure they realize the confrontation is about their *behavior*, not about them. Our kids must realize that they make mistakes and will be called on them. However, they must never be made to feel that *they* are a mistake, that they're bad people because they make mistakes.

Some other ways in which kids are often abused emotionally are name-calling, not acknowledging their needs, or enforcing inappropriate discipline, often because we interpret misbehavior as a personal affront to us. We can be especially vulnerable to personalizing our kids' behavior when their actions directly affect us. For example, when an adolescent uses our car without permission and has an accident with it, this behavior infuriates us not only because it violates limits we've set, but because it damages our property, creates inconvenience and costs us a lot of money.

Physical Abuse

Technically, physical abuse occurs whenever a child is physically damaged by interaction with an adult. Although it's legal to use corporal punishment such as spanking, it isn't an effective or healthy way to enforce limits or teach self-discipline. Any type of corporal punishment is especially damaging to kids in their late childhood or adolescence. It runs the double risk of crossing the line into physical abuse and of humiliating someone whose sense of self-esteem is already very fragile. This type of punishment often leads to escalating power conflicts between the child and parent, teaches the child fear and mistrust, is very demeaning, and diminishes self-esteem and self-respect.

Sexual Abuse

Sexual abuse occurs when family members or adults indulge in any type of sexual activity or seductive or suggestive behavior with a young person. As we become more willing to accept testimony about sexual abuse, it's shocking to realize the number of families experiencing this problem. While the perpetrators in these situations are usually men, the victims aren't always females. An increasing number of young boys are being reported as sexual-abuse victims, often as victims of an adult family member.

Family members often intuitively sense what's going on even when any kind of abusive behavior is kept secret. It's important for family members to take any suspected abuse seriously, because it's too prevalent and damaging to ignore. Bringing the abusive behavior out into the open and recognizing it as destructive behavior is the indispensable first step in helping the victim as well as the rest of the family.

When young people report abuse—physical, emotional, or sexual—they're usually telling the truth. Help is available and accessible. If you suspect or know that abuse is occurring in your family, you can get immediate help by looking under Child Abuse Services in the yellow pages of your local telephone directory or by contacting Parents Anonymous, the National Committee for Prevention of Child Abuse, or your local police, county mental health or social service agency.

This job description for parents has given you a set of guidelines and a brief discussion of your main duties as parents, with a view to helping you prevent your children from getting involved with alcohol or other drugs. If you faithfully follow these guidelines, you'll be doing your part in establishing a whole family atmosphere in which your kids can develop the indispensable lifeskills we'll cover in the next chapter—skills that will make it immeasurably easier for your kids to say no to drugs.

DAVID J. WILMES

This section is taken from *Parenting For Prevention: How to Raise a Child to Say No to Alcohol/Drugs*, published by the Johnson Institute.

Chapter Twenty

Teaching Lifeskills

Lifeskills are a whole set of *social skills*—skills that enable us to be at ease in our many and varied contacts with other people. They're an assortment of positive feelings, beliefs, and behaviors that help us handle stress and be healthy psychologically as well as physically. We're talking about such basic skills as being confident and self-reliant and being able to communicate effectively with others. These lifeskills build energy rather than drain it; they heal our wounds and strengthen us for living happily and productively, both as individuals and as members of a group. People who have these skills set goals and reach them, they manage their time well; they build a supportive network of family and friends; they take responsibility for their feelings, thoughts, and actions.

But what do lifeskills have to do with preventing alcohol and other drug problems in our kids? *Everything.* They're the best preventive medicine there is. Why? Because they're a long-range, commonsense, well-tested set of skills that develop well-balanced kids in a healthy family setting. They're not a quick fix, not a magic formula, not a one-minute-a-day program that promises effortless, painless solutions to the complex problems of parenting in a drug oriented culture. Rather, they're comparable to a long-range physical wellness program where day after day, year after year, you faithfully cling to a positive program of sound nutrition, exercise, sleep, recreation, and relaxation that slowly builds a sound body—the best *prevention* program ever.

There are six types of lifeskills this chapter will discuss: Feeling-Processing skills, Decision-Making skills, skills for Establishing Positive Behavior, Mood-Maintenance skills, Communication skills, and Refusal skills. But before we discuss these skills, we need to clarify some terms.

Basic Terms

Certain terms referring to various methods of teaching lifeskills will constantly recur in this chapter. So I want to clarify what I mean by those terms and why I think they're important.

Modeling

Modeling refers to exemplifying in our own life the lifeskills we want to teach, as distinguished from merely explaining those skills or urging our kids to develop and use them. For instance, if we make our own decisions impulsively and only for short-term gains—for example, spending $300 we can't afford on a dress we'll probably wear only once or twice—we're in effect telling our kids, "That's the way to make decisions." Since our kids tend to mimic us, modeling is the most powerful of all teaching tools, for good or ill, as popular sayings correctly remind us: "Practice what you preach"; "Actions speak louder than words"; or, as it's sometimes rather ominously worded, "What you are speaks so loudly I can't hear what you're saying."

Reinforcement

Reinforcement refers to the practice of "catching them doing it right." When our kids demonstrate that they can effectively perform a certain lifeskill, we reinforce or strengthen them in that desirable behavior by praising them immediately and openly. ("Honey, I'm really impressed by the way you've been hitting those books at night. It shows you're looking ahead and seeing what that's going to mean in the long run.") The praise can be given also by nonverbal gestures such as a hug, a literal pat on the back, a handshake, a thumbs-up gesture. Reinforcement is one of the most important teaching tools available to parents.

Consistency

This term refers to our steadiness in the messages we send to our kids. We need to be unwavering and therefore predictable in those messages, since none of us can learn a game if the rules are always changing. If we tell our kids on Tuesday that feelings are their friends, we mustn't ridicule them on Thursday for feeling and expressing sadness or fear. ("Oh, don't be such a baby. It's only a football game.")

When we're consistent in what we teach our kids, they develop a sense of security that encourages them to try out new lifeskills that otherwise might intimidate them. For instance, when we consistently practice effective communications skills, we eventually find that kids not only open up to us more, but that they also begin to demonstrate effective communication skills with others.

Encouraging Practice of Lifeskills

Practicing a new lifeskill in a low-risk setting within the family circle is an important preparation for transferring the learning to situations our kids will find at school, with friends, and in society generally. For instance, if we help our kids with the steps of decision making about saving money or choosing extracurricular activities, those same decision-making skills will be easier to use in riskier situations such as whether to drink alcohol with friends.

Techniques such as role playing or working with puppets to act out conversations or to discuss the pros and cons of life situations seen on TV will give kids a chance to think and to use various skills they'll need in real-life situations. For instance, recently when my son and I were watching one of his favorite videos, "Swiss Family Robinson," we talked about the feelings of the family at Christmas when they thought the two older boys had been captured by pirates. The experience provided him with a safe environment in which to practice identifying and sharing some feelings that are often hard to deal with: anxiety and fear.

In short, allowing our kids opportunities to play with situations that represent real life for them gives them a safe but effective laboratory for practicing new lifeskills.

Allowing Mistakes

Whatever skill we try to learn, whether it's riding a bike or making decisions, we're going to mess up once in a while. If kids are to learn new skills, they've got to know it's okay to make mistakes. We must develop a hands-off policy (no matter how itchy our hands get) that lets them skin a knee or suffer the consequences of poor decision making until they learn to make sound decisions. Allowing some mistakes, however, doesn't mean totally disregarding their activities. A parent must always be there as a guide, a resource, a shoulder to lean on.

Patience

Working with kids, especially our own, requires tons of patience. Patience seems like a gift that some of us have and others don't. Wrong. Patience is like a muscle. Some of us are given more muscle than others, but with exercise we can all develop it. In parenting my kids, the "Serenity Prayer" ("God, grant me the serenity to accept the things I cannot change, the courage to change the things I can, and the wisdom to know the difference") has helped me immensely in developing my "patience muscle." I find that instead of counting to ten, I rely on that simple prayer to help me muster at least enough patience to finish what I'm doing, get the kids and myself home, and live one more day with the satisfaction that I'm doing a pretty good job of being a parent.

Feeling-Processing Skills

Rick has just broken up with Sarah, his girlfriend. Overwhelming feelings of sadness, hurt, and anger all form one huge ball in his stomach. He can't talk to anyone: he's too embarrassed to share his feelings, and he wouldn't know what to say if he did try to express them.

In school he sees Jerry, who's well known for using alcohol and other drugs. Rick starts a conversation with him and eventually says he'd like to get high. Jerry sells him two marijuana joints and offers to smoke them with him.

Why did Rick so easily turn to marijuana? An obvious, easy

explanation is that he was feeling bad and was looking for something that would help him feel better, and right now. Alcohol or other drugs do fill that bill: They do make us feel better right now. A deeper, more helpful explanation is that Rick lacked the cluster of lifeskills called feeling-processing skills that would have enabled him to deal with his feelings, especially with his uncomfortable, painful feelings. But that's by no means the whole answer either, for behind Rick's difficulty in handling feelings is a long, tangled tradition that Rick inherited: the human race's inability to understand and handle feelings.

Our Mysterious Feelings

To start with, let it be clear that our feelings are *bodily responses* that originated in our ancestors' instinctive physical responses to the world about them—for instance, in the fight-or-flight instinct we all still experience when we sense danger stalking us. We've all noticed the physical responses characteristic of deep feelings, such as quick breaths, pounding heart, clenched fists. Our everyday language, too, recognizes the physical basis of feelings; when we mention our "gut reaction" to something, we're speaking quite precisely. Feelings are very much of the body. And there's the rub. These bodily, animal reactions of ours are very familiar and yet very mysterious and disturbing. Like the wild animals themselves, they're immensely powerful, unpredictable, hard to control. Over the centuries, then, we humans have often handled them in inappropriate ways. Sometimes we've given in totally to their urgings and indulged in orgies of drunkenness, sex, or wholesale slaughter. At other times, frightened by those excesses, we've tried to suppress our feelings entirely, pretend they don't even exist, or at best have been quite suspicious of them.

In recent decades our culture has been struggling to give feelings their proper role in a balanced life, but the old battle goes on; and frankly, most of todays' kids know very little about feelings and how to handle them. That's precisely why we need to help them develop lifeskills in that crucial area: When kids are tempted to get into drugs, they're almost invariably having problems with their feelings, not with their intellects.

The Three Stages of Processing Our Feelings

To get down to basics in understanding feelings and helping our kids understand them and deal successfully with them, let's talk about the three stages we need to go through to reach some mastery in this area: identifying feelings, owning them, and expressing (sharing) them.

Identifying Feelings: As we've mentioned, it's often quite easy to know when others are experiencing feelings, especially deep ones. Flashing eyes, scowls, a red face can be sure tipoffs. But when we're all stirred up inside, what are we *really* feeling? Recognizing and identifying our own feelings can be very difficult. Younger kids usually have to settle for something vague such as "I feel ishy" or "I feel bad." With help, though, even preschoolers can master simple ways of naming their feelings: "mad," "sad," "glad," for instance.

Owning Feelings: By "owning" feelings we simply mean acknowledging them as *ours*, acknowledging that they spring from *us* and are a part of *us*. Whether someone insults us and we react by feeling angry or embarrassed, or whether someone praises us and we react by feeling elated, what results is *our* feeling.

What that means is that we, not others, are ultimately responsible for our feelings. It's a hard lesson to learn, but it's true, and as we help our kids to see and accept that truth, we're showing them how to take control of their own lives: *I'm* the one who decides how I feel and act; I'm not at the mercy of what others decide about how I'm going to feel and act. At the same time, of course, the comforting realization that *I'm* in control of my own life means that I'm accepting *responsibility* for my feelings. That's a big step toward maturity.

Expressing Feelings: We can of course express our feelings in many ways: in artworks, poetry, stories, music, for instance. But it's absolutely indispensable that our kids develop skills in expressing their feelings in the way in which practically everyone expresses them every day: by the spoken word. Learning to say out loud "I feel hurt" or "I feel good" is a fundamental lifeskill, because without the ability to verbalize our feelings we'll find ourselves alone, cut off from the support and concern that only relationships with people can provide. And those relationships depend heavily on our ability to communicate our feelings in spoken words.

By learning to express feelings we're reaching out to others and building a bridge that creates the intimacy, togetherness, rapport, and mutual support we all need. Kids who can't *express* their feelings through speech are clearly more vulnerable to using alcohol or other drugs to *change* their feelings.

How to Help Kids Process Feelings

This section gives suggestions for helping kids process their feelings at all three stages: identifying feelings, owning them, and expressing them.

- An easy tool to help kids and to help ourselves to model appropriate handling of feelings is "I statements" such as "I feel hurt," "I feel happy, "I feel afraid." These "I statements" are nothing more than statements that begin with "I," name a feeling, and give a brief explanation. For instance, "I felt let down when I found you hadn't finished raking the lawn before you went out with Rick." By modeling statements that show we can identify, own, and express our feelings, we're teaching our kids a basic lifeskill.

- Read stories focusing on certain feelings, then talk about those feelings. *The Velveteen Rabbit*, *Charlotte's Web*, and *Winnie the Pooh* come to mind. Such stories contain many examples of how the characters live through situations that trigger important feelings. For instance, in *Charlotte's Web*, when Charlotte is concerned about Wilbur, her barnyard friend, we can talk about feelings associated with loyalty, fear, and perseverance. Stories are especially useful because all of us, and especially kids, usually have a much easier time identifying *someone else's* feelings.

- Have kids describe the feelings they get from a certain situation. For instance, have kids cut out pictures from old magazines and do a collage depicting how they felt when the home team won the basketball championship or how they felt the day they moved into the new house or when they didn't make the team. Younger kids (age 6-11) usually love to cut and paste, and even older kids (junior high and high schoolers) enjoy this activity. Pictures found in magazines and pasted on a sheet will often allow the more nonverbal kids to develop the skills they need to express their feelings openly.

- Expose kids to a rich, constructive vocabulary of feeling words. One way is to give them a sheet of feeling words and discuss them together or have kids draw a face next to each one. It's amazing how even very young kids (grades 1-3) will be able to draw faces to match specific feelings.

- Be a good listener. Often our kids primarily need a sounding board for their feelings.
- Set aside some time each day for shutting off TVs, radios, phones, record players, VCRs, and any other distractions that interfere with free expression of feelings at home.
- Support kids when they express feelings. Frank statements such as "I'm glad you could tell me that" or nonverbal support such as hugs make a real impact on our kids.
- Be patient with kids' direct or indirect expressions of feelings. ("I hate you" versus slamming the door or using sarcasm). Help them identify the feeling; invite them to share. ("You seem really angry. Can you talk to me about it?") Sometimes they find it difficult or impossible to share certain feelings with parents, so give them a chance to talk with others. They need a wide range of options. For instance, when Jean broke up with her boyfriend she chose to share the feelings with Aunt Susan. Though this was difficult for her mother to accept, it was easier for Jean to talk with her aunt than with her mother at that point in her life. What was important was that she was talking.
- Show kids that their feelings are their friends by showing them that their feelings send them signals about how they're relating at the moment to persons, places, things, or circumstances. Teach them to ask themselves questions. "How do I feel these days about my appearance? If I feel lousy about it, why? Am I just imagining that I'm too fat or that my clothes aren't right? And what's behind my feelings? Maybe I do need to eat healthier, non-fattening foods; maybe I do need some advice on how to dress." "How do I feel about my classes? If I'm feeling pretty happy, maybe my feelings

are signaling that I'm a conscientious kid who deserves to feel good about my studies."

- Avoid making judgments about feelings. Feelings are never good or bad. ("It's silly to feel that way.")
- Avoid setting consequences when kids are sharing their feelings honestly. Avoid any language or action that might seem like a threat or punishment. ("You might feel sorry now, but you'll be a lot sorrier when I'm finished with you.")
- Don't dominate the conversation. It's one thing to be a good model; it's another to take over. Appropriate sharing is fine, but when kids have feelings it's important to let them own them. ("I know exactly how you feel. Last week at work when Jerry..."—and the parent rambles on and on with his or her own story, forgetting the youngster's problem.)
- Avoid rescuing. Kids have to own their feelings and eventually make their decision about how to deal with them. Being sensitive and supportive doesn't mean rescuing. ("You'll feel better if I take you to a movie.")

The Importance of Feeling-Processing Skills

Processing feelings is a cluster of lifeskills that we must help our kids learn because critical decisions about drugs are made, as we've pointed out, in emotionally charged situations. The typical youngster really hasn't been given much understanding of feelings: what they are, how they influence us, what we can do not only to counter their possible harm to us but to use them in a positive way as our friends and powerful helpers in developing a well-balanced, strong personality.

Kids whose parents have explained feelings to them and helped them put their knowledge to work in everyday home situations will be able to identify their feelings, own them, and express them in a healthy, constructive way. Such kids are in a strong position to make important decisions wisely and firmly. Finally, because feelings pervade our whole life, handling them well is basic to developing the other lifeskills that we will discuss.

Decision-Making Skills

Shawn, a seventh grader, is walking to school with his friend Brian. Brian suggests that they skip school and go to the video arcade, then go to Brian's house and drink a few beers. He's pretty sure his parents won't miss the beers because there's a whole case of cans opened in the basement, and his parents aren't the kind to keep close track of them. Brian says, "It'll be a blast, and no one will ever know the difference. I can get my older sister to write us excuses for school and sign our parents' names to them."

Brian has been his friend since grade school, and Shawn knows it would be fun. But he also realizes that if they get caught he could be in a lot of trouble. Shawn has to make a decision.

The ability to make wise decisions is more critical than ever for today's kids, who are faced with making very adult decisions at an increasingly younger age. To help our kids develop skill in decision making, we need to be clear in our own minds—and to make clear to them—the four basic components of the process: identifying our feelings, brainstorming, sorting out pros and cons, and evaluating those pros and cons.

Identifying Feelings

We just mentioned that processing feelings is basic for other lifeskills. The first stage of processing feelings, identifying feelings, is particularly relevant to decision making. When Shawn is confronted by Brian's invitation, what he needs to do first is identify his own feelings. If he's able to do that he might identify several conflicting ones.

- I like Brian and want to keep him as a friend, and I'm afraid I might lose him if I don't skip school with him.
- It'd be fun to skip school.
- I'm afraid of what might happen if we got caught.
- I'd feel guilty and scared about skipping school, drinking stolen beer, handing in a fake excuse at school, and lying to my parents.

Decisions typically have their roots in many such complex and ambivalent feelings. Some decisions are based on feelings we have right now, others on feelings we've had in the past, still others on feelings we predict we'll have in the future. Since our feelings are so complex and even contradictory, we need to sort them out carefully and name them clearly so that we know just what they are. Then we are ready to move on to the next step.

Brainstorming

Brainstorming is nothing more than thinking and perhaps writing a list of the options available in a given situation. Shawn, for example, clearly has two primary options: either skip school or go to school. As he continues to consider options, though, others might become clear.

- I could refuse to join Brian altogether and go on to school.
- I could go to school in the morning and meet Brian at noon.

- I could skip school but not drink the beer with Brian.
- I could try to persuade Brian not to drink the beer.
- I could try to persuade Brian not to skip school.

Sorting Out Pros and Cons

The options are really quite numerous. Each option has consequences, both positive and negative, that would probably follow. We often refer to these anticipated consequences as pros and cons of the choice. It is important that we raise kids in an environment where considering the mixed consequences of our choices is a normal, natural part of everyday life. I've discovered again and again in dealing with kids that teaching them to sort out the pros and cons of their decisions is very helpful. As Shawn, for instance, ponders his options he can rather easily sort them out on that basis.

His pros for skipping school with Brian might well be:
- It would be fun.
- Brian might accept me more.
- I could brag about it to other kids.

His cons might well be:
- I might get in trouble at school.
- I might lose privileges at home.
- I'd feel guilty lying at home and at school.
- I'd feel guilty about drinking beer when I know my parents object.
- I'd feel guilty about drinking stolen beer.
- Some kids at school might think I was stupid.

It might seem clear to you and me that the cons far outweigh the pros, but how Shawn decides will depend on the next step: how he evaluates their relative weights.

Evaluating Pros and Cons

This step is the climax of the decision-making process. After all, no matter how right or wrong our decisions might prove to be, we ultimately make it on the basis of how we evaluate the pros and cons. In effect we say, "All things considered, this set looks more attractive than that set. So I'm going this way." Here are several things we can do to help our kids evaluate pros and cons wisely.

1. When we look at Shawn's list of pros and cons, we notice right away that most of the pros for skipping school bring immediate rewards such as having fun and being accepted by his peers. But all the cons bring delayed consequences such as feelings of guilt and fear of being caught. If Shawn makes his choice based on what will feel best right now (immediate gratification), he might choose to skip school. But as he learns to forgo immediate gratification for longer-term benefits, he'll very probably opt to go to school. While it's difficult for young people to think beyond this moment, it's possible with practice and guidance from parents. The message to us is clear: To help kids make choices to say no to drugs, we must help them learn to consider long-range consequences.

2. To help kids learn how to evaluate pros and cons, we also need to teach them to consider these pros and cons from a variety of perspectives. For instance:

- The perspective of one's best self alone: In view of my own values, regardless of what others think or of whatever else might happen, which decision will I be proudest of?
- The perspective of others: In view of what my parents, friends, and others might think and do (in other words, my reputation and the consequences that others might inflict on me), which decisions will I be most comfortable with?

- The long-range perspective: When I think not just of today but of tomorrow, next week, next month, even years from now, which decision will I feel best about?

3. It's difficult for kids to think about the future and to develop the habit of anticipating that every decision they make will have either immediate or eventual consequences or both. So we need to be very patient in helping them develop this crucial lifeskill. But my experience has been that with patience and practice, kids can slowly develop the ability to make choices that have positive long-term results.

4. We need more than patience. We need to keep thinking of practical ways of helping our kids learn this skill. That means weaving decision making into the fabric of our everyday family life so that it becomes an integral, expected part of their lives. After all, if the only decisions our kids make are huge, career-threatening or life-threatening ones such as the decision to use or not use drugs (decisions typically made away from home, where our influence is far weaker), they won't have developed the necessary skill to handle such major tasks all at once, and we can almost predict they'll choose poorly.

How to Help Kids Make Decisions

- Model good decision making. Talk to kids about decisions you're facing, and explain the steps you go through in making a decision. Allow them to become involved in the decisions we adults face.
- Be a resource. Rather than giving kids solutions or directions because we're sure we know what's best, be there as a resource to help them go through the four big steps in making their own decisions. Let them make the choice, but help them sort out their options and their long-term ramifications.

- Encourage kids to investigate pros and cons by playing "what if." For instance: What if I ask the girl my best friend likes to go to the game with me? What if I'm asked to be a cheerleader and my best friend isn't?
- Allow kids to make mistakes. We'd never learn to ride a bike if we didn't risk a few spills. So allow kids to make some choices you don't really agree with.
- Encourage kids to get involved in a personal-growth group, or in various activities where they'll have opportunities to make decisions and help others make decisions.
- Look for opportunities to discuss decision-making with your kids, especially in a risk-free environment where unwise choices don't really do any harm. TV programs, movies, books, comic books, the daily newspaper all offer many opportunities to second-guess choices others have made.
- Be interested in longer-term outcomes of what kids are doing. Give them encouragement by praise and other rewards for completing projects or activities they've begun; many kids have great initial enthusiasm but soon give up.
- Actually work side by side with your kids in projects that require a long time, stamina, and patience to complete. As the project unfolds, help them be invested in it by asking them how they think the two of you should go about it, and by letting them make critical choices on such matters as selecting materials and colors.
- Avoid making decisions your kids should make, such as whom to date, what clothes to buy, whether to save money for school or buy the new CD player. Even though we probably know what's best for them, it's never productive to interfere in choices that are truly their responsibility. The goal of parenting, after all, is to

prepare kids to face the real world. So we have to involve them in situations where they learn real lifeskills that will actually help them deal effectively with everyday situations.

- Don't lecture. Listen. Our role in the process of our kid's decision making is essentially to be a resource and sounding board. Kids only learn by doing.

The Importance of Decision Making Skills

For kids to avoid drugs they must be prepared to make even major decisions at a very early age. We must assume that by age eight or nine our kids may have to make critical choices related to alcohol or other drug use. These choices are complex and emotionally charged. Simplistic short-term solutions will always fall short. Kids must be equipped to make choices that will benefit them in the long run.

Skills for Establishing Positive Behavior

Let's assume that a youngster has learned those two bedrock lifeskills of processing feelings and making wise decisions. As those two skills develop, kids gradually begin making choices that will prove sensible in the long run (they're overcoming the tendency to choose only on the basis of immediate gratification). For instance, when Mike learned he had been cut from the football team, he was of course crushed. But he talked his feelings out with parents and friends and decided to join an early fall basketball team instead. Now he's working on his way toward a successful basketball season rather than becoming caught up in self-defeating behavior as a result of being cut from the football team. In other words, Mike has learned to turn problems into opportunities. This means he's already well on his way to establishing positive patterns of behavior. Here are three major ways of ensuring that he'll follow through on his decisions in a way that will enlarge and deepen this positive pattern: establishing and maintaining a positive attitude, developing and sticking to an action plan, and learning to congratulate himself.

Establishing and Maintaining Positive Attitudes

Kids who get caught in self-defeating patterns of behavior often get caught up in self-defeating attitudes as well. Our most important attitudes are those we have toward ourselves. Overly harsh, critical, judgmental attitudes about ourselves are self-defeating.

A good way of becoming aware of our attitudes about ourselves is to look at *how we talk to ourselves.* Kids who get caught up in self-defeating attitudes most often say things to themselves like: "I'm just too dumb," "I'm too ugly," or "No one cares about me." These patterns of negative self-talk reinforce patterns of self-defeating behavior because they provide an immediate excuse or rationalization for it. And naturally they keep the young person trapped.

The key to learning self-enhancing behavior lies in *establishing an attitude that reflects confidence, openness, and a willingness to try.* A helpful way to build up that positive attitude is to help kids learn to use *affirmations.* Affirmations are short, usually one-line statements that reflect encouraging, self-enhancing self-talk, such as: "I'm good person," "I'm a hard worker," "I can do most anything I set my mind to," and "I like people."

How we talk to ourselves is clearly related to *the attitude we project to others.* If we can learn to talk to ourselves in a confident, patient, and supportive tone, we'll begin to project our attitude to others. Learning to use affirmations helps us project an image of confidence and strength. This image in turn is the beginning of establishing positive, self-enhancing behavior patterns that help kids make difficult choices such as saying no to drugs.

Establishing an Action Plan

We can break a large, general goal or objective into an action plan of small steps. These steps provide the young person with small bits of success and payoffs along the way.

For example, Mark decided to continue track even though he didn't make the relay team this year. After processing his feelings of disappointment and frustration, he made that decision because he believed he could make the team next year. The hard part would be to follow through with a plan that had few payoffs until a whole year later. The solution was to establish a plan that broke the ultimate, larger goal into many action steps along the way. To do that, Mark made a chart that allowed him to record his progress daily. As he participated in his regular workouts he was able to note his progress toward his overall goal and to experience positive feelings of pride, confidence and excitement.

Learning to establish an action plan is a skill that helps kids channel their activities in a direction that will create *long-term* rewards but also carry *short-term* payoffs along the way. By establishing self-enhancing patterns of behavior our kids are also building stronger self-esteem and generating positive feelings that in turn reinforce additional positive choices.

Congratulating Ourselves

The final step in establishing positive patterns of behavior is learning to give ourselves a good pat on the back. Our culture

444

has a strong taboo against being a braggart. This taboo often prevents us from congratulating ourselves when we do well. Learning to say to ourselves "Good job!" or "I did my best," or "I deserve this award (recognition, praise)" is important if we hope to teach our kids these important ways of establishing positive patterns of behavior.

We need to show our kids how to build themselves up by congratulating themselves. We need to tell them things like, "John, you should pat yourself on the back for studying so hard." Kids can learn to congratulate themselves on many things, such as learning how to handle money, choosing good companions, getting a part-time job, practicing the flute faithfully. These are attainable, repeatable behaviors that they can perform; they don't all have to score the winning touchdown or get all A's and B's.

By helping our kids learn to reinforce themselves we help them be less dependent on constant reinforcement from others. Kids who are unhealthily dependent on the approval of others (especially their peers) are vulnerable to peer pressure when the time comes to make decisions about using or not using drugs.

How to Help Kids Establish Positive Behavior

- Become more aware of your own patterns of behavior and try to model patterns that are healthy and self-enhancing.
- Freely and openly say affirmations about kids. "I admire your willingness to practice the piano so regularly."
- Acknowledge kids' daily successes as they occur. Learning to pat ourselves on the back is first learned from others who pat us on the back.

- Teach kids to respond directly to positive feedback with simple acknowledgements such as "Thank you" and "I'm glad you like it" rather than denying or minimizing the congratulations with "It's really nothing."
- Work with kids to establish action plans they can share with you as they carry through on activities. Posting stars and stickers on charts works well with younger kids.
- When confronting negative behavior, be willing to go beyond just setting consequences. Help kids understand which part of the process (feelings, decisions, or behavior) is causing them problems.
- Be openly demonstrative with praise that acknowledges some specific aspect of a kid. "It amazes me how much effort you've been putting into that history paper." Positive feelings, hugs, and congratulations from us often become too rare, especially as our kids get older.
- Don't use money or material presents or your approval as rewards for positive behavior. These rewards undermine the establishment of the lifeskill for its own sake and give kids the unrealistic expectation that rewards always follow positive behavior.
- Avoid saying "I'm so proud of you" so that they feel it's you they have to please. Instead say "You have every right to feel proud of your effort or accomplishment. Good for you."
- Don't give others credit for what your kids do. It can sometimes be easy to congratulate a coach, a team, a teacher, or anyone else for what our own kids accomplish. No matter who has helped, kids must receive credit directly from us for their good behavior, just as they receive blame for the negative behavior.
- Don't withhold approval. Sometimes we withhold it

because we suspect our kids are being manipulative, or because they misbehaved yesterday, or because we're simply not comfortable giving praise. When our kids do something well they deserve to be congratulated.

The Importance of Establishing Positive Behavior Skills

Establishing a pattern of positive behavior is essential to prevent drug abuse with our kids. Positive behavior can become self-perpetuating and self-enhancing just as truly and powerfully as negative behavior like drug use can.

Mood-Maintenance Skills

Ben is stuck. He feels numb inside. When pushed to describe his feelings, he says he feels empty. He avoids decisions. He doesn't have the energy for thinking and analyzing. His behavior has become lethargic. He often sleeps ten to fourteen hours a day. Ben is caught in a very low-range mood of depression. Unfortunately, kids who become engulfed in these low-range moods are extremely vulnerable to using alcohol or other drugs as a means of self-medication.

Lisa is also stuck, but on the other end of the spectrum. She's obsessively active, afraid to slow down or relax. Moving from activity to activity, Lisa uses perpetual motion as a way to avoid facing her feelings. Being a perfectionist, she's afraid that if she doesn't always make sure that things get done, and done very well, people will think bad things about her. She finds herself trapped in the upper-range mood of anxiety.

What Are Moods?

Moods are sometimes described as the product of the decisions we make or the behaviors we participate in or how we deal with our feelings. Individuals who become trapped in self-defeating patterns of dealing with feelings, decisions, and behaviors usually find themselves caught in either upper-range or low-range moods. That's a set-up for kids to use alcohol or drugs.

In explaining moods to kids I often use the analogy of a car going from 0 to 100 miles per hour. The car speeds correspond to the following moods:

0	Depressed
10	Detached
20	Bored
30	Calm
40	Relaxed
50	Interested
60	Excited
70	Anxious
80	Irritable
90	Angry
100	Enraged

Most kids know that cars run most efficiently and safely at somewhere between 30 and 60 miles per hour, even though we sometimes need to drive them faster or slower. The moods corresponding to speeds from 30 to 60 miles per hour tend to be the safest and most productive for us humans as well. If we find ourselves stuck in the low-range moods of boredom, detachment or depression, we never get anywhere. People around us become impatient, and eventually we lose all momentum and direction. Conversely, if we get stuck in the high-range moods of anxiety, irritability, anger or rage, we often go off half-cocked, we can't slow down and we usually run the risk of hurting ourselves or others.

Getting stuck in these uncomfortable high or low mood ranges is easier than most of us think. If we lack the lifeskills to effectively process our feelings, make good decisions, or maintain productive behavior, we'll find ourselves more likely to become trapped in these uncomfortable moods. Moods are the products of how we deal with the challenges we face on a day-in, day-out basis. Consequently we might describe our moods are being encircled by the activities of feeling processing, decision making, and behavior control. If we lack skills in any vital area of daily life, this void can severely affect our moods, moving us to either the high or low range. Kids who get caught here tend to run a greater risk of early abuse of drugs and also run a significantly high risk of developing serious problems with drugs.

On the other hand, when kids learn lifeskills, they process their feelings properly, make decisions based on long-term needs and goals, and follow through with self-enhancing behavior. When those things happen, their moods stabilize within that middle zone of 30 to 60 miles per hour, which means they're calm, relaxed, interested, healthily excited. In working with kids, we consistently find that those who have learned to maintain their moods within the middle range are less likely either to use alcohol and other drugs or to develop problems with them.

Strategies for Mood-Maintenance

Obviously, the lifeskills discussed earlier are crucial in helping kids keep their moods in the middle range. Here are some other useful strategies parents can use to help their kids reach that goal.

Diet: Getting sound nutrition on a daily basis is essential in maintaining our moods. Almost all family physicians have literature on sound family nutrition. Or check out a book from the library or ask at your local bookstore.

Sleep: Many of the chemically dependent kids I've worked with have long histories of poor sleeping habits and sleep disturbances. Almost everyone needs between seven and nine hours of sleep per night. Getting more or less than we need tends to have negative effects on our moods.

Exercise: Kids (and adults) suffering from problems with moods, especially low-range moods associated with depression, often are inactive. Regular exercise not only keeps us fit; it also affects our moods and changes our whole outlook on life.

Relaxation: Relaxation is especially important for the child who has tendencies toward the high-range moods of anxiety, irritability, and rage. Activities that develop one's ability to relax, such as meditation, reading and various crafts, are important tools in mood-maintenance.

H.A.L.T.: A lifeskill that has been taught to thousands of recovering alcoholics as a means of making them aware of their mood swings is H.A.L.T. The letters stand for "hungry, angry, lonely, tired." The message for the alcoholic is to avoid getting too hungry, angry, lonely or tired, because that's a surefire way to fall back into drug use. This is also a technique we can easily teach ourselves and our kids.

I've also used H.A.L.T. with kids as a tool to indicate that some strange, uncomfortable things may be going on inside them:

- Hungry: "I'm hungry even though I've eaten enough."
- Angry: "I'm angry even though there's no one bothering me."
- Lonely: "I'm lonely even though there are people all around me."
- Tired: "I'm tired even though I've had enough sleep."

When kids complain, for example, of feeling hungry even though they've clearly had enough to eat, H.A.L.T. is signaling that they're experiencing feelings they haven't identified, owned, and expressed constructively, and that as a result they're slipping from healthy mid-range moods to the more unstable high-range or low-range moods. Teaching our kids to be *aware* of their moods and mood changes is a long step toward helping them *maintain* these moods in the middle range, which puts them in a much stronger position to say no to drugs.

How to Help Kids Manage Their Moods

- Model healthful eating habits. Avoid having junk food in the house and plan regular meals that include all the basic food groups.
- Establish routines for quiet time, bedtime and sleeping time that allow all members of the family to get the sleep and relaxation they need.
- Do activities with kids that teach them good exercise habits and at the same time show that exercise is fun.
- Help kids avoid confining themselves to passive activities such as watching TV or sitting on the sidelines at all sporting events. Encourage their active participation in sports, hobbies, and outdoor activities.
- Help the family openly discuss the mood levels of individual family members and of the family as a whole.
- Become aware of your own moods and be willing to discuss with the kids how those moods affect them and others around you. Modeling this willingness will teach kids a lot about maintaining their own moods in the comfortable middle range. Also, it's important to be responsive to kids as they give us feedback about our moods.
- Direct your kids to have jobs that don't interfere with proper daily habits associated with basic needs such as proper nutrition, sleep, exercise and relaxation.

The Importance of Mood-Maintenance Skills

Mood-maintenance is a lifeskill which, when undeveloped, can lead to drug problems. By definition alcohol and other drugs are *mood-altering* chemicals, and that's precisely why they're often used to maintain or change moods artificially. By teaching our kids specific and healthful ways to maintain their moods in the desirable mid-range, we significantly reduce their vulnerability to drug use.

Communication Skills

Chemical dependence is often called a disease of loneliness. Many young people try to get rid of their loneliness by turning to drugs as a means of building up their confidence so they can meet people and make friends. Satisfying interpersonal relationships, by contrast, reduce a young person's tendency to seek drugs.

Communication skills are important tools that kids need to connect with others. As we might expect, and as researchers keep telling us, kids who are good communicators are well accepted by others, so they're well on their way to establishing the personal contacts that prevent loneliness and its predictable effects, including drug problems.

Communication skills are equally important to parents as a means of building and maintaining good relationships with their kids.

The Ineffective Communicator

Kids learn their communication habits, good or bad, primarily from parents who model them. When we want to teach our kids communication skills, then, we need to look first at our own communication habits to see which are effective and which are ineffective. It helps to start by inspecting the ineffective ones, because we often unwittingly fall into them.

- **The Drill Sergeant:** The primary goal of the drill sergeant is to demand submission. The drill sergeant's communication often uses threats, punishment, ridicule, or harsh methods. The drill sergeant often uses language such as "What do you mean, you feel like crying? No son or daughter of mine is going to be a bawl-baby!" or "Being afraid of the water is no excuse for not jumping in. The only way to learn to swim is to jump into water that's over your head and learn how not to drown." The message that kids really get from drill sergeants is that it's not safe to share feelings or show weaknesses in their presence, because they'll be ridiculed or demeaned.

- **The Prosecuting Attorney:** The goal of the prosecuting attorney is to get the facts; nothing else is important. The prosecuting attorney often resorts to cross-examination or verbal trickery in an effort to get all the information.

    Son (looking sad and dejected): "I didn't make the basketball team."

    Parent: "But *why*? Didn't you put out for the coach?"

    Son: "Yeah, I think I worked hard, but the kid who beat me out was better."

    Parent: "You must have done something wrong. What was it? Either you weren't working hard enough or you just didn't care. If you'd have done your best, you'd have made the team."

    Son: "You don't understand. You just think I'm a big loser."

    The message kids get from the prosecuting attorney is "I don't count; it's not important how I feel."

- **The Egomaniac:** The goal of the egomaniac, even if it's not consciously intended, is to talk about only what he or she is interested in and not to listen at all to the other person. A typical tactic of the egomaniac is switching subjects. No matter what the young person tries to talk about, the conversation always returns to the egomaniac. He or she is incapable of listening to anything that doesn't arouse immediate interest or give gratification to him or her. The egomaniac often uses such tactics as "You think your football coach is tough on you? Well, when I was your age we used to . . ." or "I'm sure glad you made the honor roll. Did I ever tell you about the way I felt when I . . .?" The message kids get is "What's the use in trying? Whatever I do is never as good as what he (she) did."

- **The Comedian:** The goal of the comedian is to take the focus off uncomfortable topics by making others laugh. For example, if a child has been caught cheating in school, instead of dealing with the child's feelings that prompted the cheating, the comedian will make a joke to cover up the seriousness of the problem. "Well, I'm real happy you haven't murdered anyone yet. Heh, heh." The comedian often uses sarcasm or cynicism couched in humor to get his or her point across. "You sure look like a stuffed monkey in that outfit." It's frustrating when kids try to communicate with the comedian, who can always counter any criticism with "I was just having a little fun" or "Just teasing." But the method isn't funny, and it does hurt. And ultimately the comedian's approach teaches kids a terrible habit: covering up their true feelings by laughing when they're actually in trouble and hurting inside.

- **The Psychiatrist:** The goal of the psychiatrist is to analyze, diagnose, and then prescribe the appropriate action to solve a youngster's problem. "I think what's really behind these arguments with your sister is that she has developed a very passive-aggressive attitude toward you, and I think you're caught in an attention-getting ploy that will..." The psychiatrist might appear to be an effective listener but actually undermines communication by assuming too much responsibility for the child's behavior. This communicates to the child that there will always be someone to give him or her the right answer and that there's no need to learn to think for oneself.

- **The Avoider:** The goal of the avoider is the same as that of the comedian: to sidetrack uncomfortable concerns, no matter how serious they are. Instead of using humor, though, the avoider simply drops any heated or controversial topic. "Well, I certainly agree that nuclear weapons are a problem, but my dad always told me never to argue religion or politics. Did you see what the Yankees did yesterday? Eight runs in the fifth inning!" The message kids get from the avoider is that conflict and controversy are dangerous and should be avoided at all costs, even if it means covering up our feelings or violating our convictions to avoid "a scene."

Here's how each type of ineffective communicator might respond to a twelve year old who says, "I don't have time to clean my room and do my homework, too. You always expect me to be perfect."

- **The Drill Sergeant:** "You march right back upstairs this instant, and don't show your face down here until you've finished both jobs."
- **The Prosecuting Attorney:** "How much homework have you done? And why haven't you done it? If you don't get the grades you promised, there'll be hell to pay around here."

- **The Egomaniac:** "When I was your age I not only had to keep my room clean and do my homework, I had three cows to milk every morning and evening."
- **The Comedian:** "What do you mean, you can't do both at the same time? You seem to do pretty well keeping two or three girls on the hook all at the same time."
- **The Psychiatrist:** "I think your problem is in time management. Let me look at your daily and weekly schedule, and I'll figure out something for you." (As we've pointed out, this supposedly helpful response takes on too much of the youngster's responsibility. It's one thing to be sensitive to our kids' problems; it's another to take them over and solve them. This approach invites either extreme rebellion or extreme compliance.)
- **The Avoider:** "You're probably just tired. Run along and don't worry about it. I'm sure things will be better tomorrow."

These ineffective communication habits can either destroy good relationships between us and our kids, or prevent them from ever developing because we're habitually modeling habits that tend to build walls between us and our kids.

The Effective Communicator

Effective communication primarily involves both speaking and listening. But I've discovered that by far the greatest difficulty in communication between parents and kids is lack of listening skills. So I'll concentrate on that crucial area. Once we've become aware of any ineffective listening habits, we want to start building up habits that help bond us to our kids. Good listening habits make us accessible to our kids. They help us hear not only what our kids are saying but what they're not saying. Effective listeners fall into two categories: the active listener and the facilitative listener.

The Active Listener: The active listener aims at two goals: not only to hear the message being delivered but to reinforce the person delivering the message by giving him or her both verbal and nonverbal feedback. Let's say, for example, that Bill is listening to his son Tom tell about his friend Larry's car accident. Here are some examples of reinforcing the message and giving verbal feedback:

- Appropriate questions: "Where were Larry's parents when the accident happened?" "Was Larry driving the family car, or his own?"
- Clarifying content: "Do you mean Larry didn't even try to slow down, or do you mean he tried to slow down but couldn't?"
- Appropriate verbal encouragement: "Uh huh, I see." "Go on." "Tell me more."
- Good eye contact: looking directly at the person speaking in an open, nonthreatening way.
- A facial expression that indicates interest, understanding, empathy. Being responsive means laughing when things are funny and generally responding nonverbally in an appropriate way.

The Facilitative Listener: The active listener, who listens in such a way as to hear the content and at the same time to reinforce the child giving the message, is most effective when the child just needs a sounding board, an opportunity to ventilate ideas and feelings in a safe environment. Active listening will probably make up eighty to ninety percent of the listening time we spend with our kids. But sometimes our kids need more: They need help in bringing their *underlying feelings* to the surface so they can clarify them. That's where the facilitative listener comes in.

The facilitative listener uses the same skills that the active listener does but goes one step farther: by observing what's *not* put into words at all. The facilitative listener picks up *nonverbal clues* by watching for *body language* such as facial expressions (angry, sad), gestures (jiggling the feet, wringing the hands), posture (slumped), kinds of breathing (rapid, heavy exhaling), skin color (flushed, pale), and tone of voice (quiet, anxious). All these can indicate the child's real feelings—feelings that the words themselves don't indicate at all, or that the words might be trying to conceal or even falsify. The observant parent will pick up this body language, interpret what feelings it signifies, and use the clues to help the child clarify his or her feelings.

Son (looking sad, dejected, posture slumped): "I didn't make the team."

Parent: "It looks as if you have a lot of feelings about that."

Son: "No, its okay. I'm kind of mad at the coach, but I'll get over it."

Parent: "You look like you might be feeling more hurt or rejected than angry. Do you have mixed feelings?"

Son: "Well, maybe I do have some of those other feelings, but right now it's easier to be mad."

Parent: "I understand. Sometimes it's hard to feel all of our feelings at once. I'd be glad to talk with you about this later when you're more comfortable. Is that okay?"

Son: "Yeah, maybe we could take a walk after dinner."

Facilitative listening isn't easy for some of us. The temptation is either to get caught up only in the content of what's being said and consequently to disregard feelings or to become so involved in protecting our kids from their feelings that we insulate them from pain by smothering them with consolation or pat answers. ("You shouldn't take it so hard. Hey, how about going to a movie and then stopping for pizza?")

The important assumption behind facilitative listening is that our children have the capacity to work through and deal constructively with their own feelings and their own life situations. But when difficult, emotion-laden situations arise and kids are confused about their own feelings and about possible courses of action, we can be there as facilitative listeners who help them clarify their feelings and decide on sensible ways out of their problems. Kids whose parents aren't there offering such help often turn to the quick fix of drugs.

How to Help Kids Communicate

- Become more aware of your listening style. Look at the situations where you fall into ineffective listening and consider ways to listen more effectively.
- Ask others for feedback on how well you listen. Check again after working on it for a few weeks, and see if you've improved.
- Gently give your kids feedback on their listening habits. Ask them for feedback on your listening habits, too. Work with each other to establish good active and facilitative listening skills.
- Talk with your kids about relationships and the role of communication.
- When you don't have time to listen right now, make sure to get back to your kids within a reasonable time. It's important to acknowledge their problems and to commit yourself to helping.
- Don't expect yourself and your kids to be perfect listeners all the time. You all need time to develop your listening skills.

The Importance of Communication Skills

Communication skills are a basic tool in establishing healthy, satisfying relationships. Because kids (and adults) tend to use alcohol or other drugs as a substitute for relationships, our own communication skills and the communications skills we teach our kids are essential in helping them avoid drugs. Kids learn styles of communication primarily by observing others, especially parents. So the communication styles we model for them are crucially important.

Refusal Skills

Ellen, a seventh grader, was somewhat shy. When Kathy moved into the neighborhood, she and Ellen began hanging out together. Ellen liked being around Kathy because Kathy was outgoing, a lot of fun, and instinctively know how to attract boys. When Kathy offered to share some vodka with her, Ellen was surprised. Ellen had promised her parents she wouldn't use alcohol or other drugs, and she took the promise seriously, but she really liked Kathy. She also envied how easily Kathy could talk with others, and she wanted to be like her.

When Kathy assured her that a couple of drinks of vodka would make her more relaxed and confident, Ellen wanted to say no, but the words just wouldn't form in her mouth. She was caught because she was afraid. She lacked refusal skills.

Refusal skills enable us to say no when we want to say no, and to do it effectively. Both common sense and the best of current research tell us that if we want to prevent our kids from getting involved in drugs, we have to teach them, among other things, how to use refusal skills.

The Continuum of Refusal Styles

There are many ways or styles of saying no. For instance, in *Your Perfect Right: A Guide to Assertive Living,* Robert E.

Alberti and Michael L. Emmons describe a continuum of styles that range from passive to aggressive, with the desirable assertive style falling in the middle.

The Passive Refusal Style: People who use the passive style of refusal tend to say *maybe* a lot more than they say *no*. They often report feeling obligated to go along with others, or at least to appear to be going along. A typical passive refusal often sounds something like token resistance followed by compliance. "I'd really rather not, at least not right now. But if everybody else is, well, maybe." The person who uses this style would generally rather not go along with the crowd but lacks the confidence and skills to take a stand.

The Aggressive Refusal Style: People who use this refusal style typically overstate their objection and go so far as to be indignant or morally outraged at what's been proposed to them. Those who use this style often resort to insults or threats, and their whole manner shows that they don't really respect others. A typical aggressive refusal sounds like "What? Me drink that stuff? You guys must be a bunch of morons." Their indignation might seem to represent deep convictions about their beliefs and values, but it's usually more of a compensation for insecurity and feelings of self-doubt.

The Assertive Refusal Style: This is the refusal style we want to help our kids learn. It avoids the extreme, unproductive behavior of both the passive and the aggressive styles, and, unlike them, really is a skill, a truly desirable method of handling the delicate problem of how to say no. People who have mastered the assertive refusal style are in a powerful position when they're invited to get involved in drugs. They're able to let it be known firmly, forcefully, clearly, but gently that the answer is no. At the same time, though, their answer and their whole manner shows that although they don't want to get involved in drugs, they respect the people they're talking to. They don't resort to self-righteous indignation, anger, insults or threats. The end result is that they've maintained their own position but haven't alienated others or isolated themselves. Some typical assertive refusals include: "No, I can't. I want to stay eligible for football." or "No, thanks. I always have a good time without it."

How to Help Kids Learn Refusal Skills

What can parents do to help their kids learn this assertive refusal style? Here are three major recommendations: help them develop confidence, help them practice assertive refusal skills, and reinforce their individuality.

Help Kids Develop Confidence: Confidence is crucial in developing effective refusal skills. Kids who don't feel sure of themselves can't calmly and firmly assert their values and decisions. We can help them develop confidence in a number of ways.

- Express your love for them openly and often. We tend to assume that kids know we love them, but in childhood years and early adolescence they often feel unloved, unwanted.
- Give kids positive feedback on specific instances of good behavior.
- When confronting kids on negative behavior, make sure they know you're focusing on their behavior, not on them as people.

Help Kids Practice Assertive Refusal Skills: Kids develop the ability to say no at about eighteen months. During the terrible twos, "no" seems to be the only word they know. Trying as those early years are for parents, they mark the important initial attempts at assertiveness. In grade school, when peer pressure becomes very strong, youngsters increasingly need to practice refusal skills so they won't weakly go along with the crowd in everything. Parents can help by giving kids opportunities to discuss problem situations that often occur, such as saying no to a bully or to an older kid, and then role-playing such situations ("Okay, I'm a bully. I want that jacket of yours, kid."). These discussions and role-playing sessions answer many needs including learning firsthand differences between refusal styles and letting our kids know we understand the types of situations they face every day.

Help Kids by Reinforcing Their Individuality: During the pre-teen years, kids are experimenting more and more with what it means to be an individual. While this conduct may be somewhat threatening to parents, we should reinforce kids by letting them know by words and deeds that we understand and approve their natural movement toward becoming mature, independent individuals. We do this by:

- Recognizing and discussing with them their unique qualities and abilities.
- Not overreacting by laying down tough and rigid rules when kids assert their individuality with what is to us bizarre behavior (showy earrings, outlandish dress and hairdos). We should talk with our kids about their motives for such conduct, show them we recognize their need for increased independence, and all the while make it clear that we support their newly emerging sense of self. When kids clearly lack the willingness to discuss the motivation behind their behavior, we may occasionally need to set limits their newly emerging individuality must fit within.
- Never ridiculing or teasing our kids about their efforts at being individuals.

The Importance of Refusal Skills

Refusal skills are essential if our kids are to develop the ability to say no to alcohol and other drugs. Simply teaching kids to rehearse pat answers isn't enough. Ineffective refusal styles usually tend to be either overly passive or overly aggressive. The effective refusal style, the assertive, asserts the individual's choice firmly but with respect for others. Parents must help kids learn assertive styles of refusal long before the kids encounter pressures to use drugs.

The Importance of All These Lifeskills

As I've highlighted throughout this chapter all the lifeskills are crucial and interrelated. Our kids need to be able to process their feelings to make good decisions. They need to develop patterns of positive behavior and know how to maintain their moods and communicate well to be able to use assertive refusal skills.

When we teach our kids the whole array of lifeskills that I've advocated in this chapter, we're giving them basic education in how to approach life's biggest problems with a confidence that brings success. Kids with such skills and such fundamental confidence are armed with the best preventive methods ever devised against drugs.

DAVID J. WILMES

This section is taken from *Parenting For Prevention: How to Raise a Child to Say No to Alcohol/Drugs*, published by the Johnson Institute.

CHAPTER TWENTY-ONE

Parental Drug Use

Bob and Janet are 39 years old. Bob comes from a family of heavy drinkers; Janet's family never drank at all. Bob likes to unwind every evening with two or three beers as he watches TV. Janet has never approved, but Bob's drinking apparently hasn't caused any problems, so she says nothing about it. But when Danny, their fourteen year old, is arrested for possession of marijuana, he argues that using marijuana is really no different from Dad's use of alcohol. The parents are surprised and disturbed by his argument. Could Danny be right?

Excessive Drug Use by Parents

This little story raises more questions than whether Danny's marijuana is really no different from his dad's using alcohol. For instance: Is his dad's regular use of alcohol moderate or excessive? Is there anything at all wrong with it? In view of parents' duty of modeling proper behavior for their kids, must parents abstain totally from alcohol and other drugs? Or, to put it somewhat differently, is any use of drugs by parents to be considered excessive? Let's talk first about what constitutes excessive use, and why.

Excessive Regular Use

Professionals usually distinguish three kinds of excessive use: regular excessive use, recreational excessive use, symptomatic excessive use. The way Danny's dad uses alcohol really falls into the first category, excessive regular use. That's not to say he's an alcoholic or that he should go into treatment right now. But there's danger in the air. Experts in the field would probably say that he's in late Phase II of chemical use, where the user is regularly seeking the mood swing that drugs bring. While he may still think of himself as a social drinker, over time his drinking may begin to exact an emotional cost: guilt or shame due to an ever-increasing number of embarrassing incidents related to his use of alcohol. For example, during a night of excessive drinking he makes obscene remarks to one of his daughter's friends who has come to the house to pick her up. If episodes like this continue to happen, he is likely to pass into Phase III of chemical use: harmful dependence. He will have crossed the line between social use and alcoholism. At this point the red light isn't on for Bob, but the amber light is certainly flashing. Later in this chapter we'll discuss the impact of parental alcoholism on kids.

However, the question of whether Bob is an alcoholic or close to being one isn't the only question here. Bob, after all, is a *parent*, and as we've repeatedly pointed out, parents are supposed to model the kind of behavior they want their children to emulate. In this important area of drug use, what is Bob modeling? He's telling Danny, by his actions, that having a few beers every night is a perfectly normal, harmless, and effective way of unwinding at the end of a hard day; that it's the way adults do it, and no questions asked. Since this is Danny's real-life introduction to the whole area of drugs, it's no wonder he sees no difference between his use of marijuana and his father's use of alcohol—a dangerous introduction indeed.

Recreational Excessive Use

Parents who habitually overindulge at weddings, family reunions, ball games, and other get-togethers exemplify this type of excessive use. The message they send to their kids is that *the* way to loosen up, celebrate events, or have fun is to get smashed; that you can't really have fun without alcohol.

Symptomatic Excessive Use

When professionals speak of "symptomatic" use of drugs, they're referring to use that's intended to relieve symptoms connected with a specific problem. For instance, those who are exhausted, grieving a loss, depressed, lonely, fearful, or who are nervous about heavy work loads, often turn to alcohol or other drugs to get relief from that particular problem.

When those people are parents, they're modeling the wrong double-barreled message to their kids: that this is a perfectly normal, adult way of dealing with difficulties, and that it works—it's a true solution. This message contradicts, however, the sound parenting messages we've been trying to send our kids: that the way to handle life's problems is to develop basic lifeskills that enable us to process our feelings, maintain our moods in the productive middle zone, and make decisions wisely.

Parents and Total Abstinence

Must parents abstain totally from alcohol to avoid giving kids mixed messages about using it? Not necessarily. I'd like to make three points about this problem: one based on common sense, one based on a simple distinction, and one based on my own experience as a counselor.

1. Common Sense

I sometimes hear an argument that, if put into words, would sound something like "If drinking isn't okay for kids, why should it be okay for parents?" Well, lots of things that are okay for adults aren't okay for kids. Adults are supposedly mature, grown-up, and so they have both responsibilities and privileges that kids don't. Adults have the responsibility of making major decisions as a matter of course: about which marriage partner to choose, which career to follow, which city and state and even country to live in, how to invest thousands or even million of dollars, and many other things. Since adults are responsible for such heavy choices, they have to be free, basically, to make them.

Kids ordinarily have no such major responsibilities, and we shouldn't push such huge decisions onto them—or even **allow** them to take them on. Kids, especially younger ones, just aren't ready. That's why we don't think it unfair that a ten year old can't get a driver's license or sign a contract to buy a home for $100,000 or vote or tour Europe alone. And I've found that most kids understand very well that they're not ready for certain decisions and privileges until they reach a certain age and a certain stage of maturity.

When it comes to deciding whether or how to use alcohol, adults must face the major decision the way they face other major decisions: freely, but taking full responsibility for their choice. Many of them will make the wrong decision; but many also make the wrong decisions about careers and marriage partners and investments. Privileges and responsibility are the two-edged sword that adults have to carry around every day.

2. A Simple Distinction

A rather simple distinction also helps us answer whether adults have to be total abstainers: **Avoiding abuse doesn't rule out use.** Automobiles kill thousands of people every year, but we don't banish them from the Earth; we try to get people to drive them responsibly. And so with alcohol. For all the misery that often comes with it, it's still abuse, not use, that causes the misery. For some people, of course, any use of alcohol turns out to be abuse; but that's a special case, to be decided in terms of each individual. The same problem hits those exceptional individuals who are allergic to wheat or macadamia nuts: Any use is too much.

3. Experience

To me, the most convincing argument against forcing total abstinence on all parents is my own experience and that of my colleagues who have researched the subject thoroughly. What that experience shows clearly is that kids raised in families where adults use alcohol appropriately and in moderate amounts show no stronger or more numerous signs of using alcohol or other drugs than do kids raised in families where parents are total abstainers. Experience teaches us that trying to force all people to stop using alcohol (Prohibition) doesn't work. The law will never override the public conscience. Moreover, alcohol isn't destructive in itself—it's the irresponsible use of it and the resulting problems that are.

Parents and Prescription Drugs

In an age when the word "drugs" almost automatically brings to mind illegal drugs such as marijuana, cocaine or heroin, we need to remind ourselves that prescription drugs are indeed drugs and that they can cause problems or serious side effects, abuse, and even addiction. Here are some recommendations about their use.

- Use only drugs prescribed for you by a careful, competent physician, and follow the directions.
- Don't assume that all physicians are aware that drugs they prescribe might cause problems of abuse and chemical dependence. In practice, some physicians overlook that danger.
- Get a second physician's opinion if you have reason to doubt whether a certain drug is suitable for you.
- Always inform a physician about any drugs prescribed for you by another physician; there may be a danger of over-medication or of incompatible drugs.
- Check other sound sources of information about drugs; pharmacists (most of whom are very knowledgeable), well-recommended books that list and evaluate drugs; experienced nurses; sensible friends whose experience with a given drug may well be invaluable as a firsthand report.
- Never mix prescription drugs with alcohol.

In this area of prescription drugs, as in so many other areas, our *modeling* of proper use is the strongest message we can send our kids about what's appropriate for them.

Parents and Illegal Drugs

I've worked with many parents who grew up in the sixties and seventies when marijuana was so popular its use was widely taken for granted. Some of those parents still feel justified in using marijuana occasionally, arguing that it's no different from using alcohol.

When parents use marijuana, though, the message they send their kids is different from the one they send when they use alcohol moderately. Despite admitted similarities between using the two substances, using marijuana adds a new, undesirable message. For the hard fact is that marijuana is illegal. So when parents use it—or any other illegal drug—they tell their kids "We're above the law." Kids easily arrive at a more general conclusion: that limits, rules, and laws are for **others.** Mom and Dad do what they want and when they want to. Why can't I?

Parents and Secret Use of Illegal Drugs

Some parents counter the previous objection to illegal drugs with "Yes, I see what you mean. But we just don't tell our kids we're using illegal drugs. So there's no harm done." When I hear that, I'm tempted to say "You must be kidding." But I try to be polite: I remind them that it's impossible to keep such secrets from kids, who are sizing us up all the time and who have seemingly limitless resources for uncovering our secrets. When they uncover this one, we've modeled not only lawbreaking but hypocrisy as well. Hardly a prescription for effective parenting!

Effects of Parental Alcoholism on Kids

From here to the summary, I'll be talking explicitly about alcoholism because alcohol is still by far the most widely used drug among parents. Naturally, though, much of the material will apply to other drugs as well.

Alcoholism in parents has terribly destructive effects on kids, both physically and psychologically. Here are some of them in very brief form. (For more information on the effects of chemical dependence on families see Chapter 9).

Physical Effects[1]

- **FAS—Fetal Alcohol Syndrome:** One of the three most frequent causes of birth defects associated with mental retardation that occurs as a direct result of a mother's alcohol abuse or addiction.
- **FAE—Fetal Alcohol Effects:** More common birth defects such as low birth weight that can produce developmental damage to the child—e.g., learning disabilities—also associated with mother's use or abuse of alcohol.

Psychological Effects

In Margaret Cork's early but classic study on children of alcoholics, *The Forgotten Children*,[2] the author reports these

---

[1] Sheila B. Blume, M.D., *Alcohol/Drug Dependent Women: New Insights into Their Special Problems, Treatment, Recovery* (Minneapolis: The Johnson Institute, 1988).

[2] R. Margaret Cork, *The Forgotten Children: A Study of Children with Alcoholic Parents* (Toronto: Alcoholism and Drug Addiction Research Foundation, 1969).

statistics on children of alcoholic parents:

- 98% feel that relationships within the family are affected
- 97% feel that relationships outside the family are affected
- 94% feel unsure of themselves, lack confidence
- 97% feel unwanted by one or both parents
- 77% feel constantly ashamed or hurt and get upset and cry easily

In brief, the impact of parental alcoholism on children is devastating. Not only do alcoholic parents model inappropriate use of drugs, but they fail to build a home environment that gives kids the pervasive sense of security they need if they're ever to develop the basic lifeskills. Instead of developing those positive, healthy lifeskills that help the emerging adult to exercise and strengthen his or her wings, gradually become an independent adult, and in due time move out of the family circle and use those skills confidently in the outside world, the child in an alcoholic home develops **survival** skills—skills that help him or her merely to survive in that abnormal alcoholic environment. Those skills are quite the opposite of the liberating lifeskills; instead, they become a ball and chain that often keeps the young person tethered, emotionally or physically, to the family of origin.[3]

The family itself begins to center its whole life around the alcoholic—creating a dysfunctional system in which each member functions to protect the drinker and keep the problem hidden from others. The young person finds himself or herself trapped in relationships that revolve around surviving drug dependence.

---

[3] To learn more about what it's like to be raised by alcoholic parents, read *Different Like Me: A Book for Teens Who Worry About Their Parents' Use of Alcohol/Drugs* by Evelyn Leite and Pamela Espeland (Minneapolis: The Johnson Institute, 1987) or read Chapters 14 and 15 of this book.

How the Non-Drinking Parent
Can Help the Kids

Although life in a family where one parent is an alcoholic often is bleak and seems beyond all help, the non-drinking parent can do many things to help the children. Here are some of them.

- Openly acknowledge your spouse's disease. The most insidious family reaction to chemical dependence is to keep the problem a secret. Kids learn the following rules: Don't talk; don't trust; don't feel. Kids must learn to trust their own perceptions of reality and must be encouraged to act according to them. By acknowledging the existence and devastating effects of the alcoholism, the non-drinking parent breaks the no-talk rule and frees the children from their isolation so they can find ways to get their own needs met.

- Get help for yourself. Help is always available, whether it's professional or self-help. A good first step is Al-Anon. Al-Anon is a self-help, Twelve Step program that is free for anyone seeking assistance with living with an alcoholic or other drug-dependent person. Your reaching out to others will help your kids in at least two ways: You'll be more sane and consequently better able to respond to their needs, and you'll be modeling a constructive lifeskill that can help your kids learn to begin trusting others and to break the no-talk rule.

- Find a support group for your kids—a group where kids can talk with peers about their feelings and concerns. Alateen, Alatot, and various other groups for kids with alcoholic parents, such as Children Are People, are becoming increasingly available. No matter what the kids' age, they need the opportunity to process their feelings and relate to others who are experiencing troubles like their own. Such contacts help kids overcome their feelings of isolation and uniqueness—the feeling that they're drifting helpless and alone on an endless, menacing ocean.

Summary

Clearly, the choices we make regarding alcohol and other drugs will affect the decisions our kids will inevitably make about them. How we model appropriate use is therefore critical.

Despite our best attempts, it's naive to think we can keep our use a secret from our kids—a secret that includes what we use, how much we use, when and even where we use. They'll know.

Parental chemical dependence does further damage to kids because it disables the family in ways that encourage kids to develop mere survival skills rather than true, positive, lifeskills. It also sets them up to carry that dysfunctional survivor mode of living into adulthood and to pass it on to their kids.

DAVID J. WILMES

This section is taken from *Parenting for Prevention: How to Raise a Child to Say No to Alcohol/Drugs*, published by the Johnson Institute.

CHAPTER TWENTY-TWO

The Recovering Parent

Dave has been sober for four years. He went into treatment when his son Eddie, an only child, was eight years old.

Eddie wasn't involved in his dad's treatment; everyone thought he was too young at the time. But he vividly remembers his dad's drinking, especially the last year: endless family arguments, his dad coming home drunk and shouting obscenities at the neighbors, the police coming again and again after the neighbors' complaints, and finally his dad leaving, suitcase in hand, for the hospital.

Yet it seemed that Eddie was never really affected by that whole experience. He did well in school, seemed happy enough, and really helped out Mom while Dad was gone.

Now that Eddie is twelve, though, he's like a different person: withdrawn, isolated, and hanging out with a crowd of kids known for using alcohol and other drugs. Dave blames himself. He feels that his alcoholism has created a barrier between himself and his son that keeps him from being available as a parent at this crucial time in Eddie's life. When he and Eddie try to talk, Dave always ends up angry, and Eddie stares at the wall in silence.

I've seen the scenario repeated many times as recovering parents are confronted with the dysfunctional behavior some of their kids develop even though the parent is now sober.

Alcoholism and other drug dependence creates open wounds in all of those directly affected by the chemical dependent. Until recently, however, professionals in the field of chemical dependence, as well as parents themselves, have frequently ignored the wounds carried by children in these families, especially by younger children—probably because younger children do a good job of looking unaffected. We've also avoided looking at their wounds because when we do, the depth of their pain can be frightening.

Since children have been so neglected, the bulk of this chapter on the recovering parent is really devoted to them: first, to help parents understand what usually happens to kids when a parent quits drinking or using and gets on the road to recovery; and second, to focus on three major areas where the recovering parent can help heal kids' wounds. The final section of the chapter offers some other suggestions to the recovering parent.

What Happens to Kids
When a Parent Quits Using

When a parent stops using drugs and begins recovery, what happens to the children can usually be summed up in three steps.

Step 1: Putting Band-Aids on Deep Wounds

Usually no attention is paid to the pain and suffering of the children until a parent quits using. Possibly kids will participate in only one group session or perhaps in an education program at the center where the parent is in treatment. The children's immediate bleeding may be stopped and Band-Aids applied to their wounds, but the primary focus stays on the recovery process of the drug dependent parent. Providing treatment for the children is often given only cursory attention. This leaves the young person only one choice: to ignore the pain and the impact of the parent's dependence and pretend nothing is going on. This is usually fairly easy for the children, since they've been taught over and over "Don't talk, don't trust, don't feel." As the child ignores the pain, eventually the bleeding stops and the wounds form hardened scabs.

Step 2: The Scabbing Over of Wounds

As the parent continues to participate in a recovery program, the deeper wounds of the children often go unnoticed. As others often fail to acknowledge those wounds, kids develop defense mechanisms to cope with the feelings they've experienced and continue to carry as the result of the painful events that happened during the using or drinking years. For example, they pretend that the feelings from being ignored, yelled at, and sometimes beaten by a drug dependent parent don't even exist. Feelings of hurt and anger often fester and turn into deep-seated resentment. Feelings of being different, isolated, and unwanted create a sense of shame.

Even though scabs form over the wounds, children often continue to carry unresolved feelings centered around that resentment and shame. Those feelings undermine not only the relationship between the recovering parent and the child, but also the child's self-esteem.

Step 3: The Eruption

Usually those unresolved feelings erupt during early adolescence (often ages 11-14), because at this stage kids tend to act out their feelings. Outward displays of hostility, anger, and rage are common, as are feelings of self-doubt, confusion, and self-hatred. As those feelings erupt, the recovering parent and the children typically become pitted against each other as they dump their unresolved pain on each other.

Parent: "You don't care about me at all. I was up till two in the morning waiting for you to come home from that party."

Child: "What do you mean, I don't care? When you were drinking, you were never home, and you never came to one of my games. I'll always hate you for that."

Not only has the child of the chemical dependent carried unresolved pain, but the recovering parent often has had little opportunity to verbalize any of the depth of the guilt he or she has felt toward the child. With time that guilt often turns inward to self-hatred and anger. When, after years of being ignored, these festering feelings are first lanced (often in the course of the parent's treatment for alcoholism), it's not unusual or surprising that there's an emotional outpouring of feelings springing from vague, unfocused anger. But under the anger lie feelings of guilt, shame, and humiliation that need to be resolved.

At this point children can very easily develop a serious problem with alcohol or other drugs. These children are more likely to experiment with drugs at a earlier age than their friends do; worse, their experimentation will probably develop into a problem far more quickly. These children may be at high risk to develop drug problems because of the strong possibility of a genetic disposition to alcoholism or because the parent has modeled drug use as a way to cope with pain and stress. Also since the erupting pain is so powerful, mind-altering chemicals are extremely attractive and effective.

How to Help Kids Recover

The pain that parental alcoholism or other chemical dependence causes kids is predictably devastating, but the recovering parent can help in at least three major ways.

Help Kids to Face the Pain

It can be very difficult for a parent just to see the deep-seated resentment, rage, and shame that his or her chemical dependence has brought upon the children. For example, a teenage boy who was seldom disciplined by his father, but who now sees his dad attempting to assume a parental role he had abdicated in favor of alcohol, will often vehemently reject these attempts. It can be even more difficult to help such a parent face his or her own pain. But it can be done.

The ability of a recovering parent to help when his or her child is in pain as a result of parental neglect or mistreatment will depend on that parent's courage, patience and willingness to help. It also depends on the parent's ability to identify his or her feelings, accept them as his or her own, and express them. It would be hard to imagine a situation in which that feeling-processing lifeskill could be more valuable than when a recovering alcoholic parent sits down with his or her own kids to help them face and conquer their own painful feelings. The parent can signal in many ways that those feelings are understandable and normal and that he or she is willing to help the children know about them and work through them.

Those feelings won't be processed in one easy session. It will be done the way we peel an onion—one layer after another.

Child: "Why do you think you have the right to tell me what to do after all you've put this family through?"

Parent: "I'm only trying to help, to do my part. I'm not trying to run your life. I'm just trying to be your dad (mom)."

Child: "It's too late for that. I don't need you! I've learned to take care of myself. Sometimes I wish you didn't quit drinking—you think you're perfect."

Parent: "I know the pain is still there; I feel it too. You can't begin to know the hours of sleepless nights I've had wondering if I could ever make it up to you and the family. Let's agree to work through these feelings together. I'm willing to try. Are you?"

Child: "I don't know; I need to think about it. I don't want to get hurt again."

Parent: "I understand. Let's talk tomorrow after you've given it some thought."

Help Kids to Reconstruct the Past

It's common for kids to have clouded memories, sometimes no memory at all, of the drinking episodes that occurred while they lived with a drug dependent parent. Despite their apparent lack of memory, it's usually important for kids to reconstruct their past in some way.

An exercise I've used with many kids from alcoholic families is to have them bring a journal or notebook and to separate the pages into years. (Usually I suggest going by grades, since kids tend to associate memories with the school calendar, school events, and teachers.) I recommend that each night before going to bed, they spend ten to fifteen minutes relaxing and letting any memory from the family come to mind. When it does, they're to jot down words, sentences, or sketches that describe it. If this exercise is to succeed, parents need to take a real interest in it. They should ask how the journal is going and set aside time each week to discuss memories from the journal as the child is willing to share them.

As kids talk through those events, they'll begin to make sense of their history: where they've been and why things have happened to them. Much of the confusion experienced by children of alcoholic and other chemically dependent families appears to be caused by a genuine lack of understanding of how the events of their life have fitted together. This isn't surprising when we consider that so much of the life of the chemical dependent is steeped in secrecy, unpredictability, chaos, and an unwillingness to acknowledge problems with drugs.

Cooperate in Reestablishing Family Boundaries

In normal families there are clearly defined, healthy, accepted boundaries between parents and children. Parents make major decisions about where the family lives, how it spends its money, how the house is managed, how the children behave and acquire an education. Kids have a right to be loved and respected, to have all their basic physical and psychological needs taken care of. At the same time, they're expected to cooperate in family life by obeying their parents in all reasonable matters, getting along with their brothers and sisters, and performing tasks suitable to their condition, such as keeping their room in good order, doing some household chores, and running errands.

As chemical dependence takes over in a family, though, those boundaries begin to break down. I've worked with families where kids in effect became parents and parents became kids. A ten-year-old girl might be doing major housecleaning day after day and her twelve-year-old brother might be preparing all the meals. A fourteen-year-old boy might be doing all the grocery shopping and paying the family bills, and his sixteen-year-old brother might be Mom's confidante, who listens to all her troubles, comforts her as best he can, and in effect practically becomes a substitute spouse.

The recovering drug dependent parent must cooperate with both spouse and children to turn that topsy-turvy world right side up. Parents must once again act like parents, kids like kids. In short, roles must be reassigned and really accepted. Parents must be nurturers, leaders, make major family decisions. Kids mustn't be turned into miniature adults. They need time to relax, to play, to be free of making major family decisions, to grow at a natural pace. They need to be given tasks appropriate to their age and stage of development. Above all, they need love, support, encouragement, praise, acknowledgment, and acceptance.

Accomplishing all this turnaround is a task for the whole family, and the recovering alcoholic must be an integral part of it.[1]

Getting Help

Most families recovering from chemical dependence need outside help. For some, the support of self-help groups such as Al-Anon and Alateen is enough. Those with a longtime and complex history of chemical dependence will need professional help from well-qualified counselors or therapists in going through the major steps in recovery that we've just discussed: facing the pain, reconstructing the past, reestablishing family boundaries.

When selecting a therapist or professional counselor, be sure that the therapist/counselor has a good background not only in the field of chemical dependence, but also in family systems and in the developmental needs of children. Recovery of a drug-dependent parent usually means recovery of the

---

[1] For more information, see *Another Chance: Hope and Health for the Alcoholic Family* by Sharon Wegscheider (Palo Alto: Science and Behavior Books, 1981).

whole family, because the whole family has been swept into an abnormal, traumatic lifestyle.

Suggestions for the Recovering Parent

- Be willing to talk about the past when kids have questions. It may be very helpful for you to share with them why it's important for you, too, to resolve issues from the past. It can be tempting to avoid this area, but kids really need to sort out their past, and so does the parent. Questions about the past will often come years after the parent has begun sobriety.
- Go slow. Your chemical dependence has severely undermined your position as a parent. Don't expect yourself or your kids immediately to feel comfortable with or accepting of this "new" parent.
- Talk about the guilt that you, like every drug dependent parent, have felt about not having been there for your kids. Guilt feelings are powerful but unfortunately are often ignored. To reestablish yourself as a parent, you must acknowledge them and work your way through them.
- Be careful about projecting your own personal situation onto your kids. The recovering parent is tempted to overreact when kids—especially kids entering adolescence—seem to be on the verge of making the very same mistakes he or she made. The first impulse is to overreact because of guilt feelings and become overly vigilant and protective. To assume that your kids are exactly like you and therefore will fall into exactly the same traps that you fell into is a mistake. What you can do, instead, is to respond to the kids' *real*—not imagined—needs. That means you need to listen well to what

they're *really* saying, observe what they're *really* doing, size up their situation objectively. *Then* you're in a position to offer help.

- Be patient. Recovery is a process that unfolds as you confront sobriety one day at a time. Reestablishing relationships with your kids is also a long, slow process. Sometimes the kids are well into their twenties before they're able to resolve their feelings about a chemically dependent parent. Only then can they begin to realize that parents are people, too—not gods or goddesses, but imperfect human beings like themselves—who've proved it by making lots of mistakes and yet are willing to work through them.

DAVID J. WILMES

This section is taken from *Parenting For Prevention: How to Raise a Child to Say No to Alcohol/Drugs*, published by the Johnson Institute.

Publications Used in This Book

The following is a complete list of the Johnson Institute publications used to compile this guide. If you would like more information about any of these publications, call the Johnson Institute **TOLL FREE** Monday-Friday 7:00 a.m. to 6:00 p.m. CST:

1-800-231-5165
1-800-247-0484 (Minnesota only)
1-800-447-6660 (Canada only)

Alcohol and Anxiety, by Anne Geller, M.D.

Alcohol and Sexual Performance, by Anne Geller, M.D.

Alcohol/Drug Dependent Women: New Insights into Their Special Problems, Treatment, Recovery, by Sheila B. Blume, M.D.

Blackouts and Alcoholism, by Lucy Barry Robe.

Chemical Dependence and Recovery: A Family Affair.

Chemical Dependence: Yes, You Can Do Something.

Choices & Consequences: What to Do When a Teenager Uses Alcohol/ Drugs, by Dick Schaefer.

Detachment: The Art of Letting Go While Living With An Alcoholic, by Evelyn Leite.

Diagnosing and Treating Co-Dependence: A Guide for Professionals Who Work With Chemical Dependents, Their Spouses and Children, by Timmen L. Cermak, M.D.

Different Like Me: A Book for Teens Who Worry About Their Parents' Use of Alcohol/Drugs, by Evelyn Leite and Pamela Espeland.

The Family Enablers.

Intervention: How to Help Someone Who Doesn't Want Help, by Vernon E. Johnson, D.D.

Parenting for Prevention: How to Raise a Child to Say No to Alcohol/Drugs, by David J. Wilmes.

Recovery of Chemically Dependent Families.

Relapse/Slips: Abstinent Drinkers Who Return to Drinking, by Maxwell N. Weisman, M.D., and Lucy Barry Robe.

Supervisors and Managers As Enablers, by Brenda R. Blair, M.B.A.

Women, Alcohol and Dependency: I Am Responsible.

National Organizations to Contact

The following groups and organizations can provide additional information on or assistance with alcohol and other drug use.

Addiction Research Foundation
33 Russell Street
Toronto, Ontario M5S 2S1
CANADA
(416) 595-6056

Al-Anon Family Group Headquarters
1372 Broadway
New York, NY 10018-0862
(212) 302-7240

Alateen
1372 Broadway
New York, NY 10018-0862
(212) 302-7240

(For veterans)
Alcohol and Drug Dependence
Mental Health and Behavior Science and Services
Department of Medicine and Surgery
Veterans Administration
8 Vermont Avenue NW, Room 116A3
Washington, DC 20420
(202) 389-5193

Alcoholics Anonymous (A.A.)
General Service Office
P.O. Box 459
Grand Central Station
New York, NY 10163
(212) 686-1100

American Council for Drug Education
204 Monroe Street
Rockville, MD 20850
(301) 294-0600

Chemical People Project/WQED-TV
4802 Fifth Avenue
Pittsburgh, PA 15213
(412) 622-1491

Children Are People, Inc.
Chemical Abuse Prevention Program
493 Selby Avenue
St. Paul, MN 55102
(612) 227-4031

Children of Alcoholics Foundation, Inc. (COAF)
200 Park Avenue, 31st Floor
New York, NY 10166
(212) 351-2680

Division of Occupational Programs
National Institute on Alcohol Abuse and Alcoholism
Department of Health and Human Services
Room 11055, Parklawn Building
5600 Fishers Lane
Rockville, MD 20857
(301) 443-1148

Employee Assistance Professionals Association, Inc. (EAPA)
4601 North Fairfax Drive
Suite 1001
Arlington, VA 22203
(703) 522-6272

Families Anonymous
World Service Office
P.O. Box 528
Van Nuys, CA 91408
(818) 989-7841

Families in Action Drug Information Center
2296 Henderson Mill Road
Suite 204
Atlanta, GA 30345
(404) 325-5799

Hazelden Foundation
Box 11
Center City, MN 55012
(800) 328-9000

Institute on Black Chemical Abuse (IBCA)
2614 Nicollet Avenue South
Minneapolis, MN 55408
(612) 871-7878

Johnson Institute
7151 Metro Boulevard
Minneapolis, MN 55439-2122
(800) 231-5165
In Minnesota, call: (800) 247-0484

Mothers Against Drunk Driving (MADD)
National Headquarters
669 Airport Freeway
Suite 310
Hurst, TX 76053-3944
(817) 268-6233

Narcotics Anonymous (N.A.)
World Services Office, Inc.
P.O. Box 9999
Van Nuys, CA 91409
(818) 780-3951

National Association for Children of Alcoholics, Inc. (NACOA)
31582 Coast Highway
Suite B
South Laguna, CA 92677-3044
(714) 499-3889

National Clearinghouse for Alcohol/Drug Information (NCADI)
P.O. Box 2345
Rockville, MD 28052
(301) 468-2600

National Coalition for the Prevention of Drug and Alcohol Abuse
537 Jones Road
Granville, OH 43023
(614) 587-2800

National Council on Alcoholism, Inc. (NCA)
12 West 21st Street, 7th Floor
New York, NY 10010
(800) NCA-CALL

492

National Federation of Parents for Drug-Free Youth
8730 Georgia Avenue
Suite 200
Silver Spring, MD 20910
(301) 585-5437

National Institute on Alcohol Abuse and Alcoholism (NIAAA)
Room 16-105
Parklawn Building
5600 Fishers Lane
Rockville, MD 20857
(301) 443-3885

National Institute on Drug Abuse (NIDA)
Room 10-05
Parklawn Building
5600 Fishers Lane
Rockville, MD 20857
(301) 443-6480

National Parents Resource Institute on Drug Education (PRIDE)
Robert W. Woodruff Volunteer Service Center
Suite 1002
100 Edgewood Avenue
Atlanta, GA 30303
(404) 651-2548

Students Against Drunk Driving (SADD)
P.O. Box 800
277 Main Street
Marlboro, MA 01752
(800) 521-SADD

JOHNSON INSTITUTE

When the Johnson Institute first opened its doors in 1966, few people knew or believed that alcoholism was a disease. Fewer still thought that anything could be done to help the chemically dependent person other than to wait for him or her to "hit bottom" and then pick up the pieces.

We've spent over twenty years spreading the good news that chemical dependence is a *treatable* disease. Through our publications, films, video and audiocassettes, and our training and consultation services, we've given hope and help to hundreds of thousands of people across the country and around the world. The intervention and treatment methods we've pioneered have restored shattered careers, healed relationships with co-workers and friends, saved lives, and brought families back together.

Today the Johnson Institute is an internationally recognized leader in the field of chemical dependence intervention, treatment, and recovery. Individuals, organizations, and businesses, large and small, rely on us to provide them with the tools they need. Schools, universities, hospitals, treatment centers, and other healthcare agencies look to us for experience, expertise, innovation, and results. With care, compassion, and commitment, we will continue to reach out to chemically dependent persons, their families, and the professionals who serve them.

To find out more about us, write or call:
7151 Metro Boulevard
Minneapolis, MN 55439-2122
1-800-231-5165
In Minnesota: 1-800-247-0484
or 944-0511
In Canada: 1-800-447-6660